D1496338

# The Rhetorical Feminine

*Gender and Orient on the
German Stage, 1647–1742*

SARAH COLVIN

CLARENDON PRESS · OXFORD

# OXFORD
UNIVERSITY PRESS

Great Clarendon Street, Oxford OX2 6DP

Oxford University Press is a department of the University of Oxford.
It furthers the University's objective of excellence in research, scholarship,
and education by publishing worldwide in

Oxford New York

Athens Auckland Bangkok Bogotá Buenos Aires Calcutta
Cape Town Chennai Dar es Salaam Delhi Florence Hong Kong Istanbul
Karachi Kuala Lumpur Madrid Melbourne Mexico City Mumbai
Nairobi Paris São Paulo Singapore Taipei Tokyo Toronto Warsaw
and associated companies in Berlin Ibadan

Oxford is a registered trade mark of Oxford University Press
in the UK and certain other countries

Published in the United States
by Oxford University Press Inc., New York

© Sarah Colvin 1999

British Library Cataloguing in Publication Data

Data available

Library of Congress Cataloging in Publication Data

Data available

ISBN 0–19–818636–3

1 3 5 7 9 10 8 6 4 2

Typeset by Graphicraft Ltd, Hong Kong
Printed in Great Britain
on acid-free paper by
Bookcraft Ltd,
Midsomer Norton, Somerset

# PREFACE

In 1995 I submitted an earlier form of this study as a thesis to the University of Oxford. Special thanks are due to my supervisor, who was also an inspiring mentor: Dr Helen Watanabe-O'Kelly of Exeter College. Emma Dillon, Niall Livingstone, and Mark Taplin were sources of interdisciplinary advice and support.

My research on opera in Hamburg and Wolfenbüttel was facilitated by a generous scholarship from the FVS foundation of the late Alfred Töpfer. Christ Church, Oxford, later supported me academically and financially as a Senior Scholar.

# CONTENTS

# ABBREVIATIONS

JOURNALS

| | |
|---|---|
| *AMZ* | *Allgemeine Musikalische Zeitung* |
| *CG* | *Colloquia Germanica* |
| *COJ* | *Cambridge Opera Journal* |
| *DVjs* | *Deutsche Vierteljahresschrift für Literaturwissenschaft und Geistesgeschichte* |
| *GLL* | *German Life and Letters* |
| *GQ* | *German Quarterly* |
| *GR* | *Germanic Review* |
| *JMP* | *Jahrbuch der Musikbibliothek Peters* |
| *ML* | *Music and Letters* |
| *MLN* | *Modern Language Notes* |
| *MLR* | *Modern Languages Review* |
| *MR* | *Music Review* |
| *MQ* | *Musical Quarterly* |
| *OGS* | *Oxford German Studies* |
| *SIM* | *Sammelbände der internationalen Musikgesellschaft* |

LIBRARIES

| | |
|---|---|
| BL | British Library, London |
| BOD | Bodleian Library, Oxford |
| HAB | Herzog August Bibliothek, Wolfenbüttel |
| SB Berlin | Staatsbibliothek zu Berlin |
| SUB Gö | Stadt- und Universitätsbibliothek, Göttingen |
| SUB HH | Staats- und Universitätsbibliothek, Hamburg |
| TAY | Taylor Institution Library, Oxford |

# NOTE ON TERMINOLOGY
# AND ORTHOGRAPHY

In what follows I have used the terms 'male' and 'female' to describe what we construct as 'biological sex', and 'masculine' and 'feminine' to refer to conventional gender attributes. It is tempting to signpost such ideologically loaded terms as 'masculinity', 'femininity', or 'oriental' with inverted commas, but since such a procedure could easily get out of hand I have decided not to mark these words in the text that follows.

Spelling in the early modern period is *not* an exact science, and it is not feasible to signal every departure from modern expectations of German spelling and grammar. I have followed the orthography of reliable critical editions and of early printed texts exactly, with the following exceptions: m̄ and n̄ are rendered mm/nn; u/U and v/V as well as i/I and j/J are used in such a way as to correspond to normal modern usage, as is the Umlaut form ä etc., as opposed to å. I have kept the oblique sign (/), which is used in early modern texts in place of the modern comma.

# INTRODUCTION:
## MEN, RHETORIC, AND THE STAGE

Literary representations of woman and the Orient flourished in the early modern period in Europe against a background of social and political development. There were changes in the legal position of women when Roman law started to replace medieval codes during the sixteenth century: unmarried women in particular were accorded certain rights such as landowning and self-representation in court (a married woman remained legally subject to her husband in all things).[1] The new independence of single women may have given rise to a level of insecurity among men accustomed, officially at least, to control. Within marriage, the medieval conception of the interdependence of married partners was giving way to a new idea of complementary, *opposite* roles, based in the domestic and the public spheres respectively—although social realities still meant that, for most couples, these two spheres were not discrete.[2] In the public sphere (and hence, according to the notion of gendered opposites, in the masculine domain), women rulers and regents in Europe in the sixteenth and seventeenth centuries, such as Elizabeth of England, Christina of Sweden, or Marie de Médicis, were demonstrating that women were not the feeble creatures comfortable popular (male) opinion would style them, but fully able and even ambitious to wield power.

But not only was the identity of the Christian male under pressure from *within* the Christian state: the latter was also territorially threatened from the outside, by Islam. The Ottoman Empire was expanding from the fourteenth century, and Mehmet II's conquest of Constantinople in 1453 sent shock waves through Christendom. The next two centuries

---

[1] See Merry E. Wiesner, *Women and Gender in Early Modern Europe* (Cambridge 1993), 30–1.

[2] See Sigrid Brauner, 'Gender and its Subversion: Reflections on Literary Ideals of Marriage', in Lynne Tatlock (ed.), *The Graph of Sex and the German Text: Gendered Culture in Early Modern Germany* (Amsterdam 1994), 179–98 (184–5).

saw unsettled relations between the Holy Roman Empire and its religious and territorial rival, which came to a head in the second siege of Vienna in 1683, when the Ottoman forces were finally defeated. These social tensions quickly found their way onto the early modern stage, where they could be enacted and defused within the controllable world of the drama: a microcosmic representation of the *theatrum mundi*, in which the playwright pulls the strings.

This study spans the century of dramatic literature in German from 1647 (when Andreas Gryphius probably wrote his *Catharina von Georgien*) to 1742, and juxtaposes the work of unfamiliar writers with that of their currently better-known contemporaries. The texts I have considered were all written by men; the specific difficulties and concerns of women writing in the early modern period would, I think, merit a separate study.[3] For reasons of space I have had to limit my inclusion of material, and when faced with a choice between the discussion of lesser-known and better-known works I have generally opted for the former. It is on these grounds, for example, that I have chosen not to discuss Gryphius's critically acclaimed comedies in my last chapter.[4]

Early drama should be envisaged quite differently from the theatre-based, consumer-oriented spectacle that developed from the end of the early modern period in the German-speaking territories. In the sixteenth and seventeenth centuries, plays were performed either by touring troops of actors

---

[3] Interesting work is being done on the women writers of the early modern period, most of whom were not, however, dramatists. See e.g. Barbara Becker-Cantarino's edition of Anna Ovena Hoyers, *Geistliche und Weltliche Poemata* (Tübingen 1986); Natalie Zemon Davis, *Women on the Margins: Three Seventeenth-Century Lives* (Boston 1995); Helen Watanabe-O'Kelly, ' "Sei mir dreimal mehr mit Licht bekleidet": German Poems by Women to their Mentors in the Seventeenth Century', in *CG* 28 (1995), 255–64. The only work on women dramatists of the early modern period, to my knowledge, is in the joint dissertation of Susanne Gugrel-Steindl and Margarete Bican-Zehetbauer, 'Figurenkonstellation im Drama des 17. Jahrhunderts im deutschsprachigen Raum Oder: Von Tugend und Untugend, (Frauen)Schönheit und (Ohn)Macht' (unpublished doctoral diss., University of Vienna 1991).

[4] I have, however, included detailed studies of the dramas of Daniel Casper von Lohenstein, and must disagree with Cornelia Plume, in her otherwise stimulating work, that there is little more to be said on the subject of Lohenstein's portrayal of the feminine in his dramas. See Plume, *Heroinen in der Geschlechterordnung: Wirklichkeitsprojektionen bei Daniel Casper von Lohenstein und die 'Querelle des Femmes'* (Stuttgart 1996).

using improvised stage constructions, or seasonally by local citizens (*Fastnachtspiele*), or as occasional entertainment at the courts of the noble and wealthy. They also came to be used as a mode of instruction and as a public relations exercise by boys' schools, most famously in the Silesian town of Breslau (Wroclaw), whose Protestant grammar schools of St Magdalena and St Elizabeth produced the dramatists Andreas Gryphius (1616–64), Daniel Casper von Lohenstein (1635–83), and Johann Christian Hallmann (1640–?1704). School performances in Breslau are recorded as early as 1500,[5] and the striking proliferation of school drama in the Silesian town in the seventeenth century has been seen as a result of unusual political and confessional circumstances (from 1526, Silesia was Habsburg territory, but Breslau in particular had a strong Lutheran tradition) which permitted the competitive coexistence of Protestant and Catholic schools.[6]

Catholic schooling in the early modern period was dominated by the Society of Jesus, which had established its first school for German boys in Cologne in 1556, having been active in that city for twelve years. In Breslau, theatrical performances by the Jesuits and their pupils began in 1639. Jesuit drama, like the early Protestant school plays, was performed in Latin, and the inaccessibility of the Latin text for at least some members of the audience may have been one reason why the Jesuits became famous for their skilful use of nonverbal theatrical effects, including music.[7] Given the opulence of the Jesuit productions, which helped the order to extend its influence into the Catholic courts as well as raising its profile generally, it is no surprise that Breslau's Protestant school dramatists, equally hungry for influence, soon felt the

---

[5] The earliest recorded performance, on 1 March 1500, was of Terence's *Eunuch.* See Konrad Gajek (ed.), *Das Breslauer Schultheater im 17. und 18. Jahrhundert* (Tübingen 1994), p. 5*.

[6] Wilfried Barner, *Barock-Rhetorik: Untersuchungen zu ihren geschichtlichen Grundlagen* (Tübingen 1970), 323. See also Adalbert Wichert, *Literatur, Rhetorik und Jurisprudenz im 17. Jahrhundert: Daniel Casper von Lohenstein und sein Werk* (Tübingen 1991), 48.

[7] Music might e.g. add a special atmosphere to important allegorical or supernatural scenes, thus distinguishing them from the remainder of the action. See Richard Taubald, 'Die Oper als Schule der Tugend und des Lebens im Zeitalter des Barock: Die enkulturierende Wirkung einer Kunstpflege' (unpublished doctoral thesis, University of Erlangen-Nuremberg 1972), esp. pp. 4, 276.

4 INTRODUCTION

need to produce pieces in the German vernacular, accessible to a wider audience. Confessional competition seems to
have provided a stimulus for the mobilization of drama—with
all its visual, verbal, and aural appeal—as a status-enhancing,
persuasive, and thus rhetorical form.

Rhetoric, its nature and its uses, is a key concern of this
study. I shall argue that the seventeenth- and early eighteenth-
century stage provided an ideal setting for 'ideal' rhetoric;
that is, for musical and linguistic sign-systems that reflect and
project a conception of social order.[8] For the dramatists and
composers, many of whom had grown up during, or in the
aftermath of, the destruction and chaos wreaked by the
Thirty Years War, the stage of school drama and of early opera
becomes the controllable and hence ideal version of the *theatrum mundi*. In it, order can be enforced because chaos is
rhetorically defined and contained. But the process of creating meaning in drama is not of course confined to the stage:
the development of comprehensible sign-systems in theatre
(for example, what is to be perceived by an audience as order,
and what as chaos; or, what is comic) inevitably reflects and
is reflected by the society (audience) with which the stage
interacts. On early modern opera, McClary has remarked that:
'music does not just passively reflect society; it also serves
as a public forum within which various models of gender
organization . . . are asserted, adopted, contested'.[9] The same
might be said of early theatre in general. A process of mutual
confirmation, perpetuation, and fixing of 'models'—rhetorical
or metaphorical constructs—between stage and audience
occurs: a 'norm' is negotiated.

It is nothing new to claim that rhetoric and the teaching of rhetoric are central to German drama in the seventeenth century.[10] But one important aspect of early modern

---

[8] While it is possible to treat visual aspects of theatre in so far as they are obvious
from the text, work still needs to be done on the production aspect of school drama
in particular. I have not found space to treat this in any detail in this study.

[9] Susan McClary, *Feminine Endings: Music, Gender, and Sexuality* (Minneapolis, Minn.
1991), 8.

[10] The topic has been treated in some detail, notably by Joachim Dyck (*Ticht-
Kunst: Deutsche Barockpoetik und rhetorische Tradition* (Tübingen 1991 [1966]),
Wilfried Barner (*Barock-Rhetorik* (Tübingen 1970)), and by Wichert in his illuminating
study of Lohenstein (*Literatur, Rhetorik und Jurisprudenz*).

rhetoric has hardly been considered: its masculinity. For the pedagogue Christian Weise, introducing his *Politischer Redner* of 1683, the practical purpose of rhetoric is to make men of boys: 'daß die Jugend durch anmuthige Wege fortge-bracht und durch nuetzliche Übungen zu dem Nutze des Maenlichen Lebens vorbereitet werde'.[11] Curiously, most modern scholars, too, have accepted without comment that rhetoric is a male preserve.[12] Barner, for example, notes the key position of rhetoric in early modern educated society,

ihre Schlüsselposition im Hinblick auf die sprachliche Kultur der Barockepoche. Dem Unterricht fällt es zu, den Menschen in der ihm eigenen Fähigkeit zum Wort auszubilden, ihm die Konventionen des sprachlich-repräsentativen Miteinanders einzuprägen.[13]

The linguistic schooling Barner speaks of was scarcely ever available to women in early modern Germany. We must therefore assume that the 'Mensch' he refers to, who dif-ferentiates himself from the animals by means of his unique linguistic ability is—in the time-honoured tradition of misuse of the word—a man rather than mankind. Barner's assess-ment of rhetoric as a key to the linguistic culture of the epoch is convincing; the move away from Latin towards a literary form of the vernacular in the early seventeenth cen-tury would have rendered a sophisticated command of the German language all the more important to a sense of the cultural self. But such a 'self' was not, of course, available to the rhetorically uneducated: boys of the poorer classes and almost all women and girls.[14] In Western culture, women's place has been defined not in speech but in silence: having identified men as beings that have language, Aristotle

[11] Weise, *Politischer Redner/ Das ist: Kurtze und eigentliche Nachricht/ wie ein sorgfältiger Hofemeister seine Untergebene zu der Wohlredenheit anführen sol . . .* (Leipzig 1683; repr. Kronberg/Ts. 1974), 'Vorwort' (unpag.).

[12] Even Brian Vickers, in his impressive and influential work *In Defence of Rhetoric* (Oxford 1997 [1988]), does not mention this aspect of his subject.

[13] Barner, *Barock-Rhetorik*, 242.

[14] In fact intermittent attempts were made to include poorer boys in the Humanist education system via scholarship systems such as that introduced in Breslau in the 16th cent. See David Halsted, 'Education in Breslau', in *idem, Poetry and Politics in the Silesian Baroque: Neo-Stoicism in the Work of Christophorus Colerus and his Circle* (Wiesbaden 1996), 69–92 (73). Girls, on the other hand, were scarcely ever offered schooling above elementary level.

decided that women, ideally, have none.[15] Paul's epistles have also lent authority to Christian writers who wished to exclude women from the linguistic and rhetorical endeavour that, according to Toni Morrison, is central to human existence: 'We die. That may be the meaning of life. But we *do* language. That may be the measure of our lives.'[16] When we 'do' language, we define how we exist, and the long-term danger of women's exclusion is that those who are not actively involved in the process of linguistic defining are likely to find themselves defined; when rhetorically educated men construct meanings, women are all too often the ones to whom those meanings are assigned.

Perhaps the most expert rhetorician of the early modern period, Martin Luther, had warmly recommended the pedagogical use of (Latin) drama in boys' schools:

Comödien zu spielen soll man um der Knaben in der Schule willen nicht wehren, sondern gestatten und zulassen, erstlich, daß sie sich üben [*sic*] in der lateinischen Sprache; zum Andern, daß in Comödien fein künstlich erdichtet, abgemalet und fürgestellt werden solche Personen, dadurch die Leute unterrichtet . . . wie sich ein Iglicher in seinem Stande halten soll im äußerlichen Wandel, wie in einem Spiegel.[17]

Luther's emphasis on the value of school drama as a conservative or socially stabilizing force is worth noting. In Breslau, the school productions attracted criticism because of the carnivalesque situation into which they threw the town. Lessons were suspended while the performance was prepared and the stage constructed, and hawkers and visitors entered the city; drunkenness and disorderly behaviour were rife.[18] Despite this, the authorities allowed the practice to continue until 1671. While influential local enthusiasts such as Elias Major, the headmaster of St Elizabeth's, and the poet and councillor Christian Hoffmann von Hoffmannswaldau were partly responsible for school drama's survival, the Rat had

[15] 'Silence is a woman's glory'. Aristotle, *Politics* (Oxford 1923), 1. 13. 1260²ᵃ. 30.
[16] From Morrison's 1993 Nobel Lecture in Literature. Cited in Judith Butler, *Excitable Speech: A Politics of the Performative* (New York 1997), 7.
[17] Martin Luther, *Tischreden*, vol. 1 (Weimar 1912), no. 867, pp. 431–2.
[18] Wichert, *Literatur, Rhetorik und Jurisprudenz*, 49–50.

other reasons to be tolerant. The value of the play, according to Luther and presumably also in the eyes of the Breslau authorities, is that a world is constructed in which things are seen to function as they *ought*: an ideal world in which everything may be put in its proper place. The process of assigning 'proper places' on stage allows the system of order in which the dramatist believes to be seen to triumph over all other systems. It is a persuasive process, and the composition and production of the drama is, therefore, in itself a rhetorical act. This would have been attractive to Luther, but also in a later century to the councillors of Breslau, who probably felt a need to see the Protestant viewpoint communicated in response to the Catholic propaganda of Jesuit performances. And even while they caused, in real terms, a level of civic havoc, the school dramas underpinned an *idea* of civic order, by which 'proper places' are assigned within the hierarchy of authority. Halsted notes that 'the *Gymnasien* [of St Elizabeth and St Magdalena] were the primary means by which the city's élite sought to reproduce itself as a class';[19] for a long time, school drama certainly played a part in this process.

The city officials of Breslau would have been in the best possible position to appreciate the importance of the rhetorical skills taught by the school dramas. They attended performances not only of the latter but also of disputations, a less obviously theatrical form that was nonetheless closely related to the drama. Disputations are practical, applied rhetoric, in which a point or argument is proved in a competitive discussion involving two or more parties. As a pedagogical rhetorical form, they had a tradition going back to the medieval universities of Europe, and they also came to characterize literary contributions to the religious debates of the Reformation: a 'rigged' disputation, such as Hans Sachs provides in his *Reformationsdialoge*, may function as a persuasive literary form. As well as being performed separately by schoolboys, disputations become a part of the rhetorical lesson of school drama—a carefully rigged on-stage discussion will often prove a point in the face of counter-argument.

[19] Halsted, 'Education in Breslau', 69.

New work on rhetoric has defined its effect as one by which 'listeners are forced to become *like* the speaker in some way— to act or think like the speaker—without their full under- standing'.[20] Rhetoric is not a 'dry' discipline that insists on the observance of a set of formalized precepts; even in Classical theory, the truly expert rhetor is the man(!) who can flexibly adapt his self-presentation to achieve maximum effect in a given situation. The introduction of drama as a rhetorical teaching method in early modern German schools suggests a move in the Classical spirit from theory to practice. The boys of the St Elizabeth and St Magdalena schools were the sons of the administrative classes; and administrative authority, or the capacity to convince and influence, was not least what the performances that formed part of their curriculum were designed to instil in them. But the audience as well as the performers were liable to be affected by the author-pedagogue's manipulation of lan- guage and its images.

While the school stage was likely to be a fairly simple wooden structure that was erected in the town hall or in the school itself,[21] early opera is an increasingly flamboyant the- atrical development. It not only radically augments the use of dramatic music (which was already a feature of Catholic and Protestant school dramas in the German states, as well as of folk theatre), but also brings women on to the stage, a hitherto scarce occurrence.[22] This study looks principally at libretti and some scores from the major German- language opera centres at the court of Braunschweig- Wolfenbüttel and in the city-state of Hamburg; the sheer volume of the libretti makes it impossible to extend the scope of such as study as this one to all locations where German- language opera was performed.[23]

---

[20] Susan C. Jarrat and Nedra Reynolds, 'The Splitting Image: Contemporary Feminisms and the Ethics of *êthos*', in *Ethos: New Essays in Rhetorical and Critical Theory* (Dallas 1994), 37–64 (54). Italics in original.

[21] See Peter Skrine, 'German Baroque Drama and Seventeenth-Century European Theatre', in James A. Parente *et al.* (eds.), *Literary Culture in the Holy Roman Empire*, 1555–1720 (Chapel Hill, NC 1991), 49–59 (51).

[22] See W. Gordon Marigold, 'Politics, Religion and Opera: Problems of the Hamburg Opera, 1678–1720', in *Mosaic* 18/4 (1985), 49–60 (51).

[23] Another important centre, for example, was in Weißenfels; see Eleonore Sent (ed.), *Die Oper am Weißenfelser Hof* (Rudolstadt 1996).

Performances began in Braunschweig-Wolfenbüttel with a festival performance of Harsdörffer's and Staden's *Seelewig* in 1654. Until 1690 performances took place in the ducal residences at Wolfenbüttel and Salzdahlum, but from around 1687 operas were put on in Braunschweig, probably in the town hall, at fair times. In 1690, Braunschweig's *Rathaus am Hagen* was converted into an opera house proper, and local and visiting nobles were invited to performances; the public could gain access at a price. From the 1730s, however, German-language opera at Braunschweig-Wolfenbüttel gave way increasingly to performances in Italian.[24]

Despite their obvious differences, especially regarding performance conditions and intended audience, opera and school drama are not entirely discrete. Better-known librettists such as Christian Heinrich Postel and Barthold Feind acknowledge a debt to the Breslau school dramatists, whose work they consider exemplary; traces of their influence are evident in many of the German libretti.[25] By the end of the seventeenth century, when Johann Christian Hallmann was writing, the distinction between theatre and music theatre had become even less pronounced. Hallmann's *Catharina*, published in 1684, is a 'musikalisches Trauer=Spiel', while *Antiochus und Stratonica* of the same year reappears in Hamburg in 1707, adapted by Barthold Feind to music by Christoph Graupner and entitled *L'Amore Ammalato . . . Antiochus und Stratonica*. The *Adelheide* material goes full circle: Hallmann's '*Freuden=Spiel*' was inspired by a Venetian opera, appeared in 1684, and was reworked for the Bayreuth and Hamburg stages in 1724 and 1727 respectively.[26]

---

[24] See Renate Brockpähler, *Handbuch zur Geschichte der Barockoper in Deutschland* (Emsdetten 1964), 86–8.

[25] See also Haufe, *Die Behandlung der antiken Mythologie in den Textbüchern der Hamburger Oper 1678–1738* (Frankfurt a.M. 1994 [1964]), 228; Helen Watanabe-O'Kelly, 'Barthold Feind's Libretto Octavia (1705) and the "Schuldrama" Tradition', in *GLL* 35/3 (1982), 208–20; and Sarah Colvin, 'The Classical Witch and the Christian Martyr: Two Ideas of Woman in Hamburg Baroque Opera Libretti', in *GLL* 46/3 (1993), 193–202.

[26] The text of the German opera is probably by Praetorius, the music by Telemann; the Italian source is Dolfino's (text) and Sartorio's (music) *L'Adelaide* (Venice 1672). See Robert Donald Lynch, *Opera in Hamburg 1718–1738: A Study of the Libretto and Musical Style*, 2 vols. (Michigan 1980), 444. The transformation of the text between drama and opera is discussed in detail by Bernhard Jahn,

Weise's *Masaniello* of 1683 was also adapted for Hamburg by Feind and his composer Reinhard Keiser in 1706.[27] For these reasons and others I have chosen not to overplay the distinctions between early opera and drama on the German stage. Both forms of theatre have a rhetorical dynamic on which I have focused my attention; both make effective manipulative use of the audiovisual sign-systems that their stage form makes available.

Interaction between the opera at Braunschweig-Wolfenbüttel and the theatre in the neighbouring city-state of Hamburg is easily traceable: composers and their works moved back and forth fluidly between the two centres. A group of shareholders led by Senator Gerhard Schott had caused an opera house to be built on the Hamburg *Gänsemarkt* in 1677, and the first opera, Christian Richter's and Johann Theile's *Adam und Eva*, was performed in January 1678.[28] Hamburg had no court, and for this reason the theatre on the *Gänsemarkt* has often been described as the first bourgeois opera house on German soil. In fact its patrons included royalty from the neighbouring states, their ambassadors to Hamburg, and the wealthy Hamburg patricians; the best boxes were available only to upper-class applicants, who would pay an annual fee for the right to use them.[29] Hamburg was without question the most prolific German opera house of the period: Johann Mattheson, who wrote and sang for the theatre and also compiled the first directory of its output, lists 256 different operas performed at Hamburg between 1678 and 1738.[30]

'*L'Adelaide* und *L'Heraclio* in Venedig, Breslau und Hamburg: Transformationen zweier Bühnenwerke im Spannungsverhältnis zwischen Musik- und Sprechtheater', in *DVjs* 68 (1994), 651–94.

[27] See Roger Thiel, 'Constantia oder Klassenkampf? Christian Weises *Masaniello* (1682) und Barthold Feind's *Masagniello Furioso* (1706), in *Daphnis* 17 (1988), 247–66.

[28] For a more detailed history of the Hamburg opera house see Haufe, *Die Behandlung der antiken Mythologie*, 7–17.

[29] See Hans Joachim Marx, 'Geschichte der Hamburger Barockoper: Ein Forschungsbericht', in *Hamburger Jahrbuch für Musikwissenschaft 3: Studien zur Barockoper* (Hamburg 1978), 7–34 (19).

[30] See Dian Igor Lindberg, 'Literary Aspects of German Baroque Opera: History, Theory and Practice (Christian H. Postel and Barthold Feind)' (UMI microfilmed doctoral thesis, University of California 1964), 19.

Both of these northern German strongholds had escaped
the worst ravages of the Thirty Years War, and therefore found
themselves in a position, towards the end of the seventeenth
century, to indulge in the new-fangled theatrical luxury
of opera that was already popular in the Italian-speaking
courts of the South. In total, the libretti from Hamburg and
Braunschweig amount to some four hundred texts; very few
scores from the period survive, and any consideration of
dramatic music is, therefore, strictly limited by availability.
But literary scholars have tended to exclude music from their
studies of the early German libretto on the grounds that the
libretti (as the Italian word suggests) were printed as booklets,
and therefore intended to be read in isolation. Some, it
seems, were never even intended to be put to music.[31] But more
often the booklets were intended to accompany the spectator
into a performance, as a programme, and in centres like
Braunschweig-Wolfenbüttel, where Italian opera was popular, a German parallel translation might also be provided.
The collaboration between the composer and the librettist
was deliberate rather than incidental—it is easy to observe
the regular partnerships that developed—and however
interesting the text, a libretto is not complete without its
musical accompaniment. This necessitates a move towards
discussing the libretti in their musical context; Chapter 4
attempts to show how this might be done by scholars of
literature.

The texts are considered in a literary rather than a social
historical context—in so far as these two things are separ-
able—in order to demonstrate that the will to portray the other
(woman, the oriental, the 'infidel') in a fictive context is peren-
nial, and to show the process by which the images that are
invoked to describe and define it become fixed within the
communicative sign-system of drama. The focus is not so much
on the effect of society on the text as on the potential effect
of the text on society, that is, on the rhetorical and dialogic

[31] Bernhard Jahn has recently pointed to the existence of the 'Leselibretto',
a type he sees as related to the novel. See Jahn, 'Das Libretto als literarische
Leitgattung am Ende des 17. Jahrhunderts? Zu Zi(e)glers Roman *Die Asiatische Banise*
und seinen Opernfassungen', in Sent, *Die Oper*, 143–70.

power of the audiovisual medium of theatre. This is not
to say that portrayals of the non-self or other by Western
male writers were a sudden phenomenon, or limited to this
period. Men have always used their relative monopoly of the
arts to achieve self-definition by investigation and expression
of the idea of non-man. 'Man' in this sense is not a sex or
even necessarily a gender category, but an ideological position: it excludes not only (most) women, but also those who
hold different creeds or have different skin colours. In special circumstances, certain women may be granted masculine status, and the same applies, more exceptionally, to
non-Christians. In both cases the portrayal is usually functionalized in the service of the self or norm; an outsider is
accorded exceptional status in such a way that the status quo
is stabilized rather than subverted. The studies in the following chapters are not, therefore, an attempt to extrapolate
information from the texts about 'real' women or 'real'
Turks, but to analyse how ideas about gender and alterity are
constructed.

I have widened the traditional feminist perspective to
include the oriental or non-Christian. Setting another
category alongside 'woman' illustrates that the issue I am
investigating in these dramatic texts is not *structurally* one of
gender in the standard male/female sense: that is, that
woman is not the only idea to be gendered as feminine. In
the realm of ideas, gendering involves power and territory:
linguistic, domestic, and political. Linguistic territory is
mapped out by rhetoric and by control of the image. At base
the issue seems to be one of order, a precarious thing in an
unpredictable world, and order comes to depend crucially
on the construction of binary opposites, ranging from
masculine/feminine to good/evil, that have a fixed place
in a dualistic system. The construction of such ideas takes
place in rhetoric: the more conscious application of what we
might today call discourse. I would define the latter with the
late Sigrid Brauner: 'Discourses produce social meaning
and social identities which are always ideological.'[32]

---

[32] Brauner, 'Gender and its Subversion', 181.

In the early modern period, the rhetorical enacting and defining of masculinity and femininity on the stage feeds a developing discourse that is perceived as relevant not only to the behaviour of individual men and women, but to the stability of a whole society.

1

# THE RHETORICAL FEMININE (I):
# WOMEN AND MUSLIMS IN THE
# LITERARY IMAGINATION

The idea of woman need not be negative. In literature, women are as often portrayed as heroic Amazons or paragons of constancy as they are as witches and whores. The idea of the *femme forte* or heroic woman, for example, popularized especially in France in the early to mid-seventeenth century, is a construction of woman as ideally virtuous, and is specifically designed to refute established misogynist prejudices.[1] This might suggest that there is no obviously identifiable pattern in the traditional literary imagination. But it becomes apparent that this is an unsatisfactory mode of reading as soon as we stop reading the *sex* of the idea and instead look analytically at its *gender*. The female is not necessarily portrayed as feminine, the male not necessarily as masculine: nonetheless, those linguistic or rhetorical categories are important, and femininity is inevitably linked to female just as masculinity is to male in the writing imagination. Just how this works becomes clearer when we stop working simply with men and women characters, and start to observe the portrayal of such things as different religions—here Christianity and Islam—different skin colours, and different modes of rulership.

*Gendering Creed:* Catharina von Georgien

Gryphius's *Catharina von Georgien* is perhaps the purest illustration of the reception of the idea of the *femme forte* by a German dramatist. According to Gryphius, the play was

---

[1] For an authoritative account see Ian Maclean, *Woman Triumphant: Feminism in French Literature 1610–1652* (Oxford 1977).

written before his *Carolus Stuardus* (1650) or the execution of Charles I in 1649.[2] The most likely date is therefore that given by his seventeenth-century biographer, Baltzer Siegmund von Stosch: 1647.[3] The play gives a version of the last day in the life of the Armenian queen executed by Shah Abbas of Persia in 1624. Gryphius does not give a particular historical account as his source, but it seems likely that he followed the story principally as it was recorded by Claude Malingre, Sieur de Saint-Lazare, in his *Histoires tragiques de notre temps* (Paris 1635).[4]

Saint-Lazare's account is oddly inconsistent in its description of the relationship between Cha-Abas (Gryphius's Abas) and Catherine. It begins with an extended discussion of the power of erotic passion over men, and its political consequences, illustrated by the examples of Helen of Troy and Paris; the Roman Emperor Tarquin and Lucretia; and Theodoricus the Goth, who was defeated in Spain by the Moors after raping a Moorish woman. Saint-Lazare connects these with Catherine's story:

> Mais voici en nos jours un exemple non moins mémorable que ceux-là: c'est l'acte qui fut joué sur le théâtre de la Géorgie en la personne de Catherine, princesse du pays, par la passion déshonnête et cruelle de Cha-Abas, roi de Perse.[5]

This, however, is the only time that an erotic interest in the queen on the part of the Shah is suggested. The two of them are barely mentioned again in connection with each other until the events surrounding Catherine's death are narrated at the close of the account. In Gryphius's play it will be crucial that Catharina must choose between death and a sexual union with the Persian ruler; but in Saint-Lazare's

---

[2] 'Kurtze Anmerckungen über etliche dunckele Oerter seiner CATHARINE', I. 15. In Andreas Gryphius, *Catharina von Georgien Oder Bewehrte Beständigkeit*, ed. Hugh Powell, in *Gesamtausgabe der deutschsprachigen Werke*, vol. 6 (Tübingen 1966). All references are to this edition of the text.

[3] Baltzer Siegmund von Stosch, 'Danck= und Denck=Seule des ANDREAE GRYPHII' (1665), repr. in *Andreas Gryphius*, ed. Heinz Ludwig Arnold, 2nd edn. [= Text und Kritik 7/8 (1980)].

[4] See Eugène Susini, 'Claude Malingre, Sieur de Saint-Lazare, et son histoire de Catherine de Géorgie', in *Études Germaniques* 23 (1968), 37–53.

[5] Ibid. 42.

version religion is the issue. Abas sends his courtier Imancouly to Catherine,

de la tenter premièrement par toutes voies de douceur, flatterie et promesses, puis par paroles de rigueur et menaces de tourments, pour induire cette princesse à quitter sa foi et se faire maure, et au cas qu'elle refusât d'obéir à ce commandement, qu'il la fît cruellement mourir.[6]

One of the flattering promises made is that she will be kept as a wife if she will renounce her Christian faith. Saint-Lazare's emphasis, however, is on her 'marriage' with the new Muslim religion rather than with the Shah: '[le] roi . . . lui promettait des montagnes d'or, et de la tenir pour sa femme, si en quittant la vraie religion elle épousait la loi mahométane.'[7] This account, then, highlights Abas's wish to convert the Georgians for political reasons, as part of a plan to annexe the neighbouring state, and it registers Saint-Lazare's unease regarding the potential loss of a Christian outpost. Catherine, who had been Eastern Orthodox, is converted to Catholicism by an Augustinian priest just before her death, and Saint-Lazare closes his narrative with the satisfied observation that this event marked the entry of the Augustinians into Georgia to introduce the 'true' faith:

Le père Ambroise, confesseur de la défuncte princesse, ayant pris son chef, l'envoya à Tamaras Can, son fils . . . et par ce moyen les pères Augustins se sont donné entrée en ce royaume d'Yvérie, où le roi Tamaras leur a fait bâtir une église, où il voulut que le chef de sa mère fût mis dans une châsse d'or.[8]

There is no description of Abas's response to the death of his victim.

It is, therefore, Gryphius who introduces the sexual conflict into the story.[9] While the Cha-Abas of Saint-Lazare merely feigns love for Catherine,[10] Gryphius's tyrant is genuinely in the grip of erotic passion. Saint-Lazare's polarization of Christian and Muslim is maintained in the German

---

[6] Susini, 'Claude Malingre', 51.    [7] Ibid.    [8] Ibid. 53.
[9] Ingrid Walsøe-Engel has recently produced an interesting analysis of Gryphius's *Catharina* as a drama of seduction: *Fathers and Daughters: Patterns of Seduction in Tragedies by Gryphius, Lessing, Hebbel, and Kroetz* (Columbia, Oh. 1993).
[10] Susini, 'Claude Malingre', 48.

drama, but to it is added a powerful dramatic antithesis incorporated in the two characters who represent these faiths,
Catharina and Chach Abas. The opposition functions in a
secular as well as in a religious sense, and depends on gender difference: the polarity of male and female, masculine
and feminine.

What is perhaps the most highly developed polarity of
male and female in Western literary tradition occurs in
Petrarchism. Here, there is no union or merging of the poles:
the beloved (woman) remains absolutely separate and un-
attainable. Ingrid Walsøe-Engel has argued that Gryphius's
Catharina is not only the type of the pure female martyr, but
also a victim, so to speak, of the Petrarchan idiom, when its
polarities are fatally inverted:[11]

Gryphius reverses the 'normal' sado-masochistic relationship of the lovers.
. . . The lover is the supposedly abject martyr to the cruelties of his proud
mistress: for Catharina, the roles are fatally reversed. She is the martyr to
his obsessive sexual desire, and it is she, not her seducer/lover, who dies
when his demands are not satisfied.[12]

In opposing Catharina and Abas in this way, Gryphius turns
the almost peripheral martyred queen of Saint-Lazare's
story into an exemplary central character. The construction
and reversal of a Petrarchistic relationship between the two
protagonists is just one part of the antithetical structure that
is the key to the drama's effect.

Gryphius had spent the two years 1644–6 in France as
travelling companion to a merchant's son, Wilhelm Schlegel,
and Alois Haas has suggested that he found there the material for his drama.[13] Haas refers to Saint-Lazare's *Histoires
Tragiques* as Gryphius's historical source; it is likely, however,
that the German traveller also found stimuli in the literature
surrounding the so-called *querelle des femmes*. From 1643 to
1652—throughout Gryphius's visit—Anne of Austria was
Regent in France. Hers was the third period of female
regency in less than a hundred years in a country in which
Salic law forbade women to rule outright: Catherine de
Médicis had held the regency from 1561 to 1563 and in 1574,

---

[11] Walsøe-Engel, *Fathers and Daughters*, 44–53.      [12] Ibid. 52.
[13] Alois Haas, 'Nachwort' in *Catharina von Georgien* (Stuttgart 1975), 135–57 (135).

and Marie de Médicis from 1610 to 1614. The unpopularity of the latter in particular may have provided one stimulus for Alexis Trousset's misogynist text, *L'Alphabet de l'Imperfection et Malice des Femmes*, published under the pseudonym 'Jacques Olivier' in 1617, which appears to have sparked off the bout of pro- and antifeminist argument known as the *querelle des femmes*. In his authoritative study, Maclean concludes that this *querelle* was a feature principally of the first three decades of the seventeenth century.[14] But the regency of Anne inevitably encouraged further writing in praise of women, especially ruling women, and two influential pro-feminist works in the tradition of the *querelle* were published in the mid-seventeenth century, around the time of Gryphius's stay: Jacques Du Bosc's *La Femme Heroïque* (1645) and Pierre Le Moyne's *Gallerie des Femmes Fortes* (1647).

Both of these followed Boccaccio's lead (in his *De mulieribus claris* of 1355)[15] by citing an exemplary series of famous women from history and biblical history; this became a standard method of pro-feminist argument.[16] The point was to illustrate women's capacity for heroic virtue and, importantly, for government, to which end the masculine qualities of political and military prowess had to be reallocated to woman. The *femme forte* was thus created. The term originates in the first verse of the Alphabet of the Good Woman in Proverbs, but, as Maclean points out, feminist writers do not draw their conception of the *femme forte* from her description in these verses;[17] the new *femme forte* is distinctly more masculine in type, *force* being conceived of as stoic apathy (*Beständigkeit*), and *fortitudo*.

The idea of the heroic woman is an oxymoron, and striking because of the element of surprise or curiosity it engenders. Gryphius's Catharina is a doubly paradoxical figure: not

[14] Maclean, *Woman Triumphant*, 35.
[15] Boccaccio's text was also translated into German, by Stainhöwel in 1473; the translation appeared in several editions to 1576. See Boccaccio, *De claris mulieribus Deutsch übersetzt von Stainhöwel*, ed. Karl Drescher (Tübingen 1895).
[16] See Christa Schlumbohm, 'Die Glorifizierung der Barockfürstin als "Femme Forte"', in August Buck *et al.* (eds.), *Europäische Hofkultur im 16. und 17. Jahrhundert*, 1. 112–22 (114). I follow Schlumbohm's use of 'profeminist' to mean 'anti-misogynist'.
[17] Maclean, *Woman Triumphant*, 81–2.

only is she Chach's Petrarchan *dolce nemica*, she is also the
perfect example of a *femme forte*, embodying *douceur, beauté,
force* and *fierté*.[18] In a dramatic system of antitheses she is therefore bound to stand in a complex relationship to her dramatic opponent, and this works because Gryphius creates
in Chach Abas not only an *homme faible*, so to speak, but also
Catharina's *penibile amico*. Even before her first appearance,
Catharina is introduced in ideal terms that more usually pertain to the masculine. Demetrius, the Georgian ambassador,
describes her capacity as a ruler with emphatic reference
to the political and military qualities that characterize the
*femme forte*:

> O Königin der Frauen
>
> .    .    .    .    .    .    .    .    .    .    .
>
> Die Vaterland und Reich durch Faust und Recht geschützt/
> Den Strom der Tyrraney mit Stahl und Mutt gestützt          (I. 101 ff.)

Two main points of contention in the *querelle* are thus dealt
with at this early stage in the drama, namely Catharina's capacity as a woman for just government and for valour in times
of strife.

Catharina's dramatic counterpart, Chach Abas, notably lacks
these qualities. When the ambassador relates Abas's recent
political activities to Catharina, he emphasizes 'wie der
Tyrann mit List und stetem Meineyd spilt [*sic*]' (I. 580). Abas
practises the politics of calculating cowardice: 'Chach weiß
daß Reussen nicht umb eine Fraw wird kämpffen' (I. 157),
and of deceit, using those in his power to destroy one another.
We are told, for example, that the Georgian hostage Constantin is made much of by Abas and encouraged to murder
his own father and brother, yet that Abas subsequently
applauds the death of Constantin at the hands of the vengeful
Georgians (III. 117–220). His next effort is to cause a rift
between the successor he sends back to Gurgistan, Tamaras,
and his neighbour Alovas (III. 221–75).[19] The 'Reye der
von Chach Abas erwürgeten Fürsten' underlines Chach's

---

[18] Compare Schlumbohm, 'Die Glorifizierung', 114 ff.
[19] In these details, Gryphius follows Saint-Lazare's account, transforming the narrative into a lengthy history related by the heroine.

preference for less direct methods than Catharina's heroic
force of arms:

> Was nützt es seinem Stahl entrinnen;
> Wenn schwartze Gifft kont uns gewinnen?    (II. 383–4)

Nor is justice a characteristic of Abas's regime. Catharina
describes his tyrannical fury on discovering that Gurgistan
has pledged allegiance to the Ottomans rather than to
Persia, and how he vents it on the innocent courtiers who
try to dissuade him from launching a punitive attack:

> Can Alovard der ihm diß außzureden tracht;
> Ward unversehns mit Gifft an seinem Tisch' umbbracht.
> Er hiß in tollem Grimm den Curtzi Bassi prügeln/
> Und nach gehäuffter Schmach in einem Thurm verrigeln.
> Er biß als sein Gemahl ihn bat/ nicht auß dem Land
> Zu weichen/ ihr erhitzt/ die Finger von der Hand
>
> (III. 327–32)

Catharina has the heroic quality of patriotism; she is 'die
werthe Fürstin . . . Die stritt und lid [sic] für Kirch und
Thron und Herd [= Erde]' (I. 82 ff.). Abas, on the other hand,
is reproached by his shocked adviser, Seinal Can, for giving
his love for a foreign princess priority over that for his country: 'Ist ihrer Majestet was liber als ihr Land!' (II. 336). The
passion Abas indulges contrasts starkly with the stoic apathy
maintained by Catharina. Even on receipt of the news that
her freedom is imminent after eight years of imprisonment,
she controls her response and reproaches her lady-in-waiting
for an impetuous outburst of joy:

> Regire dein Gemütt. Die Freud ist vil zu groß!
> .    .    .    .    .    .    .    .    .    .
> Wir hoffen nicht zu vil und fürchten nicht zu sehr    (IV. 72 ff.)

A point of contention in the *querelle* is whether or not *raison*
(*Vernunft*) can be attributed to women. We shall see that
Lohenstein constructs *Vernunft* as the essential characteristic
of a successful male politician; in Gryphius's play it is a woman
who argues for this quality, and the ruling man who fails
to display it. This is illustrated in the dispute between
Catharina and Abas regarding erotic passion and *Vernunft*:

CHACH. Was Abas schafft muß Recht/ dafern es Unrecht/ werden.
CATH. Er schafft der Libe nicht die keinen Herren kent.
CHACH. Wir geben über uns ihr völlig Regiment.
CATH. Sie lest sich durch Vernunfft auff rechte Wege lencken.

(I. 784–7)

Chach Abas's inability to regulate his passion creates another paradoxical situation underlying the relationship of the two protagonists, namely his 'captivity' as opposed to his prisoner's 'freedom'. The captivity of the lover is a commonplace enough conceit, but in this drama the idea is given depth by the metaphysical opposition of Chach and Catharina. The imprisonment/freedom paradox of the erotic theme is paralleled in the imprisonment/freedom (and life/death) contradiction that is standard in the portrayal of the martyr. Because Catharina has the fortitude to free herself from ruling passions, she is spiritually at liberty even in physical captivity, while Chach Abas, with all the asserted freedom of the tyrant, is helplessly in thrall to the corporeal world. Within the confines of that world he is already tasting the torments of his final destination, which again will be the antithesis of Catharina's: Hell.

The opposition of male Abas and female Catharina and the cross-attributing of masculine and feminine ideas to these two central characters is a conscious device on Gryphius's part. Within the drama the protagonists themselves use gendered ideas self-consciously and rhetorically. Catharina introduces herself with reference both to her heroic (or pseudo-masculine) qualities and to her femaleness:

> Wir haben diß volbracht [*sic*]
> Was eine Fürstin sol/ was eine Fraw in Macht
> Und Mutter hat in Trew erbötig noch zu wagen    (I. 447–9)

In a discussion of the queen's resoluteness, Abas and his courtier Seinal Can exchange opposing views of the feminine:

> SEIN. Ein Weib verändert leicht.
> CHACH. Was kan verstockter seyn
>   Als ein hartnäckicht Weib?    (II. 115–16)

Both, of course, are wrong, since Catharina's determination is the *Beständigkeit* of the *femme forte*, and therefore belongs to the masculine rather than the feminine category.

The automatic association of femaleness with femininity in all its connotations is rhetorically and manipulatively used by the opposing Persian and pro-Georgian factions. The representations made to Abas by the Russian ambassador on Catharina's behalf depend for their success on the assumption that women are both worthless and ineffectual:

Czar bildet fest' ihm ein daß Abas mehr verzeih'
Als eine Fraw verwürckt; wie schuldig sie auch sey.   (II. 167–8)

The same chain of meaning is evoked by the ambassador, to point up the contrast between her behaviour and that of her persecutor: 'Hat jemals ein Tyrann so auff ein Weib gewüttet?' (V. 197). The standard martyr/tyrant antithesis of early modern drama is rendered more poignant by the attribution of feminine vulnerability to the martyr figure, but Seinal Can's last-ditch attempt to save Catharina with recourse to to the discourse of female worthlessness is unsuccessful:

Sie/ war ein frembdes Weib. Eur eigen Nutz ist groß.   (V. 331)

In Saint-Lazare's account and in Gryphius's drama Catharina is stripped naked before she is tortured, and the torture itself relates peculiarly to her sex, being concentrated on her breasts and thighs. There may be various levels of motivation for such a representation. Her waiting-women connect her nakedness with the *imitatio Christi* she is performing: 'So hat ihr Heyland selbst entblöst erblassen müssen' (V. 65). Walsøe-Engel sees in the scene an analogy with the preparation of the bride for the bridegroom's arrival, whereby Catharina's death agony later corresponds to bridal defloration.[20] There is also a visual aspect, related to her portrayal as *femme forte*: the image conjured by the report of Catharina's death is strongly coloured by her femaleness and the idea of the vulnerable, sexually available femininity associated with nakedness. She is described standing exposed to her executioners like a Botticelli Venus:

Sie stund gleich einem Bild von Jungfern-Wachs bereitet
Das Har fil umb den Hals nachlässig außgebreitet/
Und flog theils in die Lufft/ theils hing als in der Wag
In dem man auff der Brust spürt jeden Aderschlag.   (V. 69–72)

---

[20] Walsøe-Engel, *Fathers and Daughters*, 40–1.

Catharina's masculine constancy and fortitude appear all the more striking by contrast with this feminine vision. At the same time her apparent vulnerability is disarming, and helps undermine any sense of threat that an audience might feel when faced with a woman of masculine fortitude.

The image of Catharina as bride of Christ draws us into the religious aspect of her portrayal. Like *femme forte, amazone chrétienne*—another frequent epithet in the French *querelle*—is a contradiction in terms. The Amazon is a pagan figure who traditionally challenges the rule of men. In Catharina the contradiction is resolved and the threat neutralized, because her allegiance is not to her own worldly best interests but to the paternalistic values represented by her metaphysical father and bridegroom.

The precarious position of humanity in an antithetical metaphysical scheme is defined in the stage directions as Gryphius's play opens: 'Uber [*sic*] dem Schau-Platz öffnet sich der Himmel/ unter dem Schau-Platz die Helle'. The binary arrangement of these localities is reproduced in the polarity of stage space observed by Eggers:[21] in the course of the drama the front of the stage is established as the locality of Abas, the back as that of Catharina. The two scenes in which they share a locality (I. vii and the final scene) are therefore of special significance. In the first case the space shared is Catharina's prison, in the second it is Abas's royal chamber.

Act I, scene vii is the only one in the piece in which the two central characters physically confront each other. They engage in an extended rhetorical disputation typical of the school drama, in which each side puts forward an argument, pressing the audience into the role of a considering jury. Walsøe-Engel correctly describes the discourse of Catharina and Abas as 'competitive' rather than 'communicative':[22] the element of contest in the exchange is stylistically emphasized by stichomythia. She also observes of Catharina that 'her relationship to language is a cognitive one: for her, language is the unalterable reflection of an absolute, divinely-ordained truth', while Abas is 'manipulative and metaphorical' in his

---

[21] Werner Eggers, *Wirklichkeit und Wahrheit im Trauerspiel des Andreas Gryphius* (Heidelberg 1967), 29.

[22] Walsøe-Engel, *Fathers and Daughters*, 45.

use of language.[23] In a slight self-contradiction, Walsøe-Engel attributes Catharina's success in the battle of words to 'her superior command of language and her familiarity with the petrarchistic idiom';[24] but in fact Catharina triumphs not so much by her participation in an intricate rhetorical game as by simply being on the side of right. An exchange on the subject of marriage in her disputation with Abas reveals the forensic advantage Christianity lends in Gryphius's Christian world-view:

CATH. Der Christen Recht verknüpfft nur Zwey durch dises [*sic*] Band.
CHACH. Der Persen Recht gilt mehr. Wir sind in ihrem Land!
CATH. Noch mehr deß Höchsten Recht! wir stehn auff seiner Erden.

(I. 781–3)

A second disputation occurs, this time between Catharina and Iman Culi, in the third scene of Act IV. The courtier has the task of persuading Catharina to marry Abas, with the conversion to Islam this would involve. She initially puts the practical point of view that she has nothing to gain from such a marriage, but all to lose; she objects to the Shah's aberrant sexuality (IV. 141–4), and, more importantly, recoils from the idea of relinquishing her faith and her martyrdom. She defies Abas in a crescendo of Christian constancy:

Nemmt Kercker für Paläst/ für Freyheit; Ketten an/
Für Reichthumb/ kiest Verlust und was ergetzen kan
Verwächselt mit der Qual. Wagt Freund und Fleisch und Jahre!
Erschreckt für keiner Flamm! springt auff die Todtenbare!
Küst Schwerdter die man euch durch Brust und Gurgel treibt!
Wenn euch der eine Schatz deß heilgen Glaubens bleibt!

(IV. 175–80)

Iman Culi responds pragmatically, from the non-Christian perspective: 'Durchlauchtigst es ist hart für einen Wahn zu sterben' (IV. 181), and a religious contest ensues. Catharina's evocation of Christ's Passion prefigures her *imitatio* (IV. 190 ff.). The Persian puts forward a *carpe diem* argument; she counters with the *vanitas* idea:

---

[23] Walsøe-Engel, *Fathers and Daughters*, 45.    [24] Ibid. 49.

IMAN. Last uns weil wir noch hir der Zeit und Welt gebrauchen!
CATH. In einem Nun wird Welt und ihre Pracht verrauchen.

(IV. 201–2)

The rhetorical move that decides the religious encounter is again based on the a priori argument that the Christian world view is simply *right*:

IMAN. Es ist ein falscher Wahn der ihren Geist bethöret.
CATH. Die Warheit haben wir auß Gottes Mund gehöret.   (IV. 217–18)

Iman Culi, although a Muslim, is not an evil character. He expresses his good nature in sympathy and admiration for the Georgian queen, having failed to persuade her to choose marriage over execution: 'Ade denn wertte Fraw! die bessern Glückes wert' (IV. 263). The good Persian sharpens by contrast our perception of the bad one: the absolute rightness of Catharina's religious position is complemented not by Iman Culi's incomprehension, but by the absolute wrongness of Abas's.

Gryphius signals his heroine's perfection by linking her with the Christian epitome of right behaviour, in references to Christ's Passion. The roses brought by her lady-in-waiting, Salome, are transformed by a dream into a crown of thorns on Catharina's head (I. 323 ff.), and she recalls the image when she is informed of her certain execution:

Wir haben von der Cron nur Dornen zu Gewin!
Nur Dornen! die wir noch als alle Lust verschwunden
Den Rosenblättern gleich/ auff disem Har [*sic*] gefunden   (IV. 356–8)

Repeated hints of Catharina's *imitatio Christi* are confirmed in her own exclamation here: 'Schaut JEsus [*sic*] geht voran!' (IV. 351).[25]

Her Christ-like qualities are mirrored by shades of Antichrist in her opponent. Like the Abas of Saint-Lazare, Gryphius's tyrant persecutes Christians and attempts to destroy what is holy to them (I. 517 ff.). The 'Reye der

[25] Schings has argued that Catharina's 'wahres Martyrium' in the drama is set against the tyrant's 'falsches Martyrium der Leidenschaft', an anti-martyrdom. See Hans-Jürgen Schings, '*Catharina von Georgien. Oder Bewehrete Beständigkeit*', in *Die Dramen des Andreas Gryphius: Eine Sammlung von Einzelinterpretationen* (Stuttgart 1968), 35–72 (56).

Gefangenen Jungfrauen' at the close of Act I aligns the Persian ruler with the side of death and the devil, when they celebrate Catharina's crown of honour, 'trotz Chach und Tod!' (I. 865). The final scene is a clear echo of the first.[26] Although the locality is Abas's royal chamber, heavenly eternity is present in the figure of the dead Catharina, who as a ghost is restored from the disfiguration inflicted on her during her torture and execution. Hell, too, is at hand; at least in the consciousness of Abas:

> Der Erden Grund brüllt und erzittert!
> Was ist das hinter uns sich wüttert
> Wie? oder schreckt uns eitle Fantasy!    (V. 425–7)

Abas is not only on the path to damnation, but is *already* a terrestrial manifestation of the infernal, just as Catharina's earthly presence is *already* suffused with heavenly perfection.[27] Gryphius is able to play with another ironic reversal when he describes the destruction of Catharina's body by burning (V. 125); the flames that engulf her are terrestrial and temporary, those surrounding Abas, although merely metaphorical in the worldly context, are more real than her funeral pyre because they are understood to be eternal.

The introductory scene was prophetic, and its suggestions are fulfilled at the play's close, when the tangible realm of the world is revealed as no more than a dividing line between the binary poles inhabited by Catharina and Chach Abas. Abas and Catharina rule neighbouring kingdoms. Within the antithetical structure of the drama, however, Persia and Gurgistan come to represent Orient and Christendom respectively. A distinct division is apparent even in the dramatis personae. The names of those in the Georgian/Christian camp are romanized (Catharina, Serena, Cassandra, Procopius, Demetrius, Ambrosius) and therefore connote the occidental, cultured, civilized world. The Persians, on the other hand, have unfamiliar names and titles (Chach Abas, Seinal Can, Iman Culi); they evoke the fascination of the exotic,

---

[26] Schings, *Die Dramen des Andreas Gryphius*, 60.
[27] Schings notes 'das Höllenmotiv, bei der Gestaltung des Chach ja schon gelegentlich mit im Spiel'. Ibid.

but also suggest unintelligibility and therefore, in an etymological and wider sense, barbarity.

With a certain amount of 'oriental colour', Gryphius
plays with the exotic or titillating potential of the East. The
division of the stage into palace and prison provides scope
for the depiction of oriental opulence by contrast with
Christian asceticism. On a more threatening note, the
'Reyen der gefangenen Jungfrauen' that concludes Act III
hints at gruesome practices:

> Uns wird nicht vor Sirvan grauen
> Da sie Thürm auß Köpffen bauen.   (III. 489–90)

In a slightly shamefaced note to these lines—which does
not, of course, detract from their effect within the play—
Gryphius refers to two travel reports, the popular exoticizing fuel for early modern curiosity, and admits that he may
be playing up the bloodthirstiness by implying that the
skulls are those of men:

Nahe bey Sirvan sind die Uberbleibungen [*sic*] eines Thurmes von Steinen
und Todten-Köpffen zu finden/ derer Edelen abgehauen/ welche der
König in Persen bezwungen . . . Wiewol etliche der Meynung er hätte seinen
Grimm geändert/ und an stat Menschen- so vil Hundes-Köpffe dahin
setzen lassen. (p. 124)

Within the play, the reference threatens and titillates
simultaneously.

But the threat becomes more serious when religious
issues or the basic tenets of Christian society are at stake.
Gryphius's Islamic oriental Persia is (as in Saint-Lazare's
account) perceived as a predator. Catharina is the lamb,
Abas the wolf (I. 214); the metaphor is sustained when his
servant Meurab later reveals himself as a (Christian) sheep
in a (Muslim) wolf's clothing: 'Mein Kleid siht Persisch
auß/ im Hertzen steckt ein Christ' (I. 604). This is also relevant to the contest of *Sein* and *Schein*: Orient/Islam is the
superficial or external element, Christianity by implication
the inner reality.

Meurab himself is a victim of Abas's voracious sexual
appetite, the opposite pole to Catharina's chastity. A reference to animality in Catharina's description of the crime is
not accidental:

Da Meurabs Fraw von Chach in Meurabs Angesicht
So freventlich entehrt! O blitzt der Himmel nicht!
Da Meurabs zarter Sohn und Tochter diß erlitten
Was angeborne Recht' auch stummen Vieh verbitten!    (I. 483–6)

Like woman, the oriental takes a lower position in the perceived hierarchy of men and animals. In the binary scheme, the oriental falls on the side of the feminine: both Shakespeare's *Antony and Cleopatra* (1606/7) and Lohenstein's *Cleopatra* (1680) indicate the debilitating, feminizing influence of the Orient on Antony.[28] Gryphius's Meurab draws on the same idea when inciting the Georgians to resist the sovereignty of Abas in their country:

Habt ihr noch so vil Muts mit mir ein Schwerdt zu zücken;
So wollen wir diß Land Chach auß den Fäusten rücken.
Wo aber langer Dinst euch gantz zu Weibern macht;
So last mich hir allein.

(I. 609–12)

As the two kingdoms in question are geographically proximate, their division into Orient and Occident must depend on the religious disparity. Unlike Saint-Lazare, Gryphius makes no distinction between forms of Christianity (Eastern Orthodox or Catholic) and there is no conversion of the heroine at the moment of her martyrdom. This may represent a prudent suppression of detail by a Protestant dramatist, but it also avoids confusion on the question of sides: the Orient is the Islamic world and carries associations of danger and evil. With the vision of Hell in the prologue it provides (in the person of Chach) an opposing pole for the virtuous Christian world represented by Catharina and the vision of Heaven. Abas and Catharina perfectly correspond to Walter Benjamin's 'Janushäupter des Gekrönten':[29] one head turned towards the worldly, the other towards the heavenly sphere.

[28] Shakespeare's *Antony and Cleopatra* opens with a reference to Antony's change from a masculine general to the effeminate lover of a 'gypsy' (I. i. 1–10); similar associations with Egyptianness are evident in Lohenstein's *Cleopatra*, when Proculejus challenges Anton to prove 'Daß sein Gemütte nicht zu sehr Egyptisch sei' (I. 821).

[29] Walter Benjamin, *Ursprung des deutschen Trauerspiels* (1928), ed. Rolf Tiedemann (Frankfurt a.M. 1990 [1978]), 51.

In inverting the genders of his two protagonists, Gryphius uses established, gendered chains of meaning to particular effect. Abas's femininity consists in cowardice, inconstancy, uncontrolled sexuality, weakness of will, while Catharina's masculinity is expressed in valour, constancy, chastity, and an unswayable sense of purpose. Even the religions they embody acquire a gender: Islam is feminine, Christianity masculine, and in this there is a political message. Saint-Lazare clearly perceived the Islamic world as a predatory threat to Christendom, a view which Gryphius appears to share. If, however, the Muslim male is seen to incorporate the attributes of the feminine, which are placed low down in the hierarchy of values, while the Christian female is masculinized by her religion to the extent that she can achieve complete moral victory, the danger of the Orient and of the rival religion, Islam, is lessened. It is important to note here that the prior assumptions about femininity on which the effect of the *femme forte* depends remain unchanged. Gryphius's heroine embodies what is emphatically the extraordinary: the 'real' weakness of her gender is transferred to her unsuccessful oriental opponent. This transferral is made by the dramatist for the sake of persuasive effect; it is, in fact, a rhetorical device, and one we shall see recurring in later dramas, in which the threat of Islam is located more specifically in the figure of the Turk.

## The Feminized Turk

Ideas about femininity and about cultural Otherness—orientality or barbarism—were already linked in Classical drama. Hall has identified their relationship in Aeschylus, and shown that 'femaleness, barbarism, luxury and hubris are . . . ineluctably drawn into the same semantic complex'.[30] Hall also notes that a structural similarity is apparent in portrayals of virtuous barbarians and strong women in Greek literature: 'Just as the gynaecocratic Lemnians and Amazons

---

[30] Edith Hall, *Inventing the Barbarian: Greek Self-Definition through Tragedy* (Oxford 1989), 206.

of myth, and the powerful Clytemnaestras and Medeas of tragedy, were only conspicuous because Greek society was run by men, so the noble barbarians stood out in relief because their kind was normally denigrated.'[31] This pattern is of course also the basis for the apparent idealization of women in the early modern tradition of the *femme forte*: the exception reinforces the rule. There is an obvious analogy between the conception of the barbarian and that of woman in early modern Europe, too: if women are felt to pose an internal threat to Western patriarchy in the sixteenth and seventeenth centuries, then non-Christian societies threaten upset from without, especially during periods of territorial struggle. By tracing the development of literary ideas about Muslims from the fall of Constantinople, with reference to the historical events which are likely to have provoked an increased literary concern with the subject, it is possible to show how the kind of conceptual canon that Gryphius was able to exploit becomes established.

These events—notably the Ottoman expansion—do mean that the 'barbarian', from being generally Asiatic or 'Saracen', is distinctly Islamic, conceived of and described as the Turk;[32] an inaccurate category, since the Ottomans themselves would have shunned the term. They looked down on the Turcomans as an inferior ethnic group comprised of Anatolian peasants who would not even have understood the language of the ruling élite.[33] But Norman Daniel has observed a long history of such attempts within Christendom to classify a major rival: 'A twofold attack on Islam dates from early days: *luxuriosus* and *bellicosus*. . . . Christian criticism along this line goes back to at least the ninth century in both East and West.'[34]

[31] Hall, *Inventing the Barbarian*, 222.

[32] See Alev Tekinay, *Materialien zum vergleichenden Studium von Erzählmotiven in der deutschen Dichtung des Mittelalters und den Literaturen des Orients* (Frankfurt a.M. 1980), 28.

[33] Andrina Stiles, *The Ottoman Empire 1450–1700* (London 1989), 9–11.

[34] Norman Daniel, *Heroes and Saracens: An Interpretation of the Chansons de Geste* (Edinburgh 1984), 69. I am indebted to Dr David Constantine for the hint that such sentiments coexisted with a quite different early attitude towards the Turks. This is described by Terence Spencer, and appears to have been based on the medieval belief that the Turks were the descendants and avengers of the Classical Trojans. See Spencer, *Fair Greece, Sad Relic: Literary Philhellenism from Shakespeare to Byron* (London 1954), 8–9. This attitude does not appear to be reflected in early

What Daniel categorizes negatively as an attack is not always overtly or unambiguously such, however. The idea of the Turk as *bellicosus* implies both cruelty and a tyrannical impulse, but may also embrace an apparent or real admiration of the enemy's military prowess. *Luxuriosus*, with its overtones of degenerate sexuality, may suggest animality and perversity, but it also expresses an exoticizing fascination with the unfamiliar. The literary idea of the Turk, like that of the *femme forte*, is rendered complex by an apparent ambivalence. How does one account for virtuous Turks who are rewarded with death, or for idealized descriptions of Muslims: of the religious and territorial enemy? At all events, such texts must be read as the literary fruits of the long and fraught relationship between the Ottoman and the Holy Roman Empires.

Europeans and Ottomans were engaged in uneasy contact from the fourteenth century, when the latter founded their state.[35] The shock to the Christian side of Constantinople's fall to the forces of Mehmet II in May 1453 was considerable. In September, Pope Nicholas V called Christians to a new crusade, using biblical exegesis as a rhetorical weapon: he characterized the Turkish Sultan as the seven-headed dragon of Revelation, the son of Satan, thirsty for Christian blood.[36] In December of the following year, the recently established Gutenberg press produced the earliest dated printed document extant, Albrecht Pfister's *Eyn manung der cristenheit widder die durcken*. Common reference to this as the *Türkenkalender* is misleading. As Eckehard Simon has indicated, it is in fact an early political pamphlet, a deliberate incitement to resistance.[37]

---

modern German literature, probably because, having taken the Greek islands, the Ottomans moved swiftly towards the Austro-Hungarian borderlands, presenting a threat which even Classical nostalgia could not dispel.

[35] Senol Özyurt traces the progress of the conflict in her introduction to *Die Türkenlieder und das Türkenbild in der deutschen Volksüberlieferung vom 16. bis zum 20. Jahrhundert* (Munich 1972).

[36] See Eckehard Simon, 'Der Türke in Nürnberg: zur Türkenpolemik nach 1453 und "Des Turken vastnachtspil"', in Eijiro Iwasaki (ed.), *Begegnung mit dem 'Fremden': Grenzen—Traditionen—Vergleiche: Akten des VIII. Internationalen Germanisten-Kongresses*, 11 vols. (Munich 1991), 7. 322–8 (322).

[37] Ibid. 323.

Not all anti-Turkish writing is as transparent as Pfister's. Because Hans Rosenplüt's *Des Turken [sic] vasnachtspiel* (1454) does not ride the wave of overt anti-Turkish polemic, Simon decides that this is not a political Shrovetide play.[38] It is not, in the sense that it does not incite the Nuremberger to take up arms against the Ottomans. This would, in any case, hardly be an effective approach in the carnival atmosphere. What it does, however, is to use a ridiculous portrayal of the Turkish foreigner not only in the comic tradition as a means of uniting an audience of indigenous insiders in mirth, but also as a critical mirror held up to contemporary German society.[39] Much later, Montesquieu's *Lettres Persanes* (1721) herald this typical function of the Orient in Enlightenment literature: the view of one's own society and its failings achieved by its reflection in the eyes of a stranger is a deliberately alienated one, 'satirisch verfremdet'.[40] Although this approach has been discussed by critics predominantly with reference to later writing, Montesquieu has precedents other than Rosenplüt. Occidental self-reference by oriental mirroring is a feature of early travel reports, and may also account for the portrayal of the Sultan in *Des Turken vasnachtspil*. Simon may well be overlooking the satire in the depiction of a Turkish Sultan as a 'positive' character who intends to reform degenerate Christian society. That society is degenerate certainly appears to be Rosenplüt's message.[41] It is unlikely, though, that a public in the immediate aftermath of the fall of Constantinople, in the light of the tales of cruelty and persecution which proceeded from it, would have taken seriously the promises of any Turk to effect

---

[38] Simon, 'Der Türke in Nürnberg', 327.

[39] Karl Ulrich Syndram introduces the idea of the Orient as 'kritischer Spiegel' in his essay, 'Der erfundene Orient in der europäischen Literatur vom 18. bis zum Beginn des 20. Jahrhunderts', in G. Sievernich and H. Budde (eds.), *Europa und der Orient 800–1900* (Gütersloh 1989), 324–41.

[40] See Claudia Opitz, 'Der aufgeklärte Harem: Kulturvergleich und Geschlechterbeziehungen in Montesquieus "Perserbriefen"', in *Feministische Studien* 2 (1991), 22–56 (42).

[41] See Hans Rosenplüt, *Des Turken vasnachtspil*, 39 in *Fastnachtspiele aus dem 15. Jahrhundert*, ed. Adelbert von Keller (Stuttgart 1853; repr. Darmstadt 1965), vol. 1 (*Bibliothek des Litterarischen Vereins*, vol. 28), 288–304 (301 ff.).

benevolent reform in Christendom.[42] Instead they might have understood the political irony in the suggestion that the dreaded Ottoman should offer to improve on contemporary Christian government. In keeping with the lightweight genre of *Fastnachtspiel*, the threat of the Turk is defused in the various comic punishments promised in retribution for war crimes at Constantinople (*Des Turken vasnachtspil*, 295 ff.). Nonetheless, two serious political elements emerge from Rosenplüt's piece. There is criticism of the home system that tolerates social decay, and implicit criticism of the Turkish state as much worse. We must recognize that the satirical use of the Turkish outsider as a mirror can only function if the dreadfulness of the Turk is *presupposed* to the extent that his 'positive' portrayal can only be understood ironically.

In the latter half of the fifteenth and the earlier part of the sixteenth centuries the Turkish advances continued. Less than eighty years after the fall of Constantinople, the Ottoman threat to Christendom peaked again, with the first siege of Vienna in 1529. Mehmed II had moved on from Constantinople to take Serbia in 1459, Bosnia in 1463, and Albania in 1466; his successor Suleyman I ('the Magnificent') took Belgrade in 1521 and Rhodes in 1522, before defeating the Hungarians at Mohács on 29 August 1526 to make Budapest a Turkish-ruled city, and bring the Ottoman forces uncomfortably close to the central areas of the Holy Roman Empire. Three years later, from 22 September to 15 October 1529, Vienna was under siege. In a move against passive resignation or direct surrender in the face of the Ottoman advances, more and more deliberately incendiary anti-Turkish pamphlets appeared, and before the fall of Rhodes in 1522 the widely-read *Türckenbiechlin* was printed.[43] This piece of propaganda communicates a number of ideas about the aggressor which would characterize

[42] Islamic law allowed three days of unrestricted plunder, pillage, rape, and murder to the victorious soldiers in any city which had refused the chance to surrender. This was the case in Constantinople. See Stiles, *The Ottoman Empire*, 7–8.

[43] See the editors' introduction, 'Vom Kriege wider die Türken', in *D. Martin Luthers Werke. Kritische Gesamtausgabe* (Weimar 1883– ; henceforth *WA*), vol. 30/2, pp. 85 ff.

writing about Turks for at least the next two centuries: papal failings and the Turkish advances are connected, something which is taken to an extreme in Luther's writings, and the Ottomans are perceived as divine punishment for the sins of Christendom.[44] Both of these motifs are observed by Senol Özyurt in early German folk-songs about the Turk; other recurring themes include Turkish immorality and cruelty, the Turk as tyrant, and the Turk as the butt of comedy.[45] She also notes the simultaneous and contradictory interest in the exemplary qualities of the Turks, particularly as warriors, but also in their private morality.[46] These are all ideas we shall see recurring in works by Luther and other early writers.

In the sixteenth century, Catholics and Reformers express predictably opposed opinions on who is to blame for the divine application of the Turkish scourge, or *Gottesrute*. Luther and his followers blame the Pope and his See; the papalists put it down to the heresies of the Wittenberg reformer. Luther in particular acquires and develops ideas already in circulation about the Turk with his usual rhetorical adeptness, such as in his influential interpretation of the Book of Daniel. A more polemical view of the Turkish enemy emerges from the reformer's three tracts: *Vom Kriege wider die Türken*, which appeared prior to the siege of Vienna, in April 1529; *Heerpredigt wider den Türken*, which was printed just subsequently to it, in December of that year; and the *Vermahnung zum Gebet wider den Türken* of 1541, the year in which Suleyman took Ofen and the Turks again occupied a position dangerously close to the Austrian capital.

In the preface to his translation of Daniel, Luther refers to current events when interpreting the significance of the eleventh horn on the fourth beast of Daniel's dream, which since Jerome traditionally represents the fourth or Roman empire. Luther interprets:

UND das ein kleins Horn/ sol drey Hörner von den fordersten zehen Hörnern abstossen/ Das ist der Mahmet oder Türcke/ der itzt Egypten/ Asiam und Greciam hat. Und wie dasselbige kleine Horn/ sol die

---

[44] *D. Martin Luthers Werke. Kritische Gesamtausgabe*, 89.
[45] Özyurt, *Die Türkenlieder*, 36–8; 121 ff.; 124–6; 98–100, 126–7.
[46] Ibid. 41.

Heiligen bestreiten/ und Christum lestern. Welchs wir alles erfaren/ und fur unsern augen sehen. Denn der Türck hat grossen sieg wider die Christen gehabt/ und leugnet doch Christum und hebt seinen Mahmet uber alles. Das wir nu gewislich nicht zu warten haben/ denn des Jüngsten tags/ Denn der Türck wird nicht mehr Hörner uber die drey/ abstossen.[47]

The last idea in this prophetic interpretation is of course a comforting one for the increasingly insecure subjects of the Holy Roman Empire. In the *Heerpredigt*, Luther concludes his discussion of Daniel's prophecy with the authoritative words:

So wird und kan der Türke nymer mehr so mechtig werden, als das Römisch reich gewesen ist, sonst würden nicht vier, sondern funff keiserthum auff erden komen. Darümb mus der Türke kein keiser werden noch ein new odder eigen keiserthum auffrichten, wie ers wol ym syn habt, Aber es wird und mus yhm gewislich feylen odder Daniel würde zum lügener, Das ist nicht müglich.[48]

At the root of the certainty expressed in this passage is the idea of a divinely imposed (Christian) order, which must and can establish itself in the face of threatening (non-Christian) disruption.

Luther's constant associations of Pope, Turk, and devil are antichaotic admonitions, for each of the three embodies, in his view, the potential to overturn a God-given world order. Connections between dark-skinned peoples and devilishness are not new in the sixteenth century: a medieval term for devil, testified to in the work of Walther von der Vogelweide and Konrad von Würzburg, is *hellemôr* (infernal Moor).[49] Luther's tracts on the Turk firmly place the Ottomans in this category, even though he polemicizes against the Pope as worse than the Turk on the *Endechrist* scale of evil. Luther makes effective use of the alliterative possibilities of 'Türke' and 'Teuffel',[50] and he, like the author of the *Türckenbiechlin*, functionalizes the enemy as a divine scourge. The rhetorical suggestion is that the Turks have no independent purpose,

---

[47] 'Vorrede uber den Propheten Daniel', in D. Martin Luther, *Die gantze Heilige Schrifft* (Wittemberg 1545), ed. Hans Volz (Munich 1972), 1503–4.

[48] 'Eine Heerpredigt widder den Türcken', in *WA* 30/2. 160–97 (166).

[49] See Beverly Harris-Schenz, *Black Images in Eighteenth-Century German Literature* (Stuttgart 1981), 146–7.

[50] e.g. in his 'Vermahnunge zum Gebet Wider den Türcken', in *WA* 51. 585–625 (591, 594).

but have been created ultimately for the Christian good. A benificent Christian God/Father will therefore withdraw the rod once paternal discipline has been re-established.

Yet Luther is also prepared to comment on the exemplary qualities of the Turks: their military skills are praised to the shame of the Christian *Obrigkeit*, while their domestic customs are favourably compared to those of Luther's society:

> Zum vierden wirstu sehen bey den Türcken nach dem eusserlichen wandel ein dapffer strenge und ehrbarlich wesen: Sie trinken nicht wein, sauffen und fressen nicht so, wie wir thun, kleiden sich nicht so leichtfertiglich und frölich, bawen nicht so prechtig, brangen auch nicht so, schweren und fluchen nicht so, haben grossen trefflichen gehorsam, zucht und ehre gegen yhren Keiser und herrn, Und haben yhr regiment eusserlich gefasset und ym schwanck, wie wirs gerne haben wolten ynn Deudschen landen.[51]

Even the strictures on Turkish bigamy and concubinage give way to an admiration of the system which keeps women subject to what Luther sees as more effective controls than his own:

> Und wie wol solche ehe nicht ein ehe für Gott sondern mehr ein schein ist, denn eine ehe, noch halten sie damit yhre weiber ynn solchem zwang und schönen geberden, das bey yhn nicht solch fürwitz, uppickeit, leichtfertickeit und ander uberflüssiger schmuck, kost und bracht unter den weibern ist, als bei uns.[52]

Luther's admiration here is likely to be real, but still the Other is functionalized: like Rosenplüt, Luther constructs Turkish society as a convenient measure or mirror for the strengths and weaknesses of his own.

Evocations of the cruelty and tyranny of the bellicose Ottomans, rather than their pattern-card strictness in military and personal matters, predominate in Hans Sachs's writings on Turks. The first siege of Vienna provoked Sachs to compose his *Historia der türckischen belegerung der stat Wien* (1529), and the *Tyrannische that des Türcken, vor Wien begangen* (1539). He followed later military developments in the years they occurred with the *Historia des türckischen scharmützel*

---

[51] WA 30/2. 189–90.    [52] Ibid. 190.

*bey der Newenstat* (1532) and *Der ungluckhaftig scharmützel des Türcken vor Ofen* (1541).[53] Sachs invokes popular images of Turkish cruelty or inhumanity: in the *Historia der türckischen belegerung* he picks up on a favourite, almost emblematic, idea regarding Turkish behaviour towards pregnant women and children:

> Auch schnitens auf die schwangern weibr,
> Die kinder auff die spiß sie steckten
> Und sie auff gehn dem himel reckten,
> Darob eym Cristen-menschen grauset.        (p. 410)

'Die Kinder spist er an die Zäun', reports Ehrnholt (the herald) in similar vein, a citizen of doomed Constantinople in Jacob Ayrer's *Schröckliche Tragedi. Vom Regiment unnd schändlichen Sterben des türkischen Keisers Machumetis des Andern dis Namens, wie er Constantinopel eingenommen und gantz grausam tyrannisirt*.[54] In the course of this play we actually see the Turkish warriors killing the children of Constantinople, and hear them declare their disregard for pregnant women. Such slaughter of the traditionally most vulnerable members of society arouses easy sympathy in an audience and anti-pathy towards the perpetrators, but the killing of children, and of women about to bear children, is also a clear threat to the continued existence of that society. Inheritance and family are disturbed; chaos looms.

The barbarity of the Turk is seen to backfire when he attempts to avert chaos by his own, secular, means, by putting to death members of his own family. Ayrer's Machumet kills his brother in the presence of his mother early on in the piece, in order to avoid confusion in the royal succession.

---

[53] Nos. 207, 208, 210, and 211 in Hans Sachs, *Werke*, ed. Adelbert von Keller (Tübingen 1870). For Turkish themes see also no. 213, *Türkisch tyranney mit der Königin*, and no. 214, *Klag zu Got uber des Türcken krig*.

[54] In *Ayrers Dramen*, ed. Adelbert von Keller (Tübingen 1865), 2. 737–809 (738). Further references are given in the text. Johannes Praetorius later picks up on this clearly widespread idea in his propagandistic tract, *Catastrophe Muhammetica* (Leipzig 1664), when he gives a version of the events at Constantinople: 'Solches Jammer=Exempel kan man nehmen aus den schrecklichen Thaten der Türcken/ welcher die Männer nicht allein zerhacket/ sondern auch die schwangern Frauen mitten von einander geschnitten/ und ihnen ihre Leibes=Früchte heraus gerissen/ . . .' (p. 16).

The killing and its political motive are historically attested, but here the dramatist plays on the maternal presence to emphasize the unnatural or inverted force of the deed. Machumet at least has political motives; the dramatist of political *Vernunft*, Lohenstein, shows us pure uncontrolled passion when he has his Ibrahim Sultan strike two of his sons dead before their mothers' eyes, in the eponymous drama in which chaos rules until the Turks themselves, interestingly, reimpose order. A variation on the theme of family/female killing is the frequently attested execution by Mehmet II (Machumet) of his concubine in front of his troops. In Ayrer's play, this is first mentioned by Ehrnholt in his introductory speech about Machumet, who

> Thet sich an ein schöns Weibsbildt hangn,
> Die het er gar lang lieb und werth.
> Und als sich das Kriegsvolck beschwerd
> Ob des Keisers Weiblicher [*sic*] That,
> Er sie selbsten erwürget hat
> Vor aller Herren Angesicht.
>
> (*Schröckliche Tragedi*, p. 738)

In the course of the drama we are introduced to the 'schöns Weibsbildt', Hircavena, and our sympathy is directed towards her as an oppressed pious Christian. Hence when Machumet finally beheads her with his sabre following complaints from the army about his sexual preoccupation, the audience reaction is one of horror at the barbarous deed. By contrast, when Haugwitz has Soliman recall his ancestor's action, the implication is that political masculine *Vernunft* has bravely severed the debilitating, effeminizing bonds of love:

> Weil seine Tapfferkeit von Liebe eingewiegt/
> Von Liebe/ die Iren' durch ihren Glantz erweckte/
> Bis/ wie daß solche Gluth den hohen Ruhm befleckte/
> Und Ihm höchst schädlich sey/ sein Mustaph kundt gemacht.
> Drauff must das Wunder=Bild in Demant heller Pracht/
> Als eine Halb=Göttin/ vor allen Volck erscheinen/
>
> .    .    .    .    .    .    .    .    .    .    .
>
> Stracks war der Säbel bloß/ der Lil'gen=Hals entzwey/
> Und Mahomet vom Gifft der strengen Liebe frey.
>
> (*Soliman*, I. 186 ff.)

Haugwitz cites as his source Erasmus Francisci's *Trauersaal* and Gryphius in *Catharina von Georgien*. Gryphius, too, has Seinal Can present the action as heroic when he recounts the tale, but Chach Abas's response puts it in a different light: 'Er war in disem Stück ein Unmensch gleich als du' (*Catharina*, II. 323). The exemplary, popular tale is ambiguous: the reader or audience may admire the decisive unsentimentality of the warrior Sultan, but at the same time his action is taken as proof of his oriental inhumanity: the inhumanity of the non-Christian who is very nearly a beast. An animalistic metaphor in Rosenplüt is not coincidental:

> Es sol kein heiden in Cristen landen
> Nicht nüsten oder jung außprüeten.   (*Des Turken vasnachtspil*, 292)

Ayrer is at pains to establish in his drama the reasons for the Turkish victory over Constantinople, which one might expect to have been invulnerable, because protected by the Christian God. Internally, its citizens display 'Geitz' in refusing to pay their taxes; externally, the Roman Catholic and Greek Orthodox Church are at loggerheads, preventing help from arriving in time. Human culpability therefore justifies the application of the familiar scourge, 'die Göttlich Straff', as Libeta calls it (*Schröckliche Tragedi*, 749). There is another echo of Luther when Cardinal Isidorus describes the Turk as 'des Antichristi Knecht' (778). Like Rosenplüt, Ayrer uses comedy reassuringly, allowing an element of scatological humour finally to defuse the terror of Machumet: his 'schändliches Sterben' is from 'Darmgicht', or an inflammation of the bowels.

Details of non-Christian countries, their inhabitants and their customs, reached Europe in travel reports, a best-selling genre in which fact mingled inextricably with fiction. They became popular source material for contemporary dramatists: Haugwitz, Lohenstein, and Gryphius all refer to a variety of travel writers as the basis for their use of oriental detail.[55]

---

[55] Lohenstein in *Ibrahim Sultan* mentions Pietro della Valle (*Anmerck., Vorredn.* v. 9), Bellonius (ibid., v. 13–16), and Olearius (ibid., v. 428 and v. 433). Gryphius in *Catharina von Georgien* refers to Purchasius and Olearius (*Kurtze Anmerck.*, II, v. 380) and to Johannes Cartwright and Anthony Jenkinson (ibid. III, v. 490), and Haugwitz in *Soliman* to the traveller De Busbecq (*Anmerck.*, 99).

The best-known German-speaking travel writer in the seventeenth century was Adam Olearius, who published his *Offt begehrte Beschreibung der Newen orientalischen Reise* in 1647, the *Vermehrte Newe Beschreibung Der Muscowitischen und Persischen Reise* in 1656 and Jürgen Andersen's *Orientalische Reise=Beschreibunge* in 1669.[56] The last is the least well known of Olearius's efforts, but deserves some attention in the context of this discussion. What makes it particularly interesting are the circumstances of its transmission: it was Olearius who actually wrote down Andersen's story, sitting behind a screen while the traveller related it to a curious Duke Friederich of Schleswig-Holstein. The details of the account must, therefore, be seen to have been transmitted at a double remove: firstly because Andersen is recalling from memory observations made nearly twenty years previously, and which were, even then, inevitably influenced by what information culled from other reports and sources had already led him to expect, and secondly because his recollections are filtered through the mind and pen of Olearius, who was himself an experienced writer of such accounts. This renders the Andersen/Olearius account especially interesting in terms of occidental expectations of the Orient and the transmission of ideas.

Presuppositions already begin to emerge in Olearius's prologue. It is superficially a typical literary defence of *delectatio* with didacticism: the tale is 'theils mit Lust/ theils mit höchster Verwunderung zu lesen', but equally

[ist] daraus zu ersehen/ in was grosser Blindheit die Heyden noch heutiges Tages stecken/ und wir an unserm Orte für jene glückseliger zu schätzen/ daß wir in diesen Ländern gebohren/ unter Christlicher Herrschaft leben/ in der allein seligmachenden Religion aufferzogen.

(a4ᵛ)

The pedagogical Christian perspective is thus maintained. The verdant Cape of Good Hope is perceived as wasted on its inhabitants: 'wenn man in das Land kompt/ sihet man eine

[56] *Orientalische Reise=Beschreibunge Jürgen Andersen aus Schleßwig der An. Christi 1644 außgezogen und 1650 wiederkommen. . . . Heraus gegeben Durch Adam Olearium . . .* (1669), repr. ed. Dieter Lohmeyer (Tübingen 1980). Further references are given in the text.

grosse fruchtbarkeit des Erdreichs/ und ist jammer daß es
nicht von Christen längst hätte sollen bewohnet werden'
(p. 3). The technique of critically mirroring one's own society by reference to another, noted in Rosenplüt and others,
is also applied by Olearius/Andersen from time to time as
a didactic device. We are told that the Javanese practise Islam,
but are, nonetheless, 'sehr devot, daß sie manchen Christen
darmit beschämen solten' (p. 15), while more generally,
'Die armen blinden Heyden seynd in ihrem Götzendienst
sehr embsig und geschäfftig/ lassen es ihnen viel eyferiger
angelegen seyn ihre Abgötter zu ehren/ als bißweilen die
Christen den rechten lebendigen Gott' (p. 129). Japan, too,
offers an 'Exempel der Keuschheit': Japanese women who
commit suicide after being raped (p. 110), thus exemplify-
ing the model of feminine chastity familiar from the Lucretia
story.[57] The exemplary value of virtue, made striking by
its occurrence in non-European peoples, is even more pronounced in the tale of the martyred Japanese Christians:[58]
'Die gröste Verfolgung und Execution . . . hat sich angefan-
gen Anno Christi 1622. . . . und ist zu verwundern/ daß die
Japonischen Christen so beständig bey der Religion biß
zum Tode/ und mit Freuden zum Fewr gegangen' (p. 114).
When the peoples observed have no exemplary function, however, they are portrayed in terms of their animality. The mean-
ingless babble or 'baba' of an uncomprehended language
—the etymological root of the Greek 'barbarian'—is associated by Andersen/Olearius with animal noises. Of the
Cape's inhabitants we are told, 'Was die Einwohner betrifft/
seynd sie an ihrem Leben und Sittenrecht viehische wilde
Menschen . . . Auß ihrer Sprache kan man kaum vernehmen
daß es menschlich/ ist fast ehnlicher dem plaudern der
Calcunischen Hanen' (p. 5). Titillation is never far away, however: animality and oriental lasciviousness are linked when

---

[57] This is a favourite episode from Classical history which also found its way into
early opera; Keiser's and Feind's *Die Kleinmühtige Selbst-Mörderin LUCRETIA*
(Hamburg 1705) portrays the exemplary heroine in a manner tempered only
superficially by obligatory Christian disapproval of suicide.
[58] The exemplary Japanese Christians are also a theme in Jesuit drama.
Compare e.g. text II, I. 51 in *Das Jesuitendrama*, ed. Elida Maria Szarota, 4 vols.
(Munich 1979–87), vol. 2/1. 535–46.

the sight of a deformed beggar provokes generalized charges of bestiality: 'Diese Mißgeburt solte/ wie man vorgab/ von einem Hassanischen Weibe in der Stadt Dernech gebohren seyn. Ob diß dierechte [*sic*] Mutter gewesen/ weiß ich nicht/ halte sonst dafür/ daß zu solchen Mißgeburten Ursache seyn mag das Gottlose und ärger als Sodomitische Leben vieler Leute/ so in Orient/ . . . getrieben wird' (p. 28). Hints of sexual excesses in distant lands are, then, already basic to Western fascination with the Orient by the seventeenth century. The travelling subject does not admit to participation in the idyll of unrepressed sexuality, as he does in later travel literature, but Olearius/Andersen do not pass up the opportunity to attribute 1,200 wives to the Mogul in Agra (p. 40), and to conclude a damning description of the Hassanists with a titbit of information: 'sie nehmen so viel Weiber/ als sie ernehren können' (p. 51).

By the mid-seventeenth century a number of set ideas about oriental or non-Christian peoples, especially Turks, were clearly in circulation. Writers based their accounts, whether they purported to be fictional or non-fictional, on each other's work, and it is therefore unsurprising that a conceptional canon was gradually established. From *bellicosus* and *luxuriosus* had developed (sometimes overlapping) ideas of oriental inhumanity or animality, cruelty, chaos, devilishness, lasciviousness, perversion (inversion), and excess. In short, the non-Christian might embody everything the Christian must not, and such potential for transgression is naturally fascinating. On the other hand, a perceived opposite can also be exemplary, incorporating that which is to be striven after. If an oriental or heathen can achieve virtue—so the implication —how much more virtuous might a suitably motivated Christian be! Where both of these attitudes are in evidence, as in the case of Luther, we have so far deduced that this is not so much the result of truly ambivalent sentiments in the writer as the rhetorical functionalizing of the Other as an instructive mirror. Such an assumed, even unconscious presupposition of a canon of Otherness enables early modern authors to use oriental, especially Turkish characters to achieve striking literary effects.

*Turkish Types: Lohenstein's Ibrahims and Haugwitz's Soliman*

The idea of the Turk as the antithetical Other of early modern Germany is discussed by Pierre Béhar.[59] Béhar identifies the Turk as the German 'archétype du "barbare"', and distinguishes the idea of the savage from that of the barbarian Other: 'le barbare est, par définition, l'autre, c'est-à-dire non point l'être qui ne connaît point de culture—ce serait le sauvage—mais celui dont la culture est différente . . .'[60] The Turk takes on this archetypal role not only because of the territorial conflict between the Ottomans and the Empire but also, as Béhar ingeniously recognizes, because he embodies the *verkehrte Welt*: the notion of the familiar world turned upside-down. The Turkish male dresses like a woman, in flowing robes, while his wife wears trousers; he writes from right to left, not from left to right; he urinates sitting, not standing; and in battle he kills by impaling, not by beheading.[61] This perfect inversion of Christian culture constitutes from the Christian point of view perfect inhumanity: 'si le chrétien est le type achevé de l'humain, le Turc ne peut être que celui de l'inhumain'.[62] In this way we come back to the Lutheran perception of the Turk: not as a man, but as man's enemy, the devil.

If we accept Béhar's conception of the Turk as antithetical to the Christian writer of the Holy Roman Empire, then the fact that in the dramatic work of Lohenstein and Haugwitz Turkish plays share pride of place with plays about women must arrest our attention. The dramatists display an interest in investigating something perceived as *other* than themselves. While Béhar identifies a traditionally negative view in both of Lohenstein's Ibrahim plays, by contrast with the positive, exemplary portrayal of the Sultan in Haugwitz's Soliman, Helen Watanabe-O'Kelly has used the example of the court festival to illustrate 'das Ambivalente', or the tradition

---

[59] Pierre Béhar, 'La Répresentation du Turc dans l'Europe des XVIe et XVIIe siècles et l'œuvre de Callot', in *Jacques Callot (1592–1635): Actes du colloque de musée du Louvre et de la ville de Nancy des 25, 26 et 27 Juin 1992*, ed. D. Ternois (Paris 1993), 305–30.
[60] Ibid. 307.     [61] Ibid. 307–8.     [62] Ibid. 308.

of praise as well as of condemnation, in the seventeenth-century view of the Turk.[63] A certain ambivalence was a feature of *Catharina von Georgien*, in which Gryphius led us to understand that the fortitude of his heroine is all the more striking because it is cast into relief by our expectation that women are weak creatures. But there is no compliment to women in general in this; the point is that the admirable *exemplum* works because the generality of women are held to be rather despicable. We should, then, be careful in assuming that portrayals of good Turks have their roots in a positive view of this people. The idealized conception of the Turk as soldier identified by Watanabe-O'Kelly in festival and horse-breeding books is one we find an earlier version of in Luther's tracts: 'Denn der Turck ist ein rechter Kriegsman, der wol anders weis mit land und leuten umbzugehen, beyde zu gewinnen und zu behalten, denn unser Keyser, Könige und Fürsten' (*Vom Kriege wider die Türken*, 140). Discipline, too, is praised: Turks, unlike some Germans, display 'grossen trefflichen gehorsam, zucht und ehre gegen yhren Keiser und herrn' (*Heerpredigt wider den Türken*, 189). Luther's admiration may be real, but his method is transparent: the Turkish example is functionalized to shame Christian soldiers into behaving better.

Although both Lohenstein and Haugwitz are concerned with the exemplary function of a Turkish protagonist, the playwrights approach their portrayals from different angles, from what might be seen as the perspective of the 'negative' and 'positive' traditions respectively. But if we observe each of these portrayals carefully, evidence begins to emerge that these two traditions are not as distinct as they might superficially appear.

The continent of Asia is frequently allegorized in the early modern period as an exotically attired woman. This in itself cannot be taken to indicate a conceptual link between the feminine and the oriental, since the other continents, including Europe, were also depicted as female. It is none-

---

[63] H. Watanabe-O'Kelly, 'Lohenstein, Haugwitz, und das Türkenmotiv in deutschen Turnieren des Barock', in Iwasaki, *Begegnung mit dem 'Fremden'*, 7. 348–55 (355).

theless a striking image when Lohenstein opens his *Ibrahim Bassa* (1653) with an allegorical stage set showing Asia as a female figure chained by her vices,[64] and it is worth noting that the cruellest and most ruthless character in the piece is not only an oriental but a woman, Roxelane, whose vicious feminine jealousy leads her, in the manner of a Salome, to persuade the prince to kill. In characterizing Turkey and the Turks, Lohenstein uses the language we might expect. The Satanic element, with apocalyptic overtones reminiscent of Luther's Daniel preface, is introduced in the prologue, where Asia laments:

> Das zwölf-bekrönte Haupt/ des Halses Alabaster
> Pflügt unter Gog und Magogs Joch.           (p. 18)

Soliman is described by Isabelle as 'des Abgrunds Fürst' (I. 352), his henchman Rustan as 'Frucht der schwarzen Hellen' (V. 80), while the inverted antichristian nature of the Turk is illustrated in her description of the European lovers' arrest in terms of a twisted Eucharist:

> Ist dis das schöne Mahl/ auf dem man unser Blut
> Vermischt mit Speiß und Wein in die Christallen thut?   (V. 93–4)

Ideas of Turkish cruelty are luridly evoked at the end of the first act by a 'Chor der Leibeignen Christen', who list the tortures that await them in Turkish hands and seem to revel in their cumulative gruesomeness:[65]

> Wird man uns auf Galeen schmiden?
> In sidend-heissem Oele siden?
> Wird man uns braten an dem Pfal?
> Wird man in Mörseln uns zerstossen?
> Wird man umb unsre Köpffe lossen?
> Wird man uns spissen an den Stal?
> Wird man uns köpffen oder wird man uns erwürgen?
> Wird man uns unsern Leib zersegen?
> Auf Holtz-stöß und auf Röste legen?

[64] D. C. von Lohenstein, *Ibrahim Bassa*, in *Türkische Trauerspiele*, ed. Klaus Günther Just (Stuttgart 1953). Further references are given in the text.
[65] Explicit descriptions of torture highlight the cruelty of an earlier dramatic oriental, Gryphius's Chach Abas, in the 'Reyen der von Chach Abas erwürgeten Fürsten' in *Catharina von Georgien*, II. 357–416, esp. 393–400.

Mit glüend-rothen Kohln und warmer Asch umbschürgen?
Wil man uns Därm und Lung und Eingeweid aus-reissen?
Und umb das blutge Maul die fetten Hertzen schmeissen/ . . . ?

(I. 497–508)

There is no doubt in the minds of Lohenstein's Christians that their captors represent the scourge of a disciplinarian divinity: 'Wie lange peitscht uns deine Rutt . . . ?' (I. 534). This metaphor, couched in the terms of Luther's theodicy of the Turk, imposes a form of order on what might otherwise be chaotic suffering: throughout the drama, the principle of Christian order is seen in battle with the non-Christian (antichristian) principle of chaos.

The chorus following Act II is the 'Reien der Begihrde/ der Vernunft/ des Menschen'. In the play proper, the voice of chaotic passion is that of the Turkish tyrant, Soliman, and it is countered by the voice of ordered calm: that of the Europeans, Isabelle and Ibrahim. What we see on stage in this *Reyen*, then, is a dialogue between Orient ('Begihrde') and Occident ('Vernunft'), and there is potential for the costumes of 'Begihrde' and 'Vernunft' to make this visible. 'Vernunft', predictably, has the last word, and is corroborated by the voice of reasoning humanity, 'der Mensch'. In the play proper, by contrast, it is the chaotic principle that is victorious, since Roxelane and Rustan are able to provoke the Sultan into murdering Ibrahim. In this Lohenstein, keen to stick consistently to his opposition of Christian and Turk, moves away from the positive conclusion given the story by Scudéry and Zesen.[66] Turkish chaos prevails at Soliman's court; only in the *Reyen* are we reminded, as Luther predicted in his Daniel prologue, that the days of the triumphant Turk are numbered, since order must and will be restored by an omnipotent Christian deity.

By the time *Ibrahim Sultan* was published in 1673, twenty years after his first Turkish play and ten years before the second unsuccessful siege of Vienna, which seems to have confirmed a turn in the military fortunes of the Ottomans,

---

[66] Lohenstein excuses the divergence of his story from Philipp Zesen's translation of Madeleine de Scudéry's *Ibrahim ou l'Illustre Bassa* (1641) by reference to other, unspecified historians. See *Ibrahim Bassa*, 13–14.

the predictions of a Turkish decline noted in *Ibrahim Bassa* have for Lohenstein already begun to be fulfilled.[67] In dedicating the piece to his Emperor, Leopold, he is confident enough to explain: 'Diß Schauspiel entwirfft die Gemüths-Flecken und die zu unserer Zeit sichtbare Verfinsterung eines Oßmannischen Mohnden' ('Zuschrifft', 71-2). The moon of the Ottomans is antithetically opposed to 'die Sonnen von Oesterreich' ('Zuschrifft', 75). That this is part of the East/West opposition of *Begierde* and *Vernunft* observed in the earlier drama emerges from Lohenstein's metaphor, which links the light of the sun with that of reason, 'die Sonne der Vernunft' (I. 161).[68] The Turkish ruler in this play is even more obviously subject to his chaotic *Affekte* than Soliman; his perversion is illustrated by his passion for an Armenian giantess, which gives way only to desire for his brother's mourning widow, Sisigambis. In characteristic, politically didactic mode Lohenstein is at pains to establish a link between Turkish lasciviousness and the military decline of the Ottomans. Mehemet Bassa makes the correlation in the case of Ibrahim:

> Jetzt/ nun wir auß der See schon zweymal sind geschlagen/
> Durch ihren Morosin/ nimmt unser Sultan wahr:
> Es dörffe mehr Verstand/ auch schaff es mehr Gefahr
> Mit einer solchen Stadt/ als geilen Weibern kriegen.

[67] See D. C. von Lohenstein, *Ibrahim Sultan*, in *Türkische Trauerspiele*. Further references are given in the text.

[68] The metaphor is also used by Lohenstein's Cleopatra, who indicates by it the extent of Antony's decline; he has become, by implication, more 'oriental' than she is (*Cleopatra* [1661], II. 283-4). In Reinhard Keiser's and Christian Heinrich Postel's opera *Janus* (1698) Leopold is again the sun; Postel (who knew Lohenstein's work) closes his libretto with eulogic arias sung to the Emperor by 'Fama', the second of which runs:

> Verheere der Türken blutdürstiges Heer
> O Teutschlands Arm und Seele!
> Mach Ungarn von Nattern und Höllenbrut leer,
> Zerknirsche Schwert und Pfeile.
> Auf Leopold! siege, Du Sonne der Deinen,
> So wird hinfort kein Mond mehr scheinen.

The idea that the light of the sun is the true and proper light, that of the moon deceptive or misleading, is used in religious allegory before Lohenstein, notably by Hans Sachs to depict the differences between the Roman Catholic Church and the new preaching of Luther in his *Wittenbergisch Nachtigall* (1523).

Jetzt/ nun der Krieg sich schleppt/ lässt ihn der Sultan liegen/
Hengt seiner Wollust nach. Dem Divan liegt die Last
Des Krieges einig ob.

(I. 396–402)

Mehemet and the other Turks in the play, on the other hand,
appear surprisingly reasonable; but this only renders
Ibrahim's iniquity (which might otherwise simply confirm the
view of the Turkish oriental we have come to expect) the more
striking. In the other Ottomans, Lohenstein is not showing us a contrasting portrayal of 'good' Turks, but merely
pointing up the exceptional shamefulness of the Sultan's
behaviour.

Despite his obvious intention to portray Turks negatively,
Lohenstein is not immune to the fascination of oriental transgression.[69] The dramatist is keen to condemn the sexual
excesses of Sultan Ibrahim, but he is not averse to titillating
his audience with glimpses of the sensual oriental sphere.
The play proper opens in the seraglio, the concept of which
fascinated the European mind, and the audience imagination is tantalized with suggestions of nudity and lesbian sexuality when Sechierpera, Ibrahim's procuress, attempts to wake
the Sultan's interest in the young Ambre:[70]

Des Mufti himmlisch Kind jen' [Sisigambis] und auch all'absticht.
Der Zunder heisser Brunst ist selbst in mir entglommen/
Seit dem ich zweymal sie im Bade wahrgenommen.

(I. 350–2)

The voyeurism which characterizes later portrayals of the
Orient, such as Ingres's famous depiction of *Le Bain Turc*

[69] Burhaneddin Kâmil, in his dissertation on German literary portrayals of the
Turk to the 17th cent., does not find in Lohenstein's work the exoticism which later
came to characterize perceptions of the Orient. See Kâmil (British Library catalogue: Burhan Al-Din Kâmil), 'Die Türken in der deutschen Literatur bis zum Barock
und die Sultansgestalten in den Türkendramen Lohensteins' (unpublished doctoral thesis, University of Kiel 1935), 23.
[70] Lesbian eroticism and the connotations of this scene are discussed in detail
by Jane O. Newman, 'Disorientations: Same-Sex Seduction and Women's Power
in Daniel Casper von Lohenstein's *Ibrahim Sultan*', in *CG* 28 (1995), 337–55. But
in looking for authorial tolerance or even endorsement of 'transgressive' lesbian
sexuality, Newman seems to forget that lesbianism has traditionally been regarded
as less threatening than male homosexuality, and has perenially fascinated the
'controlling eye' of the male voyeur.

(1862), the very shape of which suggests the view through a peephole, is already a feature of Lohenstein's drama. At the end of Act III, while Ambre's rape is supposed to be taking place offstage, the 'Reyen Des badenden Frauenzimmers' presents us with an exoticized and eroticized scene, which may accord some visual satisfaction to an audience who are presumably both shocked and excited by the hidden dramatic events. Once again a particular kind of ambivalence or inconsistency is in evidence. Even though Turkish sensuality can hardly be seen in seventeenth-century Christian terms as a positive feature, Lohenstein betrays his fascination.

Kâmil sees in these dramas a development from a view of the Turk in general to one of the Turk in particular: the Turkish individual.[71] While this is true in so far as Lohenstein concentrates on the portrayal of one central Turkish figure, we need not assume that this figure is individualized: both Soliman and Sultan Ibrahim are typical of school drama in that for didactic purposes they embody a predictable, one-sided, and easily identifiable set of ideas. As Turkish individuals they are indistinguishable from the generality of that nationality as customarily portrayed. Real concern with the Turk as an individual does not begin to emerge on the German stage until Haugwitz creates his *Soliman* (1684).[72]

Gryphius's Catharina was the woman who behaved as a man should, and was therefore an example to men. Haugwitz's is a non-Christian who finally behaves as a Christian should, and may therefore also be seen as a pattern-card. Because a good Turk is unexpected, he ought to provide a more striking example than the admonitory Turkish figures of Lohenstein's dramas, whose behaviour is no more than predictably iniquitous. Unlike Lohenstein, Haugwitz adheres to the unhistorical literary precedents of Scudéry and Zesen, in that his Soliman is able to master his passions and stand as a shining example of *Vernunft*. It is typical of this—for his period exceptionally self-conscious—dramatist that he should wryly observe his own fiction in his 'Anmerckungen': 'massen

[71] Kâmil, 'Die Türken', 22.
[72] In A. A. von Haugwitz, *Prodromus Poeticus, Oder: Poetischer Vortrab.* 1684, ed. Pierre Béhar (Tübingen 1984).

wir . . . / weil er [= weder?] dem [*sic*] Soliman so **tugendhafft**/
noch auch den Ibrahim so **unschuldig** machen können/ wann
wir extra fictionem poeticam den rauhen Weg der Historischen
Warheit zu gehen/ hätten erkiesen müssen' (pp. 80–1).
In his edition of the *Prodromus Poeticus*, Pierre Béhar explains Haugwitz's portrayal of a virtuous Turkish Sultan as
a deliberate response to Lohenstein's earlier play: he calls
Soliman an 'Anti-Ibrahim'.[73] Béhar makes a convincing case
for Haugwitz's familiarity with *Ibrahim Bassa*, as well as identifying what he takes to be deliberate structural and conceptual
oppositions between the two plays.

Indirect reference is made to the story that informed
Lohenstein's version (in which Ibrahim's head is finally sent
to Isabelle by a tardily rueful Soliman) when Haugwitz's
Isabella voices her fears about the Sultan:

> Der/ sag ich/ der kan seyn auch endlich so verwegen/
> Daß Er des Ibrah'ms Haupt läst vor die Füsse legen    (I. 566–7)

At the beginning of the second act it emerges that her insecurity is not unfounded, when Soliman admits in a soliloquy
that he had hoped for Ibrahim's death in battle (II. 25–31);
Haugwitz's Turkish Sultan is at least potentially murderous,
and dramatic tension is maintained.

As in Gryphius's *Catharina* and in both of Lohenstein's plays,
there is in *Soliman* a sense of the opposition between Turk
and European, Muslim and Christian. In the throes of passion, under the influence of Rustan and Roxolane, Soliman
perceives Ibrahim in terms of the Christian enemy as
'Christen=Hund' (IV. 209). The indictment of the Ottoman
Empire in the threnody and *Reyen* that follow this scene is
reminiscent of the condemnation of England in Gryphius's
*Carolus Stuardus*. England is the 'Land mit Königs Blutt
durchspritzt', as we are told by the 'Chor der ermordeten
Engelländischen Könige' (*Carolus Stuardus*, I. 314). In
*Soliman* the 'Chor Der Ermordeten Groß=Veziere' is pre-
faced by a like claim: 'Es ist das Türck'sche Reich/ Fast einer
SchlachtBanck gleich' (*Soliman*, IV. 261 ff.). In Gryphius's
case the monarch, Charles I, is separate from his country,

---

[73] In A. A. von Haugwitz, 'Nachwort', 93.

as its victim. At this point in Haugwitz's drama, by contrast, the ruler is associated with his nation: backed by the ruthless pair Roxolane and Rustan, Soliman becomes the ultimate embodiment of Turkish transgressions.

In allowing Soliman to develop like this, Haugwitz builds dramatic tension which is not going to be fulfilled, although by playing on audience *expectations* of the oriental protagonist he is effortlessly able to suggest that it might be. Roxolane, too, unfolds her villainy and manipulates audience fears when she hints at Ottoman military advances towards Christendom:

> Mit Persen ists nunmehr und [= um?] seiner Macht gethan/
> Die uns bisher getrotzt/ nun muß der Christe dran.

> (III. 123–4)

Yet Haugwitz is also prepared to reassure on this topic. We are reminded more of Lohenstein's confident, current affairs-based predictions in the dedication of *Ibrahim Sultan* than of Luther's more abstract reliance on a divine plan which favours Christendom, when Soliman worries:

> Mich deucht ich sehe schon das Heer der Teutschen stehn/
> . . . . . . . . . . . .
> Denn warlich unser Glück/ das wir gewohnt mit Hauffen
> Zufinden/ scheint jetzt uns auch so verwirrt zulauffen/
> Daß wann die Christen uns recht in die Karte sehn/
> Und Carol es recht wagt/ so ists umb uns geschehn.

> (V. 186 ff.)

Early on in Haugwitz's drama, there is a familiar pairing from the store of Orient/Occident metaphor: the 'Inhalt' tells of Soliman's return to reason, 'nachdem endlich die Vernunfft nach ausgestandenen [*sic*] Gemüths=Kampffe/ seinen Begierden obgesiegt' (Soliman, A3ʳ). We would expect *Vernunft* or reason to be the occidental or masculine value, *Begierde* or lasciviousness to be oriental or feminine. Unusually, we find both ideas united in one dramatic character. Haugwitz initially appears to be developing the portrayal of a Turkish Sultan we expect: Soliman is consumed by desire for Isabella, and her Genoese compatriot Alphonso remembers caustically,

> wer kennt die Begierde
> Des Türck'schen Käysers nicht/ die eine schlechte Zierde
> Hat öffters angeflammt.                     (I. 73–5)

The chorus of the passions that concludes Act II claims mastery over both Soliman and Roxolane:

> Wer uns kennt wird sagen müssen/
> Daß uns Soliman zum [sic] Füssen
> Sambt der Roxolanen liegt        (II. 317–9)

Soliman's subservience to his passion makes him 'verkehrt', as he himself recognizes (I. 449), and as Ibrahim observes on his return to the Turkish court (II. 88). The *Reyen* of the second act is explicitly titled 'Chor der Leidenschafften/ über den Verkehrten SOLIMAN'. It is here, however, that the subtle shift which is taking place in Haugwitz's portrayal of the Turkish Sultan begins. Soliman is 'verkehrt', the inverted Turk identified by Béhar, but he is less importantly an inverted Christian than an inverted version of his own former self:

> bißher hab ich geehrt
> Was mein Gemüth geliebt/ jetzt bin ich gantz verkehrt
> Und wiedersinns gesinnt.                     (I. 448–50)

His *Verkehrtheit* is not, therefore, *necessarily* connected to his Turkishness. Haugwitz puts an unexpected defence of Soliman into the mouth of the French duke, who is associated with Ibrahim and Isabelle and hence with the positive, Christian side. The argument is that all humans are subject to perverting domination by erotic passion:

> Die Liebe übertrifft/ was die Natur sonst scheut/
> Was Freundschafft anbefiehlt/ was GOtt und Mensch gebeut.
> Die Mütter haben sich den Söhnen angehangen/
> Der Vater ist selb=selbst der Tochter nachgegangen/
> Von Brüdern ward der Crantz der Schwestern offt betrübt/
> Ja die vertraute Heerd' hat offt sein Hirt' geliebt.
> Was soll ein Fürst nicht thun der voller Liebs=Gedancken?
>
> (I. 99–105)

The bestiality hinted at by Jürgen Andersen in the *verkehrte Welt* outside European Christendom becomes a universal possibility in the duke's speech, even though this and the other sexual aberrations he lists are, for the sake of dramatic decency, immediately and energetically refuted by Isabella's maid, Emilia: 'Der dem die Tugend ziert weicht niemahls aus den Schrancken' (I. 106).

The portrayal of Soliman as an individual with more than one side to his character unfolds in this exchange. To Emilia's incredulous denial of his passion for her mistress, 'Es lobt den Soliman ja sonst die gantze Welt', the duke responds realistically: 'Er ist auch Lobens werth/ nur nicht in diesem Stücke' (I. 107–8). The Sultan's daughter, Asterie, also defends her father, insisting that he is more than a simple stereotype of Turkish lasciviousness:

> ich kenne Soliman:
> Ich weiß/ Er strafft sich selbst/ in dem Er Sie betrübet/
> Ich weiß/ daß Er zugleich Sie und den Ibrah'm liebet/
> Und beyde doch erzörnt (I. 423–6)

Unlike Lohenstein, Haugwitz does without the exoticism or vicarious eroticism typical of later orientalist writing. Lohenstein's Turkish protagonists are primarily characterized as Turks, and behave as we expect early modern literary Turks to behave. Haugwitz's Soliman is primarily an individual, and breaks the bounds of European xenophobic expectations.

Pierre Béhar explains the unusual portrayal geographically. It could, he claims, only happen on Protestant territory, where Luther had helped to detach the Church from the individual's relationship to God (although, as we have seen, Luther had also helped to shape polemic against the Turk), and only in a place like Saxony, which was further than Lohenstein's Silesia from the borders threatened by advancing Ottomans.[74] The move away from an absolute and value-laden opposition of Christian and non-Christian is, in Béhar's view, not a move towards secularization (and hence a step in the direction of the Enlightenment), but what he calls 'eine Sakralisation des Säkularen'. By this a kind of supraconfessional divine principle seems to be meant, or, in his words, 'die Anerkennung der Gegenwart des Absoluten, worauf das Gute beruht, im Grunde jedes Menschen, gleichviel, zu welcher Konfession er sich bekennt. In der ganzen Welt offenbart sich der

[74] Ibid. 108–9.

eine Gott . . .'.[75] Béhar is right, in so far as the character of
Soliman displays unusual complexity in its potential for good
and evil, and the Muslim ruler is finally accepted as exemplary by the Christians in the play, without any reference to
his religion. Yet religious irenicism and open-mindedness
do not feature in the portrayals of Rustan and Roxolane, the
real Turkish villains of the piece. Throughout the drama
we see the eventually virtuous Sultan against a background
of 'real' Turkishness: hence we must perceive him as an exception, not as the rule. Ideas traditionally associated with the
oriental or specifically the Turk thus intrude into Haugwitz's
drama; we are left facing the question why the dramatist
should allow this to happen and yet take such pains to contradict the clichés in his portrayal of Soliman. I believe that
Béhar comes closer to the poet's intention when he sees
the play as a eurocentric mirror of princes;[76] this is what
Ibrahim and Isabella, those tone-setting Europeans, are
telling us when they give their final judgement on the title
figure in the concluding lines of Soliman:

> Was hilfft herrschen Meer und Lande/
> Was hilfft reich seyn/ hoch am Stande
> Und doch von Natur ein Knecht?
> Der macht edel sein Geschlecht/
> Und soll Kron und Scepter führen/
> Der so wie Soliman sich selbsten kan regieren.    (V. 316–21)

The reference to 'Geschlecht' underlines the exceptional
nature of this Sultan in a long line of culpable Ottoman rulers.
His oriental passions and *Verkehrtheit* make him susceptible
to the more typical Turkishness of Rustan and Roxolane, and
it is only the obtrusive virtue of the pendant Christian pair
Ibrahim and Isabella (who also alliterate!) that eventually
provokes the swing from *Begierde* to *Vernunft*. Haugwitz may be
trying to break down traditional oppositions in his portrayal

---

[75] In A. A. von Haugwitz, 'Nachwort', 107.

[76] Ibid. An author with whose work Haugwitz was familiar, Erasmus Francisci,
takes precisely this approach to exotic or oriental material: it is a mirror of personal and political realities for the Self. See Francesca Ferraris, 'Exotismus und
Intertextualität: Die literarische Kuriositätensammlung' in *Intertextualität in der
frühen Neuzeit: Studien zu ihren theoretischen und praktischen Perspektiven*, ed. Wilhelm
Kühlmann and Wolfgang Neuber (Frankfurt a. M. 1994), 465–84.

of Soliman, but he is still caught in the literary conventions of his time. The Sultan is an advanced, because complex, character by comparison with Lohenstein's Turkish types; but at the same time, like Gryphius's Catharina, he is effective because he does what we do not expect of his kind, and in the end it is in terms of an exemplary mirror for Christian princes that his function is defined. The presupposition of the type forms the basis for the dramatic effect achieved; our appreciation of oriental virtue is heightened by a background of oriental iniquity.

### Turks in Opera: Bostel's Cara Mustapha Libretto

Another Ibrahim is one of the main protagonists in Lucas von Bostel's two-part opera *Cara Mustapha*, written for the opera house in Hamburg in 1686.[77] As in Lohenstein's *Ibrahim Sultan*, to which Bostel refers in his 'Historische Einleitung' (*Cara Mustapha*, part 1, 188), the character is Turkish; like Haugwitz's Spanish 'Ibrahim', however, he is also virtuous. The action of the opera is based on historical events leading up to the Battle of Kahlenberg on 12 September 1683, which concluded the second unsuccessful Ottoman siege of Vienna. Following a French source, Bostel makes the entire fiasco—historically, the forces of Mehmed IV had good chances of taking the city on this occasion—the result of Turkish passion; the attack takes place when and as it does because of the Grand Vezier Cara Mustapha's desire for a woman living in Ofen, near Vienna.[78]

---

[77] The first part of the libretto only is published in Reinhard Meyer's collection, *Die Hamburger Oper. Eine Sammlung von Texten der Hamburger Oper aus der Zeit 1678–1730*, 4 vols. (Munich 1980–4), 1. 171–248. References to the second part follow the text held by the Hamburg Staats- und Universitätsbibliothek. For a discussion of Franck's score, see Chapter 4.

[78] H. C. Wolff cites Monteverdi's *Poppea* and a two-part opera by Minato as 'die wahren Vorbilder' for *Cara Mustapha*. Wolff, *Die Barockoper in Hamburg* (1678–1738), 2 vols. (Wolfenbüttel 1957), 1. 39. His interest, however, is in the characterization of the tyrant, Mustapha, rather than that of the Turk. Lorenzo Bianconi and Thomas Walker are more specific when they suggest that Minato's operas are a source of structural inspiration for the Hamburg librettists. See Lorenzo Bianconi and Thomas Walker, 'Production, Consumption and Political Function of Seventeenth-Century Opera', in *Early Music History* 4 (1984), 209–96 (258).

In Bostel's libretto, as in *Soliman* and to an extent in *Ibrahim Sultan*, we find good Turks, bad Turks, and Christian Europeans who provide the measure of what is truly virtuous. The lovers Gasparo and Manuela take the place of Ibrahim and Isabella in the Soliman story. Like that Ibrahim (whose real, European, name is Justinian), Gasparo has an alternative Turkish persona: he appears dressed as a woman, Roxellana. We never find out the reason for his cross-dressing, nor indeed for his sudden entrance as an Amazon halfway through the second act. The latter at least is likely to be pure operatic indulgence: Amazons were considered titillating treats on the opera stage. As a Turkish pendant to the two Spaniards, we have Ibrahim and his wife Baschlari, both of whom strive—within the confines of their Turkishness—to be virtuous. Central to the piece is not the Ottoman ruler, Mahomet (Mehmed) IV, but his Grand Vizier, Kara Mustafa Köprülü, who as Bostel's Mustapha is a highly stereotypical example of Turkish iniquity.

In the prologue to part one of a two-part libretto, Bostel indicates that his source is a German translation of a well-known French text: Jean de Préchac's *Cara Mustapha, Grand Visir, Histoire, contenant son élevation, ses amours dans le Serail, ses divers employs, le vray sujet qui lui a fait entreprendre le siège de Vienne & les particularitez de sa mort* (Paris 1684). The German version had been published in Hamburg a year later.[79] The 'vray sujet' or 'wahre Ursache/ warumb er sich die Belägerung der Stadt Wien unternommen', as the translation has it, is alleged to be Mustapha's uncontrolled desire for the Sultan's married sister, Baschlari. Opera is a hyperbolic genre, and Bostel takes the idea illustrated by the Baschlari affair—namely, that the Turk is prey to his passions—to its extreme. When Mustapha defends his decision to provoke war to Selim (a character added to the story by Bostel), he does so in the strongest terms of passion:

Ich biete Trotz dem Himmel/ und der Höllen/
Ob sie sich noch so zornig stellen/

[79] Compare Werner Braun, *Vom Remter zum Gänsemarkt: Aus der Frühgeschichte der alten Hamburger Oper* (1677–1697) (Saarbrücken 1987), 122. Reinhard Meyer gives the same source. See Meyer, *Die Hamburger Oper*, 4. 155 and 162–3.

Soll dieser Krieg doch fest gestellet seyn.

   .   .   .   .   .   .   .   .

Mein trautster Selim, dir ist gnug bewust/
Wie das holdsehligste Gesicht
Der lieblichsten Baschlari meine Brust/
In Liebe hat entzündet.                    (Part 1, I. ii)

The audience is further encouraged to note the contrast
between Christian stoicism and Turkish incontinence when
a heroic aria of Manuela's is set against a desperate love
aria sung by the Sultan's mother, who is infatuated with
Mustapha. Manuela sings her stoic resignation in the garden
of the seraglio, in the unmistakable manner of the *femme forte*:

Das Kreuz/ so GOtt mir auffgelegt/
   Wil ich nicht mehr beweinen/
Ich weiß/ daß Er zu helffen pflegt/
   Wann wir es nicht vermeinen;
Drum wart' ich in Geduld/
Auff seine Hülff' und Huld/
Die Tugend sol indes allein/
Mein Trost und stete Freude seyn.    (Part 1, I. viii)

Zaime then enters to give an account of her, strikingly different, state of being:

Lieb' und Eyfer/ Gunst und Haß/
   Quählen mich auff allen Seiten/
   Daß mein Hertz ohn Unterlaß
     Muß mit ihnen allen streiten/
Lieb' und Eyfer/ Gunst und Haß!

Like Mustapha whom she loves and hates, Zaime displays the
incontinent passion we have come to expect of the Turk.

Bostel *seems* at first glance to subscribe to traditional
admiration for Turkish military skill. Mustapha's aria in
the second act can be read as an illustration of tactical
astuteness:

Darin besteht die Krieges=List/
Wann erst der Feind im weichen ist/
  Ihm in der Eil nicht Zeit zu lassen/
  Umb wieder Muth und Stand zu fassen/
Ein plötzlicher Anfall kan zagen und schrecken/
Auch bey den sonst tapfren Gemüthern erwecken.   (Part 1, II. iv)

The effect of this aria is changed, however, when we consider that the siege of Vienna failed despite the initial paucity of defending imperial forces because of crass tactical errors on the part of Kara Mustafa Köprülü: he seems to have waited far too long to attack, and hence to have given the tardy Austro-Hungarian reinforcements time to arrive. It is likely that Bostel's audience knew this, and recognized the irony.

Bostel's Mustapha is the kind of Machiavellian agitator Béhar saw negated in Haugwitz's *Soliman*. He works on a principle of ruthless self-interest in the personal and in the political sphere. He is driven by his desire for the Sultan's married sister, Baschlari, and the egotistical, passion-based nature of his lust is powerfully conveyed in an aria:

> Bluth von Feinden/
> Oder Freunden/
> Ist mir alles gleiche viel/
> Komm' ich nur zu meinem Ziel/
> Kan ich nur Baschlari sehn/
> Mag der Krieg an allen Enden/
> Morden/ Rauben/ Brennen/ Schänden/
> Ja das Reich mag untergehn!                    (Part 1, I. ii)

The patriotism which forms part of the Christian human ideal as it is embodied in *femmes fortes*, like Gryphius's Catharina and Bostel's Manuela, is conspicuously lacking in Mustapha: the latter is as extreme a Turkish anti-hero as Lohenstein's Sultan Ibrahim. Bostel's negative portrayal of the Grand Vizier approaches caricature when, in case we had forgotten it, he reiterates his will to chaos in the aria that closes Act II, this time with reference to the order of marriage rather than that of the state:

> Was meiner Liebe schaden thut/
> Muß alles untergehen/
> Solt' auch die gantze Welt im Bluth/
> In Feur und Flammen stehen/
>   Acht' ichs doch alles nicht/
> Baschlari zu erwerben/
> Soll Ibrahim jetzt sterben/
>   So bricht
> Das Band der Ehr' und Pflicht/
> Ich acht' es alles nicht.                    (Part 1, II. vii)

Mustapha's personal ruthlessness arises out of his willing slavery to passion. We see the seriousness of this when he applies the same principle politically, to the Turkish state. The high priest Muffti suggests that the divine powers are opposed to an Ottoman attack on Christian territory because it would involve breaking an oath (the treaty with Austria of 1664), but the Grand Vizier refutes the idea that the Turkish forces are bound by considerations of honour or righteousness:

> Kurtz/ Ottomann ist nicht durch Wort und Eyd gebunden/
> Er fragt nicht ob der Krieg recht oder unrecht sey/
> Wann er nur Nutzen schafft . . .
>
> (Part 1, I. v)

That these Machiavellian principles are shared by other Turks—that is, that Mustapha is to be understood as the rule rather than as the exception—is made clear when Selim and Hussain express similar views:

> **Aria**. Was heistu Eyd und Treu!
> Wird solche Fantasey
> Von grossen mehr geachtet!
> Wer jetzo in der Welt
> Nach Macht und Ehre trachtet/
> Der hält
> Den Eyd
> Für Eitelkeit/
> Die Treu
> Für Triegerey.          (Part 1, II. v)

Bostel's and Franck's opera deals with a political event—the Second Siege of Vienna—which happened just three years before its first performance in Hamburg in 1686. The audience would remember and expect to observe what were very nearly current events. This specificity stands in contrast to the kind of universalizing portrayal of history that allowed both Lohenstein and Haugwitz to make of the Orient an instructive, self-referential mirror. Any didacticism in Bostel's libretto would have come closer to political propaganda.[80]

[80] W. Gordon Marigold claims that Mustapha in this opera was identified by the audience with the King of Denmark, who was then besieging Hamburg. This does not alter the fact that the demonization of the character depends heavily on his recognizable Turkishness. See Marigold, 'Politics, Religion and Opera: Problems of the Hamburg Opera, 1678–1720', in *Mosaic* 18/4 (1985), 49–60 (58).

This makes it particularly interesting that, in the midst of predictably negative views of Turkishness, so much is made of the virtuous Turks Baschlari and Ibrahim, and it is worth investigating whether Bostel here, like Haugwitz in *Soliman*, is attempting to counter anti-Turkish polemic with reference to individual virtue (Ibrahim, Baschlari), or whether he is closer to Lohenstein in using more positive examples of Turkishness to emphasize the depths of the villain's (Mustapha's) iniquity. To this end we need to look more closely at the nature of the relationship between Muslim and Christian, and the rhetoric of the 'good heathen'.

Edith Hall, when contrasting and yet comparing Euripides' Colchian Medea with Aeschylus's Greek Clytemnaestra, explains the apparent contradiction in the portrayal of a non-barbarian woman who nonetheless 'gets out of hand' with reference to her language: 'on close examination a brilliant device is shown to have been deployed in the presentation of this 'woman of manly counsel' (Ag.II): the 'vocabulary of barbarism' has been transferred to illuminate the psychology and motivation of a Greek.'[81] By these means a dramatist can switch established categories for effect. Something similar, only the other way around, is happening in Bostel's opera. The Muslim couple, especially Ibrahim, are portrayed as distinct from the other Turks in the piece. Baschlari's near-Christian cast of mind is illustrated in a stichomythic dialogue with Mustapha in Act 1, scene vii, which is strongly reminiscent of that which takes place between the Christian Isabelle and Soliman in the first act of Haugwitz's play (*Soliman*, I. 492–526): in both cases the female protagonist defends her virtue in a display of rhetorical adeptness. There are other instances when the language used by the two couples is strikingly similar. Manuela's stereotypical Christian stoic aria in the absence of Gasparo, cited above, is echoed at the beginning of the following act when Ibrahim comforts Baschlari in the face of their imminent separation:

> Mein wehrtster Schatz/ man muß
> In allen sich des Himmels Schluß'/
> In stetiger Gelassenheit ergeben          (Part 1, II. i)

---

[81] Hall, *Inventing the Barbarian*, 203.

The duet subsequently sung by the Muslim pair contains incongruous Christian imagery: 'So lang mein Hertz die Treu verspührt/ Kan es kein Kreutz betrüben'. This may be conscious; it may equally mean that the librettist is drawing unthinkingly on a stock of 'positive' metaphor with Christian origins. The married love of Ibrahim and Baschlari is described in the same duet in positively laden terms as 'keusche Brunst', and the comparable nature of their love with that of the Christian pair, Manuela and Gasparo, is further suggested when in Act III, scene ix the two women sing an aria about love together.

The couples are, however, not quite on a par. Although Ibrahim displays only noble proto-Christian qualities by contrast with the other Turkish men, Baschlari—unlike Manuela —eventually betrays her vulnerability to passion. Her aria, 'Schickung/ warumb schlägstu mich', very nearly echoes Gasparo's (in the guise of Roxellana) 'Schickung/ ach/ es ist zu viel!' (1, I. iv). But in the second stanza, instead of expressing the stoic resignation to the will of God or Fate we might expect, Baschlari chastises her own flighty sensuality:

> Doch/ verwegne Ungedult/
>    Halt mit Klagen innen!
> Wird mein Hertz auffs neu entzündet/
> Daß es neue Quahl empfindet/
>    So habt ihr allein die Schuld
>    Meine leichte [sic] Sinnen          (Part 1, II. i)

This forms a basis for the idea that is introduced in the second part of the opera, namely that the fall of great men may be brought about by women. Selim thereby suggests that Baschlari is at the root of Mustapha's tyrannical miscalculations:

> **Aria**. Ach/ wie werden hohe Geister
> Offt zum Fall gebracht/
> Wenn die Liebe sich erst Meister
> Ihrer Sinnen macht/
> Wann die schwache Weibes=Hand
> Einen Held in Ketten führet/
> Und der herrlichste Verstand
> Von der Thorheit wird regieret.          (Part 2, II. i)

The accusation of women is reinforced by the Barac's (the fool's) comic aria in the following act:

> Ein Weib ist ein gefährlich Ding/
>   Ich halte nichts von Freyen/
> Wer weiß/ ob mirs auch nicht so ging/
>   Wann ich käm' an den Reihen          (Part 2, III. iv)

while Mustapha's own lament at the end of the opera is more specific:

> Ach hätt' ich/ allermeist Baschlari nie gesehen
> Ich würde jetzo nicht so schmählich untergehen!   (Part 2, III. xi)

The point of this is likely to be a warning against the *Affekt* of passion rather than an indication that it is directly Baschlari's fault; it is, however, worth observing that it is never suggested that the Christian Isabelle in the *Soliman* and *Ibrahim* dramas of Haugwitz and Lohenstein is even indirectly responsible for the Sultan's fall.

The death of Bostel's virtuous Ibrahim is another interesting aspect of the second part of the opera. In the first act we see him rejecting suicide as a manifestation of the Christian sin of despair:

> Doch/ wann ich in diesen Nöthen
>   Mich begreiffe/ fält mir bey/
> Daß/ aus Unmuht sich zu tödten/
>   Der Verzweifflung Zuflucht sey      (Part 2, I. vi)

In Act II he is unjustly executed in the Turkish manner, by strangulation. There is a paradox here: the structure of early opera is such that death ought not to reward a virtuous character—'goodies' survive—yet Ibrahim's final aria confirms that he has not compromised his virtue. The language is that of the Christian martyr, who can only be read as virtuous:

> Kanstu dieses Unrecht sehen/
> Daß die Unschuld muß vergehen/
> Der du in den Wolcken wohnst!
>
> (Part 2, II, 'Siebende Vorstellung')

The solution to the riddle is that Ibrahim, as a Turk, is allowed to die despite his virtue, but will as a proto-Christian be avenged on the Turkish tyrant by the God to whom he appeals in death; the Hamburg audience knew that the Grand Vizier was himself strangled on the orders of Mehmed a fortnight after his defeat at Vienna.

The murder of Ibrahim, like the imprisonment of the Viennese ambassador at the end of the first part of *Cara Mustapha*, is a small-scale Turkish victory internal to the opera's action. In this way it is similar to the temporal triumph of Soliman when he murders Ibrahim in Lohenstein's *Ibrahim Bassa*. It is made clear that such triumphs are short-term, since a Christian God will in time impose his own order and punish non-Christian transgressors. This emerges from a disputation between Mustapha and the ambassador, which develops into a theological argument:

> MUST. Mich straffe Mahomet, wenn wir die Stadt gewinnen/
> Bleibt selbst in Mutter Leib' ein zartes Kind verschont!
> ABG. Der Eyd/ und Vorsatz wird wie heisser Schnee zerrinnen.
> Wo der es nicht verhängt/ der in den Wolcken wohnt.
> MUST. Der in den Wolcken wohnt/ gedenckt euch auszurotten.
> ABG. Nicht uns/ besondern die/ so seine Macht verspotten.
> MUST. Der Ausgang zeigt/ daß er euch straffet/ und uns liebt.
> ABG. Weil er für euch die Straff' ins Höllen=Feur verschiebt.

> (Part 1, III. xi)

The battle for Vienna is shown as a conflict between the (pious) Christian and the (barbaric) Islamic principle.

That Luther's theodicy of the Turk as the instrument of a Christian divinity is still influencing German literary writing at the end of the seventeenth century is apparent from the series of sung interludes or *Vorstellungen* that are interpolated into the opera.[82] These *Vorstellungen* are similar to *Reyen*, in that they reflect or comment on the dramatic action without being a direct part of it. In the second part of the opera, the interludes serve chiefly to illustrate the horror of the Turkish advances, depicting tableau-like scenes of slaughter

[82] There is no surviving music for these *Vorstellungen*. It seems sensible to assume that they were sung because they represent exactly the kind of overtly religious interlude that would have been set to music in the influential Jesuit operas.

and destruction. In the first part of Bostel's opera, however, they represent a 'truth' or higher order that is imposed by the dramatist on his historical material.

In his commentary on the first part of *Cara Mustapha*, Reinhard Meyer remarks only on the first three *Vorstellungen*, which are separated off from the opera proper as a prologue, something more characteristic of the structure of court opera. The first two of these represent, as the stage directions indicate, material from the second and seventh chapter of the Book of Daniel, namely Nebuchadnezzar's dream figure of gold, silver, bronze, iron, and clay, and Daniel's own vision of the four creatures from the sea, the last of which is just growing its eleventh horn; the relevance of these images to the opera can be understood if we return to Luther's Daniel preface for the interpretation of the eleventh horn as a symbol of the Turk.[83] But Meyer does not comment on the third of the tableaux of the 'Vorspiel', which is equally indebted to Luther. The Christian Church is shown, pursued and oppressed by Mohammed. The reaction of the Church is that repeatedly recommended by the reformer as the most effective means of countering the Turkish scourge, namely repentance:

> KIRCHE. Ach! schöne grosser Zebaoth/
> Verzeihe meinen Sünden/
> Rett dich und mich von diesem Spott/
> Und laß dich gnädig finden
>
> (Part 1, 'Dritte Vorstellung')

In response to this, an angel appears from the clouds to cover the Church with a shield and restrain Mohammed's arm. When the latter questions the constraint, the angel explains simply:

> Es ist des höchsten GOttes Hand/
> Die stürtzt dich endlich nieder.

The stage direction follows, 'Mahomet wird durch einen Blitz in den Abgrund gestürtzt'. In this way the Lutheran prophecy that God will restore Christian order is shown to be

[83] See Meyer, *Die Hamburger Oper*, 4. 175.

fulfilled (we must assume that the defeat at Vienna is taken to be the first step in this process) and the Prophet of Islam is, in the spirit of Luther, clearly associated with Lucifer or the Antichrist.

The 'Vierte Vorstellung' occurs, in the manner of a *Reyen*, after the first act. Mehmed IV is shown dreaming; what he sees is the heretofore waxing moon of the Ottomans beginning to wane, while a rising sun quartered by a red cross outshines the light of the stars. Once again, the angel descends to explain:

> Du stoltzer Ottoman,
> Der Glantz/ den deine Macht
> Vom höchsten Licht gewann/
> Neigt sich zur finstern Nacht/
> .    .    .    .    .    .
> Die Sonne der Gerechtigkeit
> Stürtzt dich in Tunckelheit.

We are reminded not only of Luther's prophecy, 'der Türck wird nicht mehr Hörner uber die drey/ abstossen' but also strongly of the dedication in Lohenstein's *Ibrahim Sultan* (a drama Bostel refers to in his preface) in which the imperial sun of Austria, Leopold, was metaphorically invited to observe 'die zu unserer Zeit sichtbare Verfinsterung eines Oßmannischen Mohnden'.

After Act II, the fifth interlude illustrates another popular Lutheran idea: the divine scourge. The now-familiar angel as the voice of truth reminds us and the oppressed Austrians shown in the tableau, 'Sehet/ wie Gott straffen kann'. The first part of the opera closes with a sixth 'Vorstellung', which finally makes the connection implicit in the preceding five between the reimposition of divine order and the defeat of the Ottomans at Vienna. The victorious Count Starenberg and his soldiers conclude this part of the opera with the assertion that this is not only a military but a theological victory: 'GOtt hat es gethan!' By divine judgement, the Christian side has been proved right.

Bostel's and Franck's opera should have heralded a new era in the life of the Hamburg opera house when it reopened in 1686 after an economically dictated closure. In fact it was one of the operas banned by the Wittenberg theologians who were applied to the following year for a final resolution of the *Opernstreit*, the theological argument over opera that had dogged the Hamburg theatre since its opening in 1678. The question was whether opera was morally damaging, or merely an *adiaphoron*; in most cases the Wittenberg judges took the latter view. *Cara Mustapha*, however, they rejected on the grounds of 'Anstößigkeit in puncto pii et honesti'.[84] The latter charge presumably refers to the too-explicit expressions of Turkish passion; the exact origin of the former is less easy to pin down. Despite the Lutheran elements in the libretto, which seem clearly enough to indicate a movement towards the fulfilment of a Christian world plan, did the Wittenberger find offensive the inclusion of two virtuous Turks in the piece? In his intention, Bostel is probably closer to Lohenstein than to Haugwitz: the virtue of his Ibrahim points up by its exceptional nature the culpability of the other Muslims rather than standing as an individual example of suprareligious integrity. But if opera was to defend its status as a non-corrupting medium, perhaps even one good Turk was one too many.

## Conclusion

It is a reasonably straightforward process to identify the negative preconceptions of non-Christians, especially Ottomans or Turks, which become established in the literature of the early modern period. We have observed that a number of ideas about the Ottoman enemy were evolved for propaganda purposes. Yet Olearius's/Andersen's travel report illustrates that similar preconceptions applied to peoples who posed no direct political or territorial threat to the West. It seems that a level of insecurity is a general feature of writing about that which is culturally and (to an extent) physically different, and expresses itself in the need to represent it as inferior. This can be achieved by suggesting that real or supposed differences are in fact defects in the Other—woman,

---

[84] See Haufe, *Die Behandlung der antiken Mythologie*, 96.

for example, as *vir imperfectus*—or, in the case of religious differences, by wheeling on the circular argument that Christianity is right, and a Christian God will therefore protect his people at the expense of all others.

The latter method is Bostel's in *Cara Mustapha*. In a recent work on Lohenstein, Adalbert Wichert reminds us 'daß Dramen nach der Struktur von juristischen Prozessen auf Beurteilung hin konzipiert sind und vielfach Prozesse zu ihrem Gegenstand machen'.[85] Wichert is discussing forensic rhetoric —the rhetoric of proof in a legal dispute—whereby the listeners (or, in drama, the audience) are the deciding jury. But Bostel, following Luther's rhetorical method, ultimately circumnavigates the problem of proof in his choice of judge: the Christian God, whose judgements are pre-defined as right and true. Even before this, however, Bostel is helped by the discourse that is already in place forty years earlier, in Gryphius's *Catharina von Georgien*, by which Islam is gendered feminine, Christianity masculine: for all his threatening military (and seafaring)[86] prowess, the Muslim is subject to passion, which is politically emasculating unless correctly countered with *Vernunft*.

With reference to the late seventeenth-century encyclopaedist of exotica, Eberhard Werner Happel (1647–90), Lynne Tatlock has noted an impulse to address specific cultural anxieties in the economically dynamic *Hansestadt* of Hamburg: to stabilize an insecure Self in a changing world by reference to the Other, which is defined as the *real* location of chaos.[87] Happel, whose works were best-sellers, was keen to present his reading public with 'true facts', which he uncovers or reveals to them in text and numerous illustrations.[88] The visual aspect is theatrical, the method forensic. Following Bostel, Lohenstein, and *their* predecessors,

---

[85] Adalbert Wichert, *Literatur, Rhetorik und Jurisprudenz im 17. Jahrhundert: Daniel Casper von Lohenstein und sein Werk* (Tübingen 1991), 267.
[86] The Turks had palpable effect on the economy of Bostel's Hamburg, whose merchant sailors all too often fell into the hands of Turkish and Algerian pirates. See Lynne Tatlock, 'Selling Turks: Eberhard Werner Happel's Turcica (1683–1690)', in *CG* 28 (1995), 307–35.
[87] Ibid. 309 ff.
[88] See e.g. Happel's *Gröste Denckwürdigkeiten der Welt Oder so-genannte RELATIONES CURIOSAE . . .*, 5 vols. (Hamburg 1683). TAY.

Happel is able to construct the Turk as chaotic and arbitrary, and as the reassuring opposite pole of German Christendom.

Christian writers nonetheless take the trouble to construct the occasional virtuous Muslim. It seems that there are (to ruin a metaphor) *two* other sides to the negative coin of the Other, namely admiration and fascination (or titillation).[89] The first of these two flip-sides, admiration, is the more deceptive, as Luther's praise of Turkish soldiers exemplified: in fact the Turks are rhetorically functionalized to provoke feelings of shame and competition in the imperial troops, and the interest is therefore firmly focused on the Christian subject and his world, rather than on the Muslim object and his. Andersen's story of the Japanese Christians and post-rape suicides, Lohenstein's courageous Ambre, Haugwitz's Soliman, and Bostel's near-Christian Ibrahim fit the same kind of pattern, since each of these portrayals constitutes an instructive example to a Christian European readership or audience. These figures contradict our expectations, which run along the lines female—Orient—non-Christian —Machiavellian or unprincipled leadership, and male— Occident—Christian—just and principled rulership. On a didactic level, therefore, the unexpectedness of a strong-minded woman or a virtuous Muslim renders the figure more striking than a more predictably ideal (Christian, male) character might be, and hence far more effective on the stage.

The same may be said of the heroic woman, Catharina, who in fact reflects back an ideal of Christian *male* behaviour. When anti-misogynists such as Pierre Le Moyne tried to enhance the reputation of women by depicting them as *femmes fortes*, contemporary gender discourse left them no alternative when attempting to create a positive picture but to reassign traditionally *masculine* attributes. There is evidence of a similar problem in idealized portrayals of non-Christians, such as Haugwitz's Soliman or Bostel's Ibrahim. The latter stands out from his fellow Turks because he is characterized in Christian terms. Even Haugwitz is only able to accord Sultan

[89] See Francesca Ferraris and Sabine Wagner, 'Stellung und Funktion des Exotismus in der deutschen Literatur der Frühen Neuzeit', in *Frühneuzeit-Info* 3/2 (1992), 113–14.

Soliman a laudatory portrayal by turning him into a kind
of mirror for Christians: his function as a pattern-card for
Christian rulers is finally established because it is identified
by the Europeans, Ibrahim (Justinian) and Isabelle.

In Lohenstein's Turkish dramas, as in elements of the travel
report and possibly in the torture scene of *Catharina von
Georgien*, another kind of flip-side is beginning to emerge:
the erotic fascination of the Western writer with his oriental
or female subject. German literary culture in the seventeenth century was male-dominated, and appears to have
constructed masculinity as, among other things, the ability
to subordinate the sexual urge to reason, or *Vernunft*. Sensuality is distanced from the masculine, and in an antithetical
universe must therefore be relocated on the side of the
feminine, where we also find the oriental and the Muslim.
The rhetoric of this is simple and effective: as woman are subjugated by men, so too, in an ideal world, are the potentially
alarming ideas of sex and the Orient. Gendering—as the next
chapter will explore in more detail—becomes a means to
rhetorical control; in literature, at least, the Other can be
pinned down by rhetoric while its fascinating unfamiliarity
is explored.

# 2

# THE RHETORICAL FEMININE (II): SEPARATING THE WOMEN FROM THE BOYS

Gryphius's and Lohenstein's conceptions of Turkish and other Islamic characters indicate the extent to which their texts rely on an idea of society that is pre-defined as Christian. For Christian, male writers in a hierarchical, masculinist society, otherness is not only equated with wrongness, but is 'naturally' located in binary opposition to the Self; that is, in women and non-Christians. As in a hall of mirrors, this inverted reflection is perceived as an excess that is instructive or interesting in so far as it refers back to the Self.

But even the apparently clear reflection of an ideal may not be as straightforward as it seems. This was the case in *Catharina von Georgien.* Gryphius's heroine is not simply a pattern-card among women, because many of her ideal qualities are in fact masculine and might be less desirable in a woman whose circumstances were different: bourgeois rather than royal, perhaps, or with a husband living. Ian Maclean has shown that in Renaissance thought different standards of virtue apply not only to women and men, but to women in different social strata:

men may be virtuous in practising eloquence, liberality, courage, magnificence; women by being silent . . . economical, chaste, modest. . . . The moral virtues assigned to women are suitable to a member of the bourgeoisie or lesser nobility; . . . The princess is, as it were, a man by virtue of her birth, and hence the masculine standard of morality applies to her.[1]

[1] Ian Maclean, *Woman Triumphant. Feminism in French Literature 1610–1652* (Oxford 1977), 19–20.

Ideals and anti-ideals may therefore be quite closely related, and need not be consistent. Ideal behaviour in one
instance can easily be perceived as transgressive behaviour
in another; the line between extraordinary heroism and
threatening inversion of the gender ethic is fine and ill-
defined. By investigating portrayals of women on both sides
of the line, we can look further at the rhetoric of gender
and of order on the early modern stage.

## The Misogynist Tradition in Literature

Classical philosophers as early as the Pythagoreans attributed chaotic potential to women, ordering abilities to men.[2]
Chaos is the destructive opposite of a civilized identity, and
naturally comes to be associated with the demonic, as does
the female. By the late medieval period in Europe the
literary idea of the female demon was widespread. There are
recurring themes in these male nightmares of the feminine, but whether Lilith, Empusa, or Lamia, what unites them
'is their power to destroy men, either by magically under-
mining their vitality or by sucking their blood'.[3] The notion
of bloodsucking all too clearly reflects male sexual anxiety
about the loss of precious bodily fluids to the 'insatiable'
female, and characterizes writing on witchcraft.[4] This is
likely to be linked to castration phobia—women are perceived as a threat to the male vitality that is symbolized in
the phallus—but it circumscribes feminization in another
sense, too, as women themselves are the sex more usually
defined by the loss of bodily fluids, such as menstrual blood
and breast milk.

A medieval tendency which survives into much later literature is to polarize the ideal and the demonic in portrayals

---

[2] See Glenda McLeod, *Virtue and Venom: Catalogs of Women from Antiquity to the Renaissance* (Ann Arbor 1991), 38.

[3] Hoffmann R. Hays, *The Dangerous Sex: The Myth of Feminine Evil* (London 1966 [1964]), 141.

[4] Lyndal Roper describes the early modern 'economy of bodily fluids' which became the basis for many witchcraft accusations. See Lyndal Roper, *Oedipus and the Devil: Witchcraft, Sexuality and Religion in Early Modern Europe* (London 1994), 208.

of women.⁵ The connection between woman and the
demonic or the devil is made with clarity by Der Stricker
(?–1250): in his narrative poem *Von einem übelen wîbe* the
unruly wife is possessed, and her 'taming' is described in terms
of an exorcism.⁶ She subsequently confesses to the priest:

> mir hâte der tiuvel gar benomen
> beide vorht und minne,
> wîsheit und rehte sinne.        (160–2)

In a longer poem, *Von übelen wîben*, a more general accusation is levelled at womankind, which extends the idea of
female guilt for the Fall from Eden to suggest that women
still threaten men's salvation:

> diu übelen wîp hânt geladen
> die werlt mit einem solhen schaden
> der manegen an die sêle gât.        (43–5)

Again there is a special relationship between women and the
devil, who gives them the power to subvert and invert the
God-given order of the sexes:

> daz gît den übelen wîben kraft
> daz si niht rehte meisterschaft
> von den mannen müzzen dulden.        (505–7)

The threat posed by such women is grotesquely illustrated
in the image of the phallic woman that Der Stricker evokes:

> sie wirbet spâte unde vruo
> mit übele und mit guote
> über lût und mit dem muote
> daz si die êre bejage
> daz si daz lenger mezzer trage.        (118–24)

⁵ See Barbara Becker-Cantarino, ' "Frau Welt" und "Femme Fatale": Die Geburt
eines Frauenbildes aus dem Geiste des Mittelalters', in J. F. Poag and G. Scholz-Williams
(eds.), *Das Weiterleben des Mittelalters in der deutschen Literatur* (Königstein/Ts. 1983),
61–73 (61–2). Claudia Honegger has also investigated the dual conception of woman
in the middle ages with particular reference to the cult of the Virgin, which she
describes as 'die Andere [*sic*] Seite des entstehenden "Hexenwahns"'. See Honegger
(ed.), *Die Hexen der Neuzeit: Studien zur Sozialgeschichte eines kulturellen Deutungsmusters*
(Frankfurt a.M. 1978), 56.
⁶ Franz Brietzmann remarks on this in his edition of the text. See Brietzmann,
*Die böse Frau in der deutschen Litteratur des Mittelalters* (Berlin 1912 [= *Palaestra* 42]),
122. All references are to this edition of the text.

The narrative voice in this poem conceives not only of women but also of non-Christians as potential allies of the devil and opponents of the Christian male. This is the force of the claim, obviously intended to shock, that of women, Jews, and heathens, women are the most pernicious:[7]

> ir [= women's] übele hât sô grôze kraft:
> die juden und die heidenschaft
> die bekêret man al gemeine
> ê man ir alters eine
> bî lebendem lîbe erwerte
> die mortlîchen vlinsherte
> die ir eiterigez herze hât                    (651–7)

The modern editor of these poems, Franz Brietzmann, re-marks that conjugal conflict in Der Stricker's work is in fact microcosmic symbolism: man and wife come to represent God and the Devil, and 'nicht Mannesherrschaft oder Frauenregi-ment sind die Endstadien des Hauskampfes, sondern Himmel und Hölle, ewige Seligkeit oder Verdamnis [sic]' (p. 124). The problem clearly *does* revolve around 'Mannesherrschaft oder Frauenregiment', however; the point is that Der Stricker is able to add great authority to his argument for the sub-jugation of women within marriage by associating the male/female relationship with that between God (order, salva-tion) and the devil (chaos, damnation). The idea of woman presented in these poems is implicitly—or rhetorically and deliberately—related to the medieval conception of *Frau Welt*, which links woman with both worldly temptation and ultimate damnation. Woman's part in (men's) loss of salva-tion automatically locates her in opposition to the bringer of salvation, Christ. She is not only potentially in league with the devil or Antichrist, she may even figure as an incarnation of the latter, a 'Gegenspielerin Christi', as Becker-Cantarino has described Grimmelshausen's Courasche.[8]

An illustrated broadsheet published in 1617 provides a striking instance of the reception of the medieval idea of

---

[7] Links are also frequently made between Jews and witches in European accounts of witchcraft in the early modern period. See Honegger, *Die Hexen der Neuzeit*, 81.

[8] Becker-Cantarino, ' "Frau Welt" ', 65.

woman in the seventeenth century. The picture is antithetical:
on the right-hand side (and therefore on the side of order
and the norm) a young man is shown in front of a glorious
castle, whose narrow entrance is the destination of cross-
bearing, childlike figures toiling along a precarious path.
On the left, the side of inversion and the sinister, a richly
dressed woman is standing. She is close enough to the
picture's centre to have her arm around the young man, and
is distracting his gaze from the glowing castle and the cross-
bearers towards a flowery landscape. But on closer investigation we find a snake among the flowers, and the wide arch
far left, through which a crowd of corpulent adults is push-
ing, barely conceals the fiery jaws of Satan in its depths. The
woman's role is elucidated in the text:

> Der junge Mensch ist zweiffels voll/
> Unwissend/ welchen Weeg er soll
> Zu gehn fürnemmen/ dann das Weib/
> So hie gebildet schön von Leib/
> Im zeiget der Welt Stoltz und Pracht.
> Und ihm weltliche Wollust macht/
> So hönig süß/ bildet ihm ein/
> Wie er mög allzeit frölich sein/
> Und gut täg haben in seim Leben/
> Wann er ihr Gehör solte geben/
> So führt sie ihn den Weeg zur Höllen.[9]

This broadsheet documents contemporary preconceptions;
there is no question in the mind of the illustrator or author
but that woman—inversion—vice—hell, and man—order—
virtue—heaven are naturally antithetical chains of meaning.

Aegidius Albertinus's *Hortus mulieribus* was published
in 1630, and is a compendium of the dangers and failings embodied by women. But Albertinus does not only
demonize the female. In 1611 he published his *Himlisch
Frawenzimmer. Darin dz [sic] Leben zwey und funffzig der aller-
heiligsten Junckfrawen und Frawen*, a catalogue of ideal female
virtue. In this, physical and spiritual chastity are presented

---

[9] In Wolfgang Harms *et al.* (eds.), *Illustrierte Flugblätter des Barock: Eine Auswahl*
(Tübingen 1983), 34–5.

'as the *summum bonum* of feminine virtue';[10] but it is worth
noting that this involves in every case the choice of death
over life; chastity may be the *summum bonum* in women, but
moribundity is apparently its guarantee. Chastity is, at all
events, a key concept. Lyndal Roper's analysis of notions of
gender and virtue in the early modern period in Germany
finds that 'female virtue is understood in bodily terms and it
ultimately means chastity; male virtue, by contrast, is plural
and concerns a host of qualities which must be manifested in
public'.[11] Gryphius's Catharina, a royal widow and therefore
not subject to any terrestrial male authority, could display
heroic chastity in her fight to be allowed to submit only to
the metaphysical authority of God. The self-presentation and
reception of historical women in the early modern period
seems to have followed the same pattern: while the unmarried
queens Elizabeth I of England (1533–1603) and Christina
of Sweden (1626–89) were accepted as models of the
masculine spirit in the female body, Empress Maria Teresia
(1717–80) figured instead as *Landesmutter*, in a role that could
not threaten the ultimate authority of her husband.[12]

Even within an antithetical world-view that is intimately
related to a perceived gender polarity, it is impossible to maintain that women are consistently vicious or chaotic—indeed,
the *femme forte* was designed explicitly to contradict the
extreme misogynist view—or that men are without exception
virtuous upholders of order. The writers I shall consider
in this chapter do not on the whole attempt to do this.
They investigate ideas of masculinity and femininity, within
both men and women, and in doing this they communicate
a persuasive assessment of which combinations of these
ideas will result in civilized order, and which in social and
political chaos.

---

[10] Lawrence S. Larsen, 'Una Poenitentium: Levels of Sin and Sanctity in
Albertinian Women', in James Hardin and Jörg Jungmayr (eds.), *'Der Buchstab tödt—
der Geist macht lebendig': Festschrift zum 60. Geburtstag von Hans-Gert Roloff*, 2 vols. (Berlin
1992), 2. 697–708 (699).
[11] Roper, *Oedipus and the Devil*, 107.
[12] Heide Wunder describes the self-stylization of these prominent women.
See Wunder, *'Er ist die Sonn', sie ist der Mond': Frauen in der frühen Neuzeit* (Munich
1992), 206.

*The Problem of the Virile Virgin:* Epicharis

Gryphius's Catharina performed heroic actions in the service
of patriarchal authority, divine rather than terrestrial. Both
her royal rank and her constancy in this service counter-
balance the 'natural' infernal sensuality of woman, rendering
her a virago or 'virile virgin' (despite her widowhood), in the
Classical sense.[13] Lohenstein's *Epicharis* (published 1665)[14]
depicts a heroine who is both related to and distinct from
Catharina. Just as Chach Abas was feminized to play against
a masculine Catharina, so the Roman men in Lohenstein's
play are shown at a disadvantage by Epicharis's virility. But,
unlike Catharina, Epicharis is neither a Christian (and therefore not acting as the terrestrial arm of a patriarchal authority) nor a sovereign, and Lohenstein's play illustrates the
problems of interpretation that arise when women who are
*not* legitimized to do so act outside the controls society places
on their sex.

   Like Catharina, Epicharis displays aspects of the martyr,
and the most prominent of these is her chastity. She, too,
demands to prove herself through suffering:

Braucht siedend Oel und Hartzt/ Strang/ Schwefel/ Pech und Flammen.
. . . . . . . . . . . . .
Die Marter soll mein Ruhm/ der Tod mein Siegs-Krantz seyn.

(III. 540 ff.)

The reference to her 'Krantz' reminds us that Epicharis will
go to death as a virgin, giving her a bridal status similar to
Catharina's—like Catharina, she is stripped and undergoes
the 'defloration' of torture.[15] This explains her apparently

---

[13] McLeod, *Virtue and Venom*, 40.

[14] Unless otherwise stated, all references to Lohenstein's dramas are from Klaus
Günther Just's editions: *Türkische Trauerspiele* (Stuttgart 1953); *Römische Trauerspiele*
(Stuttgart 1955); *Afrikanische Trauerspiele* (Stuttgart 1957).

[15] Jane O. Newman suggests that when Epicharis is stripped for torture the
spectators confront the 'naked truth' of her female identity behind the masculine
heroism. This again suggests a parallel with Gryphius's heroine. See Newman, 'Sex
"in Strange Places": The Split Text of Gender in Lohenstein's *Epicharis* (1665)', in
Lynne Tatlock (ed.), *The Graph of Sex and the German Text: Gendered Culture in Early Modern
Germany* (Amsterdam 1994), 349–82 (357). But I disagree with Newman's assertion that Epicharis's chastity is a front for 'her real allegiance . . . to the male-identified
political identity as a member of the conspiracy against Nero'; on the contrary, her
chastity *signals* the ideal status that sets her apart from her fellow conspirators.

sexual relationship with death, which has been considered problematic:

> Umb Pfal und Folterbanck/ empfind ich größer Lust/
> Als Acte/ die gleich ruht dem Käyser auf der Brust.    (IV. 85–6)

Despite the non-Christian context, the language of the martyr play signals the heroine's ideal status. But Lohenstein does not show us his protagonist acting under the protection of a higher authority. Catharina triumphs in a metaphysical sense because she is following a divinely ordained path; Epicharis, as the *Reyen* after Act IV of Lohenstein's drama makes clear, is not even acting with the support of that other metaphysical power, Fate. Gillespie remarks pertinently that Epicharis does not entirely fit the martyr type because her methods are violent.[16] In fact she embodies a virility that is closer to that of a royal heroine as defined by Maclean than to the more passive stoic virtues of the martyr saints.

Epicharis's central position in Lohenstein's play should not distract our attention from the fact that this is a drama about the need for heroism in *men*. Roman manhood has degenerated under Nero, and '[Epicharis's] political program is literally to reconvert the Romans into a heroic race'.[17] Romans are traditionally the epitome of manliness, so much so that even Roman women have been known to display heroic masculinity, as Epicharis recalls:

> Steckt nichts mehr Römisches in Römischen Gemüttern?
> Wo ist die edle Zeit/ da man durch Flammen lief/
> Da auch ein Weib den Stahl auf den Tirannen schlief
> Und durch die Flüße schwam.    (I. 40–3)

She uses the rhetoric of gender in two ways: firstly to shame the men and spur them into action:

> Ich selbst wil greiffen an
> Wo mehr kein Männer-Hertz in eurem Busen stecket    (I. 78–9)

---

[16] G. E. P. Gillespie, 'Lohenstein's Epicharis: The Play of the Beautiful Loser', in Gillespie, *Garden and Labyrinth of Time: Studies in Renaissance and Baroque Literature* (New York 1988), 193–224 (161).

[17] G. E. P. Gillespie, *Daniel Casper von Lohenstein's Historical Tragedies* (Columbus, Oh. 1965), 47.

and secondly to imply her innocence when accused of conspiracy: 'Mein schwacher Arm benimmt den Lügen allen
Schein' (II. 330). The audience or reader is nonetheless aware
that standard expectations of femininity do not pertain to
Epicharis. Sulpitius suggests that her masculinity is such
that she is scarcely credible as a woman:

> Wird künfftig uns die Welt wol Glauben meßen bey?
> Daß sie Epicharis ein Weib gewesen sey;
> Die klüger als ein Mann/ behertzter ist als Helden!    (II. 421–3)

Her Roman virility casts the men's lack of it into a particularly unfavourable light; they are described in the unflatter-
ing terms of the feminine. In his summary or 'Innhalt' [sic]
Lohenstein condemns Piso's 'weibische Heucheley' (p. 157),
and within the play Antonius Natalis warns the other conspirators against Proculus, using a metaphor which implies that
even masculine rhetoric may disguise feminine infirmity:

> Dem Proculus zu viel zu trauen/ ist nicht Rath:
> Der von der Zung ein Mann/ ein Weib ist in der That.    (I. 341–2)

During a rueful orgy of self-accusation late in the play, the
failed conspirators apostrophize themselves as 'Weiber' (IV.
297), an insult that is picked up by Subrius Flavius as a means
of (dishonestly) denying his involvement in the plot:[18]

> So bildet euch nicht ein/ ihr furchsamsten der Knechte/
> Die man mehr Römer nicht/ nicht Männer heißt mit Rechte/
> Daß Flavius sich hett euch Weibern beygesellt
>
> (IV. 383–5)

Women are now perceived as better Romans than these
men, as the response of Julius Turgurinus indicates: 'wir sind
kaum noch des Weiber-Nahmens werth' (IV. 389). The
truth of this is demonstrated not only by the indomitable
Epicharis, but also by Atilla, who exhibits considerably more
bravery in this scene than her son.

---

[18] Tacitus attributes a similar remark to Subrius Flavus, with the particular slant
not reproduced by Lohenstein that a soldier would not ally himself with effeminate civilians. See Tacitus, *The Annals of Imperial Rome*, trans. Michael Grant, 2nd edn.
(London 1989), 377.

Lohenstein's sources for the play are Tacitus, in whose account Epicharis is a freed woman of uncertain origin who participates in the Pisonian rebellion, and very probably Desmarets de Saint-Sorlin's novel *Ariane*, in which she is more central and an originator of the plot.[19] One interesting detail, offered by Tacitus and taken up by Lohenstein, is that Nero finally chooses to surround himself with German guards because Romans can no longer be trusted; it is possible that the German dramatist is distancing himself and his own masculinist civilization from the degenerate, feminized Rome portrayed in the play.

As Rome's ruler, Nero is the most effeminate and servile character of all. Gillespie has described the antithetical opposition of Nero and Epicharis: 'His is "ein knechtisches Gemütte" (V, iii, 548), though draped in purple; while she, "eines Griechen Magd" (V, iii, 551), undertakes magnanimous actions'.[20] Another element in this opposition is Epicharis's heroic chastity, which contrasts not only with Proculus's lust, but more particularly with Nero's (homo)sexuality; she reveals elliptically, 'daß der ein Weib sein wil' (I. 616).[21] Servility and femininity in the Emperor are scornfully observed and linked by his would-be assassin, Subrius Flavius:

Man fall ihn an/ wenn er durch knechtische Gebehrden
Und Weibischen Gesang sich Gauklern beygeselln
Und zum Gelächter wird der Welt für Augen stelln.          (I. 668–70)

This portrayal of Nero both as woman and fool evokes carnivalesque misrule. It is no wonder that heroic Roman men are behaving like women, and women like men, when their ruler himself embodies inversion in every sense. Flavius later hurls the accusation of misgovernment at the Emperor directly:

---

[19] See Bernhard Asmuth, *Lohenstein und Tacitus* (Stuttgart 1971), esp. pp. 63–71, and Gerhard Spellerberg, 'Eine unbekannte Quelle zur Epicharis Daniel Caspers von Lohenstein', in *Euphorion* 61 (1967), 143–54. Peter Skrine has suggested another source, namely Guilliam van Nieuwelandt's *Claudius Domitius Nero* (1618); see Skrine, 'A Flemish Model for the Tragedies of Lohenstein', in *MLR* 61 (1966), 64–70.

[20] Gillespie, 'Lohenstein's Epicharis', 215.

[21] Lohenstein gives the background to this rather coy reference in a note; Nero, dressed as a woman, apparently took a youth called Pythagoras to his bed. See the 'Anmerckungen', 276.

Nun aber du durch Morden
Zum Bruder-Henker bist/ zum Mutter-Mörder worden/
Nun du zum Gauckler dich/ zum Sänger hast gemacht/
Der Hure zu Gefalln dein Ehweib umbgebracht . . .        (IV. 431–4)

Further reversals emerge in Act V, when we see that the ruler
is in fact ruled by his subject Tigillinus and his wife Poppaea
(V. 202–3), both of whom ought properly to be subordinate.
The *Reyen* that follows Act IV suggests that the problem is
not limited to Nero: Rome herself and the Sybil describe a
list of Roman emperors in terms of the animals that connote
their bestial inversion (IV. 683–732). We are led to deduce
that the current reversal of the order of gender in Rome is a
reflection of the perversion of orderly rule by its emperors.
The tyrant and his associates betray their perverted perception in false accusations of witchcraft. Both heroic female conspirators in *Epicharis* are misperceived as witches: Epicharis
by Nero (III. 555) and Atilla by Poppaea (IV. 261). The despicable Piso claims to have been won over to the conspiracy by
Natalis's 'Zauberey' (IV. 554), while Fenius Rufus attempts
to escape punishment with a similar accusation, claiming that
Natalis bewitched him with a wax image (V. 457–9) and, in
the manner of a vampire or lamia, sucked 'Vernunfft und
Blutt aus Seel und Ohr' (V. 460). Such accusations do not
feature in Tacitus's account; but they are typical of early
modern witchcraft trials, and therefore automatically connote
perverse or chaotic behaviour.

Despite—or because of—her heroism, Epicharis differs
from Catharina in that she is distinctly on the borderline
between the ideal and the alarming.[22] Menhennet argues that
this is the culmination of a tension already present in the
pendant play, *Agrippina* (1665), in which the central figure
appears both as a ruthless sexual schemer and a martyred

---

[22] Jean-Marie Valentin has found a Jesuit version of Lohenstein's play that demonstrates just how easily the same material can be given a negative interpretation. See
Valentin, 'Une représentation inconnue de *L'Epicharis* de Lohenstein (Sion, 1710)',
in *Études Germaniques* 24 (1969), 242–8. Elida Maria Szarota recalls that, in the
Cologne performance of Epicharis in 1978, the central protagonist was portrayed
as a potential terrorist. See Szarota, *Stärke, dein Name sei Weib!: Bühnenfiguren des 17.
Jahrhunderts* (Berlin 1987), 214.

mother.[23] Epicharis does not fit either of these types, but her position as a woman revolutionary is delicate. Her virility is a problem: 'Seen from a seventeenth-century perspective, she plays a man's role. . . . ladies do not lead revolutions in the seventeenth century. Their role in this sphere is rather that of victim.'[24] Finally, of course, Epicharis *is* a victim, of Nero's tyranny, and although critics have baulked at Lohenstein's cavalier treatment of his heroic revolutionary, we cannot assume that her death implies a condemnation of her motives or behaviour, even though Seneca protests against the social inversion inherent in the conspiratorial idea: 'Hat ein vernünftig Volck je wolln sein Haupt beherrschen?' (I. 507); the attempted regicide portrayed in this play is clearly the inevitable result of imperial misrule, and Nero, rather than Epicharis, is at the root of the revolt.[25]

I am not convinced, however, that Lohenstein's drama really is *primarily* a case study of regicide or tyrannicide.[26] Epicharis leads the Pisonian rebellion in this play not in order that Nero might be overthrown—we all know that he was not —but so that shame may be cast on all men (except perhaps Seneca) from the Emperor downwards. Nero's tyranny is a problem, but it is a problem which has its roots in the greater malaise that is attacking Roman civilization. This Emperor, as the *Reyen* following Act IV makes clear, is not an exception, but the culmination of an imperial Roman tradition of misrule. Civilization has been perverted, and the effeminization of the Roman male (to which Tacitus, too, makes reference),[27] highlighted by the virility of a Roman woman, is the sign and result of chaotic inversion. Far from condemning Epicharis

[23] Alan Menhennet, 'The Death of Lohenstein's Agrippina', in *Quinquereme* 6/1 (1983), 28–38 (28).
[24] Alan Menhennet, 'Virtue and Vanity: Thoughts on the Beginning and End of Lohenstein's *Epicharis*', in *OGS* 16 (1985), 1–12 (10).
[25] Pierre Béhar interprets *Epicharis* in the light of the historical events in Silesia between 1650 and 1660, as the Swedish occupying troops departed and the Emperor began to clamp down on Silesian Protestantism; hence the negative portrayal of the despotic Roman emperor in the play and the 'glorification' (in Béhar's words) of a potential tyrannicide. See Béhar, *Silesia Tragica: epanouissement et fin de l'école dramatique silesienne dans l'œuvre tragique de Daniel Casper von Lohenstein (1635–1683)*, 2 vols. (Wiesbaden 1988), I. 43–4.
[26] Ibid.; Menhennet, 'Virtue and Vanity', 3.
[27] Tacitus, *The Annals of Imperial Rome*, 373, 379.

for her part in the rebellion, Lohenstein goes out of his way
to excuse her masculine behaviour, borrowing from Saint-
Sorlin's *Ariane* to make of the freed woman of Tacitus's
account a probable noblewoman, in whom a heroic spirit
would appear more acceptable. I do not share Gillespie's conviction that Epicharis has the 'tragic flaw' of 'still believing,
contrary to the evidence . . . that the liberation of society from
oppression is a necessary, attainable enterprise'.[28] The only
tragic flaw in Epicharis—in the sense that it is the one that
necessitates her dramatic downfall—is that she is not in fact
a man. Early on in the drama it is hinted that a female-led
conspiracy will lead to complications. Antonius Natalis concludes the relation of the episode of Marcellinus, who killed
for jealousy, with an axiomatic warning:

> Der Frauen Schönheit ist ein zeher Seelen-Leim/
> An dem die Flügel selbst der Tugend kleben bleiben.   (I. 154–5)

There is no suggestion here, as there was in Der Stricker's
poems, that women deliberately undermine men's spiritual-
ity and virtue. Femininity is perceived as an inevitable cause
of chaos, and both Epicharis (because she is a woman and
beautiful) and the male conspirators (because they are
effeminate) have a hand in bringing about the final scenes
of torture, misrule, and chaos in the drama.

The large number of dramatis personae alone suggests that
Epicharis was intended as a school production. In the tradition of school drama (at least as observed by Lohenstein and
Weise) it is politically instructive. Seneca delivers the sententious line that is one pedagogical tenet of the piece: 'Der hat
Vernunft/ der Mord und Unheil nicht spinnt an' (V. 25), but
the rhetoric of masculinity and femininity is equally instructive. Epicharis explains her plans for Nero:

> Ich wil den ersten Dolch auf diesen Panther schärffen
> Und lehrn: Daß auch ein Weib Tyrannen stürtzen kan.   (I. 328–9)

and Proculus recalls,

> Boudicea führt der Britten Heers-Kraft an/
> Und lehrt: Daß ihr Geschlecht auch Römer stürtzen kan.   (II. 121–2)

---

[28] Gillespie, 'Lohenstein's Epicharis', 214.

The word 'auch' in each of these extracts betrays that the heroic woman is functioning here as a mirror for unheroic men. But the problem in this drama is that a masculine woman who is not legitimized, like Catharina, by a divine Father, is potentially as much a representative of inversion or chaos as a feminine man; the flip-side of Epicharis's female activism is demonstrated by the slave woman Corinne, who persuades her husband to betray their master to Nero in the name of 'Gefahr und Kühnheit', and for material gain (II. 291). As a woman acting independently, Epicharis can never replace a masculine man and act in collaboration with Fate or Providence to restore order to an effeminized, degenerate, chaotic society, because her success would only confirm that society's inversion. Epicharis fails in her endeavour, and the potential threat of her unsupervised virility is thus contained; but at the same time she provides an example of virile heroism to shame those men who cannot match it.

### Sex and Rhetoric: Lohenstein's Venusian Heroines

Epicharis is rhetorically adept, and Lohenstein allows his heroine a large proportion of the long rhetorical speeches in the play. When competitive disputations take place, such as with Nero and Tigillinus in Act II (311 ff.), Epicharis is clearly the winner, even though her rhetorical adeptness, like Catharina's, is finally simply quashed by the brute force of her tyrannical opponent. Both heroines have a degree of linguistic mastery more usually—and acceptably—found in men; in both it is excusable because they are in fact functioning as mirrors of the masculine. It is also rendered far less threatening by the fact of their chastity: in using rhetoric, the tool of the male, neither Catharina or Epicharis simultaneously *deliberately* uses sex-appeal, which is perceived as the tool or weapon of the female. With reference to Renaissance rhetoric, McClary has noted that 'a man skilled in oratory was powerful, effective in imposing his will in society at large. A woman's rhetoric was usually understood as seduction, as a manifestation not of intellectual but of sexual power'.[29] Those of Lohenstein's heroines who are *not* exemplary masculine figures—Cleopatra, Sophonisbe, and Agrippina—are adept in precisely this art of 'seductive' rhetoric. This has important implications in the context of school drama.

Rhetoric is all about authority: the speaker's capacity both to teach and to persuade. Classical rhetoric, as it was formalized by Cicero and Quintilian, defines three ways in which the rhetor may influence an audience. The first is by instruction (*docere*), although this capacity is shared by philosophy and other academic disciplines. The second and third are exclusively the rhetorician's province: the arousal of pleasure or gentle emotions (*delectare, conciliare*) and the excitement of passion (*movere, concitare*).[30] The notorious *Schwulststil* of seventeenth-century drama, lamented by critics until quite recently, comes into perspective when we consider that the last and most persuasive of these rhetorical arts, the arousal of intense emotion in the listener or audience, is held to depend on mastery of the exalted and pathetic style, the *genus grande*, which makes generous use of figures and tropes such as metaphor and metonymy. *Ornatus*, linguistic ornament, is generally thought to enhance rhetorical efficacy; Vickers has noted that, in Latin, *ornamentum* signifies ' "equipment or accoutrements", a soldier's "gear" or weapons'.[31]

The standard textbook of rhetoric in seventeenth-century German Protestant schools was from Holland: Gerhard Johannes Vossius's *Rhetorices Contractae*, first published in 1606.[32] Like other contemporary handbooks of rhetoric, this one taught the Classical five-point scheme that divides the rhetorical process into *inventio* (the conception of the subject and the argument), *dispositio* (the structuring of these elements), *elocutio* (the choice of style), *memoria* (committing to memory), and *actio* or *pronunciatio* (the delivery). The most

[29] Susan McClary, 'Constructions of Gender in Monteverdi's Dramatic Music', in *COJ* 1/3 (1989), 203–23 (207).

[30] Gert Ueding, *Klassische Rhetorik* (Munich 1995), 74–5.

[31] Brian Vickers, *In Defence of Rhetoric* (Oxford 1997 [1988]), 284.

[32] Comenius's *Janua* and *Vestibulum* were also introduced in the Breslau *Gymnasien* in the 17th cent. See David Halsted, *Poetry and Politics in the Silesian Baroque: Neo-Stoicism in the Work of Christophorus Colerus and his Circle* (Wiesbaden 1996), 77.

obvious function of school drama is the rehearsal of *memoria* and *actio*, the essentials of public speaking. But the plays also exemplify the standard Humanist teaching method by which the theory (*doctrina* or *praeceptum*) is illustrated by *exempla* before the process culminates in *imitatio* on the part of the student. School dramas were generally written for the boys by senior members of the teaching body or local establishment, and the imitation of rhetorical conceptions, structure and style—that is, the appropriation of an authorial and authoritative use of language by the students—is a vital part of the pedagogical effect. The boys who perform are learning to manage meaning.

Authoritative language relies, among other things, on a highly developed control of the linguistic image. Early modern writers reveal a theoretical interest in the use of artefacts such as emblems, metonymy, and metaphor; one practical argument in their defence is the mnemonic efficacy of the image, described by Francis Bacon in 1605:

> Emblems bring down intellectual to sensible things; for what is sensible always strikes the memory stronger, and sooner impresses itself than the intellectual . . . And therefore it is easier to retain the image of a sportsman hunting the hare, of an apothecary ranging his boxes, an orator making a speech, a boy repeating verses, or a player acting his part, than the corresponding notions of intention, disposition, memory, action.[33]

Bacon's intention is to produce something which is striking and memorable, and hence both teaches and persuades; such a use of the image is clearly a rhetorical endeavour.

Early modern emblems were a popular genre in which a visual image (*pictura*) was printed beneath a heading (*inscriptio*) and assigned meaning in a text (*subscriptio*). One of the most famous collections of emblems, which was also known to Lohenstein, was Andrea Alciati's *Emblemata*, first published in 1531.[34] As Bacon suggested, emblems provide

---

[33] Francis Bacon, 'De dignitate et augmentis scientiarum', in *The Works of Francis Bacon*, ed. James Spedding *et al.*, vol. 1 (London 1889), 649.

[34] An extended version of Alciati's collection was published in Germany in 1661, namely Joachim Camerarius's *Centuriae quatuor Emblematum*. See Charlotte Brancaforte, *Lohenstein's Preisgedicht 'Venus': Kritischer Text und Untersuchung* (Munich 1974), 102.

a mnemonic stimulus, and they certainly illustrate the extent
to which imagery can become an accepted authoritative
force. The *pictura* represents an idea, while the text constructs its meaning: a picture of Medea with her children,
for example, is standardly construed as signifying untrustworthiness and merciless cruelty.[35] Eventually this significa-
tion becomes so familiar that it is perceived as 'truth', and the
reader is encouraged to extend the application of the construct from the specific situation depicted in the emblem to
a wider sphere of experience. Schöne has famously demonstrated that the emblem is the basis for dramatic metaphor
in the seventeenth century: both audiences and readers had
already learnt from the familiar emblematic form to see objects
and occurrences as deictic, as having significance beyond
the superficial in the world and on the stage.[36] The efficacy
of the emblem lies in the breadth of its significance, which
transcends the apparent content of the image: 'Die res picta
des Emblems besitzt verweisende Kraft, ist res significans'.[37]
Schöne answers the question why the dramatic pedagogues
of the seventeenth century make such widespread use of visual
and linguistic imagery by demonstrating the function of the
emblem as 'Beweismittel'.[38] It is striking that he uses the language of the lawcourt to describe how the linguistic image
works: 'forensische Rhetorik' is what Adalbert Wichert has
recently called Lohenstein's persuasive use of language.[39]

The late Italian Renaissance had seen the development
of the 'closed' stage, a framed *Guckkasten* that replaced the
raised open platforms in the round traditionally used by
itinerant players; this new stage probably entered the German
states with the Jesuits, as the order extended its influence. Its
quadrangular, almost two-dimensional form—like a frame—
leads the viewer to perceive the dramatic action as pictorial
or emblematic. The stage in itself can therefore function
as a sort of *pictura*, while the changing images it houses are
persuasively (or rhetorically) elucidated by the *subscriptio*

[35] See Albrecht Schöne, *Emblematik und Drama im Zeitalter des Barock* (Munich
1964), 113.
[36] Ibid. 59.    [37] Ibid. 21.    [38] Ibid. 64 ff.
[39] Adalbert Wichert, *Literatur, Rhetorik und Jurisprudenz im 17. Jahrhundert: Daniel
Casper von Lohenstein und sein Werk* (Tübingen 1991), 267.

provided in the dramatic text.[40] Béhar has called the theatre
of Daniel Casper von Lohenstein 'pictorial dramaturgy': a
recreation of a historical event in a series of tableaux, or a
fresco.[41] By creating these historical and allegorical tableaux
on stage, the Baroque dramatist is able to exploit the implicit
authority of the precedent in history, or ancient mythology,
in a way that is structurally related both to the *argumentum
emblematicum* (in that the significance of a specific instance is
applied to a new or wider situation) and to the principles of
forensic or juridical rhetoric: the historical or mythological
occurrence constitutes proof by precedence that what the
dramatist depicts is indeed the way of the world.[42] Emanuele
Tesauro, a literary theorist of the seventeenth century, called
tragedies 'Metaphore rappresentanti Attioni Heroiche con
Habito, e Voce, e Gesto, & Harmonia',[43] and it certainly
seems that the metaphor, emblem, or image is central to the
semiotics as well as the rhetoric of the seventeenth-century
stage. We shall take as a case study of this the idea of Venus
in Lohenstein's dramas of great women.

Venus is more complex than another popular allegorical
female figure of the early modern period, *Frau Welt*. The latter is lovely face-on, hideous from the rear: one need only
turn the figure around to reveal the danger and decay she
threatens. Venus, by contrast, embodies beauty from every
angle; but in the work of writers such as Lohenstein she, too,
has a more threatening side. This may be discovered not
merely by physical rotation, as in the case of *Frau Welt*, but
rather by analytically turning the idea to reveal the warning
it communicates. The gallant associations of sensual love with
Venus might lead us to assume that the allegory is harmless
and flattering. Even in the gallant poetry of the period,
however, the idea of Venus is used with ambiguous effect. It
functions as a descriptive metaphor for stylized beauty in the

---

[40] Schöne, *Emblematik und Drama*, 217 ff.

[41] Pierre Béhar, 'Vt Pictura Poesis: Lohenstein où la dramaturgie picturale', in
*Pictura et Poesis, TRAMES, collection allemand*, 3 (Limoges 1989), 27–63.

[42] Alciati, author of the *Emblemata*, was himself a lawyer. See Wichert, *Literatur,
Rhetorik und Jurisprudenz*, 269–70.

[43] Emanuele Tesauro, *Il Cannocchiale Aristotelico O Sia Idea Dell'Arguta Et Ingeniosa
Elocutione* . . . (Turin 1680; repr. ed. A. Buck, Bad Homburg 1968), 732.

Petrarchan and Marinist tradition, but also allows the poet to disclaim responsibility for his behaviour: the suggestion is that he is exposed to the irresistible power of Cupid's arrow, which is directed by the beloved in the guise of Venus. The gallant fiction, therefore, is that the responsibility for the poet's passion lies with the object and not with the writing subject. Lohenstein was clearly familiar with this rhetorical *topos*, and critical of it: in the first act of *Ibrahim Sultan* (1673), the Turkish tyrant plays on the idea of a divinely inspired and therefore excusably indulged passion for his sister-in-law, Sisigambis, by metaphorically offering her a golden apple, as Paris did Venus (I. 65–6).

But even for Classical authors the figure of Venus could well connote danger. Vitruvius testifies to this in the first book of his *De Architectura*, in which he discusses town planning and the choice of sites for the forum and the temples of the gods:

Aedibus vero sacris, quorum deorum maxime in tutela civitas videtur esse, et Iovi et Iunoni et Minervae, in excelsissimo loco, unde moenium maxima pars conspiciatur, areae distribuantur. Mercurio autem in foro aut, ut Isidi et Serapi, in emporio . . . itemque Veneri ad portum. Id autem etiam Etruscis haruspicibus disciplinarum scripturis ita est dedicatum, extra murum Veneris, Volcani, Martis fana ideo conlocari, uti non insuescat in urbe adulescentibus seu matribus familiarum veneria libido . . .[44]

This idea is received in early modern literature. Emblem collections, for example, reveal a conception of Venus as a threatening figure: one emblem depicts a naked female form posed on a shell rising from the sea. The *inscriptio* reads 'KAKA TPIA' ('the dangerous threesome'), and the *subscriptio* explains:

> La mar, el fuego, y la muger, tres cosas
> Son, segun que lo dixo el mote Griego,
> Por todo estremo malas, y dañosas,
> Si con prestreza no se atajan luego:
> Huid nauegaciones peligrosas,
> Acudid a matar con agua el fuego,
> Muchos no escapan del tercer contrario,
> Por que les viene a ser mal necessario.[45]

[44] Vitruv. 1. 7. 1. I am indebted for the reference to Dr Ulrich Schmitzer (Nuremberg).

[45] In Arthur Henkel and Albrecht Schöne (eds.), *Emblemata: Handbuch zur Sinnbildkunst des XVI. und XVII. Jahrhunderts* (Stuttgart 1967), cols. 1544–5.

This alarming aspect of the goddess of love is also transmitted in a standard work on Classical mythology known
to Lohenstein: Natale Conti's *Mythologiae [ . . . ] libri decem*
(1561–4).[46] One entire chapter of Conti's work, namely
Chapter 13 of Book IV, is dedicated to the legends surrounding Venus. The author mentions the popular story of
her marine origins: 'Nata esse dicitur èspuma maris' (p. 261),
and, on a more threatening note, cites sources indicating
that her power is greater than that of the male gods, even
Jupiter (p. 379). The legend of the judgement of Paris, when
Venus triumphed over Juno and Pallas on Mount Ida, Conti
assumes to be so well known that he does not bother with
a detailed account of events, but instead concentrates on
the allegorical or moral sense of the myth, concluding his
narrative with an interpretation of the fable:

> Veruntamen dolosum illud iudicium universo Troianorum, imperio
> postea fuit calamitosum, qm [*sic*] stulta sunt omnia iniqua, sed omnium
> maxime Veneris opera quae fiunt. (pp. 258–9)

A warning against the influence of Venus is thus issued,
and the negative connotations of the goddess are developed
when, with reference to Euripides, Conti puts forward an
alternative suggestion for the origin of her Greek name,
Aphrodite: 'non solum spuma [Greek: *aphros*], sed etiam ab
insania [*aphrosyne*] Veneris nomen deduci possit' (p. 259).

Other fears betray themselves when Conti describes the
debilitating effects of sexuality (gendered feminine through
Venus) on the otherwise active male:

> omnium sanè voluptatum, quibus homines vexantur, maxima & deterrima
> est libido rei Venereae, quae opes dilapidat, obest memoriae, vim oculorum
> labefactat, stomachum frigidiorem & imbecilliorem efficit. (p. 259)

This is not simply the expression of a moralistic stance on
sexual indulgence. If we refer back to the judgement of Paris
it becomes clear that more important things are at stake: for
if men are incapacitated by love or sex, order and the state
are jeopardized, and the fate of Troy looms again.

---

[46] Natalis Comes [= Natale Conti], *Mythologiae, sive explicationis fabularum, Libri
decem* [ . . . ] (Frankfurt 1588; first edn. Venice 1561–4). Further references are
given in the text. Just gives references testifying to Lohenstein's knowledge of the
work; see *Römische Trauerspiele*, 302.

Natale Conti's understanding of the Venus myth as a warning of the danger posed to men by their sexuality is a strand in its reception that can be followed in two texts from the earlier part of the seventeenth century, Heinrich Kornmann's *Fraw Veneris Berg* (1614) and Nicolas Renouard's *Le Jugement de Paris* (German translation 1638).[47]

Kornmann's account seems to be indebted to Conti's, but the author also relates many other details pertaining to Venus, and includes a list of seventy names by which he claims she is or has been known. These range from the familiar 'Cypria' to less common epithets such as 'Barter/ die Männliche', which evokes an unsettling sense of masculinity in the female goddess. Kornmann's version of the judgement of Paris is hardly more extensive than Conti's, and concludes with the same interpretation of the myth as an allegory of the destructive potential of sexuality for civilized society:

> daß Paris die Wollust dem Reichthumb und Weißheit hat wöllen fürziehen/ . . . darauß dann der zehenjährige Trojanische Krieg in der Stadt Troja endtlichen Verderbnuß und Untergang entstanden. (pp. 124–5)[48]

As its title indicates, Nicolas Renouard's work treats only the episode of Paris on Mount Ida.[49] It demonstrates a reception of the myth and of the nature of Venus strikingly

---

[47] Heinrich Kornmann, *Mons Veneris, Fraw Veneris Berg/ Das ist/ Wunderbare und eigentliche Beschreibung der alten haydnischen und Newen Scribenten Meynung/ von der Göttin Venere . . .* (Frankfurt a.M. 1614); Nicolas Renouard (trans. anon.), *Le Jugement de Paris, Das Urteil des Schäffers Paris* (Leipzig 1638).

[48] It is nonetheless worth noting that Kornmann's extensively researched work also shows a reception of positive values associated with Venus. Chapter 15 is entitled 'De mulieribus, virginibusque Veneris castis & pudicis. Von den keuschen Weibern unnd Jungfrawen/ so von wegen ihrer Schöne sind Veneres geachtet worden' (p. 217): in this chapter, 'Venus' is a title of honour even for biblical women.

[49] The Judgement of Paris was a popular episode. Hans Sachs's play of 1532, *Ein comedi, das judicium Paridis*, treats the events on Ida with a familiar slant, although here not only Venus but Juno, too, is rejected by the dramatist in favour of the intellectual qualities of Athena/ Minerva. The herald concludes:

> Auß disem merckt beschlich nun,
> Das man auff weißheit halte mehr,
> Weder auff reichthumb, gwalt und ehr
> Oder auff weltlich lust und freudt,
> Welche endtlich werden zerstrewt
> Mit trübsal grosser bitterkeit!

In *Hans Sachs*, ed. Adelbert von Keller (Tübingen 1873), vol. 7 (*Bibliothek des litterarischen Vereins* vol. 115), 1–64.

similar to Lohenstein's. Christian feminine qualities such as chastity and modesty do not feature in Renouard's version; instead the author concentrates on the sensual or erotic quality of beauty which the goddess embodies, a quality which is only briefly allowed to titillate before being shifted towards the negative almost in the same moment as it is evoked. Thus the superficially gallant compliments made with reference to Venus in the dedication, 'An das Lieb-würdige Frauenzimmer', are qualified in a didactic tone:

Venus ist gezwungen zugestehen/ daß weil ihr Angesicht neben den ewrigen ohne Anreitzung bleibt/ sie den Apffel/ so sie vormals von Paris uberkommen hat/ euch schuldig sey. Denselben aber für ihr davonzu-tragen/ ist der jenige Ruhm so ihr am wenigsten schätzet: weil der Vortheil/ so ihr von den andern zwo Göttinnen [= Juno and Athena, i.e. dignity and wisdom] habt/ euch weit köstlicher und angenehmer ist. (p. 1ᵛ)

In this text we also find the key word *Vernunft*, which is central to Lohenstein's conception of sex relations. The preface continues:

Lasst uns der Venus zu ehren keine Altär auffrichten; ihre Gewalt ist unserm Willen unterworffen: Lasst uns unsere Schwachheit nicht anklagen und ihre Siegs-Zeichen erheben; sie erhält keinen Sieg/ welchen die Macht unserer Vernunfft ihr nicht benehmen könnte. . . . Unsere Gebuhrt setzt die freye Bewegung unserer Gemüther zwischen die Juno/ Minerva und Venus. Sie gibt uns die freye Wahl/ wie dem Paris. (p. 2ᵛ)

There is an echo of this in the exchange between Antyllus, Antony, and Caelius in the first act of Lohenstein's *Cleopatra*:

ANTYL. Gedult/ Vernunfft und Zeit schafft endlich Heil und Rath.
ANTON. Nicht/ wo Vernunfft und Zeit kein Regiment mehr hat.
      .    .    .    .    .    .    .    .    .    .    .    .

CAEL. Wo läßt der hohe Geist sich endlich hin verleiten?
    Man muß der Liebe Macht mit Ernst und Witz bestreiten.
      .    .    .    .    .    .    .    .    .    .    .    .

    Nein nein! Der Himmel ließ dem Paris freien Willen.

(I. 942 ff.)

In contradistinction to the gallant use of the metaphor, the idea of Venus in these texts signifies a threat to men's authority through their sexuality. It signals a need for men to exercise *Vernunft* in order to resist subjugation to their own lust, which may appear as the power of the female object. The Venusian becomes an identifiable category which evokes a particular kind of danger and suggests a solution: *Vernunft* or the control of the erotic impulse. In the terms of rhetorical theory, the Venusian in Lohenstein is a *locus* (or *topos*): a predefined signifier which is associated with a cluster of unspoken but authoritatively implied ideas. *Loci* or *topoi* acquire their authority from the sense of a proven precedent, and feature prominently in forensic rhetoric.[50] In school drama, they both persuade and instruct. We need, therefore, to look at both the rhetorical form and the metaphorical content of the Venus idea.

Daniel Casper von Lohenstein's central women protagonists are typically political figures who challenge male dominion. With the exception of Epicharis, they regard sexuality as a tool for their ambition. They are all frustrated in their intentions, however, and die having principally achieved the *fama* that attaches to their deaths; the male-dominated status quo is finally preserved. They are not tragic figures in the Classical sense: Cleopatra (*Cleopatra*, published 1661; revised version 1680) is a plotter who meets her match in Augustus, the faithless Sophonisbe (*Sophonisbe*, performed 1669; published 1680) is defeated in her moment of triumph by a kind of *deus ex machina* in the form of Scipio, and Agrippina's wickedness (*Agrippina*, published 1665) is only exceeded by that of her opponent, Nero. Epicharis, by contrast, is too faultless to be tragic, a heroic figure who is betrayed by the men with whom she conspires (*Epicharis*, published 1665).[51]

Cleopatra, Sophonisbe, and Agrippina are for the main body of each drama subject to negative typification by other, usually male, characters. The category to which they are

---

[50] Quintilian systematized these forensic categories as *loci a persona* and *loci a re*; see Ueding, *Klassische Rhetorik*, 57 ff.

[51] I differ with the critics who have recently been engaged in the attempt to find faults in Epicharis to account for her downfall. A simpler explanation would be that in the context of school drama and its didactic oppositions (exemplified by Catharina and Chach Abas in the previous chapter), Epicharis does not need to be an admonitory figure, because Nero is. It is this which allows Lohenstein to make of Agrippina in the pendant play something of a martyr figure in death, since she has handed over the role of negative example to her son.

assigned (or the *locus* by which they are rhetorically determined) is that of ambitious and powerful women, defined
primarily in Classical metaphors such as Circe, Medea, the
Sirens, and especially Venus. Dominant use of the Venus metaphor, most notably in *Cleopatra*, suggests that this image is
particularly important in Lohenstein's dramatic conception
of the feminine.

Renouard showed anxiety about the physical consequences
of sexuality in men; Lohenstein is principally concerned with
its politically debilitating influence. This is what emerges from
Augustus's speech following the death of Mark Antony in
*Cleopatra*:

> Der Liebe Gifft ist doch das giftigst unter allen;
> Wie manchen hohen Sinn hat doch die Pest verzehrt/
> Wie manche Länder hat die Glutt in Rauch verkehrt!    (IV. 42–5)

The fire imagery associated with love is significant; we shall
observe it again in connection with Helen of Troy, who is
linked mythologically with the Judgement of Paris, and hence
also with Venus.

In *Agrippina*, Venus signifies the excitement of lust. When
Nero's ambitious courtier Otho wants to make his wife,
Poppaea, attractive to the Emperor, he characterizes her as
the goddess of love (I. 140). The same associations are evoked
when Agrippina is rescued from a shipwreck engineered by
Nero, after her attempt to seduce him has been frustrated:
in the *Reyen* following Act 3, she rises from the waves like a
kind of Botticelli Venus, supported by nymphs:[52]

> Bringt Schwestern/ bringt ein Muschel-Schiff der Schnecken/
> Daß diese Venus fährt an Port
>
> (III. 501–2)

An interesting contradiction emerges from this scene, for the
very moment at which Agrippina is most clearly characterized as Venus is also the moment at which the defeat of what
Venusian or sexual power she had over Nero is confirmed.

Even Epicharis, who does not actively use her sexuality, is
associated with the goddess of love. Proculus employs the idea

---

[52] See Gillespie, *Lohenstein's Historical Tragedies*, 56–74.

94    SEPARATING THE WOMEN FROM THE BOYS

of Venusian origin persuasively in an effort to convince her
that he loves her despite her birth, which they both believe
to be inferior:

Man fragt nicht/ welche Schooß
Der Schnecke/ welches Schilf das Muschel-Kind beschloß
Wenn sich ihr Werth nur zeigt.                                (II. 61–3)

Here the associations are gallant and flattering rather than
threatening, but later it is Proculus's anger at his sexual rejection by Epicharis that causes him to betray the Pisonian
rebellion; thus Venusian sex-appeal still makes political waves.

But the heroine most closely linked with the goddess of
love in Lohenstein's work is Cleopatra. The Egyptian queen
was at least as popular a figure as Venus in European literature of the early modern period; Voßkamp has counted
twenty-eight Cleopatra dramas before Lohenstein's first version of 1661, including Hans Sachs's tragedy.[53] Like Venus,
her name would have triggered associations which were not
necessarily negative; some dramas idealize Cleopatra's suicide
as proof of true womanly love.[54]

Authorial notes in both the earlier and later versions of
Lohenstein's drama reveal his knowledge of the traditional
association of the mythological Venus and the historical
Cleopatra. He cites Plutarch as his source:

[53] Wilhelm Voßkamp, 'Daniel Casper von Lohensteins *Cleopatra*: Historisches
Verhängnis und politisches Spiel' in Walter Hinck (ed.), *Geschichte als Schauspiel:
Deutsche Geschichtsdrama: Interpretationen* (Frankfurt a.M. 1981), 67–81 (69). Sachs's
drama, *Ein tragedi mit zwölff personen: Die königin Cleopatra aus Egipten mit Antonio,
dem Römer*, is reprinted in *Hans Sachs*, ed. Adelbert von Keller and E. Goetze
(Tübingen 1892), vol. 20 (*Bibliothek des litterarischen Vereins*, vol. 93), 187–233. Béhar
sees Lohenstein's drama as a competitive response to Benserade's *La Cleopatre* [*sic*]
(Paris 1636); see Béhar, *Épanouissement et fin*, 130–2.
[54] In Sachs's play, Cleopatra's staged suicide is a test of Antony's love for her
rather than a deliberate attempt to kill him. Although Sachs feels obliged to condemn both suicides and to present them as the result of worldly ambition and lust,
Octavian (Augustus) admires the queen's death, calling her 'das kün männlich
weib' (ibid., 231). In Germany it is only *after* Lohenstein's drama that the assumption is made that Cleopatra is a negative character. An interesting case is Johann
Mattheson's opera *Cleopatra* (Hamburg 1704); the librettist, Feustking, feels impelled to describe the queen in condemnatory terms in the prologue, even though
his libretto does not support such a description. See Sarah Colvin, 'The Classical
Witch and the Christian Martyr: Two Ideas of Woman in Hamburg Baroque Opera
Libretti', in *GLL* 46/3 (1993), 193–202 (197).

Von Cleopatra erzehlet Plutarch . . . Sie sey auf dem Flusse Cydnus dem
Antonio . . . entgegen geschifft: sie aber habe unter einem goldgestickten
Gezelte in der Gestalt/ wie die Venus gemahlt wird/ gelegen. Umb sie
herumb hetten Knaben wie Cupidines ihr Lufft zugefachet. (*Anmerckung*,
IV. 583)[55]

The apotheosis of the ancient Egyptian queen in the eyes of
her people forms a historical basis for Lohenstein's dramatic
portrayal of her sexuality in terms of a divine power. For
the Egyptians in the play, as well as for Antonius, she is
'[ein] Ebenbild der Isis' (V. 520), to which even Augustus,
the pattern-card for masculine *Vernunft*, feels drawn by 'ein
Magnetisch [*sic*] Drat' (V. 521). Cleopatra herself associates
her sexuality with divinity, although she is politic in attributing the real power to Augustus:

> Ja ich vergöttere mich gantz/ weil Gott August
> Mein himmlischer Osir an mir wil schöpfen Lust/
> Und mich zur Isis macht.                                  (II. 87–9)

Lohenstein's intention to portray Cleopatra's influence as
preternatural is indicated by an alteration made in the later
version of the play, by which her royal attendants address the
queen as 'Göttin', an escalation from 'Prinzessin' in the 1661
edition.[56] More specific references to Venus are also frequent,
such as when Proculejus uses the metaphor to imply that
Cleopatra is deliberately using her sexuality to dominate
Antonius:

> Itzt ist er einer Knecht/ die nur durch Schminck und Pracht
> Hilfft ihrer Heßligkeit; die sich zur Venus macht/
> Ihn aber zum Vulcan.
>
>                                                         (II. 535–7)

The suggestion that cosmetics and ornament are being used
to disguise what is really hideous shifts the Venus metaphor
(and therefore Cleopatra) towards the indisputably negative
idea of *Frau Welt*.

---

[55] Compare Lohenstein's notes to II. 536 and to *Cleopatra* (1661) ed. Ilse-Marie
Barth (Stuttgart 1965; henceforth *U*), IV. 463.
[56] III. 89; compare *U* III. 81. Hans Sachs clearly used the same source; compare
Sachs, *Cleopatra*, 192.

Metaphors relating to water are prevalent in the play. As a standard cipher for the inconstancy of things worldly, water is metaphorically related to *Frau Welt*. According to the medieval and early modern theorists of the human constitution or *humores*, water is also the element of woman, to whom a phlegmatic temperament is generally ascribed on the basis of a cooler, moister physical constitution.[57] It is, of course, also related to the Venus theme: Conti and Kornmann described the origins of the goddess and her name in the waves. This idea is likely to have been familiar to Lohenstein, and the water imagery in Cleopatra therefore underpins the connections made between the Egyptian queen, the goddess of love, and the inconstancy of things worldly. The connection between water, Venus, and danger is also interesting in the light of Cleopatra's role as siren ('illa.siren.africana' is how the dedication of the 1680 edition describes her). Augustus's reference to her 'bezaubernd Lied' (IV. 299) extends the reach of her threatening potential beyond the individual Romans to the Roman Empire as represented by the warships which dominate so much of the Roman dialogue in the play— and thence to civilization in a more general sense.

Lohenstein's interest in the mythology of Venus in this play is clearly not equivalent to the flattering comparisons made by the gallant poets. Cleopatra is a 'verfluchte Zauberin' (V. 179); this echoes his description of the goddess in the poem 'Venus' as a 'schlaue zauberin [*sic*]'.[58] The Venusian element in Lohenstein's dramatic idea of woman is to be understood as erotically fascinating, but also highly dangerous. This emerges with some clarity in his treatment of the legend of the Judgement of Paris.

If a 'weak spot' in the dominant male is felt to be touched when men are exposed to female sexuality, one might illustrate the problem by showing a man faced with the choice

---

[57] Early medical theorists based their assumptions on the work of Galen (AD 129–99), who identified four basic bodily humours (blood, phlegm, yellow gall, black gall) and devised a doctrine of temperament based on the dominance of these in the human body.

[58] Lohenstein, 'Venus', in *Benjamin Neukirchs Anthologie. Herrn von Hofmann-swaldau und andrer Deutschen auserlesene und bisher ungedruckte Gedichte erster theil*, ed. Benjamin Neukirch (1697), repr. ed. Angelo George de Capua and Ernst Alfred Philippson (Tübingen 1961), 290–345 (here line 372).

between various desirable worldly commodities, such as political power, wisdom and military success, and sexual gratification. Exactly this occurs in the legend of Paris, to which Lohenstein dedicates 35 lines of his 'Venus' poem, the entire *Reyen* following Act II of *Cleopatra*, and the first *Reyen* in *Sophonisbe*. The legendary situation is preposterous. A mortal, Paris, is allowed by the gods to pass judgement on three immortals: Juno, Pallas (Athena), and Venus. Exploiting his incongruous privilege further, the mortal demands that he (fully dressed, one assumes) should judge over them naked.[59] The sexually related nature of the situation is also apparent in the object of discord, the *Zankapfel*, to which Pauly's encyclopaedia attributes 'eine lascive, wenn nicht priapeische Bedeutung',[60] and which for the Christian Lohenstein was a symbol of original sin.

Paris's legendary choice underlies the *Reyen* which follow the first act of *Sophonisbe*. As in the Classical legend, the apple of discord is here cast by Eris, 'die Zwytracht . . . / Durch die Sagunth und Troja kam in Brand' (I. 513 ff.), but here the prize is intended not for the most beautiful competitor, but for the most powerful (line 520), and the location is not Mount Ida but 'die Seele der Sophonisbe'. The contestants are eight abstracts: love, revenge, hatred, joy, desire, shock, envy, and fear, and the winner is not, as one might expect in the context of the legend, love or desire, but revenge. Lohenstein thereby signals at this early stage in the drama that Sophonisbe, despite her sensual or Venus-like appeal, is not primarily interested in love. In political terms, her feminine sexuality might give her the edge on her male rivals—after all, in the legend, sensual Venus defeats the more 'masculine' goddesses, rational Pallas and regal Juno—and it is therefore worth noting that when Lohenstein next refers to the legend of Paris's choice, at the end of *Sophonisbe*, it is in the form of a reassuring admission from

---

[59] Lohenstein, like Renouard, chooses the version of the legend in which all three goddesses appear naked. In other versions, especially in visual depictions, it is only Venus who removes her garb. See *Paulys Real-Encyclopädie der Classischen Altertumswissenschaft*, ed. Georg Wissowa and Konrat Ziegler, vol. 18/2 (Stuttgart 1949), cols. 1496–9.

[60] Ibid., col. 1496.

the heroine. For Sophonisbe, defeated by Scipio's rhetoric of *Vernunft*, the golden apple brings death by poison, rather than triumph:

> ... kein güldner Apfel habe
> So angenehmen Saft/ ...
> Als Masanissens Tranck          (V. 310 ff.)

The metaphor makes the point that the irrational sensual potential of the feminine, represented by Venus on Mount Ida, can be negated if men (in this case Scipio, directing Masanissa) will counter its influence using their rhetorical skills and ideal masculine *Vernunft*.

But where (oriental) Masanissa is successfully masculinized under Roman auspices, Lohenstein's Antonius undergoes the opposite process; he falls prey to the feminine influences of Cleopatra and Egypt, and is destroyed. Like Sophonisbe, Cleopatra only *appears* to be the incarnation of Venus; in fact she is driven by the political ambition of a Juno and the wit of an Athena. Her response to Antonius's choice of her love over political power hovers between scorn and disbelief: 'Anton gibt Thron und Kron für eine Frauen Gunst' (II. 435), and she contrasts his attitude with her own ambition and intelligence:

> Die Lorbern mögen stets die klugen Frauen zieren/
> Für welchen Männer-Witz meist muß zu scheitern gehn!   (II. 430–1)

Cleopatra's clearheadedness is thrown into stark relief by the emotional confusion suffered by Antonius. His dilemma is allegorized in the *Reyen* of the judgement of Paris that closes this act and forms the structural centre of the drama. In an animated tableau of the familiar legend, Lohenstein shows us a man faced with three female figures who incorporate different aspects of human potential, competing for his approval.[61] Juno and Athena argue their case with reference to the traditional spheres of male authority, the former basing her argument on the power held by her husband:

---

[61] Schöne gives the emblematic background to this scene. See Schöne, *Emblematik und Drama*, 168–9.

Wäre was Schöners an andern zu finden/
Hette mich Jupiter ihm nicht vermählt.
Willstu nun Jupitern Irrthums nicht zeihen/
Mustu mir Schönsten den Vorzug verleihen. (II. 689–92)

Athena, born not from her mother's womb but her father's head, and therefore the most masculine of the goddesses, offers her reward in the male domain of history:

Ich aber bin die vergötternde Tugend/
Welche die Thaten den Sternen gräbt ein.
Wilstu nun ewigen Nach-ruhm erlangen/
Muß ich als Schönste den Apfel empfangen. (II. 695–8)

Eschewing politics and posterity, only Venus conducts her argument in an area stereotyped as feminine—corporeal love:

Kronen sind dörnicht/ die Waffen gefährlich.
Aber mein Paradies schwimmet voll Lust. (II. 699–700)

She is also the first of the three to break with convention by throwing off her clothes. Paris's choice, therefore, falls on the goddess who not only proffers the most feminine reward, but at the same time displays a revolutionary or subversive tendency which contrasts with the positive attitudes towards the masculine status quo shown by her two peers. A victory of the feminine is brought about, the destructive nature of which will emerge from the prize Venus promises: Helen of Troy.[62] The victorious goddess expresses her triumph in threateningly anti-masculine imagery:

Brechet nun Zepter und Lantzen in Stücke!
Wünschet der siegenden Venus Gelücke! (II. 751–2)

Paris's rejection of Juno and Pallas has a deeper significance in the context of their arguments: he has caused injury to an accepted, positively understood, and distinctly male world order, or, in metaphorical terms, insulted the gods: 'Thörichter Richter! Verächter der Götter!' (II. 753).

[62] The link between the idea of Cleopatra and that of Helen is not new; it is made by Lucan in the *Pharsalia*. See Lucy Hughes-Hallet, *Cleopatra: Histories, Dreams and Distortions* (London 1991), 81.

The *Reyen* signals more than Cleopatra's Venusian qualities. Blame is allegorically attributed, and it lies with Antonius, who, unlike the other Romans in the play, has failed to recognize those more masculine aspects of human potential in the Egyptian queen which are allegorically represented by Juno and Pallas. He is in thrall to sexuality in a way that is clearly classed as effeminate.

Lohenstein is not unsympathetic towards the emotions which lead to such a choice as is allegorized in the judgement of Paris. In the 'Venus' poem he expresses a certain support for the decision:

> Ich lache derer wahn/
> Die ihn/ ich weiß nicht wie/ mit was für worten schmähen/
> Daß er nicht gold/ noch macht/ noch weißheit angesehen.
> .   .   .   .   .   .   .   .   .   .   .   .
> Gewißlich stimm' ich hier auch Paris meynung bey:
> Daß eine schöne frau ein halber himmel sey.          (718 ff.)

But it is worth noting that the real threat of Venus is shown to lie in men's responses to the erotic impulse. Paris chooses Venus, and Antony chooses Cleopatra; in both cases the dramatist implicitly refutes the gallant fiction that the female object, rather than the male subject, is culpable. In *Epicharis* it is spelt out that the Venusian path to destruction originates within the traitor Proculus, and not the heroine:

> SULPITIUS ASPER.                    Weil sein unkeusches Bitten
>   An ihrer [= Epicharis'] Keuschheit Schimpf und Schiffbruch hat erlitten/
>   Ward seine blinde Brunst durch Rach und Grimm verzehrt.
> LUCANUS. Die Gunst wird Gall und Gifft/ ja Venus wird verkehrt
>   In eine Furie/ wenn sie verschmeht sich schauet.
>
>                                              (III. 47–51)

When Paris makes his choice in *Cleopatra*, the scorned goddesses remind him in admonitory tones of a traditional idea, the transcendental nature of the masculine by contrast with the earthbound animality of the feminine:

> Gläube/ dein Wahn vergeringert uns nicht!
> Hoheit und Tugend wird Sternen-werts steigen/
> Wann sich die Wollust zur Erde muß neigen.    (II. 756–8)

Venus appears to represent the irrational, earthbound, un-cultured, and therefore uncivilized animal principle which is feared in (male and female) sexuality. But Venus is also unquestionably feminine, and it would be naïve to argue that problematized femininity, while present in the male, is not more obviously associated with the female in these plays. Lohenstein may make his feminized male protagonists responsible for their own fates if they cannot free themselves from sexual reliance on a woman, but he nonetheless clearly perceives woman and not man as the location of dangerous sex.

Sex and rhetoric are the two major weapons in the hands of Lohenstein's battling protagonists. Yet the ethos (in Clas-sical rhetoric, the good reputation that renders the speaker worthy of our attention) of the rhetorically adept woman is immediately undermined when she brings sex into play. The consequences are both immanent and transcendent: in political terms, she will fail as a rhetorical agent, but she will also suffer punishment for her manipulation of male desire. Dramatic closure depends on the suppression of the Venusian potential that endangers male ascendancy. Later in the play *Cleopatra*, the radical subjugation of Venus is demon-strated by the queen's cathartic suicide: Cleopatra redeems herself in the context of the drama through the destruction of her own transgressive corporeality. The symbolic nature of the act (in which a snake recalls the apple of the Fall and of Paris's judgement) is emphasized by a change in the later version of the drama, in which Lohenstein eroticizes the queen's death by directing the asp's bite to the breast rather than the arm. He justifies this variation from the text of 1661 in a note, with specious reference to a Hebrew source (*Anmerckung*, V. 299).[63] But Cleopatra explains its real significance:

> Sie hat den Arm verschmeht/ sie dürstet nach den Brüsten.
> Komm her. Weil ich den Tod verdient mit meinen Lüsten.

> (V. 299–300)

[63] Hans Sachs prudently (or prudishly) chose to stick to the version where the snake bites the arm (*Cleopatra*, 229). The idea of the breast is testified to in medieval illuminations of Cleopatra's death, but the moral use to which Lohenstein puts it is striking, and presumably compensates for the prurient nature of the visual image.

In her rational subjugation of body to mind, which takes the radical form of suicide, Cleopatra is in fact *masculinized* in death, and can thus appear before us as a virtuous ruler, free of her subversive femininity. Butler has noted that:

the ontological distinction between soul (consciousness, mind) and body invariably supports relations of political and psychic subordination and hierarchy. The mind not only subjugates the body, but occasionally entertains the fantasy of fleeing its embodiment altogether. The cultural associations of mind with masculinity and body with femininity are well documented . . .[64]

When Lohenstein's ruling women challenge male authority, corporeality challenges rationality or *Vernunft*, and from this perspective it is easy to see why the former must be defeated. The corporeal (feminine, sexual) is perceived as a dangerous, because decivilizing, influence, as the legend of Helen and the destruction of Troy illustrates, and it is therefore the task of those who uphold civilization to subdue it.[65]

  A key element in these dramas is the triumph of masculine language, characterized as rationality or *Vernunft*, over the disruptive, sexualized corporeality of the feminine—an aspect of human nature which, it seems, must be controlled in women *and* men. It is clear enough from these dramas that Lohenstein is not writing in the same misogynist tradition that denied women rulership qualities, such as provoked the French *querelle* and gave rise to the counter-conception of the *femme forte*.[66] While I am sceptical of attempts to interpret Cleopatra as a kind of Protestant saint, who enters into an *unio mystica* with Antony in death,[67] or to read Lohenstein's

[64] Judith Butler, *Gender Trouble: Feminism and the Subversion of Identity* (New York 1990), 12.
[65] The danger posed by women to civilization is illustrated with particular reference to Cleopatra and Helen of Troy in the *Malleus Maleficarum* (the so-called *Hexenhammer* of 1487). See Hughes-Hallet, *Cleopatra*, 167.
[66] Maclean, *Woman Triumphant*; Pierre Darmon, *Mythologie de la Femme dans l'Ancienne France* (Paris 1983). An account of misogynist writing in Germany in the early modern period is given by Philip Wadsley Lupton, 'Die Frauengestalten in den Trauerspielen Daniel Casper von Lohensteins [*sic*]' (unpublished doctoral thesis, University of Vienna 1954), esp. pp. 27 ff. This tradition in writing persisted at least until 1700; it is testified to in an extreme form in an anonymous text entitled *Theatrum Malorum Mulierum, Oder Schau=Platz Der Bosheit aller bösen und Regier=süchtigen Weiber über ihre Männer . . .* (Hunßfeld: Carl Kalte=Schahl [?] c.1700).
[67] Wichert, *Literatur, Rhetorik und Jurisprudenz*, 100.

characterization of protagonists as gender neutral,[68] the women in these plays are undeniably politically and rhetorically capable—they are, in some senses, *femmes fortes*, and hence potentially admirable. But we cannot simply skirt around the question of what moves Lohenstein to portray great women who are doomed to lose to their male opponents, and why the sexuality that is associated with these women evokes such obvious connotations of danger. Cleopatra, Sophonisbe, and Agrippina all lack the essential ingredient of chastity that can shift even a pagan heroine like Epicharis away from the side of femininity, chaos, and the devil, and towards the side of masculine virtue and god-given order. While Lohenstein for the most part eschews the anti-female rhetoric of the *querelle des femmes* (which is dangerously close to becoming a distraction in Lohenstein studies), he *is* drawing on an older, German tradition of misogynist thought, as testified to in the writing of Der Stricker and others. This tradition recognizes women's capacity for energy and action, while at the same time deeply distrusting female activity because it is an appropriation of 'daz lenger mezzer', or a usurpation of phallic power. Ambitious women who use the sexual weapon that is held to be their special preserve threaten to upset the order of the sexes, and hence to undermine civilized society.

In the pedagogical dramas of Lohenstein we see that, in order to meet the threat of the feminine, corporeal, or animalistic impulse, the authority of a Scipio or an Augustus is required. It is here that rhetoric comes into its own. The rhetorician, as Lohenstein ably demonstrates, will recognize and categorize the relevant material (*inventio* and *dispositio*), and use language persuasively, even forensically (*elocutio*, with recourse to tropes—such as metaphor—and *loci*). The potential for chaos in *wrong* users of seductive rhetoric (exemplified by Sophonisbe, Cleopatra, and Agrippina) will thus be recognized, contained, and countered. It is this, the masculine art of controlling language, which should ideally be imitated by the schoolboys of Lohenstein's Breslau as future

---

[68] Compare Cornelia Plume, *Heroinen in der Geschlechterordnung: Weiblichkeitsprojektionen bei Daniel Casper von Lohenstein un die 'Querelle des Femmes'* (Stuttgart 1996), esp. p. 222.

administrators, and which will help them to conserve what
is perceived as the God-given, civilized stability of a patriarchal status quo.

Yet the ethics of the rhetorical art, especially of the creation
of politically expedient 'truths', are called into question in
the work of a dramatist who has been described as no more
than an epigone of Lohenstein and Gryphius: in Haugwitz's
fascinating version of the story of Mary, Queen of Scots.

## The Political Masculine: Haugwitz's Maria Stuarda

August Adolph von Haugwitz (1647–1706), though he was
not himself one of the famous Silesian dramatists, was perfectly familiar with their work, coming as he did from the
neighbouring Saxon province of Lausitz. While Saxony had
nothing equivalent to the prestigious school performances
in Breslau, students in Leipzig did perform drama at fair times.
Haugwitz's plays were probably written with such occasions in
mind, although they were also performed at court.[69] There
is no doubt that they were written in the Silesian tradition;
Haugwitz has even (quite unfairly) been accused of being
merely an epigone.

With regard to the paradoxical title of the Mary Stuart
play, *Schuldige Unschuld*, one editor, Heitner, has suggested
that the phrase was appended later by a poet who became
suddenly aware of the historical controversy surrounding
the guilt or innocence of Mary Stuart after his drama was
complete.[70] Heitner supports the standard view of Haugwitz
as Gryphius's less talented epigone, but his assertion regarding the title is contradicted by the notes to the play, which
indicate that it is a deliberate artifice inspired by one of
Haugwitz's sources for the Mary Stuart material, Erasmus
Francisci's *Traur-Saal*:[71]

---

[69] See Pierre Béhar, 'Biographie', in Haugwitz, *Prodromus Poeticus, Oder Poetischer
Vortrab (1684)*, ed. Pierre Béhar (Tübingen 1984).

[70] See August Adolf [*sic*] von Haugwitz, *Schuldige Unschuld oder Maria Stuarda*,
ed. Robert R. Heitner (Bern and Frankfurt a.M. 1974), p. 12*.

[71] 'Die XII. Geschicht von Heinrich und Maria Stuart/ König und Königinn in
Schottland und andren', in *Der zweite Traur-Saal steigender und fallender Herren* [ . . . ].
*Fürgestellt/ durch Erasmus Francisci* (Nürnberg 1669) is based on the historical report
of the Netherlander Lambertus van den Bos.

Schuldige Unschuld.) Den Titul dieser Tragoedia betreffend/ so apparens quaedam contradictio in adjecto, wird selbiger in dem praeambulo, so unser Francisci im Anfang der Erzehlung dieser Historia aus dem Niederländischen Autore hinzusetzet/ mit mehrern gerechtfertiget/ weil nehmlich bey dieser Königin Maria das lateinische Sprichwort: Laudatur ab his, culpatur ab illis, absonderlich war zuseyn befunden worden ... (*Anmerckungen*, 77)

Heitner's suggestion that the full title imitates Andreas Gryphius's *Ermordete Majestät. Oder Carolus Stuardus* is not unreasonable; Haugwitz readily acknowledges his admiration for his Silesian forerunner, and introduces word-for-word fragments of Gryphius's dramatic verse into his own alexandrines.[72] But in 1684 we are not yet in an age when plagiarism was a negative, or even relevant, concept, and Haugwitz certainly has an independent dramatic intention: the concept of 'schuldige Unschuld' is of equally conscious, central importance to his drama as 'ermordete Majestät' was, in the earlier work, for Gryphius.

*Maria Stuarda* depicts not one female protagonist, but two, Mary Stuart and Elizabeth I of England. Strong superficial similarities exist between these two figures, since they are both royal, both female, and both reported to have been possessed of beauty and political ambition. Two striking differences separate them: Christian dogma, and the historical chain of events which enabled one to have the other executed. Haugwitz, a Protestant dramatist, differs from his Jesuit contemporaries in choosing not to focus on the religious differences,[73] and instead weaves into his drama the antithesis of

---

[72] *Anmerckungen*, II. 82. See also Béhar's appendix (p. 165* ff.), and Otto Neumann's comparison of Haugwitz's text with Francisci, Gryphius, Zesen, and Lohenstein, in 'Studien zum Leben und Werk des Lausitzer Poeten A. A. von Haugwitz' (unpublished doctoral thesis, University of Greifswald 1937), 161 ff. and 225 ff.

[73] Two versions of a Jesuit drama on the Mary Stuart theme are reprinted in Elida Maria Szarota, *Das Jesuitendrama im deutschen Sprachgebiet: eine Periochen-Edition: Texte und Kommentare*, 4 vols. (Munich 1979–87), vol. 3/2. 1145–64. See also Béhar in *Prodromus Poeticus*, 68–75*. A slightly earlier Protestant treatment of the theme can be observed in Johannes Riemer's *Von hohen Vermählungen* and *Von Staats=Eiffer* (both *c.*1680), in Riemer, *Werke*, ed. Helmut Krause (Berlin 1984), 2. 405–70 and 471–519. As this treatment is also fairly neutral, I am inclined to disagree with Béhar's view that Haugwitz's version is a result of deliberate religious irenicism, and instead to suggest that the contemporary view of the historical events simply did not lend itself to a strongly pro-Protestant portrayal.

*Sein* and *Schein*, an opposition which structures his portrayal of the two queens in a remarkably complex manner. Each is individually representative of the antithesis—Maria seems guilty and is actually innocent, while Elisabeth preserves an appearance of innocence and is, in the terms of the drama, culpable—and each represents on a wider scale a set of values to which the same opposition is applied. When the divine right of monarchy is injured, or 'Thron durch Thron verletzt' (II. 274), Haugwitz presents us with the apparent victory of the terrestrial throne, represented by Elisabeth and her court, by contrast with the actual victory of the heavenly throne which is celebrated by Maria in her martyrdom.

The linguistic play on the paradox, 'schuldige Unschuld', anticipates not only an antithetical structure in the drama, but also the ambiguous function of language in the *Schein*-world of the court, where innocence and guilt are determined by rhetorical sleight-of-hand. Here even Elisabeth, who attempts or appears to manipulate, is in fact manipulated into playing Pilate to Maria's *imitatio Christi*. Haugwitz critically investigates the rhetoric for which Lohenstein has provided didactic *exempla*, and allows problems to emerge, particularly those faced by women who attempt to exert rhetorical influence in a language whose metaphors function against them.

In contradistinction to Vondel, in whose *Maria Stuart* of 1646 the English queen does not appear on stage at all,[74] Haugwitz divides the acts of his drama more or less equally between Elisabeth and Maria, and the dramatic action does not end (as it does in Gryphius's *Carolus*) with the death of the martyred monarch, but with Elisabeth's final appearance after the execution, an element of dramatic structure that we shall find again in Schiller's *Maria Stuart* of 1800. Haugwitz's play does not appear to follow the pattern that has been taken to characterize the early modern martyr play, whereby all but the central protagonist are 'Foliefiguren', created to provide dramatic symmetry.[75] This may be true of

[74] Vondel's *Maria Stuart of Gemartelde Majesteit* is likely to have been one source of inspiration for Haugwitz's drama. See Béhar's 'Nachwort' in *Prodromus Poeticus*, 60–3.

[75] For example by Erik Lunding in 'Das Schlesische Kunstdrama: Eine Darstellung und Deutung' (unpublished doctoral thesis, University of Copenhagen 1939), 20.

something like Gryphius's *Catharina von Georgien*, in which all that is admirable and Christian is embodied by Catharina, all that is heathen and despicable by Shah Abas. But Haugwitz creates a central opposition of a different kind: it is not between Muslim and Christian, Catholic and Protestant, or even male and female. The symmetrical structure of *Maria Stuarda* is achieved by the antithesis of Machiavellian political leadership as incorporated by Elisabeth and her advisers, and the Christian ideal of rulership embodied by Maria. Profane or worldly is opposed to heavenly kingship.

Within this structure, the English court is for Haugwitz the location of the superficial, where political dissimulation alone triumphs, as Davidson's inexperience illustrates (III. ii). The Aristotelian unity of place becomes (as the unity of time so often is for Gryphius) an instrument of Baroque antithesis, for Haugwitz distinguishes the scenes in Maria's cell from the court scenes by a different use of language. Elisabeth and her court beat about the bush in complex rhetorical periods, but Maria is so direct that the gentlemen who come to inform her of her condemnation and imminent execution are unable to persist in their self-righteous posturing, and leave abruptly (IV. i). This linguistic opposition of the two queens makes it impossible to support Heitner's interpretation of Maria's joyful acceptance of her martyrdom as dissimulation.[76] On the contrary, it is essential to the antithetical structure of the play that the English queen's rhetorical *Schein* should be balanced by the unambiguous *Sein* of her Scottish counterpart.

Maria may be the eponymous heroine, but it is Elisabeth who opens and closes the dramatic action, and the rhetorical complexities of *Sein* and *Schein* centre on her. A close

---

[76] Haugwitz, *Schuldiger Unschuld*, ed. Heitner, 43*. Were Maria dissimulating, this would have serious consequences for our interpretation of the figure, since dissimulation in women is one of the things feared and hated by influential theorists of the period. Aegidius Albertinus writes, 'Die Heucheley unnd Falschheit der Weiber/ erscheint sogar in ihrem eusserlichen Geschmuck und Anstrich: unnd [*sic*] in allen ihren Trachten und Geberden suchen sie nichts anders/ als dass sie das jenige/ was sie seyn/ dissimuliren/ vertuschen und verbergen/ und was sie nicht seynd/ gleichssnen und ertichten mögen: Daher soll keiner ihrem eusserlichen schein und Worten trawen' (*Hortus Mulieribus*, 1630, p. 78). I think it is sufficiently clear that Haugwitz intends Maria to represent an exemplary *exception* to this type.

examination of the language and structure of the two acts
in which she alone of the two women appears, namely the
first and the third, shows that Elisabeth's domination of her
court is superficial, or *Schein*, by contrast with the subtle
but actual dominance of her counsellors. This makes an
interpretation of the drama complex, particularly in terms
of Elisabeth's motivation. In his introductory summary or
'Inhalt', Haugwitz puts forward the opinion that Elisabeth
intended Mary Stuart to be executed, and even gave the orders
for the decapitation herself:

Maria gebohrene Königin von Schottland . . . wird gezwungen/ nach
England zuflüchten/ allda sie anfänglich von der Königin Elisabeth
ziehmlich wohl empfangen/ und tractiret/ nachmahls aber . . . auff Befehl
der/ ihren Todt (als wäre sie übereilet worden/ und die Hals=Straffe
wider ihren Willen vorgangen [*sic*]) betraurenden Königin Elisabeth/
zum unerhörten und allen gekröhnten Häuptern sehr nachtheiligen
Exempel/ mit dem Beil enthauptet worden. (A4$^{r\text{-}v}$)

Yet, in the first act of the drama, he shows us Elisabeth in
private conference with her advisers, apparently attempting
to defend Maria, and questioning the need to execute her.
Such a contradiction between the stated motivation and
the portrayed behaviour of the English queen can only be
resolved with reference to the role in Maria's destruction
played not only by Elisabeth, but also by her rhetorically active
advisers, the *Königliche Rath*.

The play's *Vorredner* is the personified figure of Eternity,
who highlights the contrast between earthly and heavenly
ambition using crown, sceptre and robe as symbols of kingship, and constructs an emblematic opposition of politics and
Christianity as representatives of the realms of *Schein* and *Sein*
respectively. It is immediately clear to which side Elisabeth
belongs when, following Eternity's final call for the renun-
ciation of worldly splendour, the stage opens to show the
English queen on the throne. Her first speech anticipates
terrestrial *fama* of the kind achieved by Lohenstein's pagan
heroines:

Wir/ die wir uns durch uns der Sterbligkeit entrissen/
Wir/ die die grosse Welt auch todt wird rühmen müssen . . .   (I. 111–2)

Elisabeth's self-portrayal as a heroic woman (a concept made striking, like that of 'schuldige Unschuld', by the implied oxymoron) has an interesting effect in this first speech. Haugwitz shows us a woman who not only perceives herself as an exception to her sex, but so identifies with the masculine heroic values she incorporates that she portrays her female rival in the light of a threatening Other, replacing gender polarity with a distinction between 'Frau' and 'Weib':

> Wir/ die wir wunderns werth/ auch dieses übertroffen/
> Was man von einer Frau kan ungewöhnlich hoffen/
> .    .    .    .    .    .    .    .    .    .    .    .    .    .
> Sind durch ein eintzig Weib/ durch ein gefangen Weib
> Nunmehr so weit gebracht/ daß wir vor unsern Leib
> Fast selbsten furchtsam seyn                        (I. 115 ff.)

There are familiar allegorical implications when Elisabeth describes Maria's influence as that of 'Eris' (I. 126). This was the Fate who cast the apple of discord at the wedding of Peleus and Thetis, the same apple awarded by Paris to Venus for the sake of Helen, who reputedly caused the fall of Troy. The counsellors later pick up on this fear and exploit it rhetorically, casting the Queen of Scots as a dangerous, inflammatory figure (I. 152; I. 244).

Although Elisabeth initially dominates Act I, in the course of the second scene her single-line speeches contrast with the long rhetorical periods of her advisers. It is here that Haugwitz's awareness of and interest in language, rhetoric and *Schein* really begins to emerge, as he allows us to observe the courtly dissimulation which is implicitly set against a Christian idea of *Sein*. In her bombastic self-characterization, Elisabeth uses the word *Schein* in connection with her monarchic virtue in a way which is ironically ambiguous, given the role she is about to play:

> Wir/ die wir dargethan durch unser Tugend Schein/
> Daß auch ein leichtes Weib kan Cronen wichtig seyn/ . . .    (I. 113–14)

Elisabeth's 'Tugend Schein' may also be read as political dissimulation, and it makes scene ii, in which she discusses the fate of Mary Stuart with her counsellors, particularly relevant to an interpretation of her motivation and her control, as

a woman, of courtly rhetoric. Both Béhar and Heitner have
taken Elisabeth's reactions in this scene at face value, as an
indication of her real wish to defend the life of her rival.[77]
If one looks at the episode as a whole, their interpretation
cannot be contradicted; when, immediately after the conference, Elisabeth is left alone on stage to express her deep
disturbance at the death sentence which has effectively been
passed, it is likely that Haugwitz intends her sentiments to
be taken seriously, since no object of a possible dissimulation
is present:

> Soll dann der eigne Nutz selbst die Natur vertreiben/
> Soll ich mein eigen Blut die Königin entleiben/
> Die Königin/ die mir und meinem Reiche traut?
> Hat wohl die grosse Welt was grausamers geschaut/
> Als diese That wird seyn?                          (I. 283–7)

At the beginning of the conference scene, however, it is by
no means clear that Elisabeth's intention is to defend Maria.
Her extended lament over the trouble the Queen of Scots
is causing her, her metaphorical characterization of Maria
as the mischievous and dangerous Eris, as well as Haugwitz's
summary of events in the 'Inhalt', lead us to expect that the
English queen would wish her counsellors to press for an
execution, even if she does not want to bear the responsibility for it. Our initial impression in this scene is indeed that
Elisabeth is encouraging her advisers to voice the need to
dispose of Maria. She first presses Bacon, who beats about
the bush, yet with a wealth of suggestive images of danger:

> ELISABETH.                          Wir kennen eure Treu/
>   Erklährt uns/ was euch dünck't ohn' alle Furcht und Scheu.
> BACON. Princesse/ Sie verzeih/ wir sind etwas zulinde/
>   Wir sehn die nahe Glut und Sturm der stolzen Winde/
>   Und steuren gleichwohl nicht/ und da wir doch den Brannt/
>   Der unser Reich ansteckt/ in unsrer Macht und Hand.
>
>                                       (I. 149–54)

Encouraged by Bacon's hints, Elisabeth puts the question
again, this time more directly, in such a way as to make her
expression of shock at the direct answer she receives from

---

[77] Haugwitz, *Schuldiger Unschuld*, ed. Heitner, 49*; Béhar, *Prodromus Poeticus*, 70*.

Patritius Gray understandable only in terms of dissimulating *Schein*:

ELIS. Wie kan man sich dann nun/ sagts nur/ der Frau befreyen/
    Die uns scheint unsern Todt und Untergang zudräuen.
PATR. GRAY. Man scheide Kopff und Leib.
ELIS.                          Ach allzuherber Schluß.

(I. 155–7)

It transpires during her interview with Davidson in Act III that the 'Schluß' Elisabeth would have preferred is secret murder, rather than official execution. Yet in the course of the stichomythic dialogue that follows her exchange with Gray, Haugwitz turns the tables on the English queen, and shows us this masculine woman achieving an uncomfortable awareness of her own femaleness, such that she finally feels sympathy for her counterpart in a way that the arrogant Lohensteinian queen of the opening speech could not.

In arguing for Maria's execution, Elisabeth's counsellors betray a particular view of Mary Stuart as a female monarch. Elisabeth herself, who just a few lines previously was boasting of her position as an exception to the feminine rule, cannot but feel the similarity in categorization. The men who would manipulate her with their rhetoric are in a delicate situation, treading a tightrope between creating the images of danger necessary to persuade her of the threat Maria poses, and yet distinguishing between the powerful woman they want executed and the one to whom they are subject. Their rhetorical success is demonstrated when, at the close of Act I, Elisabeth repeats the ideas with which they have provided her, in her soliloquy as well as in her interview with the French ambassador.

The argument opens and closes with the suggestion that Mary Stuart's death is necessary for the survival of Elisabeth and England (Bacon, I. 145–7; Leycester, I. 225; Patritius Gray, I. 280–1). This is augmented by a series of metaphorical and allegorical categorizations of Maria, all implying her threatening potential. Her destructive power is classed as that of fire or a tempest (Bacon, I. 152); the figure of Helen of Troy is indirectly present in the inflammatory image. The idea of many deaths for the sake of one such catastrophic figure is picked up by Leycester as the discussion closes (I. 244).

Elisabeth's recognition and acceptance of the metaphor is confirmed when she makes the implied image concrete in her accusation of Maria, in conversation with the French ambassador:

> Sie habe Brittens Reich mit innerlichen Flammen
> Gleich Troja angesteckt                                     (I. 367–8)

Hattan (I. 162) and Burglay (I. 166) join the argument against Maria with a rhetorical *locus*: the idea that women, especially beautiful women, cannot be trusted. In the terms of the commonplace, beauty automatically results in pride, lust, and ambition;[78] hence Elisabeth's counsellors refer to Maria's arrogance (Beal, I. 170), and to her sexual self-indulgence. But they are skating on thin ice, for the English queen, herself a woman, is sceptical of metaphors of the feminine. She begins by accepting the idea of untrustworthiness, and, in keeping with the masculinist perspective revealed in her first speech, directs her advisers' attention towards male authority: 'Man muß nicht so auff sie als auf den Bürgen schauen' (I. 163). Beal, however, makes the tactical error of voicing his reliance on the captive Mary Stuart's feminine weakness, and accidentally strikes a chord of experience in Elisabeth (the historical figure was herself held captive by her sister, Mary Tudor) which leads her to recall the applicability of such ideas to herself, as well as her rival:

> BEAL. Ein eingekärkert Weib ist leichtlich zubezähmen.
> ELISABETH. Der Kärcker schleust den Leib/ nicht das Gemüthe ein.
> .   .   .   .   .   .   .   .   .   .   .   .   .   .   .
> Ein höchstgekröhntes Haupt darff keine Straffe leiden.
>
>                                                    (I. 168 ff.)

---

[78] In Hallmann's *Mariamne* (1670; in *Sämtliche Werke*, ed. Gerhard Spellerberg, vol. 1, Berlin 1975) Salome is able to convince Herod, and later Antipater, of the heroine's guilt by similar means:

> Was ist ein schönes Weib?
> Ein Teuffel/ nicht ein Mensch/ so bald ihr zarter Leib/
> Durch Hochmuth auffgebläht/ sich in ein Zucht-Haus wandelt   (I. 89–90)

The idea is also used by Albertinus when giving advice to husbands-to-be: 'Wer sich begert zu verheyraten/ der sol keines Wegs dahin sehen/ damit das Weib ausbündig schön sey/ dann gemeiniglich seynd die übernatürliche schöne Weiber geneiget zum bösen' (*Hortus Mulieribus*, 247).

That Elisabeth's protest is motivated by personal insecurity at the similarity she senses, and not by any abstract ideal regarding the divine ordination of monarchs, is indicated by Leycester's response. He intervenes to smooth over Beal's *faux pas* by reinstigating a difference between the two queens:

LEYCESTER. Und dennoch muß man auch die Häupter unterscheiden.
ELISABETH. Maria trug so wohl deß Scepters Glantz/ als Wir.
LEYC. Sie hat sich längst beraubt der Königlichen Zier

(I. 172–4)

From this point on, however, it is clear that Elisabeth feels an affinity with the Queen of Scots which is more than political *Schein*. She defends her rival against the accusations of the *Rath* with a pragmatic disregard for their deliberately ominous reminders of Maria's abuse of men and institutions, even reattributing the guilt to the men involved:

WALSINGHAM. Wer lobt/ daß sie so bald mit Stuard Heyrath schloß?
ELISABETH. Weil Stuard Edel/ war der Fehler nicht so groß!
WARWIK. Wer lobt/ daß sie so groß den Lautenisten [i.e. Rizzio] ehrte?
ELIS. Mit dessen klugen Kopff sie Murrays Tücken wehrte.
BEAL. Wie daß sie mit Gewalt die Schott'sche Kirche höhn't?
ELIS. Mit dem hat Murray nur die Mäuterey beschön't/
BACON. Wie daß sie dann die Macht deß Königs selbst vermindert?
ELIS. Weil dessen Trägheit nur deß Reiches Heyl verhindert.

(I. 177–84)

Elisabeth's overt pragmatism here contrasts strongly with the approach of her advisers. They stress Mary Stuart's sexual and moral culpability, rather than her political activities (I. 185 ff.), but Elisabeth's refusal to accept their interpretations of Maria's behaviour in terms of what is expected of a woman, rather than what is expected of a monarch, reflects an uncomfortable awareness of her own paradoxical position as woman and ruler.

Towards the end of this first scene, while Elisabeth's speeches remain short, those of her counsellors become longer and more elaborate. She is still sufficiently in control to stop Beal's attempt to override all argument when he suggests rhetorically that Maria's crimes are general knowledge (I. 233 ff.), yet she is no longer able to counter

Walsingham's direct use of emblematic authority to indict her rival:

> Man wasche wie man wil/ man ändert doch den Mohr
> An seiner Farbe nicht.                                    (I. 238–9)[79]

It is interesting that Walsingham, wishing to express convincingly the degenerate nature of the Queen of Scots, should associate her with blackness. In this he simultaneously avoids Beal's mistake of reminding Elisabeth of feminine similarities between herself and Maria, and yet manages to imply that one of the queens has essential failings by linking her with another early modern Other: the Moor. Haugwitz finally spells out the nature of the affinity which is troubling Elisabeth through Patritius Gray: 'Und vielleicht schreckt sie ab die Gleichheit von Geschlecht' (I. 269), an intimation of feminine weakness which the speaker subtly contrasts with the decisive political execution of Lady Jane Grey by another Catholic Mary (I. 271 ff.). The mention of Elisabeth's half-sister Mary Tudor here is calculated to increase her animosity towards her present rival.

In the monologue which follows this exchange, it is apparent that Elisabeth's attempts to use the *Schein* of language to secure the murder of Mary Stuart, while keeping her own hands clean, have backfired. The rhetorical categorizations of the feminine by the *Rath* have shaken her own 'masculine' perspective on the Queen of Scots, and engendered a sense of affinity which makes Elisabeth insecure:

> Soll dann der eigne Nutz selbst die Natur vertreiben/
> Soll ich mein eigen Blut die Königin entleiben/
> Die Königin . . . ?                                       (I. 283–5)

At the same time they have pressed upon her, with the authority of metaphor and emblem, combined with hints of feminine weakness which indirectly threaten Elisabeth with the possibility of a fate similar to Maria's, the necessity of an execution. Having first expressed her distrust of linguistic

---

[79] This emblem featured in Alciati's collection (see Henkel and Schöne, *Emblemata: Handbuch zur Sinnbildkunst*, cols. 1087–8), and is reproduced by Albrecht Schöne in connection with his discussion of the *argumentum emblematicum*; see Schöne, *Emblematik und Drama*, 20.

*Schein,* as it is contained in the written word: 'Ein leichter Vers und Brieff/ Und falsch gemachtes Buch/ die können nichts beweisen' (I. 206–7), Elisabeth is forced to use exactly this authority as 'proof' of Maria's guilt, in an attempt to justify herself (or her counsellors' triumph over her) to the French ambassador: 'Und gleichwohl zeugens Schreiben/ Die man so leichtlich nicht wird wider hintertreiben' (I. 339–40). It is particularly pathetic that Elisabeth should voice the arguments of her counsellors not only, like a puppet, in this interview, but also in her soliloquy, in which she clings to their reasoning to soothe her own unease:

> O grausames entschliessen!
> Ja grausam/ doch gerecht: Ich führe ja den Schwert
> Nicht blos zum Scheine nur vor Staat/ vor Kirch und Heerd.
> .   .   .   .   .   .   .   .   .   .   .
> Und wenn ich länger noch dem Rasen solt zusehn/
> So wär' es ümb die Kirch'/ ümb Mich und Reich geschehn.
>
> (I. 288 ff.)

Instead of being mistress of the *Schein* of political rhetoric, Elisabeth falls victim to it herself. Her weakened position is clear in Act III, which Haugwitz structures to show the English queen surrounded by the men who would control her. It begins with an interview between the Bishop of Ross and the French ambassador, both of whom want to prevent Maria's execution, yet recognize the extent to which Elisabeth is being manipulated:

> GESANDTE. Die Köngin [*sic*] wanckt noch was/ doch schürt man hefftig zu:
> .   .   .   .   .   .   .   .   .   .   .
> So/ das sie endlich wird/ und zwar gezwungen/ müssen
> Das Urtheil/ so sie noch jetzt auffgezogen/ schliessen.
>
> (III. 11 ff.)

This is followed by a very brief appearance from Elisabeth, in which she again tries to use rhetorical dissimulation, this time to manipulate Davidson into perpetrating the secret murder of her rival. She fails, however, because the inexperienced courtier does not play the game of *Schein.* Like Maria with the *Rath,* he rhetorically disarms and thus silences his opponent with honesty:

DAVIDSON. Durchläuchtige Princeß! Ich bitte/ Sie verzeih':
Sie denck'/ daß nich allzeit/ was nutz'/ auch ehrlich sey:
. . . . . . . . . . . .
Kurz: Sie muß undanckbar/ entweder unrecht seyn.
ELISABETH. Genug hiervon.

(III. 163 ff.)

Elisabeth's rhetoric fails with Davidson, but that of her counsellors succeeds. They are able to persuade him to risk carrying the responsibility for Maria's death, and in doing so they openly categorize their own queen in terms of her (negative) femininity: 'Ein Weib hägt niemahls nicht beständige Gedancken' (III. 218). This contrasts strikingly with the subtle hints employed in her presence in Act I. Thus the English queen is rhetorically outmanœuvred at every turn. Her awareness of this emerges in her refusal to commit herself in clear language to Maria's execution. Indecision (I. 406; III. 174; III. 217) characterizes her behaviour until, in her final appearance after the death of her rival, she is sufficiently in control of the situation to forbid (temporarily) both Davidson and the *Rath* any further use of the powerful medium of speech:

Schweig/ Ehrvergeßner Mensch! Die Worte sind verlohren;
. . . . . . . . . . . .
Nicht ein Wort

(V. 422 ff.)

As Lohenstein's dramas illustrated, the *Reyen* in seventeenth-century German tragedies provide a location, separate from the action, for the dramatist to clarify his communicative intentions. Unsurprisingly, the *Reyen* in *Maria Stuarda* reflect particularly the problems of rhetoric and the feminine raised in the play. They follow the same antithetical structure relating to the two women as the acts themselves: the chorus of courtiers praising Elisabeth's political prowess at the end of Act I is echoed by the captive handmaids of Maria, who proclaim her piety and virtue after the second act. The idea of courtly hypocrisy presented by the Classical 'Reyen der Syrenen' in Act III is developed in the fourth chorus of

Christian lament over the misuse of political issues to support political *Schein*.[80]

The first *Reyen* provides a gloss on Haugwitz's portrayal of the rhetorical manipulation of Elisabeth by her counsellors. They have succeeded in creating an image of Mary Stuart which implies that her execution is a necessity, and the stanzas of the *Reyen* are arranged dialectically, to question standard images relating to women. The first two stanzas list a series of negative categorizations of the feminine, the third touches on the problem of female rule. Like Le Moyne and others who sought to put forward an idealized view of woman in response to misogynist accusations, Haugwitz uses mythological and historical examples of womanhood—the Amazons and Semiramis—to defend the idea of the female represented specifically by Elisabeth in the last four stanzas. Stanza 5 presents the English queen as Pallas, familiar from the judgement of Paris; she is the goddess who is born from her father's head, and therefore embodies masculine wisdom without feminine weakness. This relates interestingly to Haugwitz's historical portrayal. Elisabeth, as the arguably illegitimate daughter of Anne Boleyn, was only able to survive and come to power by constantly associating herself with her father, Henry VIII; so the daughter of Zeus and, metaphorically speaking, the least feminine of the goddesses is well suited to this most masculine of queens.

Given Haugwitz's educated awareness of language and rhetoric, as well as his travels in France, we can assume that the literary arguments listed in the *Reyen* represent a deliberate pastiche of the recent *querelle*.[81] At the start and close of the chorus the 'truth' of certain metaphors or commonplaces is questioned, first with reference to the spoken, then the written word:

> Ists war/ was man sonst pflegt zusprechen      (I. 407)
> .      .      .      .      .      .      .      .
>
> Drumb ist es nur ein blosses dichten/
> Was wir von Weiber Schwachheit richten . . .   (I. 455–6)

---

[80] Probably influenced by the 'Chor der Religion und der Ketzer' which follows Act IV of Gryphius's *Carolus Stuardus*.

[81] Haugwitz had visited Paris in 1669, and was presumably acquainted with the literature surrounding the recent *Querelle des Femmes*.

By deliberately exaggerating the negative view of woman in the first two stanzas, Haugwitz retrospectively casts doubt on the ominous categorizations of Maria effected by Elisabeth's counsellors in Act I. Sycophantic pro-female rhetoric, of the kind practised by those seeking favour with a woman ruler, is also undermined: the courtiers' lapidary praise of exceptional womanhood that concludes this *Reyen* misses its mark (or is ironically transferred) when it is Maria, and not Elisabeth, who subsequently appears.

Haugwitz's *Reyen* differ from the usual pattern in that the dramatist withholds an unambiguous indication of his view of the dramatic situation. This is demonstrated by the 'Reyen der Syrenen' (Act III), in which Elisabeth is described as a hypocrite, whose only wish is to see Maria executed; but Elisabeth's soliloquy in Act I contradicts this, and so does her similarly expressed (and therefore arguably genuine) lament following the execution.[82] The *Reyen* is preceded by Beal's determined declaration that Mary Stuart shall die, and Haugwitz thereby hints again at the extent to which Elisabeth is subject to the will of her male courtiers. It is worth noting that the last word in the play is had not by Elisabeth, but by a counsellor who ratifies the execution in the face of her protest. Haugwitz's portrayal thus remains ambiguous; Elisabeth is more or less directly responsible for Maria's death, and is—to a certain extent—condemned by the dramatist. She is, however, shown to be paradoxically less free than her captive. Maria achieves a victory of religious and personal freedom in her pseudo-martyrdom, while Elisabeth remains a prisoner in the web of courtly politics. As the sanguine nature of the *Rath's* final speech implies, she cannot escape from the intricate game of dissimulation.

In making Elisabeth the prisoner of rhetoric, Haugwitz reveals an attitude less positive than Lohenstein's towards this courtly and political skill of men. Language must be used

[82] The frontispiece of the 1683 edition shows a turbaned figure looking down from the gallery into the execution chamber. If this is intended to represent Elisabeth, it would function as a confirmation of Haugwitz's claim in the 'Inhalt' that Elisabeth knew of Maria's death, and that her angry protests at the end of Act V are therefore to be understood as dissimulation. Given the confusion that her counsellor's rhetoric has stirred up in her, her lament may nevertheless be genuine, without representing a contradiction in the terms of the drama.

with care if, as the title of his drama suggests, it is a game of paradox and ambiguity. After the dedications of the play, Haugwitz includes a quotation from de Cailière, in which the author cautions against the irresponsible use of the language of literature, 'la Poesie':

La Poesie doit estre nostre divertissement & non pas nostre passion . . . Que ce soit par sottise on [= ou] par Raison, c'est toujours une habitude si vieille & si universellement etablie, qu'on n'en scauroit desabuser [*sic*] le monde, de sorte QU'IL SE FAUT SERVIR DE CE TALENT AVEC BEAUCOUP DE CIRCUMSPECTION. (A3ᵛ)

This is an interesting echo of a traditional unease regarding rhetoric and elocution,[83] and it seems to reflect Haugwitz's own sense that language and the authority inherent in authorship is not something to be taken lightly. In a dedicatory poem to Erasmus Francisci, Haugwitz tries to deflect the danger of his own work being received with 'passion', rather than as a 'divertissement', by using the *topos* of authorial self-deprecation to suggest that his writing need not be taken seriously:

Was aber schreibt von ihr [= Maria] mein allzufrecher Kiel/
Aus einem traurigen macht er ein Freuden=Spiel/
Weil sein gantz albres Thun verdient belacht zuwerden.     (A1ᵛ)

It seems that the love of paradox and ambiguity that is reflected in the structure and language of *Maria Stuarda* is closely related to Haugwitz's sense of the power of language, through which appearance may take the place of reality, and the opposition of guilt and innocence turned around. The result in this case is that a woman who, in the terms of the drama, is an embodiment of Christian piety, is executed in the name of Christian justice.

*Conclusion*

In the first chapter we saw how the 'rhetorical feminine'— a mode of linguistic classification that defines its object in

---

[83]  Both Plato and, in Haugwitz's century, Thomas Hobbes were suspicious of the rhetorical art. See Vickers, *In Defence of Rhetoric*, 18.

terms associated with the female, as the subordinate 'other' of the male writer or speaker—can be used to relieve the sense of threat engendered by a religious or territorial rival. Because the Other is understood as the negative or non-ideal version of the Self, the writer has a useful literary device up his sleeve; for the surprise element in a *positive* portrayal of Muslims, Turks, or women will automatically cause an audience to sit up and take notice. The method is therefore didactically effective; Luther used it when he held up Turkish courage and customs as an example to the German troops, and Lohenstein uses in it *Epicharis*, when he shows us a heroine who is more masculine than the men who surround her.

In *Cleopatra, Agrippina*, and *Sophonisbe*, rhetoric is again at work, with a different slant. Even though these women are politically active and share at least in the patriotism of the *femme forte*, they cannot be seen as exemplary because they lack the essential feminine quality of chastity. Chastity or the lack of it has always been the single most important factor in the masculinist idea of woman; as the myth of the Judgement of Paris reveals, the erotic impulse is the one thing that is feared to render man subject to the woman he is anxious to construct as his inferior. Epicharis is notable for her chastity and for her silence (in the face of torture);[84] the use of sex or the 'rhetoric of seduction' is what makes Lohenstein's other great heroines so dangerous, and necessitates their defeat not only by men but at the hands of a greater, metaphysical entity, Fate, which is shown to be working against them. In one sense at least this is not merely a convenient dramatic fiction. Haugwitz's drama of Elizabeth I and Mary Stuart demonstrates that there *is* a powerful force hindering women. Not Fate, but the established network of ideas that is masculinist discourse, consciously applied in rhetoric, will finally disable them.

It is worth remembering that in school drama both male and female parts were played by boys. Given the insistently

---

[84] Newman notes that Lohenstein, as well as his sources, play up Epicharis's silence under torture as a 'rejection of stereotypical female garrulity'. See Newman, 'Sex "in Strange Places"', 361.

masculine script of Lohenstein's dramas in particular, we might expect boys dressed as women to provoke fears about effeminization—the accusation that this was indeed the effect of cross-dressing was, after all, 'the hallmark of Renaissance anti-theatricality',[85] complemented by anxiety regarding the accidental kindling of homoerotic love.[86] In the light of our analysis of *Catharina von Georgien* and *Epicharis*, we may assume that these characters posed relatively few problems. Even though they are women, they are portrayed both as masculine and as examples of sexual continence. But we might expect their deliberately seductive counterparts in *Sophonisbe*, *Agrippina*, and *Cleopatra* to have provoked a more significant level of unease. In a note to the scene in *Sophonisbe* (I. 378 ff.) in which Vermina is costumed as a woman, Lohenstein refers to the biblical veto in Deuteronomy 22: 5, 'Daß die Weiber nicht Waffen, die Männer nicht Weiberkleider tragen sollen'. Both the human sacrifice that is to be performed in this scene and the act of cross-dressing, then, are clearly to be understood as barbaric inversions of civilized order; but Lohenstein does not appear to make a more general connection with the problem of boys playing women in school drama. In the lengthy scholarly *Anmerckungen* to this and other dramas, no attempt is made to problematize the practice. We must assume that the lesson to be learned through playing the female role was, in the context of school drama, sufficiently important to outweigh considerations regarding the potential feminization of boy actors.

What these dramas were teaching goes beyond a history lesson and practice in public speaking. It is closely involved with rhetoric, metaphor, and the persuasive construction of 'truth'. Modern metaphor theory postulates a link between metaphor and drama, since dramatic objects, like metaphor, function both on a linguistic and on a visual level. Metaphor is a form of communicative shorthand that is well suited

[85] Laura Levine, *Men in Women's Clothing: Anti-Theatricality and Effeminization 1579–1642* (Cambridge 1994), 1.
[86] Jane O. Newman, 'Innovation and the Text which is not One: Representing History in Lohenstein's "Sophonisbe" (1669)', in *Innovation und Originalität* (*Fortuna Vitrea*, vol. 9), ed. Walter Haug and Burghart Wachinger (Tübingen 1993), 206–38 (220–1).

to the drama's compressed form, and its power has been described by one recent theorist as 'ein die Substruktur der Sprache und damit ein die "Substruktur des Denkens" konstituierender Faktor'.[87] In using and developing existing ideas such as Venus or Helen of Troy, while providing an interpretation of these ideas in such a way as to lay claim to *truth* (via the *argumentum emblematicum*, the stage image as emblem, the authority of the historical or mythological precedent), Lohenstein provides the schoolboys of Breslau with a set of rhetorical *loci* which, even though they depend heavily on ideas of the feminine, may—as we see in *Epicharis*—be used against women or men. This is one aspect of *imitatio* that is central to the pedagogical dramatic exercise. The other aspect is the acquisition of the rhetorical technique that enables the speaker to construct such truth categories for himself, and hence to appeal to and metaphorically manipulate the 'Substruktur des Denkens' present in his audience or opponent. These are the tools of power that will enable the grammar school boys to preserve the status quo when they enter the administrative posts they are destined for.

Modern scholars have suggested that Lohenstein, like Haugwitz, is critical of rhetoric. With reference to *Ibrahim Sultan*, Wichert argues that Lohenstein is sceptical of the efficacy of language as a means of controlling a tyrant, who will simply disregard it in favour of brute force,[88] while Halsted sees in his work evidence of a problematization of rhetoric, and argues that its use for sexual purposes in *Agrippina* constitutes a criticism of the moral basis of the *ars disputandi*, and hence the moral basis of the Protestant schools who teach it:

What is at stake is the relationship between rhetoric and moral structures and, by implication, the relationship between rhetoric and power. . . . Most interesting is the implication that rhetoric in general, including Nero's heroic images, might be merely seductive.[89]

---

[87] Holger Pausch, 'Zum Forschungsstand', in Pausch (ed.), *Kommunikative Metaphorik: Die Funktion des literarischen Bildes in der deutschen Literatur von ihren Anfängen bis zur Gegenwart* (Bonn 1976), 5–15 (7).

[88] Wichert, *Literatur, Rhetorik und Jurisprudenz*, 250.

[89] David Halsted, 'From School Theater to Trauerspiel: Lohenstein's *Agrippina* as systematic analysis', in *Daphnis* 22 (1993), 621–39 (635).

Both critics are in fact referring to the rhetoric of characters —Ibrahim Sultan, Agrippina, and Nero—who are to be understood as feminine, and therefore (as Halsted notices) as proponents of seduction and chaos, rather than of the masculine rhetoric of order.[90] If rhetoric can lead to the abuse of power, whether by sexually attractive women or by brutal tyrants, then it is all the more important that school drama should exemplify the proper use of the persuasive art to stabilize a morally ordered society. Lohenstein's African plays at least are to be understood in this way; the dramatist uses Augustus and Scipio—as rational Roman males, the epitome of masculinity—to demonstrate the political use of rhetoric with consequences which are understood to be advantageous to world history. The ideas of femininity that these men control are, like the emblematic negro in *Maria Stuarda*, a rhetorical tool in their hands; but, unlike Haugwitz, Lohenstein suggests that such tools can and should be used to preserve an ordered social hierarchy.

The memory of the Thirty Years War will have made the orderliness of civilized society of primary concern to a dramatist like Lohenstein. Haugwitz, born just twenty years later, is clearly more interested in the problem of language itself than in its ordering potential. The self-referential nature of Haugwitz's literary concerns is, nonetheless, remarkable in such an early writer. He is very clearly critical of rhetorical *Schein*: instead of exemplary orators, we are confronted in his play with an investigation of rhetoric's effects. Yet even from this perspective, women are again inevitably the losers in the linguistic game: Maria is sent to her death without ever really participating in the rhetorical struggle, while Elisabeth is left with a disturbing sense of her paradoxical position as a female ruler, since the language of her counsellors implies that power and femininity are (and should be) distinct. Their success in manipulating both her and her courtier Davidson—where

---

[90] An interesting exception to the feminine rule is Kiosem in *Ibrahim Sultan*, whose political and rhetorical adeptness finally saves the day and restores peace at the Turkish court. Newman has read Kiosem as a parallel to Lohenstein's Duchess, Louise of Silesia, who was also 'the wife and mother of sovereigns' and a political player in her own right. See Jane O. Newman, 'Disorientations: Same-Sex Seduction and Women's Power', in *CG* 28 (1995), 337–55 (350 ff.).

she failed—confirms this. Where Lohenstein encouraged us to infer that a woman should not be allowed entry into the related masculine domains of language and authority if a stable social order is to be maintained, Haugwitz illustrates the problems these domains will, anyway, always cause women, because the metaphors they would control are designed to defeat them.

# 3

# READING THE SIGNS:
# RHETORICAL *LOCI* AND
# STAGE SEMIOTICS

Depictions of the Turk or Muslim as feminine (in the face of a real fear of the Ottomans 'masculine' military prowess), or of personally ambitious women as dangerous Venus fly-traps, represent—as we have observed—the rhetorical arrangement of ideas into recognizable categories, or *loci*. The structure of the process imitates proof by precedent; we know (for example) that Helen is associated with the fall of Troy, therefore any woman associated with Helen is also automatically associated with the fall of civilizations. As such ideas gain familiarity they acquire the deictic authority of the emblem: just a fleeting reference will guide the audience or reader towards an intended meaning. Within the compressed form of the drama, this can constitute a useful kind of shorthand.

We saw in *Maria Stuarda* and in *Catharina von Georgien* that the portrayal of antitheses in drama—in these cases, conflicting protagonists—can do much to signal an underlying, or indeed overarching, dramatic meaning: *Sein* as opposed to *Schein*, or right as opposed to wrong religious allegiance. Each side of the antithesis will help delineate the other more sharply. An antithetical system of categorization—for example, women as feminine, weak, inconstant, and men as masculine, unwavering, just—also permits for striking literary effects through reversal and paradox, which contradict audience expectations: hence the impact of the *femme forte* and the virtuous Turk.

When a character reveals the inability to categorize appropriately—when, for example, Nero and his associates in *Epicharis* assign the rebellious heroine to the category of the witch—it is clear to the audience that this is in fact an indication of the Emperor's degenerate and perverted perception, rather than the uncovering of a truth about

Epicharis. This chapter will look further at the meanings of categorization and opposition on the early modern stage, and investigate the dramatists' use of forensic signals—the categories or *loci* that prove the dramatic point—to guide the audience towards a 'correct' interpretation of the on-stage world.

## A Black-and-White Interpretation of Hallmann's Dramas

> Black faces may have hearts as white as snow;
> And 'tis a general rule in moral roles,
> The whitest faces have the blackest souls.[1]

The idea of the *femme forte* relied on preconceptions of woman as the 'weaker vessel' (1 Pet. 3: 7) for its paradoxical impact. The 'general rule' postulated in these lines from *Lust's Dominion* (1599) similarly profits from contradicting the pre-existing assumption that blackness is associated with moral degeneracy.[2] Both ideas function because language is ambiguous and the way it is used, analogical. Weakness may be weakness of spirit or a relative weakness of the body in women, darkness that of night, feared by humans, or dark skin protecting them from climatic conditions. In each case the signifier may shape our understanding of what is signified.[3]

The idea that whiteness of skin is a desirable thing, blackness undesirable, is well established in Europe by the early sixteenth century. Andrea Alciati's famous emblem collection of 1531 includes under the title *IMPOSSIBILE* an illustration in which two Europeans are attempting to wash a black man. The caption reads:

---

[1] Thomas Dekker *et al.*, *Lust's Dominion* (1599), V. iii. 9–11.

[2] The standard use of blackness in early English drama as 'a signifier for various forms of socially unacceptable behaviour' is discussed by Ania Loomba with reference to Webster's *The White Devil* (1612). See Loomba, 'The Color of Patriarchy: Critical Difference, Cultural Difference, and Renaissance Drama', in Margo Hendricks and Patricia Parker (eds.), *Women, 'Race', and Writing in the Early Modern Period* (London 1994), 17–34 (27).

[3] It is interesting that fears associated with whiteness (cold, emptiness, nothingness) have—in Western literature at least—not been equated with a need to fear or abhor white-skinned individuals, although they are testified to in works like Melville's *Moby Dick* and Stifter's *Bergkristall*.

Abluis Aethiopem quid frustra? ah desine, noctis
Illustrare nigrae nemo potest tenebras,

which in the German edition is translated:

> *Vergebne Arbeit.*
> Was badt sein Moren lang umb sunst?
> Hör auff es ist verlorn all Kunst
> Dann niemand der duncklen Nacht kan
> Dick Finsternuß erleuchten thon.[4]

The image achieves a proverbial status, and reappears not only in early German drama but in English Elizabethan and Jacobean writing; in Fletcher's *The Knight of Malta*, for example, a black maid is referred to elliptically as 'my little labour in vain'.[5] In both cases dark pigmentation is associated not only with the darkness of night, but also with undesirable personal qualities.

The synonymity of blackness and unpleasantness or even wickedness, and whiteness and innocence or goodness, arises not least out of a Christian tradition of attaching values to these colours. The writer of St Matthew's Gospel describes the lightness and whiteness of the Angel of God (Matt. 28: 8); it is therefore predictable that the fallen angel Lucifer and his associates should be linked with darkness or blackness. In medieval mystery plays, blackness (occasionally redness) and animality are the standard characteristics of a devil.[6] In such a metaphorical context blackness cannot be regarded as a desirable state, and in one popular sixteenth-century legend it is assumed to be a punishment: blacks were widely believed to be the descendents of Ham in the Genesis story, their dark skin colour the punitive wages of sexual excess.[7] One is reminded of the biblical idea that biological

---

[4] In *Emblemata: Handbuch zur Sinnbildkunst des XVI. und XVII. Jahrhunderts* ed. Arthur Henkel and Albrecht Schöne (Stuttgart 1967), col. 1087. Compare also ibid., col. 1088.

[5] See Eldred D. Jones, *The Elizabethan Image of Africa* (Charlottesville, Va. 1971), 48.

[6] Maximilian Josef Rudwin, *Der Teufel in den deutschen geistlichen Spielen des Mittelalters und der Reformationszeit* (Göttingen 1915), 104. See also Luis Schuldes, *Die Teufelsszenen im deutschen geistlichen Drama des Mittelalters* (Göppingen 1974), 99, 130.

[7] Ruth Cowhig, 'Blacks in English Renaissance Drama and the Role of Shakespeare's Othello', in *The Black Presence in English Literature*, ed. David Dabydeen (Manchester 1985), 1–25 (1).

womanhood, especially childbearing, is in fact a punishment for feminine lasciviousness.

Typical early modern prejudices are voiced by the characters in Shakespeare's *Othello* (1603/4). The hero is repeatedly described in satanic terms, particularly by Iago,[8] and the rift that will destroy both Othello and Desdemona is anticipated in metaphors of black and white. Iago also draws on the animalistic ideas associated with blackness when he suggests that their sexual union is an unnatural, bestial affair.[9] The content of Shakespeare's drama does not necessarily suggest that its author agreed with the prejudice of such as Iago. Yet he is interested in the oxymoron of good blackness and bad whiteness in the characters of hero and antihero, and in the dramatic impact of oxymoron: the 'noble Moor' emphasizes by contrast the wickedness of white Iago.

Metaphorical threads of light and darkness, black and white run through Johann Christian Hallmann's (1640–?1704) dramatic work. In his *Mariamne* (1670), the oppositions of the drama are less firmly centred in the protagonists than in the plays of Gryphius and Haugwitz; instead they flicker rhetorically through the characters' language in a manner suited to a tale of courtly intrigue. Its heroine is held up in the manner of a *femme forte* as an example of inner as well as outer beauty, and of fortitude in the face of death.[10] Her main opponent is not Herodes but his sister Salome, who plays a scheming Iago to Herodes' misguided Othello.

The play is set in a specifically pre-Christian era, as Hallmann informs us with exactitude in the introductory pages: 'Die Geschicht hat sich begeben im Jahr der Welt 3922. fünff und zwanzig Jahr vor unsers Erlösers Gebuhrt.'[11] The

---

[8]  *Othello*, I. i. 88; I. ii. 72; I. iii. 102; II. i. 224–5; V. ii. 129–30.

[9]  Ibid., I. i. 85–6; I. ii. 69–70; I. iii. 101; II. i. 232–3.

[10]  Mariamne is chosen by Pierre Le Moyne for inclusion in his *Gallerie des Femmes Fortes* as an example of perfect fortitude. The author notes that at the time of his publication she is already an established dramatic figure. See Le Moyne, *La Gallerie des Femmes Fortes* (Paris 1647), 99. Szarota includes in her collection a Jesuit drama, *Mariamne* (Munich 1661) in which the heroine demonstrates her stoic patience and chastity; see Szarota, *Das Jesuitendrama im deutschen Sprachgebiet: Eine Periochen-Edition*, 4 vols. (Munich 1979–87), vol. 2/2. 1887–99.

[11]  Johann Christian Hallmann, *Mariamne*, in *Sämtliche Werke*, ed. Gerhard Spellerberg, vol. 1 (Berlin 1975). Henceforth referred to as *Werke*. All references are to this edition of the text.

two central characters, Herodes and Mariamne, are Jews; forcing them towards the opposite poles of tyrant and martyr is the Iago-like figure of Herodes' sister Salome, whose cunning is linked with her womanhood in a way that recalls Lohenstein's Cleopatra.[12] On one occasion Salome also links her dangerous wit with her Jewishness: having characterized her own intelligence as 'Frauen-List' (I. 168), she gloats over the impending downfall of Mariamne's family, and her own anticipated ascendancy: 'Die kluge Jüdin geht den Africanern vor' (III. 250). Her quick-wittedness may be stereotypically Jewish, but as a form of *ratio status* it is also untypically feminine, and therefore threatening. Salome, like so many dramatic (anti-)heroines, has the impact of the unconventional, and Pheroras is voicing the expectations and reactions of Hallmann's audience when he expresses astonishment at the courage and intelligence of his female sibling: 'Ich starr' ob deinem Muth und dem so klugen Munde!' (I. 239).

Salome's language or 'kluger Mund', identified here by her brother, is crucial. Her success in dividing Herodes from Mariamne depends on her ability to manipulate discourse. In her first rhetorical skirmish with the king, her method is that of Shakespeare's Iago: she subtly employs the rhetorical tactic of *reticentia* to arouse and then disingenuously to satisfy the curiosity of jealousy:[13]

> Es ist der Klugheit lehre/
> Nicht jedes zu erzehl'n/ was im Pallast geschicht:
> Jedoch weil meine Treu dem Bruder mich verpflicht/
> Und das hochheil'ge Recht mir selbst die Wort' einbindet/
> So red' ich sonder scheu
>
> (I. 368–72)

Salome's rhetorical expertise, employed entirely for personal ends, is transgressive in a woman and a clear signal that this character must be categorized as dangerous.

---

[12] Compare for example *Cleopatra*, II. 430–1:

> Die Lorbern mögen stets die klugen Frauen zieren/
> Für welchen Männer-Witz meist muß zu scheitern gehn!

[13] Compare *Othello*, III. iii. Brian Vickers has identified Shakespeare's use of this figure; see Vickers, *In Defence of Rhetoric* (Oxford 1997 [1988]), 337.

Two attributes, one profound and one superficial, initially protect Mariamne from her sister-in-law's machinations: her virtue and her beauty. Hallmann suggests in his prefatory summary or 'Eintheilung des Trauerspiels' that her husband is in thrall to the external quality, her 'unvergleichliche Schönheit' (p. 206); the dramatist, by contrast, is at pains to match this with an inner beauty or 'tugendhaffte Seele' (p. 208). The point is driven home in the song of Mount Zion that forms the prologue. Like a *Reyen* or the introductory verses to *Catharina von Georgien* spoken by the allegorical figure of Eternity, this scene is external to the action and communicates the authorial understanding of the drama. We therefore cannot doubt Zion's claim that the beautiful appearance of Mariamne is a reflection of her true self: 'Der Schönheit Konterfey/ der Spiegel reiner Sitten' (I. 71).

It is this association that Salome attacks and inverts. She replaces it rhetorically with the commonplace that beauty is arrogant, and she manipulates masculine insecurity with the intimation that beautiful women deliberately enslave and humiliate those who admire them:

> Was ist ein schönes Weib?
> Ein Teuffel/ nicht ein Mensch/ so bald ihr zarter Leib/
> Durch Hochmuth auffgebläht/ sich in ein Zucht-Haus wandelt/
> Das mit der Majestät als einem Sclaven handelt.

> (I. 89–92)

This is addressed to Antipater, not Herodes, but the king's familiarity with Salome's alternative metaphorical associations emerges in a later conversation with Mariamne. Shaken by her refusal to submit to him sexually, Herodes questions the meaning of her beauty: 'Sind solche Furien in dem so schönen Leib?' (IV. 193), and in the scene that follows Salome is quick to press home her advantage, developing the threat of her initial argument:

> So gehts! Die Schönheit pralt nicht nur mit stoltzen Sinnen/
> Sie darff auch endlich wol Gifft/ Mord und Todschlag spinnen!

> (IV. 267–8)

Salome thus switches the attributes of beauty and virtue into a negative opposition. Her approach to Mariamne's other

particular quality, the radiance or light that is associated with
her, is similar. For Herodes, his wife is 'unsre Sonn" (II. 157),
for her waiting-maids 'sie/ die den Sternen selbst an
Klarheit gehet vor' (II. 125). As the first character in the play
to speak, Salome's method is to twist these ideas of life-
giving warmth and clarity, characterizing Mariamne's radiance as 'Zauber-Licht' (I. 86), and the queen herself as an
'Unglücks-Stern' (I. 97). Mariamne is no longer the sun, but
a destructive and portentous comet (I. 99), an image taken
up by Antipater in Act IV to defame Mariamne by contrast
with the king's former mistress, his mother Dosis:

Was ist der Juden Printz? Nichts als ein blosser Schatten!
Weil die Cometen sich in Salems Schloß begatten/
Und Dosis meine Sonn' (ach leider!) ist verjagt          (IV. 295–7)

Salome's reversals create a tension between on-stage and off-
stage cognition of meaning. On stage, and (we must assume)
censoriously observed by the audience, she mixes and reverses the interpretation of established signals, juggling
with ideas of true and false light. She thereby perverts the
perceptions of other characters, and creates a kind of cognitive chaos.

Mariamne's first words point up a contrast between the comfort of light and the sorrows of darkness, as she awakes with
the opening of Act II from a dream:

DEm Himmel sey gedanckt/ daß Licht und Tag erwacht/
Daß die betrübte Zeit der schatten-braunen Nacht/
Das schwartze Sorgen-Meer/ weil Titan scheint/ verflossen!   (II. 1–3)

Her words purport to describe the fading moonlight as day
approaches, but the association of the moon goddess with
purity and chastity means that they also prefigure her own
impending loss of reputation:

Uns hat ein grimmer Traum und schreckliches Gesicht
Den süssen Schlaf verkürtzt: Dianens Silber-Licht
Begonte nach und nach den Spiegel zu verliehren       (II. 25–7)

Mariamne's maid dismisses the dream with a reassurance that
the light of her royal marriage is the true light, that of the
dream, false:

So lasse sie demnach/ Printzeß/ die Sorgen fahren!
Es müsse sich mit ihr die Freuden-Sonne paaren/
So in verwichner Nacht ein fälschlicher Comet
Mit Nebel überdeckt.                              (II. 119–22)

Yet the reassuring image fails to take into account Salome's metaphorical machinations. The 'Freuden-Sonne', Herodes, demonstrates his loss of the cognitive ability to distinguish between malevolent and benevolent light when he accuses Mariamne's parents of not being what they seem:

Wer hätte wol vermeint/ daß solche Mörder-Tücke/
Solch gifftig Berg-Werck solt' in euren Hertzen seyn/
Die zwar von aussen stets beliebten Sonnen-Schein/
Inwendig aber nur Cometen angezündet?            (III. 56–9)

The queen's appeal on their behalf is to the clarity of her husband's mercy:

besänfft'ge dein Gesicht/
Und gib vor Nebel uns ein Demant-helles Licht!   (III. 209–10)

This has, however, been so dimmed and confused by the cunning of Salome that Herod can no longer respond, or even recognize that the opposition of *Sein* and *Schein* he has identified is inverted, creating guilt where there is in fact innocence. Only light of the infernal kind that consumed Chach Abas still burns in Herodes, as his captain indicates at the end of this scene:

Laßt ab! wir müssen eilen!
Sonst blitzt der Fürst auff uns mit schwefellichten Keilen.

(III. 239–40)

The king now irradiates the destructive rays of the tyrant. This is spelt out after a musical interlude at the beginning of Act IV. Following the traditions of Jesuit theatre, Hallmann uses music (in this case a descant lullaby accompanied by strings and crumhorn (storto), a double-reed windcap instrument) to herald a supernatural scene, isolating it from the remainder of the action.[14] When the ghost

---

[14] On similar uses of music in opera, see Richard Taubald, 'Die Oper als Schule der Tugend und des Lebens im Zeitalter des Barock: Die enkulturierende Wirkung einer Kunstpflege' (unpublished doctoral thesis, University of Erlangen-Nuremberg 1972), 4.

of King David appears, it defines the slippage between appearance and reality that has taken place in Herodes, and the perversion of true light this has led to:

> Ruht hier der außerlesne Fürst?
> Der Sanfftmuth Conterfey/ der so gerechte Richter/
> Den stets nach reiner Tugend dürst?
> Bricht Erde! Blitzt und kracht ihr güldnen Himmels-Lichter!
> . . . . . . . . . . . .
> Wilstu/ Tyranne/ denn die Silber-klare Lufft
> Durch unversättlichs Tödten
> Erfüllen mit Cometen?
>
> (IV. 31 ff.)

Mariamne, too, objects in terms of degenerate radiance to the change Herodes' behaviour has wrought in their marriage:

> Das Eh-Bett wird erhöht
> Durch keusche Liebes-Glut/ nicht Blut-bemahlte Kertzen!    (IV. 186–7)

The traditional image of the king as a glorious and nurturing sun is inverted.

Light and darkness are ever more persistent themes as Mariamne's death approaches. Herodes is now convinced that her radiance is in fact destructive, and perceives it as equivalent to darkness at his court:

> Jedoch der Glantz erbleicht/ wenn Irrlicht und Comet
> Im Fürstlichen Pallast mit gifft'gem Schimmer steht/
> Und mit Pech-schwartzem Dampff trotzt die erlauchte Sonne.
>
> (V. 5–7)

An ironic idea of 'bringing to light' motivates the trial of Mariamne. Salome's accomplice, Antipater, suggests it when advocating the torture of Mariamne's servants: 'So ists: Ein Laster wird durchs andre klar gemacht' (IV. 333), and it is developed by Hillel when the Rabbis are gathered to judge her:

> Nichts wird so klein gesponnen/
> Es bricht doch endlich auß und kommt ans Licht der Sonnen.
>
> (V. 95–6)

The sexual dominance implied in the idea of 'uncovering' (which is also a feature of colonialist discourse)[15] reassures Herodes that what he perceives as his loss of conjugal power can yet be made good. The irony is that the perverted perception Salome has engendered at the court forces the true light in Mariamne towards the 'schwartze Traur-Gerüst' (V. 501) and the 'beschwärtzte Bahr' (V. 553): the darkness of the grave. But in a paradox that echoes the life in death and freedom in captivity of Gryphius's martyred Catharina or Haugwitz's Maria, Mariamne's radiance re-emerges in death, fulfilling the prediction of the Jewish priest who takes her to her execution:

> Bleibt Kron' und Infel gleich auff dieser wüsten Welt/
> So wird doch ihre Seel' in dem gestirnten Zelt
> Weit heller als die Sonn'/ und Mond'/ und Sternen gläntzen.
>
> (V. 477–9)

Even Herodes is able to recognize the (past) reality of Mariamne's light after her death: 'Wer hat mein Licht verlescht?' (V. 726). He is left in the dark chaos of 'falscher Schein' (V. 806) that misleads the tyrant. The connection between corrupt kingship and the inability to perceive true light is developed in a final *Reyen*, in which the allegorical figure of Tyranny explains:

> Wen das Glücke stets bescheint/
> Dem ist's seltzam/ wenn er weint/
> Und vor Sonnen sieht Cometen.   (V. 886–8)

The effect Hallmann achieves with the metaphorical polarity of Mariamne and Herodes—true and false radiance, and light and darkness—is summed up within the play by Alexandra, in the only words of comfort she can offer her daughter:

> Je schwärtzer ist die Nacht/
> Je schöner sihet man in den saffirnen Zimmern
> Das Diamantne Heer der güldnen Sternen schimmern.   (IV. 518–20)

---

[15] Patricia Parker has noted that the idea of 'bringing to light' characterizes the male European approach to the feminine or oriental Other in the early modern period. See Parker, 'Fantasies of "Race" and "Gender": Africa, Othello and Bringing to Light', in Hendricks and Parker, *Women, 'Race', and Writing*, 84–100.

Mariamne's virtue thus shines the more brightly because it is set against the darkness of tyranny.

The sign-system of light and dark is an effective one; but it slips easily over into xenophobic ideas of black and white. In a reconstruction of Lohenstein's novel, *Arminius*, Thomas Borgstedt has recently provided a compelling reading of the Dido episode. Borgstedt suggests that the lovers' respective skin colours in this episode, and the dispute that occurs over the relative merits of black and white constitute 'ein erstes Leitmotiv der Erzählung'.[16] Lohenstein here associates blackness with lust but not with beauty, and with the oriental world, connoting cruelty, barbarity, and superstition.[17] Similar ideas of blackness and the oriental develop out of ideas of light and darkness in *Mariamne*. The play's setting is exotic; Hallmann's dramatis personae include two eunuchs, two African archers, and two black page boys as visible adjuncts of the Near Eastern court. Mariamne herself, however, is emphatically white; we hear of her 'Glieder Schnee' (II. 37), 'Alabast der Glieder' (I. 107), 'Glieder Helffenbein' (II. 205), and 'Schwanen-weisse Brust' (I. 413). For Herodes she is 'weisser . . . als Schnee und Elephanten Zähne' (II. 191), but her whiteness is more than a commonplace of female beauty. It connotes her chastity, like the moon in Act II. Her eunuchs are tortured to ascertain her sexual purity or, metaphorically speaking, her whiteness:

> Ob auch die Königin durch schnöde Liebes-Thaten
> Den Alabaster Leib befleckt mit Tyridaten            (IV. 555–6)

After her death, when the purity of her reputation has reasserted itself, Mariamne appears to Herodes in a snow-white dress (V. 738) to fulfil the metaphorical prediction made in Act II: 'Die Farbe bleibet stets dem Kreiden-weissen Schwane' (II. 148).[18]

---

[16] Thomas Borgstedt, *Reichsidee und Liebesethik: Eine Rekonstruktion des Lohensteinschen Arminiusromans* (Tübingen 1992), 223.

[17] Compare ibid. 224–6.

[18] The metaphor is clearly an established one, since a variation of it, in the form of a reversal, is used by Aaron the Moor in Shakespeare's *Titus Andronicus* (1594) to describe indelible blackness: 'For all the water in the ocean | Can never turn the swan's black legs to white | Although she lave them hourly in the flood' (IV. ii. 101–3). The implication differs from that of the 'washing the Moor' emblem because Aaron perceives black colour as a positive, not a negative, attribute.

Associations of blackness specifically related to devilish-ness determine Herodes' position in the binary scheme of colour imagery. Mount Zion tells us by way of introduction that the king is inspired by 'der Höllen Mohr' (I. 61), whose empire, according to the *Reyen*'s prophecy, is also his destiny (IV. 612). Herodes' words of reassurance to his wife are an ironic, because for him unconscious, falsehood:

Hier ist kein Zaubrer ja/ kein schwartzer Teuffel nicht/
Der unsre Zythere/ die Mariamn' anficht.                    (IV. 153–4)

Salome characteristically inverts the 'correct' metaphorical system when she connects Mariamne and blackness, using the image of Cleopatra:

Wenn nicht Antonius die Mohrin so geküsset/
Hätt' er nicht in dem Dolch'/ sie in dem Molch gebüsset.

(IV. 271–2)

In Mariamne's defence of her parents, who stand accused of treason, it emerges that the analogy of blackness in this drama extends to the oriental or non-Christian. She at-tempts to placate Herodes:

Wer ists/ auff den du tobst? Ein Frauen-Bild und Priester!
Kein rauher Araber/ kein scheußlicher Philister/
Kein toller Götzen-Knecht/ kein schwartzer Mauritan.

(III. 211–13)

The implications of her speech are various, but can fairly be summarized: as a woman Alexandra is beneath anger, Hyrcanus as a man of God above it; both are Jews and nationals (Mariamne is attempting to play down the family rivalry between the Edomites and the Maccabaeans); both are white and worship the one God. They are therefore to be viewed positively in opposition to the idea of the foreign, black 'unbeliever' Mariamne rhetorically conjures.

Within the play, the Maccabaeans at least are aligned with positive ideas of whiteness and godliness. After the deaths of Alexandra, Hyrcanus, and Mariamne, however, the *Reyen* at the end of Act V causes our perspective on the Jewish world to shift. As non-Christians, the Jews are transferred to the side of the unbeliever, and Palestine is threatened by the allegorical figure of 'Unglauben':

> Ich lege dir den ersten Grabe-Stein/
> Mein Eiffer wird auff dich das erste Richt-Beil schärffen/
> Wenn du den Tempel wirst entweihn/
> Und in verblendtem Wahn deß Höchsten Sohn verwerffen.
>
> (V. 897–900)

Mariamne is pre-Christian, but the historical perspective is deliberately anachronistic. Herodes' Jewish court sends Mariamne to the grave, and with her—as the drama's metaphorical system implies—the white light of truth that is potentially Christian. Her pseudo-martyrdom is an *imitatio Christi* that prefigures rather than emulates; her truth is denied as Christ's will be, and the Jews who perpetrate the denial because they perceive incorrectly are (and, we infer, will be) left in infernal darkness.[19]

In associative moves from Roman paganism to the epitome of the non-Christian, the Saracen, Hallmann classifies Palestine (addressed directly here) as Orient:

> Dich wird des Titus Grimm vertilgen/
> Drauff Adrian durch Götzen-Dienst verführ'n;
> Heraclius beym Omar dich verliehr'n/
> Bis Bullion dich krönt mit Wolfahrts-Lilgen:
> Doch Saladin bricht diese Blum' entzwey
> Durch Gwidons Schuld/ Raimunds Verrätherey.
> Dann wirstu stehn in Sarazen'schen Banden    (V. 923–9)

At this point the drama refers outside itself, and a familiar opposition of stage and auditorium is evident:

> Allein es wird sich ändern dieses Spiel;
> Dein Heiland ist in Oesterreich vorhanden/
> Dein Salomon/ dem GOtt und Welt ist hold/
> Der Christen Schutz/ der Grosse LEOPOLD!    (V. 931–4)

Like Lohenstein in *Ibrahim Sultan*, Hallmann finally confirms that there is a polarity between on-stage and off-stage

---

[19] This contradicts Emrich's thesis: 'Die große geschichtsphilosophische "Verhängnis"-Konzeption Lohensteins taucht bei Hallmann nirgends auf'. See W. Emrich, *Deutsche Literatur der Barockzeit* (Königstein/Ts. 1981), 203.

world, Orient and Christendom, in such a way as to flatter and reassure the latter.

The sign-system of dark and light, blackness and whiteness that dominates in *Mariamne* is present as dramatic shorthand in Hallmann's less well-known plays. The familiar image of 'washing the moor' is applied in *Urania* (1666) to evoke useless endeavour.[20] In *Adelheide* (1684), 'den Mohren überweissen' describes the attempt to make something unpleasant appear less so.[21] Blackness gains metaphysical significance as the garb of devilishness in *Urania*, when the chaste shepherdess of the title opposes black and white to evoke the idea of the wolf in sheep's clothing: 'der Höllen=Mohr wil offt in Engel sich verkleiden' (III. 339), while in a fit of madness King Seleucus of *Antiochus und Stratonica* (1669) insults a group of black dancers with a similar interpretation of colour:[22]

> Was wolt ihr schwartze Raben/
> Ihr garst'gen Teuffel doch in unserm Himmel haben?
> Geh MINOS! PLUTO geh! geht in den HöllenPful!        (III. 183–5)

For Hallmann, blackness and sensuality are connected ideas; the 'wise man' Hierander in *Urania* offers his sententious opinion: 'der Dieb laufft nach dem Schatz/ der Mohr nach einer Frau' (II. 323), and the allegorical (and presumably white) figure of *himmlische Liebe* in *Sophia* (1671) explains: 'Der Himmel liebt nicht schwartzen Geilheits=Dunst'.[23] Black lust works in predictable opposition to the metaphorical 'Keuschheits=Lilge' which links whiteness and chastity in this drama and in *Liberata*.[24]

---

[20] Hallmann, *Siegprangende Tugend Oder Getrewe URANIA*, III. 434. In *Werke*, vol. 3/1 (Berlin 1987). Further references are given in the text.

[21] Hallmann, *Die Schaubühne des Glückes Oder Die Unüberwindliche ADELHEIDE* (pub. 1684), I. 116. In *Werke*, vol. 3/2. Further references are given in the text.

[22] Hallmann, *Die Denckwürdige Vater=Liebe Oder Der vor Liebe sterbende ANTIOCHUS Und Die vom Tode errettende STRATONICA*, in *Werke*, vol. 3/1. Further references are given in the text.

[23] Hallmann, *Sophia*, III. 410. In *Werke*, vol. 2 (Berlin 1980).

[24] Hallmann, *Liberata*, I. 364–5. In ibid. Further references are given in the text. Compare *Sophia* IV. 190 and *Mariamne* V. 607.

Blackness and whiteness most obviously dominate the metaphorical system of the late play *Liberata* (1699).[25] It is worth noting that *Liberata* was written in the same year the Treaty of Karlowitz was signed, which sealed the retreat of the Turkish threat from Europe; religious politics are evident in the drama. Without mentioning Karlowitz, yet almost certainly in the context of the Treaty, Hallmann appends a dramatized epilogue or 'Application' in which he wishes his Emperor continued success in the territorial and religious battle:

Die allerunterthänigste APPLICATION dieses Schau=Spiels/ als worinnen Unsrem Aller=Genädigsten Kayser LEOPOLDO von der Triumphirenden Kirche die GLORIEUSE Bekehrung aller Heyden zum Christenthum durch Seinen Sieg=prangenden Scepter verwüntschet [= gewünscht] wird. (p. 239)

He is forced to admit that the 'Bekehrung aller Heyden' is a future ideal rather than a current state of affairs, but continues undeterred to paint a picture of mass conversion which, in its sensationalist references to arbitrarily chosen deities, suggests a debt to the popular and inaccurate travel reports for information on the subject of non-Christian religions:

Was würde doch das Aller=Durchlauchtigste Ertz=Hauß von Oesterreich bey allen vier Theilen der Welt in eine grössere ADMIRATION bringen/ als wann Dessen unüberwindlichen Scepter nicht nur die allbereit ziemlich gedemüttigte Saracenen/ sondern auch die weit=entlegneste heidnische NATIONES, welche vor den wahren Drey=einigen GOTT den Teuffelischen AMIDA, FOTOCO und VITZLIPUTZLI anbeten/ in reiner Andacht Fuß=fällig verehren müsten? (pp. 239–40)

The dramatic action of *Liberata* takes place in Portugal, where the ruler, Alphonsus, is an opponent of Christianity, but finally converts after his daughter, Liberata, has died for her Christian faith. The play's central concern is with the

---

[25] Later plays, of which only the programmes are still available, are *Alexander Magnus* (1700), *Laodice* (1700), *Ariaspes* (1700), *Lionato* (1704), *Paulina* (1704), and *Salomon* (1704). *B* and *C* versions of *Catharina*, from the later period of Hallmann's creative life, are also testified to in programmes, as well as *B* versions of *Heraclius* and *Sophia*; these versions are not dated.

religious opposition of Christians and the non-Christian world. Colour is an essential element in its semiotic system, especially in Hallmann's portrayal of the Princess Liberata: her whiteness indicates her purity and martyr status, and is described in conjunction with the news of her impending execution:

> Ach! Sol der Leibes=Bau der schönsten Liberaten/
> Vor dehm selbst Alabast/ Schnee/ Schwan/ und Kreid' erbleicht/
> .    .    .    .    .    .    .    .    .    .    .    .    .    .    .
> Durch unerschöpffte Pein der grimmen Glut verschwinden?
>
> (IV. 112 ff.)

The first confrontation between white and black occurs with the arrival of three applicants for the hand of the princess: Ferdinand of Sicily, Arimantes of Egypt, and the Persian ambassador Tiridates. While she is politely firm in her refusal of (white) Ferdinand, Liberata is less tolerant of her two black suitors, whose appearance provokes from her the exclamation: 'Der Mohr und Pers' erscheint! O unbeliebtes Zeichen!' (I. 375). Her reasoning is that while an exclusive devotion to God forbids her marriage to Ferdinand (I. 360), an alliance with either of her dark-skinned suitors would be an offence against Nature. In a dialogue with Arimantes she argues that black can never be equally allied to white:

> ARIMANTES. Warumb wil Sie mit mir kein Ehlich Bündnüs schlüßen?
> LIBERATA. Er frage die Natur/ Vernunfft/ und das Gewissen.
> ARIMANTES. Es ist ja Arimant ein Mensch wie Liberat.
> LIBERATA. Doch daß die Menschheit hier nicht gleiche Staffeln hat.
> ARIMANTES. So sol ich Ewig mich in diesen Flammen quälen!
> LIBERATA. Ein Rabe kan sich nicht mit einem Schwan vermählen.
>
> (I. 383–8)

This echoes Brabantio's objection that Desdemona's choice of husband is 'against all rules of nature'.[26]

Black magic provides another titillating ingredient for Hallmann's drama. Gryphius had set a precedent for this in *Cardenio und Celinde* (pub. 1657), a play Hallmann declares to be exemplary.[27] Episodes involving magicians and

---

[26] *Othello*, I. iii. 101.     [27] In the prologue to *Urania*, p. 11.

magic crop up in *Urania* and in *Adonis und Rosibella*, as well as in *Liberata*;[28] such scenes clearly had audience appeal. Arimantes' recourse to a magician after his rejection by Liberata affirms the association of blackness with devilishness. Hallmann has him identify his colour as a visible sign of allegiance to Satan in the fight against white in all its metaphorical senses:[29]

> Ist Arimant ein Rab' und Liberat' ein Schwan?
> .    .    .    .    .    .    .    .    .    .    .    .
> Ich will ein Rabe seyn und einen solchen Raben/
> Der alle Schwanen trotzt/ zu meinem Beystand haben.    (II. 101 ff.)

The Persian prince, Tiridates, also confirms by his actions the connection between dark skin and evil character. When he has corrupted Alphonsus's courtier, Octavius, and persuaded him to assist in the abduction of Liberata, the two of them appear 'alß verlarvte Mohren' (II. x) to perform the act. The racist analogy here is spelt out by their Portuguese captors when the pair are brought to account:

> RAMIRO. Die Larven schicken sich sehr wol zu diesem Laster/
>    Weil schwartzes Meineyds=Gifft hier ist das schönste Pflaster!
> PALAMEDES. So ists; Ein schwartzes Hertz hegt auch ein schwartz Gesicht/
>    Drumb haben billich Sie der Mohren Schwärtz erticht!
>
> (II. 295–8)

In response to Tiridates' claim to diplomatic immunity, Alphonsus indicates that blackness qualifies the normal rights of the individual; by dint of his colour and his actions the Persian is 'Ein Mohr/ und kein Legat!' (II. 345).

---

[28] Ibid. III. 9 ff.; *Die Sinnreiche Liebe, Oder Der Glückseelige ADONIS und Die Vergnügte ROSIBELLA* (1671), in *Werke*, vol. 3/1, II. 54 ff.; and *Liberata*, II. 101 ff. Parts of this episode are borrowed almost word-for-word from the earlier play, *Urania*, including the list of accessories required by the magician in order to perform the necessary spells.

[29] It would be possible to argue here, as Cowhig does with reference to *Othello* (Cowhig 'Blacks in English Renaissance Drama', 4), that Arimantes' reaction is a retaliation against racial prejudice. My feeling is that Hallmann's approach is considerably less sophisticated than Shakespeare's in this respect, and that it would be unsuitable to attribute any kind of intended character defect, including racial prejudice, to his martyr *Liberata*. It seems far more likely that her view on the matter is considered the correct one by the dramatist.

The religious conflict, too, is structured by images of black and white. Elida Maria Szarota has put forward the theory that the play is constructed around the symbol of the cross, an idea she supports with reference to four motifs in the action (the persecution of Christians by Alphonsus; his incestuous love for Liberata; the efforts of the suitors to obtain her; the final victory of Christianity through her martyrdom and Alphonsus's conversion), and to the symbolism based on the number four in the deaths of Liberata and her three suitors.[30] One could add that there is a symmetrical opposition in the four deaths which make up Szarota's cross: Liberata and Ferdinand die nobly as white Christian martyrs, Arimantes and Tiridates perish shamefully as black unbelievers (the former commits suicide when his love-charm fails to take effect). The religious polarity is structurally supported in this symbolic opposition of colour.

Hallmann's exploitation of the meanings of colour leads him to a striking reversal: King Alphonsus is finally shocked out of his incestuous love for Liberata by perceiving her as black. The metaphorical importance of Liberata's physical whiteness has already been remarked, and she emphasizes the equation of blackness with 'Heidenthum' when revealing her Christian beliefs to her father:

> Kurtz: Liberatens Seele
> Hat gänzlich sich befreyt von der pech=schwartzen Höle [*sic*]
> Deß schnöden Heidenthums
>
> (III. 189–91)

Alphonsus's response when he sees Liberata as black encompasses the same ideas of devilishness, infernal magic, and sheer ugliness as are linked with blackness throughout the play:

> Steckt eine Zauberin/
> Ein brauner Mohren=Kopff in Liberatens Kleide?
> Wie? Hat in schwartzes Pech der Wangen zarte Kreide/
> In einen Raben sich der Stirnen Schwan verkehrt?
> Wird eine Furie vor Engel Unß gewehrt?
> Ist diese Göttin dann zu einem Teuffel worden?    (III. 498–503)

---

[30] Elida Maria Szarota, *Geschichte, Politik und Gesellschaft im Drama des 17. Jahrhunderts* (Berne 1976), 100–1.

The divine preservation of Liberata's white purity or chastity by means of apparent blackness is a doubly paradoxical conceit. Instead of connoting lust, black here averts it, and in an interesting turn of events the non-Christian Alphonsus perceives his Christian daughter in the same repulsive light as she previously viewed the non-Christians Arimantes and Tiridates. There is no criticism of Liberata in this; black and white and their meanings have simply been inverted, as an indication that Alphonsus is plagued by false, non-Christian perception. Like Herodes, the tyrannical King of Portugal can no longer distinguish between appearance and reality, true and false colour. Correct perception in this play depends on the discernment of guilt or innocence; guilt, predictably, being black, and innocence white. The Persian and the Egyptian are guilty of non-Christian belief and of wicked behaviour that is inseparable from orientality or blackness (there is no hint of a miscarriage of justice when Alphonsus executes Tiridates on the grounds that he is 'Ein Mohr/ und kein Legat'). Liberata is, of course, guiltless, and in the terms of the drama her innocence ought to be visible in the whiteness of her body. She explains correct perception:

> Die Lilgen im Gesicht/
> Die Rosen auff dem Mund sind/ grosser König/ nicht
> In braunen Kohl verkehrt/ die Alabaster=Wangen
> Sind nicht mit dunckler Nacht noch schwartzem Pech umfangen/
> Deß Halses Helffenbein/ der Wangen weisser Schwan
> Hegt keinen Raben nicht!
>
> (III. 513–18)

The Christian point of view as a measure of true cognition, familiar from the disputations in *Catharina von Georgien*, is applied to a debate between Liberata, Alphonsus, Ramiro and, Rodrigo (IV. x). The latter three wrongly associate black magic and devilishness with Christianity; Liberata laments the 'Einfalt sonder Grund' (IV. 297) that is at the root of their imperfect perception, and indicates the remedy: 'Daß man den wahren GOTT in diser Welt sol ehren' (IV. 300).

Even without the correcting voice of Liberata, Hallmann's audience ought by this point to be familiar enough with the pattern of metaphorical oppositions to recognize

that Christianity must be understood in antithesis to all
things black. The paradox of Liberata's blackness remains
one of false perception; Hallmann never makes the suggestion made by the Elizabethan playwrights and by Haugwitz
in *Soliman*, that dark skin colour and noble character might
really go hand-in-hand.

In the metaphorical systems of these plays certain par-
allelisms between ideas of woman and of blackness and
orientality emerge. Hallmann's dramas were written during
a period when a continuing fascination with travel reports
coexisted in European minds with the fear and abhorrence
of anything outside European Christendom that had grown
out of the Crusades and Ottoman wars. *Theodoricus* (1666),
*Urania, Mariamne, Antiochus und Stratonica, Sophia, Heraclius*
(pub. 1684), *Adelheide, Catharina* (pub. 1684), and *Adonis und
Rosibella* were all composed after the new outbreak of hos-
tilities with the Ottomans in 1663–4, during the tense decades
of the Turkish advance before their final defeat at Vienna
in 1683. For all that, Hallmann reveals a certain fascination
with the exotic non-Christian milieu. At the Syrian court of
Seleucus in *Antiochus und Stratonica*, attendant Moors provide
colourful stage extras. The voyeurism of a curious audience
is further indulged in the 'Reyen der Panquetirenden Syrier'
that provides a finale (V. 557 ff.): the banquet is doubtless
of lavish proportions, and the participants clothed in rich
oriental garb. The luxurious extravagance which the Orient
epitomizes is evoked by Hierophilo, the shepherd who
introduces *Adonis und Rosibella*:

> Es prange wie da wil Molucc' und Martrapan;
> Die Ost-See schmücke sich mit Perlen und Korallen/
> Der Fürst in Potosi mit tausend Silber-Ballen;
>    .    .    .    .    .    .    .    .    .
> Es mag der grosse Chach in lauter Spiegel-Zimmern/
> Behenckt mit dichtem Gold/ alß eine Sonne schimmern/
> Und der Chineser Printz erheben sein Quinsay!          (I. 6 ff.)

This, however, is not an expression of admiration. The
comparison with Elysian simplicity drawn by an idealized
shepherd (Hierophilo = lover of things holy) reveals that
Hallmann's Orient is here a *vanitas* metaphor:

Doch kan Elysien uns mehr Vergnügung reichen/
Und jener Irr=Licht muß vor unsrem Glanz erbleichen.    (I. 15–16)

There is an obvious parallel with the *Reyen* of shepherds
and shepherdesses that concludes Act IV of Lohenstein's
*Cleopatra* (1661; in the 1680 version the chorus is composed
of gardeners), who praise the pastoral life by contrast with
the Egyptian court:[31]

> Wie selig sind/ di den Schmaragd der Auen/
> Für der Paläste Gold erwehln!

Extravagant *Schein* is set against simple virtuous *Sein*. The
sensual gratification audiences are offered in portrayals of
Eastern opulence is paired with the hint of corruption or danger concealed beneath the colourful exterior.

Interestingly, there are elements in the pastoral plays
*Urania* and *Adonis und Rosibella* that show Hallmann metaphorically associating danger with the idea of woman as well
as with that of the oriental. The two dramas are linked by a
number of structural motifs: in both, a nymph is in love with
and pursues a shepherd; in both, a lover enrols forbidden
aid to achieve the erotic object; both plays use comic elements such as the fool and dialect, and are poised on the
brink of tragedy before the plot is happily resolved. Hallmann
borrows passages from the earlier of the plays (*Urania*),
including an entire *Reyen*, for inclusion in the later one.

Each of the dramas demonstrates a ruling passion, the
negative force of which almost brings the action to a tragic
end. In *Urania*, the passion is lust, embodied by Infortunio
and Amande; in *Adonis und Rosibella* it is anger, exhibited by
Rosibella's father Silvander. In each case the *Reyen* following
the second act takes the form of a disputation regarding the
dominant passion in question. The chorus of shepherds in
*Urania* marks lust as a passion particularly of the female:[32]

---

[31] Daniel Casper von Lohenstein, *Cleopatra*, ed. Ilse-Marie Barth (Stuttgart 1965),
IV. 511–12.

[32] These *Reyen* appear again as an interlude in the second act of *Adonis und Rosibella*.
Here, however, Hallmann is obliged to tone down the message, since Rosibella is
associated with Leopold's new wife Claudia and may therefore on no account be
taken to task for her pursuit of Adonis. Cupid is therefore later proved wrong in
his judgement on the nymphs (cf. III. iv).

Seht nur der Sachen Ursprung an:
Eh' VENUS trat auff TELLUS Bahn/
Hat zur Geburthsstat sie erwehl't
Der Wellen Saltz/ dem Durst vermähl't.
„Weil nun die Liebe Saltz und Durst stets mit sich führet/
„Wird in den Töchtern auch stets Saltz und Durst gespühret.

(II. 479–84)

In the text, the *gnomische Häkchen* are sufficient indication of the truth and wisdom of the shepherds' claim. In
the parallel *Reyen* from *Adonis und Rosibella*, Anger appears,
accompanied by black attendants: 'sechs Mohren/ so blutige
Säbeln/ Dolche/ gespannte Bogen/ auffgestrichene Pistolen/
Feuer speiende Fackeln/ und derogleichen tyrannische
Werckzeuge führen' (p. 361). Thus in one play the dangerous
passion is gendered, in the other, coloured. It is therefore
unsurprising that metaphors relating to women and blacks
are also intertwined. The same chorus of shepherds in
*Urania* applies the traditional emblematic idea of the Moor
to female sexuality, intimating that it is useless for women
to try to deny on the grounds of cold bodily humours that
they are ruled by lust:

Da doch eur Frost nur stets nach Flammen rennet;
Der Mohr bleibt schwartz/ ob man ihn wäsch't      (II. 433–4)

Not only the lustfulness attributed to the Moor, but sexual
perversity and bestiality, associated in *Othello* with blackness,
are understood in this *Reyen* as characteristics of woman:

Weil AGRIPPIN wil mit dem NERO baden/
SEMIRAMIS ihr Leib=Pferd schmückt/
PASIPHÄEN ein Stier erquick't.      (II. 436–8)

There is, however, a clear hierarchical disparity between the
idea of woman and the idea of the oriental or black in these
dramas. While Hallmann is never tempted by the concept of
the 'noble Moor', he readily subscribes to the equally paradoxical idea of the *femme forte*. Liberata is one, as is made obvious when she routs Arimantes in the persona of Judith.[33] Both

---

[33] *Liberata*, III. 486 ff. Judith is a familiar example of the *femme forte* and appears
for example on the frontispiece of Lescalopier's *Les Predications* (1645). See Ian
Maclean, *Woman Triumphant: Feminism in French Literature 1610–1652* (Oxford
1977), plate 16.

in this episode and in her martyr's death she, like Gryphius's
Catharina, demonstrates the power of Christianity even in
the weak frame of woman. By overpowering black Arimantes
she shows that Christianity lends a masculinizing force that
enables the Christian woman to defeat the devilish oriental
male. Having routed him with his own sword, Liberata exults:

> Jo Triumff! Triumff! Stimmt Freuden=Lieder an/
> Weil GOTT an seiner Magd solch Wunder hat gethan!
> Es ist der Feind besigt/ sein toller Trotz verletztet    (III. 489–91)

Hallmann is using the stage as an emblematic *pictura*, com-
prising plenty of familiar deictic details. Liberata has
become a kind of female St Michael, and the defeat of black
by white clearly signals the victory of God over the devil.

Liberata has no oriental counterpart like Catharina's
Chah Abas; the tyrant who causes her martyrdom is her father,
another Portuguese.[34] Unlike Haugwitz and Lohenstein, Hallmann chooses neither to create a great oriental villain, nor
to challenge traditional metaphorical associations with non-
Christian peoples. His dramatic ideas of black and white
follow established precedents, and are important in this discussion primarily as an indication of the extent to which
certain associations had taken root as commonplaces in
German literature by the end of the seventeenth century.
Liberata's triumph is all the more striking because she is a
woman, and it is the paradox of her strength allied with her
femaleness that impresses and shames Ferdinand into following her example, and Alphonsus into finally converting
his people to Christianity. Fortitude in woman, we understand,
is *proof* that a miracle has occurred.

## Warning Signs: Literary Witch-Burnings and Other Cautionary Tales

One of the false associations made by Alphonsus with
regard to his daughter, Liberata, is with the idea of the witch

---

[34] This interest in a religious opposition that is internal to the nation may reflect
Hallmann's conversion to Catholicism after 1684. *Liberata* is certainly more in the
style of the Jesuit dramas than Hallmann's earlier plays, such as *Mariamne* or the
pastoral pieces.

(*Liberata*, III. 498). The black character, Arimantes (whose blackness is associated with the side of the sinister, sexual, and female) is also shown dabbling in magic (II. 101 ff.). The association of women with witchcraft is closely linked to the association of women with the devil, and has an equally long tradition. Witch figures such as Circe and Calypso are passed down from Greek antiquity, and the story of Calypso in particular anticipates the connections between female sorcery and female sexuality which later find expression in depictions of the *femme fatale*.

The early Church in Europe regarded those who believed in witchcraft, not simply the 'witches' themselves, as criminals deluded by the devil. A change occurred in the thirteenth century, when most notably Thomas Aquinas put forward the view that demons really are able to injure human beings, and to impede sexual intercourse.[35] The first instances of an ecclesiastically driven persecution of witches appear to have taken place from the last third of the fifteenth century; the notorious *Malleus Malificarum*, written by two Dominicans, was first published in 1487.[36] The substitution of the feminine ending *-arum* for *-orum* in the title of this extreme misogynist text is not accidental: its authors suggest that women are the sex most prone to anti-Christian behaviour, using the doubtful etymological analogy *femina/fe-minus*. The numbers of witches accused, tortured, and executed accelerated from the second half of the sixteenth century, and reached a high point between 1560 and 1630.

Blackwell observes the importance of textual discourse in the witch trials, and emphasizes the role of the printing press in the rhetorical institutionalization of a set of ideas: 'gerade das ist der Kernpunkt, daß der Text (ob Bibel, Gelehrtenschrift über Weiber und Hexerei, selbstanerkanntes Bekenntnis oder veröffentlichte Urgicht) als Institutions-

---

[35] Aquinas, *Quaestiones quodlibetales* xi, 10; cited in Julio Carlo Baroja, 'Witchcraft and Catholic Theology', in Bengt Ankarloo and Gustav Henningsen (eds.), *Early Modern European Witchcraft: Centres and Peripheries* (Oxford 1993 [1990]), 19–43 (27).

[36] Jakob Sprenger and Heinrich Institutoris, *Der Hexenhammer*; new edn. trans. and ed. J. W. R. Schmidt (Munich 1993 [1982]). This work appeared in 29 editions between 1487 and 1669.

instrument gewaltsam benutzt wurde . . .'[37] The *Urgicht* or
confession itself was usually produced by torture of the victim until the statement given conformed to the authorities'
expectations. The document, which was often disseminated
at the subsequent execution, was strongly normative. The perversions it described were the inverted reflection of a norm,
and therefore provided an affirmation of a preconceived
notion of order as opposed to chaos. Indeed, an antithetical world-view informs the whole conception of witchcraft.
Accounts of sorcery, like the trial reports and *Urgichte*, have
standard elements. The celebration of the black mass, kiss-
ing the rump of Satan, the murder of children, and a general
association with death rather than life are typical examples.
Witchcraft is the epitome of inversion, an attack both on divine
order and on masculine *Vernunft*.[38] Clark has summarized the
linguistic context in which such accounts were intended to
make sense:

What was demanded was an act of recognition with three distinguishable
elements: first, a general awareness of the logical relation of opposition,
without which inversion could not be entertained; secondly, a familiarity
with the relevant linguistic and symbolic conventions under which a specific action might be seen as one of inversion, the most important of these
being the 'world upside-down'; and the grasping of just what positive rule
or order was implied by any individual act of ritual witchcraft.[39]

The idea of the witch is, therefore, another rhetorical category, and lends itself to the portrayal of women who invert
the hierarchical order, or turn the world upside-down.

[37] See Jeannine Blackwell, ' ". . . Die Zunge, der Geistliche und das Weib": Überlegungen zur strukturellen Bedeutung der Hexenbekenntnisse von 1500–1700',
in Sylvia Wallinger and Monika Jonas (eds.), *Der Widerspenstigen Zähmung: Studien
zur bezwungenen Weiblichkeit in der Literatur vom Mittelalter bis zur Gegenwart*
(Innsbruck 1986), 95–115 (99–100).
[38] See Ines Brenner and Gisela Morgenthal, 'Der Sabbat als Ort der
Verschwörung der Frauen gegen Ordnung und Vernunft', in Gabriele Becker
*et al.* (eds.), *Aus der Zeit der Verzweiflung: Zur Genese und Aktualität des Hexenbilds*
(Frankfurt a.M. 1977), 212–17.
[39] Stuart Clark, 'Inversion, Misrule and the Meaning of Witchcraft', in *Past and
Present* 87 (1980), 98–127 (104).

*The Witch Fortuna:* Cardenio und Celinde

In early modern representations, Fortuna is the goddess who can spin the globe and human affairs upside-down with a flick of her capricious wrist; she is traditionally depicted with a wheel, which she will turn to hurl her victims from top to bottom or bottom to top. In some illustrations the wheel is a ball like the earth, signalling that Fortuna has the power to spin the world upside-down, and turn order into chaos.[40] We need not, therefore, be surprised when we find her characterized in Andreas Gryphius's *Cardenio und Celinde Oder Unglücklich Verliebete* (*c.*1648/50)[41] as a witch.

Despite the apparent parity of the alliterating names in the title, Gryphius's drama provides an uneven portrayal of its two central characters. Critical responses to the work have highlighted this, but have also reflected modern gender prejudice by concentrating their interpretive attention on Celinde's sexual crime.[42] Othmar Müller, for example, decides: 'Im Unterschied zu Cardenio verkörpert Celinde den sinnlichen Trieb schlechthin. Obgleich Cardenio aus seiner Einsicht keine Konsequenzen zieht, bekennt er sich dennoch zu seinen Freveltaten, Celinde dagegen ist so verwirrt, daß sie überhaupt nicht mehr denken kann.'[43] Celinde, that daughter of Eve, is predictably (and reprehensibly) enslaved by her sensuality, although it does not occur to Müller to see this in the historical context of her gender. In a more recent work, Blake Lee Spahr adopts a similar approach, with even less sensitivity: for him, Celinde is a 'tart little whore', where Cardenio is merely 'volatile'.[44]

---

[40] See Michael Schilling, *Imagines Mundi: Metaphorische Darstellungen der Welt in der Emblematik* (Frankfurt a.M. 1979), and Gottfried Kirchner, *Fortuna in Dichtung und Emblematik des Barock* (Stuttgart 1970).

[41] Andreas Gryphius, *Cardenio und Celinde* (pub. 1657), ed. Hugh Powell, in *Gesamtausgabe der deutschsprachigen Werke*, vol. 5 (Tübingen 1965). Further references are given in the text.

[42] A notable exception is M. R. Sperberg-McQueen's outstanding article on this text: 'Deceitful Symmetry in Gryphius's *Cardenio und Celinde*: Or What Rosina Learned at the Theatre and Why She Went', in Lynne Tatlock (ed.), *The Graph of Sex and the German Text: Gendered Culture in Early Modern Germany* (Amsterdam 1994), 269–94.

[43] Othmar Müller, *Drama und Bühne in den Trauerspielen von Andreas Gryphius und Daniel Casper von Lohenstein* (St Gallen 1967), 120.

[44] Blake Lee Spahr, *Andreas Gryphius: A Modern Perspective* (Columbia, Oh. 1993), 70.

In fact both Cardenio and Celinde are shown to err in a
way that is linked to their sexuality. In the *Reyen* following
Act I, lust ('erhitzte Brunst'; I. 561) and revenge ('Rach=
Lust'; I. 565) are sent out by the devil; and, in the context
of the information we have received in the previous scenes,
these demonic passions must be seen in connection with
Cardenio rather than Celinde. By the time the chorus closes
the next act, however, we recognize that she, too, is in the
grip of 'geile Brunst' (II. 277), a passionate inflammation
that is infernal, as a reformed Celinde finally confirms:

> Ade verfälschte Lust! Ade nicht reine Flammen!
> Ihr Vorbild höllscher Glut!                    (V. 349–50)

Gryphius does suggest that Cardenio is, initially at least, as
much at fault as Celinde as regards their sexual liaison: he
even turns around the alarming metaphor of the siren
(later used by Lohenstein for Cleopatra) to make of Cardenio
an Odysseus, who might have resisted. Cardenio confesses
to Celinde:

> Strit lieblichste Syren ihr artiger Gesang
> Mit ihrem Harffen=Spiel/ mit ihrer Lauten Klang;
> Mir stund mit jenem frey die Ohren zu verstopffen   (V. 371–3)

The sin that is specifically Celinde's is not sensuality, but inconstancy. She is the inverted mirror-image of the female martyr whose admirable chastity is just one expression of her
exemplary *Beständigkeit*. We are introduced to Celinde as a
character affected by 'Wanckelmut' (I. 387; I. 488); from this
it is a short step for her into the arms of the sorceress Tyche,
whose name also means Fortuna. According to stoic teaching, Fortuna endangers life on earth, and stoic constancy
resists her. She is also a product of the antithetical imagination, and a perpetrator of inversion.

Celinde becomes involved with Tyche, the witch, as a result of her unrequited sexual passion for Cardenio. Instead
of practising the stoic continence Gryphius's Catharina led
us to expect of ideal Christian womanhood, she meddles
with fortune and the supernatural; this is clearly an offence
against divine order; the same one, interestingly, as is

perpetrated by Hallmann's black Arimantes in *Liberata*.[45]
Our initial glimpse of Celinde on stage ought to warn us of
her dangerous, feminine impulse to chaos: we first see her
tearing the strings from her harp in passion, and thereby
destroying the order of music, that is associated with the
harmony of the divine.[46] The repulsive perversions of the
sorcery she will soon embrace are listed for us when Tyche
explains her handiwork:

> Die Geister/ die die Welt die noth Geheimnüß lehren;
> Muß man mit reinem Blut erkiester Menschen ehren:
> Die forderten von dem ein ungeboren Kind/
> Vom dem die Mutter selbst.
> . . . . . . . . . .
> Man hat ein zartes Kind noch lebendig geschunden/
> Und auff das weiche Fell mit Blut die Schrifft gesetzt:
> Die den und jenen Geist bald zwinget bald ergetzt.
> Man hat deß Knaben Haupt umbdrehend abgerissen     (II. 189 ff.)

Standard ideas about witchcraft, such as the illicit move to
turn life into death and the destruction of the mother/
child relationship, are evident; Gryphius presents us with the
grotesque image of fortune as a perverted, disruptive, destructive witch. It cannot be coincidental that, of the drama's
antithetical title pairing, male and female, it is the female
element (Celinde) who is aligned with the side of sinister
disorder. This probably reflects not so much individual
misogyny as an established analogy in Gryphius's mind; the
'language of contrareity' prompts the dramatist's hand.

We have already established that in the dramatic system
of paradox and antithesis the idea of the inverted, demonized feminine may reinforce the idea of order or the ideal.
Gryphius's introduction to this piece suggests that its central antithesis is not between Cardenio and Celinde, but
between Celinde and Olympia. He explains:

Mein Vorsatz ist zweyerley Liebe: Eine keusche/ sitsame [*sic*] und doch
inbrünstige in Olympien: Eine rasende/ tolle und verzweifflende [*sic*] in
Celinden, abzubilden. (p. 100)

[45] Sperberg-McQueen notes pertinently that 'love-potions are the last resort of
those who have been disempowered by society'; in a white, male text these are black
and female characters. See Sperberg-McQueen, 'Deceitful Symmetry', 287.
[46] See Chapter 4.

Sperberg-McQueen has identified a certain dramatic sleight-of-hand here, and has suggested that Olympia and Celinde are 'really sisters under the skin: both demonstrate that women require male control'.[47] Nonetheless, as the type of the wife who is submissive to God and her husband (III. 87–94), Olympia provides a reassuring opposite pole to Celinde's chaotic promiscuity. She is a point of reference in the drama, a reminder of the ordered world of Christian marriage that Celinde, Tyche, and inconstancy disrupt.

That marriage is a means of conquering the world's chaos is the message of Gryphius's central *Reyen* in *Cardenio und Celinde*. Here time, man, the four seasons, and the four ages of man present us with an animated, on-stage emblem. The chorus has been seen as puzzling, with no obvious thematic correlation in the play;[48] in fact, even though Fortuna/ Tyche is not physically present in this *Reyen*, there is a link to be found in emblems between the goddess with her wheel and man's four ages.[49] Such a link—which was presumably, like Lohenstein's images, familiar both to Gryphius and to his emblematically aware audience—makes sense of a chorus that is both structurally and semiotically central to the play. The 'Mensch' (a man!) who features in the *Reyen* is seen rejecting a series of female partners (who are simultaneously the four seasons) in the insatiable hope that good fortune will bring him ever more attractive choices. But the way of the world, or fortune, is that human beings are destined for death, and 'der Mensch' finally finds himself faced with the grim death's head of the last season, Winter. This of course anticipates what is about to happen to Cardenio, when he follows the spectre of Olympia until she unmasks as a grinning skeleton: a *Frau Welt*, who is also related to the Fortuna figure. In this *Reyen* and in the action of *Cardenio und Celinde*, Gryphius demonstrates the threat inherent in the false promise of Fortuna, or libido, as opposed to the stabilizing order that marriage represents.

[47] Sperberg-McQueen, 'Deceitful Symmetry', 284.
[48] This *Reyen* has worried critics. A summary of their problems is given by Nicola Kaminski, *Der Liebe Eisen=harte Noth: "Cardenio und Celinde" im Kontext von Gryphius' Märtyrerdramen* (Tübingen 1992), 45–6.
[49] See Schilling, *Imagines Mundi*, 126–7.

*Flames of Passion: Vengeful Women*

Within the sexual and social relations exemplified in marriage and in Gryphius's Olympia, it is the role of women to be passive and accepting. Women who invert this order are on the side of chaos and the devil, and hence automatically witchlike. Förtsch's and Postel's *Die heilige Eugenia* (Hamburg 1695), portrays stoic virtue and passionate vice in a manner similar to, if more extreme than, Gryphius's. According to the librettist, Postel, the story is based on the life of St Eugenia, and adapted from an Italian opera performed in Viterbo in 1686.[50] In his introduction to *Cardenio und Celinde*, Gryphius explained his precise intentions in constructing the characters of Celinde and Olympia; Postel, having explained in *his* introduction that he has added a flying chorus of the church and the angels 'vor [= für] Liebhaber der Machinen', makes a more serious statement of intent that is heavily reminiscent of his dramatic predecessor:

Da in der Persohn der Eugenia die wahre Gottesfurcht benebenst andern Christlichen Tugenden vorgestellet und belohnet werden: Durch die Melanthia wird eine unkeusche Liebe und zuletzt ein rachgieriges Gemüht vorgezeiget und bestraffet.

Melanthia, the priestess, is not only like Celinde in her pursuit of unchaste love: she is also associated with infernal powers and witchcraft.

The opera depends for much of its effect on the way in which the two types that Eugenia and Melanthia represent are played off against each other. Eugenia parades the familiar, masculine qualities of the *femme forte*: her statue in the temple is in the guise of the armoured Pallas (I. i). She has subjugated her feminine sensuality to the extent that, when she first appears disguised as a pilgrim, the opera's buffoon, Festus, weighs up the possibilities: 'Ists nicht ein Bähr [= Bär]/ so ists ein Sack der gehen kan' (I. vi). She nonetheless possesses a beauty that confirms her inner

---

[50] Johann Philipp Förtsch (music), Christian Heinrich Postel (text [trans.]), *Die heilige EUGENIA, Oder Die Bekehrung der Stadt ALEXANDRIA zum Christentum* (Hamburg 1695 [1688]). Libretto: SUB HH. Further references are given in the text.

virtue, and Melanthia reveals an ambiguous (inverted) sexuality by expressing desire both for the image of Pallas/Eugenia in the temple and for the disguised saint. Emulating Celinde, Melanthia tries achieve her erotic goal with a magic spell. The lesbian nature of her love, although unconscious (she believes that Eugenia is a man), adds to Postel's evocation of inversion.

Melanthia is not ideally masculine, a *femme forte*, but instead usurps the role of the male in an act of vengeance. When Eugenia rejects her erotic advances and attempts to convert her to Christianity, Melanthia has her arrested, and gives vent to her alarmingly vengeful character in an aria:

> Verachtete Liebe wird Eyfer und Grimm.
> Laß Ehre/ laß Himmel/ laß Treue zerbrechen/
> Kan sich die verschmähete Schönheit nur rächen/
> Ist niemahls das schrecklichste Laster zu schlim [*sic*].    (III. ix)

Melanthia's machinations leave Eugenia on the brink of execution—a potential martyr, as her aria has already signalled to us:

> Ich eile zum Leiden
> Auff GOttes Geboth/
> Umarme mit Freuden
> So Foltern als Todt.    (III. i)

This is, however, an opera and not a martyr drama, and Postel responds to the convention that demands a happy ending by playing the popular card of revealed identity: Eugenia is recognized (she is in fact the mayor's daughter) while standing on her pyre, and rescued in the nick of time. Melanthia, on the other hand, is suddenly struck down by flames, and confirms her status as the antichristian antithesis of the heroine as she burns. Her ex-lover, Sergius, reports on the scene:

> Sie brandt'/ ach weh! und ließ zwar Thränen rinnen/
> Gestehend ihre Schuld/ doch war dabey
> Grausahme Lästerung. Sie sagte mir/
> Daß zwar der rechte GOtt dein Christus sey/
> Der dich ihr zu erkennen geben/
> Doch ihr geschworner Feind.    (III. xvi)

Melanthia's death by fire is a witch's death, ordained not by the worldy authorities but by a *deus ex machina* that causes her spontaneous combustion. Both Chach Abas and Celinde were metaphorically consumed by the flames of *their* infernal passions; Melanthia literally falls prey to the element that connotes her association with hell. The burning of the witch may thus be seen as a 'hair of the dog' antidote to the power she is feared to command: because her influence is believed to be both sexual or passion-driven and based in hell, her destruction by fire is a means of disarming her with her own weapons.

Because of the conventions that rule early German opera, and demand a cheery ending to the most violent and sinister action, Postel's saintly Eugenia cannot transcend worldly chaos in a martyr's death. Instead her opponent dies by divine ordination in the manner of a witch, taking the place in the flames she had intended for her victim. In a way that is typical of opera, reward and punishment here are immediate rather than projected into a life beyond physical death (as was usual in in the martyr drama): the fires of Hell are visible and immanent on stage. When Eugenia is rescued and Melanthia perishes, we understand that a world order that rejects women as avengers and as passionate lovers or lesbians has been actively affirmed by a higher authority that chooses accurately between two antithetical female types.

Hell (we still say) has no fury like a woman scorned. Sometimes a writer will conceive of an exceptional situation (such as in the biblical story of Judith), but the active vengefulness of women is more often than not a signal of their chaotic potential.

This is certainly the message of a drama written in 1662 by Hieronymus Thoma: *Titus und Tomyris . . . Beygenahmt Die Rachbegierige Eyfersucht.*[51] In *Titus and Tomyris*, as in *Die heilige Eugenia*, the revenge theme is closely linked with the portrayal of an evil woman (revenge itself, following the grammatical gender of the word in German, is personified in the second *Reyen* of the piece as female).

---

[51] Hieronymus Thoma, *Titus und Tomyris oder TRAUER=SPIEL Beygenahmt Die Rachbegierige Eyfersucht* (Steffen 1662). HAB. Further references are given in the text.

Although Thoma makes no reference to Shakespeare, his play is obviously a version of the *Titus Andronicus* material, in which Tomyris corresponds to Shakespeare's Tamora, and Octavian to Saturninus.[52] Thoma clarifies his position *vis-à-vis* his material in a concluding paragraph:

Dieses ist es nun hochgeneigter Leser/ was ich von diesem Stük [*sic*] auf-setzen wollen/ in dem ich an Octavian einen zubrünstig verliebten leicht-glaubigen [*sic*] Fürsten/ an Tomyre ein Rachbegierig=grausam=falsches Weibsbild/ an Tito einen frommen/ getreuen Heerführer/ ... und an Aran/ einen verzweifelten Ertzbößwicht abreissen wollen. (p. 103)

The inconsistency in his portrayal, which is also a feature of Shakespeare's drama, is in the depiction or categorization of the (anti-)heroine. In *Titus Andronicus,* the sacrifice of Tamora's son Alarbus to the god of war is described by her as 'cruel, irreligious piety' on the part of their Roman cap-tors (I. i. 130), something with which an audience or reader must agree. Thoma's Tomyris, too, is initially oppressed by the Romans. During the dramatic exchange in which they attempt to force her to marry the Emperor Octavian, our sympathies are with the foreign queen, for Titus suggests that the emperor's behaviour need know no bounds, using lan-guage that more usually connotes tyranny:

TOM. Ist bey den Römern recht dz [*sic*] man ein Weib soll zwingen

TIT. Wer zwingt sie?

TOM.                    Die so mich zur Liebe wollen dringen.

TIT. Was der gekrönte schafft/ bleibt bey uns allzeit recht

(I. iv)

The queen's favourite, Aran, is threatened with death if she will not comply. His response must also attract audience sym-pathy, because it is couched in the steadfast language that would usually signal a virtuous martyr:

---

[52] See William Shakespeare, *Titus Andronicus* (1594), ed. J. C. Maxwell (London 1993 [1968]). Maxwell notes that Shakespeare's Tamora may in fact have her name from Tomyris, queen of the Messagetae (ibid., p. xxx). This is particularly inter-esting because Shakespeare was not the originator of the Titus Andronicus mater-ial; it is possible that Thoma had the story from an older source that had kept the name of the historical foreign queen. This seems even more likely when one con-siders the fact that the conflict between the imperial princes Bassianus and Saturninus is an addition of Shakespeare's, and does not feature in Thoma's drama. See ibid., p. xxix.

> Ein unverzagter Geist
> Ist der durch Angst und Noth und durch den Tod selbst reist.   (I. iv)

We might even be led to confuse the motivation of Tomyris with that of a true *femme forte* when she exhorts herself to defend her kingdom in a rhetorical self-address that ought to connote heroic patriotism and hence an ideally masculine woman:

> Auff Tomyris! Auf auf! kanstu noch länger sehen?
> Daß Frembd' in deinem Land? auf deinen Güttern gehen?
> Leg hin das weibisch' Hertz/ wirff alle Furcht hinbey!
> Und tritt was auf dich tritt/ mit starkem Fuß entzwey.        (II. iv)

So far, the dramatic signals seem to point the audience or reader towards a positive interpretation both of Tomyris and of her henchman, Aran.

Yet from the start of Thoma's play, other signals warn us that Tomyris is a potentially threatening figure. As a warlike, beautiful queen she is the Petrarchan *dolce nemica* or, in Octavian's words, 'holdseligste Feindin' (I. i). She reveals Amazonian traits when she refuses marriage to the Emperor: 'Wir lassen uns nicht binden | Mit einem solchen Band' (I. iv). Most threateningly, she admits in a soliloquy to the power that beauty and the ability to dissimulate lend a woman, and thus to a command of the rhetoric of seduction:

> Was kan nicht eine Frau die Rach im Hertzen heget/
> Fürwar mehr als ein Mann der Spieß und Pfeile träget/
> Sie stellt sich freundlich an/ und nehmt die Hertzen ein/
> Und wann sie die besitzt/ so geußt sie Gifft darein.          (II. iv)

Her effect on the Emperor Octavian is de-masculinizing, as the second priest explains:

>                            Schaut diesen Fürsten an
> Der manchen Mann erlegt/ und jetzt nicht zwingen kan
> Ein schlecht gefangne Frau                                     (I. ii)

The contrast between Octavian and Tomyris highlights his weakness, and their situation—the erotically dominated Roman male in danger of effeminization at the hands of a strong-minded, exotic female—echoes that in the Antony and Cleopatra story. There are in fact a number of passages in

Thoma's drama that recall Lohenstein's *Cleopatra*, the first version of which was published just one year earlier, in 1661. In the mind of the audience or reader, they ought to sound all the warning bells regarding the Venusian woman and the rhetoric of seduction that Lohenstein was so careful to install. In *Titus und Tomyris*, II. iii, for example, the queen and the emperor greet each other:

> TOM. Mein Liecht.
> OCT.            Mein Schatz.
> TOM.                        Mein Fürst.
> OCT. Mein Engel.
> TOM.            Meine Wonn.

The form of the greeting is remarkably like that exchanged by Cleopatra and Antonius in Act I, scene ii of Lohenstein's play, and implies by association that Tomyris, like Cleopatra, is dissimulating. Like Cleopatra, Tomyris has the political adeptness and linguistic ability that, in a woman, is itself a threat; in one long, polished speech she persuades Octavian to have the sons of Titus executed. His response clearly puts her in the same category as Lohenstein's heroine: 'Sie Venus unsrer Zeit' (III. iii; compare *Cleopatra*, 1661, IV. 463). Her soliloquy in the following scene is an equally clear echo of Cleopatra's:

> – – – – – – So bricht
> Der Männer Witz vor uns/ so müssen sie uns weichen/
> Wann wir mit Schönheits=Blitz auf ihre Seelen streichen/
> Dann schwindet ihre Macht/
> .    .    .    .    .    .    .    .    .    .
> Ach du bethörter Printz/ du gibst vor einen Dunst
> Den Zepter/ ach du gibst vor einer Frauen Gunst
> Leib/ Leben/ Freund und Glük [*sic*]

> (III. iv; compare *Cleopatra*, 1661, II. 278–84)

Like Cleopatra, Tomyris is particularly dangerous because she is intellectually conscious of the way women can use their erotic appeal to disarm men in power.

Just as Lohenstein's Augustus finally recognizes and categorizes the type Cleopatra represents, and thus rhetorically defeats her, Octavian's eyes are finally opened to Tomyris. She, like the Egyptian queen, is a deceptive siren:

Du grausame Syren/ wie lieblich sind die Reden/
Die doch mit scharffem Gifft/ das drunder lieget/ töden.   (V. vi)

The central chorus of sirens that follows Act III has already warned of this tendency in women, contending that the latter are in fact more dangerous even than they:

Wir konnten zwar durch unser Singen/
Durch unsrer Zungen süssen Klang/
Gar manchen so in ängste [*sic*] bringen/
Daß er gewünschet Stahl und Strang.
Doch kan ein Weib mit Liebes Sachen/
Die Männer mehr bethöret machen.   (III, *Reyen*)

According to the chorus, woman's effect on man is socially chaotic:

Sie machet daß man gute Sitten
Verwirfft/ und das Gesätz veracht/

and in the terms of the play women have power not only to corrupt the individual but the state. Tomyris herself summarizes the dramatic lesson she represents in a soliloquy:

dan lehrnt wie einer Frauen/
Die von der Rache brennt/ so gar nicht ist zu trauen.
Merkt Römer/ durch die Spiel [*sic*]/ die wir gerichtet an/
Wie ein gefangnes Weib eur Macht verwerffen kan.   (V. i)

Here, as so often in the drama of the period, the Romans represent all that is male and masculine, and yet vulnerable to subversion.

The utter inversion of order that Tomyris embodies is confirmed, should any doubt remain, in the person of her favourite, Aran. Unlike Shakespeare's Aaron, Thoma's Aran is not literally black. He is, however, figuratively black: Titus arraigns him, 'Du schwartzer Ehren=Dieb bist Pfal und Feuers werth' (IV. iv). Like Aaron, he finally confesses his own wickedness in all its gruesome detail, but unlike Shakespeare's villain also repents. Nonetheless, his words prior to his execution by fire do not anticipate atonement or forgiveness, but the analogous fires of hell:

So recht! rast über mich/ ich hör die Straffen rasseln/
Ich höre nun mein Feur/ das ihr mir setzt/ schon prasseln.   (IV. iv)

Like Melanthia in Postel's opera, Aran suffers the witch's death that is the price for infernal machinations. The relationship between Tomyris and Aran therefore places the queen firmly on the side of the devil; as a vengeful and therefore perverted woman, we are to understand her as related to the type of the witch.

A level of confusion in the use of dramatic or linguistic signals in this play suggests that Thoma was not in control of stage rhetoric to the same extent as his dramatic predecessors, Lohenstein and Gryphius. Aspects of the martyr, the Venusian woman, and the witch jostle in his depiction of Tomyris and Aran, even though these characters are finally shown to belong indubitably to the latter categories. A similar confusion of rhetorical semiotics, demonstrating the pitfalls that these potentially very effective sign-systems involve, is evident in a later play, *Rosimunda*.

In 1676 a member of the literary society of the 'Pegnitz-Schäfer' with the pen-name Amyntas (= Jakob Hieronymus Lochner) published a drama with the title *Rosimunda oder Die gerochene Rächerin*.[53] The slant of the play is not immediately clear. As the action opens it is Rosimunda's husband Alboinus who seems to be the villain: he forces her to drink from the skull of her dead father, whom he has apparently murdered, and reveals himself as an enemy of Christians. There are overtones of *Hamlet* when the ghost of the dead man, Kunimundus, appears to his daughter and calls on her to avenge him. Unlike Hamlet, however, Rosimunda is a woman, and it is not legitimate for her to practise vengeance, as the resolutely womanly Diletta reminds her:

> Der Barbern Unrecht läst so strenges Recht nur zu.
> . . . . . . . . .
> Wie kan ein Frauen=Hertz in Diamant verharten?     (II. i)

There are reminiscences of the heroic woman in Rosimunda's spirited response, which still leaves us in some doubt as to which of the two women is to be condemned at this stage:

---

[53] Jakob Hieronymus Lochner ('Amyntas'), *Rosimunda oder Die gerochene Rächerin. Trauer=Spiel/* . . . (Frankfurt and Leipzig 1676). HAB. Further references are given in the text.

> Wie mag ein blödes Weib in einen Hasen arten?
>
> .   .   .   .   .   .   .   .   .   .
>
> Es sterbe der Tyrann.

Diletta closes the discussion with a characterization of Rosimunda as bestial (and therefore inverted), and a declaration of allegiance to her own femininity:

> Hilff Himmel! daß ja nicht diß Tyger Striche spinne
> Und meine traute Seel zu ihrer Rach gewinne.

When the men of the play discuss Rosimunda's predicament and her intentions their considerations are also gender-specific. Duke Faroaldus compares her situation to that of Orestes, but this apparent justification of her revenge is actually an intimation of the special threat women can pose:

> FAROALDUS. Orestes stillte nicht den Rach=beflammten Muth/
> Bis er mit Mutter=Mord den Vater=Mord gerochen.
>
> .   .   .   .   .   .   .   .   .   .   .   .
>
> GISULFUS. Orestes ist ein Mann/ und Rosimund ein Weib.
> FAROALDUS. Der Weiber List und Witz geht für den stärksten Leib.
>
> (II. ii)

Faroaldus therefore betrays Rosimunda to King Alboinus, but Rosimunda finally commits the regicide with Diletta's husband Helmiges, who is now her lover. The response of the men to her deed is shame; as a woman she has highlighted their weakness, and Gisulfus laments:

> Was soll für eine Farb das Schandmahl übermahlen/
> Das nur ein einig Weib uns Helden angebrandt?
> Pfui! daß der Trutz der Welt durch eine Weiber=Hand
> Im Blut besudelt liegt! was wird der Feind wol sagen/
> Daß eine schwache Frau das Haupt uns abgeschlagen.   (IV. vii)

Echoes of *Epicharis* again leave us wondering here whether Rosimunda is not, after all, to be admired. But Faroaldus takes up the theme of specifically female revenge and enlarges on its alarming, uncontrollable nature:

> Ja wenn ein Frauen=Hertz von erster Lieb erkalt/
> Und der entzündte Sinn auff Rach und Morden dencket/
> So wird ihr Überwitz vergebens nur umbschrencket.
> Ihr Seyn ist listig=seyn: List wird auch durchgebracht/
> Wann Argus gleich um sie mit hundert Augen wacht.   (IV. vii)

Rosimunda is now an unmistakably negative character. Using her sexual appeal to achieve political ends in the manner of a Cleopatra or indeed a Tomyris, she tries to persuade the imperial envoy Longinus to help her murder Helmiges and regain the throne. Longinus, however, recognizes the type that Rosimunda represents, and categorizes it metaphorically in a way that Lohenstein would applaud: with reference to Circe and the Sirens:

> Was wil so süsses Singen?
> Wie? wil mich Rosimund auff eine Falle bringen.
> Der stürtzt sich in den Tod/ der den Sirenen traut.
> Wie? wann mir solches Grab auch diese Zirze baut?  (V. ii)

This is a clear signal that the men are showing *Vernunft*, the quality that can defeat even women's wiles. The tables are thus turned on Rosimunda, who is finally outwitted by Helmiges and forced to drink the poison she has prepared for him. Her demonic, destructive status at the close of the play is signposted in the image of a bloodsucking vampire:

> ROSIMUNDA. Ihr Götter helfet mir!
> HELM. Dir/ die mit trocknen Augen
> Aus zweyer Männer Tod wil Lust und Leben saugen?  (V. iii)

It is finally given to Alboinus (who began the play as villain!) to clarify the lesson to be learned from Rosimunda:

> Hier kan die Welt anschauen
> Ein Muster grauser Rach/ ein Laster=Bild der Frauen  (V. iv)

Like Thoma, Lochner betrays a certain lack of control of available dramatic and rhetorical techniques, particularly of the antithetical system that was later so thoroughly exploited by Hallmann. This is most obvious in his opposition of Alboinus and the queen: the former needs to be wicked at the beginning of the play so that revenge can be provoked, but in the course of the action he and Rosimunda swap the roles of aggressor and victim. Vengeance is required, but Lochner's final message is that a woman is unsuited to be its agent; the dramatist regains rhetorical control with close reference to Lohenstein, and his message is forensically 'proven' within the play with reference to the *locus* of women's natural enslavement to the passions, which will always turn vengeful women into rampant vampires, or justice into chaos.

## Exemplary Structures: Martyrs and Marriage

We have already observed that not all representations of woman on the early modern stage are negative. Characters like Gryphius's Catharina and Lohenstein's Epicharis demonstrate, as Henry Higgins might put it, that a woman *can* be more like a man. But while such figures may reflect back in an admonitory fashion on schoolboy actors and men in the audience, they are hardly a suitable model for most early modern women. As other protagonists such as Mariamne have also begun to demonstrate, however, there is a feminine ideal that more closely fits society's conception of a 'normal' woman's role. In terms of theatrical semiotics, this ideal is anchored in two closely related dramatic structures: martyrdom and marriage.

### Martyred Mothers

Some of the most positive values associated with femaleness are those associated with motherhood. In the Christian tradition, mothers are seen to be fulfilling the appointed function of women and atoning through the pain of childbirth for their part in original sin, while the alarming potential of their sexuality is felt to be contained to some extent by the restrictions of pregnancy and child care. Grimmelhausen's recommendation to husbands in 1666 epitomizes an attitude of insecurity, even if it is tongue-in-cheek: 'man soll [seiner Frau] alle Jahr einen jungen Erben zweigen und also etwas zu thun geben.'[54] The idea of the Virgin Mary ensures that there is a special link between motherhood and saintliness or even purity. In dramatic terms, the unique relationship between mother and child offers scope for effective writing: Lohenstein makes much of the inversion and perversion of

---

[54] Hans Jacob Christoffel von Grimmelshausen, *Satyrischer Pilgram*, ed. Wolfgang Bender (Tübingen 1970), 85.

such a relationship in his *Agrippina,* for example. Particular effects can be created when the relationship is shown to be transcended by a higher bond of love even than that we normally expect between mother and child: this is the message of the martyr drama of the Christian mother.

During the decade 1634–44, Andreas Gryphius produced a translation of a French play by Caussin that had appeared in 1620. The German version was entitled *Beständige Mutter/ Oder Die Heilige Felicitas.*[55] Felicitas, like Gryphius's later heroine, Catharina, is a widow, and therefore not subject to the authority of a husband: like Catharina, she chooses instead to submit to the metaphysical authority of Christ. She is the only woman in the play, and the mother of seven sons. Felicitas also shares certain masculine heroic qualities with Catharina. She has the kind of rhetorical ability that I have suggested was the proper preserve of men. Her persecutor, the Roman Emperor Marcus Aurelius (AD 121–80), hints as much during his interrogation of her, with a sarcastic observation, 'Der Mund geht trefflich wol' (II. 59)—although Felicitas in fact speaks far less in the course of the play than her sons, for whom the more extensive proclamations of Christian constancy are reserved. From the first act, Felicitas is set up as an exception to the feminine 'rule'. In a discussion of her illegal Christian beliefs, Aurelius and a pagan priest exchange commonplaces about womankind:

AUREL. Die Frauen wechseln leicht' und unversehens die Sinnen
PRIST. [*sic*] Verstockter wird man nichts/ als Frauen finden können

(I. 124–5)

The audience, however, has already heard the Christian bishop Anicetus identify Felicitas as heroic: 'Weib Männern vorzuziehen' (I. 71), and will therefore recognize that both the emperor and the priest are misled in their assessments of her. Later in the play Felicitas's femininity is deliberately tested, this time by her sons' torturer Publius, again with unexpected results. Publius explains the experiment:

[55] In *Gesamtausgabe der deutschsprachigen Werke,* ed. Marian Szyrocki and Hugh Powell (Tübingen 1966), vol. 6. Further references are given in the text. Powell suggests the date of the translation in his introduction to this volume; see ibid., p. viii.

> Ich wil die Stunde schauen
> Ob hier ein Löwen Hertz/ ob hier ein Hertz der Frauen/
> Und Mutter Sinnen sind
>
> (III. 199–201)

But Felicitas's role as mother has already transcended worldly expectations. She has become 'der Märtrer Mutter' (II. 99), whose concern is not for the temporal but the eternal well-being of her children, and she therefore encourages her seven sons to embrace rather than to escape torture and execution.

Complementing Gryphius's portrayal of Felicitas as a heroic Christian mother is her demonization by the non-Christian Romans of the play. The structure is predictably antithetical, and indicates the false or inverted perception associated with non-Christian religions we have already identified. In Act I, a Roman citizen called Apollo is rejected by a young woman whom Felicitas has advised to practise Christian chastity. Chagrined, he accuses Felicitas of winning the woman, Erinna, through a form of witchcraft:

> den mehr den schönen Leib/
> Den hat Felicitas (vermaledeytes Weib?)
> Mit ihrem Gifft befleckt/ und so fern eingenommen/
> Daß sie der Meisterin gar weit bevor ist kommen     (I. 109–12)

But Apollo's language quickly reveals that he and not Felicitas is the representative of chaotic forces. He describes the revenge he will take by disrupting Erinna's Christian wedding with a brutal, twisted version of marital consummation:

> Ich wil durch Flamm' und Dampff ins Brautbett ein mich dringen/
> Das rauchen soll von Blut! stoß durch die Heyrath=Zier
> Diß Schwert in ihre Brust.
>
> (I. 124–6)

The accusation of witchcraft, levelled here by Apollo, genuinely reflects early perceptions of Christianity, as Gryphius would have been aware. Marcus Aurelius is convinced that the seven sons of Felicitas are 'bezaubert' (II. 218). The miracle performed for the heroine in Act III, when an idol is destroyed by the divine hand at her request, is misperceived by the other Romans as black magic, Felicitas herself

as a witch (III. 84–93). Publius specifically makes the connection with the devil, describing the Christians as 'verstockt
Geschlecht der Hölle' (III. 156). In his notes to the play,
Gryphius reminds us that the early Christians were even
accused of the ritual murder of children (an accusation more
often levelled at Jews in Gryphius's day, although he chooses
not to mention this). He illustrates the point in Apollonius's
attack on the Christians:

> Der Kinder reines Blut rufft Rach und klagt sie an!
> Die sie (wer ist der diß ohn schrecken hören kan?)
> Abreissen von der Brust/ und bey dem Abendessen
> Zu theilen in viel Stück' und ohn' entsetzen fressen!
> .   .   .   .   .   .   .   .   .   .
> Denn wird was die Natur selbst einsetzt: umbgekehrt.   (IV. 25 ff.)

The final accusation of inversion is correct with reference
to the deed—children are to be given life and nurtured, not
murdered and used as nutrition—but incorrect, we understand, with reference to Christian practice. It is also ironic,
since it is finally the Romans in this play who kill seven
children, inverting the process of their mother's natural
fertility. As the corpses are carried from the stage, Marcus
Aurelius mocks Felicitas:

> Wo ist die Mutter nun! die Kinder=reiche Frau?
> Heißt dieses fruchtbar seyn!                    (V. 274–5)

It is likely that Gryphius's *Felicitas* provided at least part of
the inspiration for an opera composed by Johann Wolfgang
Franck in 1679 for the Hamburg stage, *Die Macchabaeische
Mutter mit ihren Sieben [sic] Söhnen.*[56] The action of this opera
is located in Syria, where King Antiochus is persecuting
Jews for their faith, among others the Jewish mother Salome
and her seven sons. A number of other similarities also hint
at the influence of *Felicitas.* The opera opens with a prologue in which the Church triumphant supervises Michael's
defeat of the devil as dragon, in a spectacle reminiscent of
the *Reyen* of the Church militant and the angels in Gryphius's

---

[56] Johann Wolfgang Franck (music), Hinrich Elmenhorst (text), *Die Macchabaeische Mutter mit ihren Sieben Söhnen* (Hamburg 1679). Libretto: HAB. Further
references are given in the text.

drama. In a miracle scene, lightning destroys an idol before the elderly Jew Eleasar can be forced to sacrifice to it.
Salome, like Felicitas, is sexually attractive to her persecutor
(in this case the king's favourite, Sosander), and Sosander,
like the Emperor Aurelius, misjudges his captive because he
applies feminine criteria to a woman who clearly displays
(ideal) masculine traits:

> Ich weiß daß Ihr die Weiber auch wohl kennt/
> Denn wenn man meint/ sie stehen wie die Eichen/
> Pflegt doch der schwache Muth
> Durch schlechten Sturm zu weichen.                    (III. ii)

The courtier Bacchides, to whom this is addressed, echoes
Anicetus's (correct) judgement on Felicitas, cited above,
when he replies:

> Es zeiget uns ihr offt vergossnes Blut
> Daß Weiber offt den Männern vorzuzihen [*sic*].

Salome's seven sons, like those of Gryphius's heroine, proclaim their religious constancy in the face of both bribes and
threats, and their language is clearly that of the martyr: Areth,
for example, claims

> groß Verlangen
> Die Geisseln/ Kreutz und Streiche zu empfangen.   (III. viii)

During the agonizing deaths of their children, both
Felicitas (*Felicitas*, III. 301–18) and Salome sing hymn-like
arias. Salome's is a rendering of Psalm 42:

> Wie ein Hirsch die Quällen
> Bey den Unglücks=Fällen
> Suchet mit Begier;
> So dürst meine Seele/
> In der Marter Höle/
> Grosser Gott nach dir.
>
> (*Die Macchabaeische Mutter*, V. i)

She too transcends our expectations of the maternal
instinct by encouraging her sons to embrace death:

> So recht! O meine Liebe Frucht!
> So wird der Weg zum Himmel recht gesucht.   (V. iv)

As in *Felicitas*, the children's ghosts finally appear to justify their mother's apparently unnatural advice, demonstrating the superior state of eternal well-being they have achieved. There is a final link with Gryphius's 'beständige Mutter' in the closing scene of the opera, when Salome and her children are crowned by the allegorical figure of Constantia; constancy is clearly the virtue that this martyred mother, too, best exemplifies.

The same virtue is central to another play that may have been known to Franck or his librettist, Hinrich Elmenhorst: Johann Christian Hallmann's *Sophia* (1671). Hallmann indicates that his material is 'aus den Kirchen=Geschichten bekant' (p. 8), but the histories of both St Sophia and St Felicitas also feature in Albertinus's *Himlisch Frawenzimmer* (1611); this is another possible source for any of these works, and further demonstrates the popularity of the 'martyred mother' prototype.[57]

Sophia, too, is a widow. This appears to be an important feature of the mother-saint, as it connotes maternal status in conjunction with chastity. Links with the Virgin Mary suggest themselves, and enhance the hagiography. Sophia is also —like Felicitas and Salome—physically attractive; this gives her the opportunity to *prove* her virtue when under sexual siege from the Roman Emperor, Hadrian.

Hallmann's play feels more obviously like a parable than *Felicitas* or *Die Macchabaeische Mutter*, chiefly because of its strong allegorical elements. The heroine is subjected during the action (not in a *Reyen*, as we might expect) to an onslaught by the personified figures of Flesh, World, Death, and the Devil. This culminates in their recognition of her quasi-allegorical status, based on her name (Greek *Sophia* = wisdom): 'O überweises Weib!' (IV. 85), although in line with

---

[57] Compare Larsen, 'Una Poenitentium', 700. Larsen also notes that Albertinus places mothers 'higher up on his hierarchical ladder of sanctity' (ibid.). Susanne Gugrel-Steindl suggests a further likely source for the play: Laurentius Surius's (1522–78) *Vitae Sanctorum, Mensis Augustus Tomus I: Martyrium Sanctorum Mulierum Sophiae et eius filiarum Fidei, Spei et Charitatis, ex Simeone Metaphraste* (Cologne *c.*1570/75, German trans. Joan a Via, Munich 1577). See Gugrel-Steindl and Margarete Bican-Zehetbauer, 'Figurenkonstellation im Drama des 17. Jahrhunderts im deutschsprachigen Raum Oder: Von Tugend und Untugend, (Frauen)Schönheit und (Ohn)Macht' (unpublished doctoral diss., University of Vienna 1991), 116 ff.

the other martyred mothers discussed here, Sophia's essential virtue is not so much her wisdom as her constancy. Hallmann explains:

In diesem Trauer=Spiele wird dir vorgestellet ein Beyspiel ruhmwürdigster Beständigkeit. Das lüsternde Fleisch/ die lockende Welt/ der dreuende Tod/ der schreckende Teuffel werden von einer Ohnmächtigen Frau; unschätzbares Reichthum und Ehre/ annehmlichste Wollüste und Geschencke/ grausamste Foltern und Hencker von zärtesten Kindern besieget. (p. 8)

As we have come to expect, the dramatic emphasis is on the surprise element: stoic constancy is far more striking when practised by weak women and defenceless children. In *Catharina von Georgien*, Gryphius demonstrated the power of God 'in dem schwächsten Werckzeuge',[58] and Hallmann sees a similar miraculous paradox in the example of the early Christians:

So heftig hat die Liebe gegen dem gecreutzigten CHRISTO zu selbiger Zeit die Christlichen Seelen beherrschet/ daß nicht nur beherzte Männer/ sondern auch unmündige Kinder und schwache Weibesbilder jeden Augenblick bereit gewesen/ ihr Leben vor den zuckersüssten Nahmen JESUS aufzusetzen/ und solch Bekäntniß mit ihrem Blutte zu besiegeln! (p. 8)

The pedagogical ruse employed here ought to be familiar. Where Catharina provided a spur especially to men to equal the resolve of a weak woman, Hallmann's persecuted Christians cast shame on their privileged descendants, who fail in their faith in a world where Christianity is safe, because established. The names of Sophia's daughters: Fides, Spes, and Charitas (also testified to in Albertinus's account) provide Hallmann with an opportunity for such lines as 'Spes ist nicht zu bezwingen!' (III. 106).

Hallmann's drama plainly shows the influence of *Felicitas*. In the first scene the Christian martyrs listed by the Roman bishop include a mother and her seven sons (I. 71–2).[59] Like

[58] Andreas Gryphius, *Catharina von Georgien. Oder Bewehrete Beständigkeit*, ed. Hugh Powell, in *Gesamtausgabe der deutschsprachigen Werke*, vol. 6 (Tübingen 1966), 133. Further references are given in the text.
[59] The mother's name is Symphorosa. While the link with Sophia is clear, it could not of course be Sophia herself because Hadrian antedated Marcus Aurelius.

Gryphius's Aurelius, Hallmann's Emperor Hadrian is egged on by his priests and counsellors to persecute the Christians, and in Act II Palladia and Honorius complain that Sophia has been urging young women to practise Christian chastity. Nonetheless, the emperor is erotically drawn to Sophia, and like Aurelius he has her children tempted to relinquish their faith before they are tortured. Further similarities emerge when Charitas is misinformed that her sisters have succumbed to pagan blandishments, and all the children are finally executed in a gruesome manner while their mother looks on and offers encouragement. The inversion of natural fertility is again in evidence, and Hallmann makes the same link as Gryphius with the Classical figure of Niobe (whose seven sons and seven daughters were slain by angry Gods, in punishment for her maternal arrogance), when Hadrian mocks Sophia:

> Du andre Niobe/ du Kinder=reiches Weib/
> Hat sich dein Auge nun/ dein aufgeblasner Leib
> Durch dieses Freudenspiel zur Gnüge recht erquicket?    (V. 173–5)[60]

The children's ghosts finally appear to comfort their mother and confirm her faith in the efficacy of martyrdom.

Unlike Felicitas, Sophia has female children. They nonetheless express more or less the same sentiments as the seven boys, proclaiming their unswerving constancy and their thirst for martyrdom and eternal life. They are not only untypical of children, but also—like their mother—of their sex. In the second scene of Act III, Fides, Spes, and Charitas are tempted with and reject all the things women are held to be most susceptible to: personal ornament, sweetmeats, and sensuality. Within the metaphorical system of the play, temptation itself is feminine: Sophia apostrophizes the worldly evils that besiege her as 'Ihr Teuflischen Sirenen!' (IV. 75). Her constancy is therefore unfeminine, as Hadrian's unfulfilled prediction emphasizes:

> Denn Frauen ändern leicht auch in dem Glauben sich/
> So bald ihr Geist empfindt den süssen Liebes=Stich.    (III. 299–300)

---

[60] Compare *Felicitas*, IV. 79–85.

The sympathetic empress, Julia Sabina, tries to use com-monplaces of gender to excuse Sophia's Christianity and obtain her a pardon: 'Es wird den Frauen leicht ein Irrthum eingeflößt!' (II. 222). This is rhetoric, however; Julia Sabina is fully aware of the extraordinary status of Sophia among women. Away from the emperor, she compares her with a group extraneous to patriarchal society, the famous Amazons:

> O mehr als ädles Weib! O starcke Amazone!
> Dir weicht Harpalice mit ihrer Sieges=Krone/
> Und Rhodogune legt vor dir die Palmen hin!    (IV. 151–3)

But the threat that such praise might imply to a stable gen-der hierarchy is immediately softened when the empress reminds us that Sophia is not in fact a pagan Amazon, but subject to the authority of Christ (the martyr's bridegroom) and God the Father:

> Dein Christus muß fürwahr besondre Kräfte haben/
> Der schwache Frauen auch in höchster Angst kan laben!    (IV. 155–6)

The pagans' perception of Christianity in *Sophia* is similar to that described in *Felicitas*. Honorius and Palladia accuse Sophia's mentor, Bishop Alexander, of bewitching the three children. This idea would transform Sophia from a chaste matron into a warlock's dam:

> HONORIUS. Der Zaubrer hat diß Gift den Kindern eingeflößt?
> PALLADIA. Der Hexenmeister ist der Grund=Stein solcher Plagen.
>
> (I. 222–3)

Septitius Clarus denigrates the Christians as 'Zauber=Volck' (II. 87), and later accuses Fides, Spes, and Charitas of practising 'Zauberey' (III. 257), while Hadrian reveals his perverted perception of Sophia when he misconstrues the source of her religious impassionment:

> Welch Teufel hat doch wohl den grausen Blitz erwecket
> In der so edlen Seel'/ und Lilgenreinen Brust?    (II. 148–9)

His response to the miracle that preserves Sophia's chastity is equally misguided, for he assumes that the divinely sent thunderclap that prevents him from raping her is the result of witchcraft and the devil (IV. 271 ff.). Sophia is now perceived by the Romans as a weather witch (IV. 282), a type familiar to a seventeenth-century audience from contemporary witch trials. In an exchange between the heroine and one of her torturers, ideas of true and false light are used to signal proper (Christian) and inverted (pagan) perception:

SEPTITIUS CLARUS. Sie schaut vor Sonn' und Stern ein falsches Irrlicht an!
SOPHIA. Diß Irrlicht führet uns zur rechten Sternen=Bahn!

(II. 283–4)

It is, figuratively speaking, a lack of sight that leads Antoninus to suspect witchcraft again when Fides' pyre miraculously will not burn; Sophia laments, 'O blinde Aberwitz!' (IV. 432). The inverted nature of the pagan Romans is plainest, however, when a final 'meal' of her children's heads and blood is brought to Sophia in prison. Not only has the natural order of fertility been reversed (with an echo of the idea of ritual murder), but there is a sense of a perverted Eucharist in the separate offerings of flesh and blood. Sophia's response, which is entirely positive—she accepts the offering as proof of her children's salvation—is an indication of the power of Christian belief to transcend the inversion and chaos of an antichristian world.

The idea of the martyred mother clearly gives the dramatist the potential to play on expectations of motherhood and womanhood. Felicitas, Salome, and Sophia are all beautiful, and the idea of the beautiful moribund woman is of course an effective *vanitas* metaphor; this is especially obvious when Sophia is shown standing tied among the flowers of the imperial garden in Act IV of Hallmann's play. It is important that the beauty of these women does not present a threat, because they—unlike Lohenstein's heroines—do not use it to manipulate men through the sex instinct. In this sense, beauty is necessary as *proof* of a heroine's virtue. We are led to infer that both as mothers and as committed Christians their sexuality is reassuringly constrained, and they therefore achieve a kind of Marian purity. Because gender conceptions are based on antithesis, these women are perceived as embodying strength in weakness, which in a Christian context functions not as a concettistic paradox but as an inspiring miracle. Their heroic children extend the scope of the miracle, but also indicate, as exceptions to the rule, the parallels in the perception of women and children: both are naturally feeble and easily swayed. Finally, the martyred mother and her children illustrate a terrifying reversal of the order of motherhood: the provision of life and nurture is transformed by their persecutors into the provision of death. The barbarity or inverted nature of the perpetrator and his values or religion is revealed; his society is clearly one of misrule.

The death of the children in the absence of a protecting (terrestrial) father implies a serious threat to ordered society, which depends on lineage and inheritance, especially when the children represent such a patrilinear triumph as seven sons. Even the number seven may have significance. The threesome Fides, Spes, and Charitas is not only a reference to the cardinal virtues (1 Cor. 13: 13), but has obvious trinitarian overtones. Seven is a number more often connected with sin than virtue in the Christian tradition: the Beast of Revelations has seven heads, and the world and the devil tempt man with seven deadly sins. There may be an element of atonement, therefore, in the idea of the mother with seven sons. Woman's punishment in the Genesis story is the pain of childbirth, and the mothers in these dramas suffer that pain twice, through their children's deaths as well as their births. Felicitas receives credit for her son's martyrdom as well as her own, and is hence accorded the 'acht= fache Märter Krone' (V. 520). The link between woman, world, and devil that is concentrated in the idea of the witch is decisively broken by this double process of atonement, and the martyred mother figures unambiguously as an ideal. It is perhaps an ideal which appears to be far distant from the audience's reality, and therefore to fit oddly into the tradition of didactic drama; the structural link between these heroines and the reality of the early modern audience only emerges when we recognize the parallels between the apparent antitheses of stage martyrdom and stage marriage for the early modern heroine.

*Ideal Wives*

The institution of marriage gained in status after the Protestant Reformation. What had, in pre-Reformation terms, been regarded as a concession to human weakness, was now promoted as the ideal basis of a godly society or '[die] zentrale gesellschaftliche Ordnung der Geschlechter, die zugleich als "erste Ordnung Gottes" definiert wurde'.[61] Heide Wunder sees the new significance of marriage as complementary to the developing structures of patriarchal authority in post-Reformation society:

Die Rolle der Ehe nach der Reformation . . . gewann ihre Bedeutung auch im Zusammenhang mit der Herausbildung neuer Herrschaftsstrukturen im frühmodernen Staat. . . . Der Ehemann wurde zum Ansprechpartner der Obrigkeiten und gewann dadurch innerehelich gegenüber der Frau an Autorität.[62]

Especially in seventeenth- and early eighteenth-century German opera, marriage and martyrdom are, structurally speaking, often much the same thing for the heroine. The central importance of St Paul's writings for the Reformers may help to explain this: if, in the famous Pauline dictum, Christ is in authority over man(-kind) and men over woman-kind (1 Cor. 11; Eph. 5: 22–4), then women may find their guardian either as brides of Christ (martyrs) or as terrestrial wives. Within the martyr structure, the central protagonist suffers for the sake of her saviour (Christ), is prepared to sacrifice herself for him, and is finally rewarded for her constancy with divine union. Within marriage, the structure is secularized but otherwise identical.

In 1722, Händel's and Mattheson's *Zenobia Oder Das Muster rechtschaffener Ehelichen Liebe* was performed in Hamburg.[63] The story's source is a brief section in Book 12 of Tacitus's *Annals*,[64] but the title provides a clear enough indication of

[61] Heide Wunder, *'Er ist die Sonn', sie ist der Mond': Frauen in der frühen Neuzeit* (Munich 1992), 67.
[62] Ibid. 74–5.
[63] Georg Friedrich Händel (music), Johann Mattheson (Text [trans. of Nicola Francesco Haym's *Radamisto*]), *ZENOBIA Oder Das Muster rechtschaffener Ehelichen Liebe* (Hamburg 1722). Libretto: SUB HH. Further references are given in the text.
[64] See Tacitus, *The Annals of Imperial Rome*, rev. edn. trans. Michael Grant, (London 1989 [1956]), 275.

the German writers' focus of interest. Both central female characters, Zenobia and Polissena, are exemplary blueprints for selfless wifehood. The former, as in Tacitus, begs for death from her husband when she is unable to accompany him on the flight from their enemies, so that the marriage will never be dishonoured through her capture (and, presumably, rape). Polissena, who does not feature in Tacitus's account, displays self-subordinating conjugal behaviour. Despite just having received news of her husband's, Tiridates', infidelity, she rejects an offer of love from Tigranes, and reaffirms her abject devotion and obedience to her errant spouse. This is emphasized in the distinct form of an aria (Matheson's translation parallel):

| | |
|---|---|
| Tu vuoi ch'io parta; io parto | Du befiehlest/ ich soll fortgehen; |
| Idolo del cor mio; | Ich gehe denn/ du Abgott meines |
| Mà senza core: | Hertzens; aber ohne Leben: |
| Partirò; mà nel partire | Ich will scheiden; allein die |
| Il desio de rimirarti | Begierde/ dich wieder zu sehen/ |
| Accresce il mio dolore. | Vergrössert meinen Schmertz.    (I. ii) |

Tiridates is finally saved 'by the love of a good woman': he escapes execution as a tyrant because Polissena is prepared to forgive him.

The Zenobia material is also used by Verocai and Schürmann in their opera, *Zenobia und Radamistus*, for the Braunschweig fair in 1742.[65] The ideality of their Zenobia, too, consists in her submitting utterly to the men around her. The action begins after the events portrayed in Tacitus (and in Mattheson's libretto), and in the course of the opera's action Zenobia remains true to her husband Radamistus despite believing him responsible for the death of her father. In a prologue we are informed that Zenobia accepted her father's choice of husband even though she was in love with another man, 'welches' (as the librettist spells out for us) 'zwar eine grosse Tugend ihres kindlichen Gehorsams/ aber eine noch grössere ihrer Treu gegen ihren Ehgemahl anzeigete'. Zenobia herself confirms this when in the second act she is

---

[65] Giovanni Verocai (music), Georg Kaspar Schürmann (text [trans.]), *Zenobia und Radamistus* (Wolfenbüttel 1742). Libretto: HAB. Further references are given in the text.

confronted with her former lover, Tiridates. She rejects him with the explanation:

> wenn man mir gelassen freye Wahl
> Wär einzig Tiridates mein Gemahl/
> Mein Abgott/ mein Vernügen und mein Glück:
> Doch/ da mein Vater/ Himmel und Geschick
> Das vest [*sic*] verknüpfte Band hat wollen trennen/
> Will meine Tugend nicht vergönnen
> Dich ferner anzusehen                                    (II. iii)

Again it is the martyr's choice of fidelity and obedience over personal well-being (modelled by Olympia in *Cardenio und Celinde*) that elevates the heroine to the status of an ideal.

## Conclusion

Drama and opera acquire much of their effect through the deployment of opposing ideas, often incorporated in conflicting characters, on the stage. This was the case in Gryphius's *Catharina von Georgien*, where Catharina and Abas embody the 'masculine' and 'feminine' values of Christianity and Islam respectively; it was also a feature of Lohenstein's dramas, in which a woman's 'rhetoric of seduction' is pitted against the male rhetoric of *Vernunft*; and it reaches a peak on the opera stage, where a central protagonist is scarcely thinkable without his or her positive or negative counterpart. All of this sits comfortably with the antithetical world-view that is characteristic of the early modern period in Europe, a view that is based in rhetoric and philosophy, and finds expression in a 'language of contrariety' that signals what is inverted or chaotic and what is orderly, or the right way up.[66] Such a language is at the root of the discourse of witchcraft. A widespread preconception of a fundamental antithesis of order and chaos is what permits deliberately paradoxical constructions like the *femme forte*, the good Turk, or the 'noble Moor'.

Woman is, it seems, of interest on the stage as a signifier of ideal order as well as a harbinger of chaos. The women

---

[66] Clark, 'Inversion, Misrule', 105.

protagonists in the martyr plays of Gryphius and Hallmann point to an order that is not of this world: their function is deictic rather than present. It is also significant in a worldly sense, however, for the parallel ideas of mankind in submission to Christ and woman in submission to man constitute an ever-present paradigm of social order.

Opera, more dependent on the goodwill of a paying audience than school drama, demands a happy ending and hence resists martyr plots. Franck's *Macchabaeische Mutter* is an exception: the death of the heroine on the early opera stage is highly unusual. More typical female paragons are Zenobia and Polissena, who signal a distinctly present ideal of order in marriage, an order based on women's voluntary acceptance of their subordinate status in a hierarchical conjugal arrangement. The chorus of united couples that generally concludes opera replaces the chorus of angels who affirm the heroine's status at the end of the martyr drama.

At the other end of the scale, the anti-heroine may dominate. This is more often the case in drama than in opera: Thoma's Tomyris is a central, admonitary figure who (unlike Gryphius's Celinde) has no virtuous counterpart in the piece, and the rapaciousness of Lochner's Rosimunda is hardly counteracted by the colourless Diletta figure. The radical negation of order that these transgressive women incorporate may again be understood as dramatic deixis, since audience comprehension of the chaos they represent in itself implies that an opposing pattern of order exists as a yardstick: Gryphius and Thoma confirm the existence of this pattern in the statements of intent they append to their plays.

The Olympia/ Celinde opposition in Gryphius's play—which defies categorization as *Lustspiel* or *Trauerspiel*—anticipates a structural pattern in the portrayal of women which is highly developed in early opera. In opera, the wicked woman seldom stands alone. Melanthia is distinctly outshone by Eugenia in Förtsch's and Postel's piece, and her chaotic force no longer requires an audience to infer order negatively reflected, because it is immediately counteracted on stage by the corrective presence of an ideal. Again, the signals point to an immanent rather than a deferred human state: the order Eugenia represents is expressed through obedience to God, and she survives while her disruptive counterpart perishes, a clear enough indication that order, punishment, and reward are located in this (operatic) world, not outside or beyond it.

The links between Hallmann's dramas and early modern opera have been noted.[67] They encompass not only his use of music, but also of fireworks, machines, and other extravagant stage effects, and of libretto-like verse and structure. They may also be relevant to his use of imagery. Relative brevity is essential in the opera libretto. Certain metaphorical complexes, which include such things as the elements of the *imitatio Christi* as well as ideas of white purity and black evil, martyrdom and tyranny, and high and low singing voices form a sign-system that communicates meaning to an audience while relieving the dramatist or librettist of the necessity for textual elaboration. This sign-system has, as we have seen, its roots in literary and emblem history: such metaphorical signals must have precedents so that their meaning is generally understood before they can function as shorthand. Part of the operatic 'feel' of Hallmann's work lies in the fact that he avails himself to a far greater extent than his Silesian predecessors, or Haugwitz, of such a sign-system. His aim is clearly to emulate the kind of striking effects achieved by dramatists like Gryphius, something which is only realized in what is probably his least operatic work, and certainly the one in which metaphorical oppositions are at their most subtle, *Mariamne.* As tends to happen in early modern opera, where the use of established structures is extreme, dramatic intensity is lost rather than heightened when metaphorical systems are over-used.

Antithesis and opposition, the mainstays of the drama, have the potential to be deeply reassuring devices. The structure of opposition in the dramas and libretti discussed so far is

[67] e.g. by Elsie G. Billmann, *Johann Christian Hallmanns Dramen* (Würzburg 1942), 26; by Gernot Uwe Gabel, 'Johann Christian Hallmann: Die Wandlung des schlesischen Kunstdramas im Ausgang des 17. Jahrhunderts' (unpublished doctoral thesis, Rice University 1971), 81, 208 ff.; by Szarota, *Geschichte, Politik und Gesellschaft*, 85; by Kristine Krämer, 'Johann Christian Hallmanns Trauer-, Freuden- und Schäferspiele' (unpublished doctoral thesis, University of Berlin 1978), 151 ff.; and by Peter Skrine, 'An Exploration of Hallmann's Dramas', in *GLL* 36/3 (1983), 232–40 (238–9).

one of threat and reassurance: dramatic closure depends on order being immanently or deictically restored. Such a system is particularly well suited to early opera, because this popular form is in search of applause or audience satisfaction and therefore, even more than drama, demands the constant reaffirmation that the world order within which that audience defines itself is both secure and *right*. We shall see more of this in the next chapter.

# 4

## PERSUASIVE SOUNDS:
## THE RHETORIC OF WORDS AND MUSIC

To treat opera and drama together in one study is to venture
into extensive territories. But it is in the development of early
opera that early modern stagecraft, with all of its rhetorical or persuasive aspirations, is pushed to its limits. Here we
find another potent element working on the text and the
audience's senses: music.

Rhetoric is traditionally linked to theories of the human
passions, or *Affekte*. Both Aristotle and Quintilian consider
rhetoric's power to move the listener in a way that depends
on his or her physiological disposition or temperament.[1] Early
modern rhetoricians show an even stronger interest in the
passions, and in the power of the orator to guide or manipulate them: one of the most widely used rhetorical text-
books of the period, Gerhard Johannes Vossius's *Rhetorices
Contractae* of 1606, devotes one entire volume (of six)
largely to the study of the passions.[2] Music theorists could
not be immune to the rhetoric bug. Their treatises reveal a
remarkable degree of reflection on the emotive or 'affective'
potential of their art; the composers and librettists of early
opera, in particular, feel impelled to theorize about the
power of a new and exciting genre.

Of the hundreds of early German libretti that survive, most
now lack a score. This is an inevitable result of the practice
of the day, whereby a great number of libretti were printed
as programmes for a performance, but only a few and often
sketchy manuscript copies of the score were produced for
musicians used to improvisation. The missing music has served

---

[1] In Book Two of Aristotle's *Rhetoric*; in *De Oratore* (2. 44. 188–91); and in
Quintilian (6. 2. 20–36).
[2] Brian Vickers, *In Defence of Rhetoric* (Oxford 1997 [1988]), 278.

as a reason for those working on the opera libretto to direct
their attention overwhelmingly to the texts.[3]

Some arguments from the period do seem to support
the right of the modern scholar to focus exclusively on the
libretto. Barthold Feind's much-cited dictum, for example,
has been understood as a plea for the supremacy of the
text: 'Denn eine Opera ist ein aus vielen Unterredungen
bestehendes Gedicht/ so in die Music gesetzet/ als welche
der Verse wegen allhier gebraucht wird/ nicht aber
ümgekehret/ . . .'[4] But Feind is a librettist. The Hamburg
composer and theorist Johann Mattheson, in his first theoretical publication just five years later, approaches the
libretto from a different perspective, emphasizing the transforming effect—for better or worse—that music and staging
can have: 'Manche Opera siehet gar schön aus im Buch/ allein
wenn sie aufs Theatrum kommt/ klingt es gantz anders'.[5]
A decade later, Mattheson deals even more assertively with
current ideas about music and text. The second volume
of his *Critica Musica* (1722–5) contains a commentary on
Heinrich Bokemeyer's *Versuch von der Melodica*, in which
Bokemeyer, a cantor in Wolfenbüttel, expounds contemporary ideas in a facile manner.[6] An example is sufficient
to illustrate the tone of Mattheson's commentary (printed
with Bokemeyer's text):

[3] Notable exceptions are Hellmuth Christian Wolff, *Die Barockoper in Hamburg*
(1678–1738), 2 vols. (Wolfenbüttel 1957); Robert Donald Lynch, *Opera in
Hamburg 1718–1738: A Study of the Libretto and Musical Style*, 2 vols. (Michigan 1980);
Mara Renée Wade, *The German Baroque Pastoral 'Singspiel'* (Berne 1990). More exclusively libretto-based studies include Arwed Woldemar Bartmuß, 'Die Hamburger
Barockoper und ihre Bedeutung für die Entwicklung der deutschen Dichtung und
der deutschen Bühne' (unpublished doctoral thesis, University of Jena, 1924);
Wolfgang Huber, 'Das Textbuch der frühdeutschen Oper: Untersuchungen über
literarische Voraussetzungen, stoffliche Grundlagen und Quellen' (unpublished
doctoral thesis, University of Munich, 1957); Eberhard Haufe, *Die Behandlung der
antiken Mythologie in den Textbüchern der Hamburger Oper 1678–1738* (Frankfurt a.M.
1994 [1964]); Gloria Flaherty, *Opera in the Development of German Critical Thought*
(Princeton 1978).

[4] Barthold Feind, *Deutsche Gedichte* (Hamburg 1708), repr. ed. W. Gordon Marigold
(Bern 1989), 80.

[5] Johann Mattheson, *Das Neu-Eröffnete Orchestre . . . Mit beygefügten Anmerckungen
Herrn Capell-Meister Keisers* (Hamburg 1713; facs. repr. Ann Arbor 1993), 162.

[6] Johann Mattheson, *Critica Musica* (Hamburg 1722–5; repr. Amsterdam 1964),
2. 291 ff.

[Bokemeyer] **Von dem Texte**. Der Text, worunter man die Worte verstehet, so gesungen werden, ist das edelste und vornehmste Stück einer guten Music . . .

[Mattheson] Der Text ist gar kein Stück der Music, vielweniger das edelste oder vornehmste. Denn die Music kan auch ohne Text bestehen, und alle Passionen oder Gedancken, mit dem blossen wohl=zusammen =gefügten Klange, ausdrücken. (p. 295)

Mattheson is clearly not prepared to stand for music's relegation to the status of a mere textual prop. Recent scholarship echoes Mattheson's view: Ellen Rosand, for example, finds the early modern libretto 'glaringly, and self-consciously incomplete' without its musical setting.[7] The questions remain how opera texts for which the music is no longer extant can be approached, and, in the case of a literary study like this one, how the student of literature can best appraise those libretti for which scores (but, unfortunately, few recordings) are available.

Printing and sales records suggest that early libretti were intended to be read primarily as programmes during a performance. There were those, like Gottsched, who collected them as books, but even so they were generally read by an audience who had some knowledge and experience of music in the opera house; this would naturally change their perception of the texts. This chapter sketches the idea and the implementation of early operatic music, so that in recognizing some of the possibilities early modern poets and composers found in music, in theory and in practice, we can consider how it might affect our reading of the libretti.

### Theory: Music's Power

Any consideration of the extensive and enthusiastic treatment given to rhetorical devices by music theorists of the early modern period must be tempered by the awareness that each treatise as a whole is a rhetorical endeavour, an exercise in theoretical persuasion savoured by its author. The idea

---

[7] Ellen Rosand, *Opera in Seventeenth-Century Venice: The Creation of a Genre* (Berkeley 1991), 34.

of music, like that of woman, the oriental, or anything else, is a linguistically constructed idea; we cannot assume that theory equals practice. For this reason I shall not undertake a direct application of theories to scores in order to 'prove' points about musical figures or rhetoric in early opera. Instead I shall concentrate on the growing sense of music's potential to work on human beings, the theoretical under- standing of it as a kind of 'language', and the will of the composer and the librettist to work together to achieve the greatest possible effect.[8] Underpinning all this is a basic sense of and need for order.

Early modern theory documents a sense of music's scienti- fic and philosophical importance in a divine scheme. The association of music with the divine and the worship of the divinity is an ancient one, and particularly important to music theorists of the period was the notion that terrestrial musical harmony is capable of echoing divine harmony or order. Librettists and composers share this sense of music's meaning, which is discussed in the fictitious conversation that introduces one of the earliest German libretti, *Seelewig* (1644). The author, Georg Philipp Harsdörffer, has a speaker draw attention to the naming of music's inventor in the first book of the Bible (thus putting its origin firmly in the Christian tradition), and another instructs us: 'die Music ist hier auf Erden der Echo oder Wiederhall der himmlischen Freuden.'[9]

Behind early conceptions of music's order lies an aware- ness of the connection between music and numbers. Music was classified in antiquity as one of the *quadrivium* of math- ematical disciplines, with arithmetic, geometry, and astronomy. Order was therefore its essence. This is made evident in one

---

[8] The musicologist Jahn has recently suggested that, while musical rhetorical theory is not in itself a reliable basis for interpretation, it can cast helpful light on the early modern score. See Bernhard Jahn, 'Ist die musikalische Figurenlehre eine Hermeneutik? Probleme und Perspektiven beim Umgang mit einem analytischen Verfahren aus der Barockzeit', in *Germanica Wratislaviensia* 93 (Wroclaw 1992), 172–90. For useful examples of such analysis and a brief discussion of musical rhetoric, see Gary C. Thomas, 'Musical Rhetoric and Politics in the Early German Lied', in (ed.), James M. McGlathery *Music and German Literature: Their Relationship since the Middle Ages* (Columbia, Oh. 1992), 65–78.

[9] Georg Philipp Harsdörffer, *Frauenzimmer Gesprächspiele*, vol. 4 (Nuremberg 1644), repr. ed. Irmgard Böttcher (Tübingen 1968), 47.

of the most widely read theoretical works of the seventeenth century, Athanasius Kircher's *Musurgia universalis* (1650).[10] The second volume of Kircher's work has a frontispiece whose motto reads (after Hermes Trismegistos): 'Musica nihil aliud est, quam omnium rerum ordinem scire.'

The music theorists' ideas about order reflect their Classical sources. The translation of ideas of divine order and harmony into the Christian tradition does not obscure their origins in Platonic theory, and in Pythagorean theses of harmonic number.[11] Renaissance Humanist interest in such writings is one important element in the development of early opera, and the philosophical climate in which the librettists and their composers were working can be understood by tracing briefly the path of this interest in Italian and, later, German thought. Considerable influence on the theoretical beginnings of opera is attributed to the Florentine group called the *Camerata*. One of its members, Vincenzo Galilei (father of the astronomer Galileo) was in contact with a noted classical scholar, Girolamo Mei, and produced a book called *Dialogo della musica antica et della moderna* (1581). The title betrays his interest: the idea was to progress from the old contrapuntal style to a neo-classical music, which would distinguish itself as Greek music was believed to have done, namely through the perfect union of words and melody.[12] The Italian theorists were much concerned with Classical ideas about music's power to affect the listener, especially in combination with poetry. Plato's claim that speech has priority over harmony and rhythm[13] led Zarlino to contend that music must take its meaning from the text, and that only music involving the voice can

[10] Athanasius Kircher, *Musurgia universalis* (Rome 1650); trans. Andreas Hirsch, *Philosophischer Extract und Auszug aus . . . Athanasii Kircheri von Fulda Musurgia universali* (Schwäbisch-Hall 1662). See also Ulf Scharlau, *Athanasius Kircher (1601–1680) als Musikschriftsteller: ein Beitrag zur Musikanschauung des Barock* (Kassel/ Marburg 1969), esp. pp. 67–8.

[11] In *Timaeus* it is suggested that the motion of *mousike* and *philosophia* may delight because it imitates divine harmony, and that this helps restore order and concord to the soul. See Warren Anderson, 'Plato', in Stanley Sadie, *New Grove Dictionary of Music and Musicians* (London 1980; hereafter *New Grove*), 14. 853–7.

[12] See Donald Jay Grout, *A Short History of Opera*, 2nd edn. (New York 1965), 34–7.

[13] *Republic* 399–400; cited in Enrico Fubini, *The History of Music Aesthetics*, trans. M. Hatwell (Basingstoke 1991), 126.

have affective power (in the sense of the emotions or *Affekte*).[14] The Platonic idea may later be at the root of Barthold Feind's sense of the priority of the text in opera.

Another important element in the consideration of music's potential was the Aristotelian belief in its capacity to bring about catharsis or purgation in the listener.[15] Writers such as Tasso and Guarini extended the notion to encompass even those poetic works with happy endings, thus helping to secure the credentials of early opera. All this reveals not only a sense of the order inherent in music, but also the power of the composer to project that order for the listener. The nature and quality of music's power was a central issue.

The physiological influence of music on human beings is discussed in philosophical and scientific as well as musical treatises. Towards the end of the fifteenth century, Ficino surmised that music and poetry achieve their effect because they are carried by air, and are therefore travelling in the same element as the human *spiritus*. Through the sense of hearing, the *spiritus* transmits the movement of music to the soul. Ficino's ideas were received indirectly by sixteenth-century Humanists in the work of Mei and of Lorenzo Giacomini; their influence as well as that of Descartes can be observed in Kircher's *Musurgia*, where the author attempts a medical explanation of the process by which humans respond to music.[16] This brings us to the hub of the early modern idea of music, namely its capacity to touch or even manipulate human emotions: the *Affekte*. The so-called *Affektenlehre* in early modern music theory has attracted much critical attention in the last hundred years, and evidence of a systematic doctrine was collated enthusiastically during the first few decades of the twentieth century only to be emphatically refuted more recently.[17] Modern scholarship suggests that the kind of clearly defined doctrine suggested by the term *Affektenlehre*

[14] See Warren Anderson, 'Aristotle' in *New Grove*, 1. 587–91.

[15] Politics, 8. 5. See Barbara Russano Hanning, *Of Poetry and Music's Power: Humanism and the Creation of Opera* (Ann Arbor 1980 [1969]), 21, 29.

[16] Kircher's detailed and complex explanation of this phenomenon is lucidly summarized by Scharlau, *Athanasius Kircher*, 222–4.

[17] George J. Buelow has the last word in his essay 'Johann Mattheson and the Invention of the Affektenlehre', in George J. Buelow and Hans Joachim Marx (eds.), *New Mattheson Studies* (Cambridge 1983), 393–408.

—that is, a system which dictated specific musical devices for the achievement of specific emotional responses—never existed. This does not, however, constitute a denial that composers and librettists were genuinely fascinated by the means to excite emotion that they believed music, poetry, and the human susceptibility to *Affekte* put at their disposal.

'Affection' (the excitement of the *Affekte*) was thought to occur through the movement of the *spiritus animalis* described by Descartes.[18] In a discursive scientific prologue to his libretto, *Simson* (Hamburg 1709), Barthold Feind explains that the body is influenced by the movement of the blood and the Cartesian 'Lebens=Geister', 'welche . . . die innerliche [*sic*] Gemüths=Bewegungen nach den Temperamenten erregen'.[19] Like Kircher and Descartes before him, Feind believes that the process of affection is influenced by the natural temperament or *humores* (bodily fluids or humours) of the subject, which will cause a different degree and quality of response in different people. While the affections need to be controlled, they are not generally held to be negative. Feind emphatically approves of the human capacity to be moved, and defines the *Affekte* themselves as 'Eigenschafften der vornehmsten und ersten Krafft des menschlichen Gemühtes'.[20] Dramatically they are 'das Haupt=Werck . . . und die Schau=Spiele/ darinnen solche nicht anzutreffen/ [lieffern] uns nichts/ als leere Schalen'.[21] In keeping with the didactic spirit of the age, this judgement is justified by the belief that the affections constitute mankind's bridge to virtue; Feind's Hamburg contemporary, Mattheson, counts the recognition that 'die Gemüths=Neigungen der Menschen die wahre Materie der Tugend [sind]' among the basic precepts of musicianship.[22] Mattheson is echoing a contemporary conviction when he

[18] René Descartes, *The Passions of the Soul*, trans. Stephen H. Voss (Indianapolis 1989), 22.

[19] Barthold Feind, 'Von Erregung der Gemüths=Bewegungen in Schau=Spielen', prologue to *Der Fall des grossen Richters in Israel/ SIMSON*, music by Christoph Graupner (Hamburg 1709). The libretto and prologue are repr. in Reinhard Meyer, *Die Hamburger Oper*, 4 vols. (Munich 1980–4), 1. 255–333.

[20] 'Von dem Temperament und Gemühts=Beschaffenheit eines Poeten', in Feind, *Deutsche Gedichte*, 1–73 (14).

[21] Feind, 'Von Erregung der Gemüths=Bewegungen', 266.

[22] Johann Mattheson, *Der Vollkommene Capellmeister* (Hamburg 1739), repr. ed. Margarete Reimann (Kassel 1954), 15. Hereafter referred to in the text as *Capellmeister*.

finds it 'unstreitig' that 'das rechte Ziel aller Melodien nichts anders ist, als eine solche **Vergnügung des Gehörs, dadurch die Affecten rege werden**' [Mattheson's bold].[23] Music stirs the emotions by imitating them, as Johann Adolph Scheibe tells us in his succinct definition 'von der *Music* überhaupt':

> Die *Music* ist eine gelehrte Wißenschafft, welche nebst der Untersuchung der Klänge zugleich zeiget, wie aus solchen durch eine gute *Melodie* und *Harmonie* die *Affecten* der Menschen ausgedrucket und erreget, verschiedene Bewegungen der Natur aber nachgeahmet werden können und sollen.[24]

This echoes Aristotle's suggestion that the most natural imitation of human emotion is simultaneously the most persuasive and the most likely to stir a response in the listener.[25] The emotive power over fellow human beings that mastery of music can put in the hands of the composer is keenly felt by Reinhard Keiser, possibly the best-known German operatic composer of his day. He expresses his awareness of it with specific reference to opera music, or *musica scenica*:

> die Affecten des Zorns, des Mitleidens, der Liebe, samt den Eigensch-aften der Großmuth, Gerechtigkeit, Unschuld und Verlassenheit stellet sie [= *musica scenica*] in ihrer natürlichen Blöße dar und macht durch ihre verborgene Krafft dazu alle Gemüther rege, ja sie zwingt fast die Hertzen heimlich zu einer Passion nach Willen, . . .[26]

Since we have noted that a rigid *Affektenlehre* did not generally underlie early modern composition, it would be superfluous here to attempt a summary of all the devices put forward by composers and theorists as suited to the expression of particular emotions. Some will be discussed below with reference to musical rhetoric; but most composers who express an opinion do not claim that any one method is binding, since there is an awareness that music is, anyway, received differently by different people. Musical interpretations based

---

[23] Johann Mattheson, *Kern Melodischer Wißenschafft* (Hamburg 1737; repr. Hildesheim 1976), 66. Hereafter referred to in the text as *Kern*.

[24] Johann Adolph Scheibe, *Compendium MUSICES Theoretico-practicum*, repr. in Peter Benary, *Die deutsche Kompositionslehre des 18. Jahrhunderts* (Leipzig 1961). Benary dates the work, which is repr. from Christoph Graupner's copy, as pre-1736.

[25] Vickers, *In Defence of Rhetoric*, 297.

[26] Reinhard Keiser, introduction to *Componimenti Musicali* (Hamburg 1706), cited in Rolf Dammann, *Der Musikbegriff im deutschen Barock* (Cologne 1967), 227.

on affective systems have been attempted—a fairly recent example is Rosamond Drooker Brenner's essay on Keiser's operas—and, as in Brenner's case, have tended to attract criticism as over-interpretation.[27] With reference to Brenner's article, Klaus Zelm doubts whether the appearance of passages in quick time or a particular key really does express the composer's awareness and implementation of a musical *Affektenlehre*; he suggests that such things may in fact spring primarily from practical musical considerations that have a long tradition. Zelm prefers the view 'daß Keiser, trotz gelegentlich sensibler Ausdeutung des Affekts, sich nicht sklavisch an eine außermusikalische Doktrin band, die er vermutlich in Einzelheiten gar nicht kannte'.[28]

Zelm's deliberately practical approach, although perhaps overstated, is instructive. The ideas that form the kernel of affective theories of music in the seventeenth and early eighteenth centuries—the ideas, that is, which are most frequently repeated—are in practice accessible even to the non-expert mind. A Bach scholar and proponent of the *Affektenlehre* early this century, Gotthold Frotscher, notes that the musical expression of an emotion recalls the physical movement of the person experiencing it: 'So erscheint die Freude mit bewegten Rhythmen, die Trauer etwa mit schleichenden chromatischen Gängen'.[29] Common sense or even common sensitivity is the key: Mattheson follows Kircher in sensing joy as an expansive, sorrow as a constricting emotion, and translating this naturally into musical intervals:

§.56. Da z.E. die Freude durch **Ausbreitung** unsrer Lebens=Geister empfunden wird, so folget *vernünfftiger und natürlicher Weise*, daß ich diesen Affect am besten durch weite und erweitete Intervalle ausdrücken könne. §.57. Weiß man hergegen, daß die Traurigkeit eine **Zusammenziehung** solcher subtilen Theile unsers Leibes ist, *so stehet leicht zu ermessen*, daß sich zu dieser Leidenschafft die **engen** und **engesten** Klang=Stuffen am füglichsten schicken. (*Capellmeister*, 16. Mattheson's bold, my italics.)

---

[27] Rosamond Drooker Brenner, 'Emotional Expression in Keiser's Operas', in *MR* 33 (1972), 222–32. Reviewed by Klaus Zelm in *Die Opern Reinhard Keisers: Studien zur Chronologie, Überlieferung und Stilentwicklung* (Munich 1975), 200–2.
[28] Ibid. 201.
[29] Gotthold Frotscher, 'Die Affektenlehre als geistige Grundlage der Themenbildung J. S. Bachs', in *Bach-Jahrbuch* (1926), 90–104 (102).

The composer is not so much dictating a method here as using physiological and musical theories to explain what is, anyway, his instinct. An approach like this leaves room for flexibility: in another theoretical text, Mattheson notes that wide intervals are equally well suited to the expression of 'desperates Wesen', since they may be experienced as 'verwegen' and 'unbändig' (*Kern*, 91). Such considerations of audience reception lead us into the area of musical rhetoric.

The emulation of a perceived Classical unity of words and music was one theoretical impetus in the development of early Italian opera. Since Renaissance thinkers found such fascination in the rediscovery of the Ancients, it is not surprising that music theorists, too, began to consider their object of study in the light of the most influential Classical legacy in the early modern period: rhetoric. In 1537, a Protestant cantor called Nicolaus Listenius appended to the Boethian division of *musica theoretica* and *musica pratica* a further category, *musica poetica*, or the technique of composition.[30] In *musica poetica* theory and practice move closer together, and the new name suggests a kind of music which is interpretable and manipulable in the manner of a language: a persuasive, rhetorical music. Joachim Burmeister's *Musica Poetica* of 1606 is one attempt to classify musical rhetoric. The work lists musical figures which are analogous with the rhetorical figures of antiquity (anaphora, anadiplosis, and pleonasm, for example).[31] Similar systematic attempts followed, none of which achieved definitive status, but by the last decades of the century Christian Bernhard, a pupil of Schütz, is moved to exclaim, 'daß auff unsere Zeiten die *Musica* so hoch kommen, daß wegen Menge der *Figuren*, absonderlich aber in dem neu erfundenen und bisher immer mehr ausgezierten *Stylo Recitativo*, sie wohl einer *Rhetorica* zu vergleichen'.[32] In his seminal *Buch von der Deutschen Poeterey* of 1624, Martin Opitz

---

[30] See Carl Dahlhaus, 'Musica poetica und musikalische Poesie', in *Archiv für Musikwissenschaft* 23 (1966), 110–24.

[31] Joachim Burmeister, *Musica Poetica* (Rostock 1606), repr. ed. Martin Ruhnke (Kassel 1955), 55–65.

[32] Christian Bernhard, *Ausführlicher Bericht vom Gebrauche der Con- und Dissonantien* (Hamburg[?], c.1682), in Joseph Müller-Blattau, *Die Kompositionslehre Heinrich Schützens in der Fassung seines Schülers Christoph Bernhard* (Kassel 1963 [1926]), 132–53 (147).

had structured his discussion of German poetics according
to the Classical rhetorical principles of *inventio* ('erfindung'),
*dispositio* ('abtheilung der dinge'), and *decoratio* ('zuebereitung
und ziehr der worte'). Describing the principles of composition in the early eighteenth century, Johann Mattheson
maps out a rhetoric of music along these lines. In his early
theoretical work, *Das neu-eröffnete Orchestre* (1713), he notes:
'Es gehören sonst zu einer Composition dreyerley: Invention,
(die Erfindung) Elaboratio, (Die Ausarbeitung) Execution,
(die Ausführung oder Aufführung) welches eine ziemliche
nahe Verwandschafft mit der Oratorie oder Rhetorique . . .
an den Tag leget.'[33] Mattheson's *Kern Melodischer Wißenschafft*
(1737) demands 'dispositio', 'elaboratio', and 'decoratio' in
composition. Musical rhetoric is also a technique he requires
of the *Vollkommener Capellmeister* (1739); here Mattheson adds
'elocutio' (the use of musical pauses) to the list.

Opitz gave poetic guidelines on the use of metre, advocating the use primarily of trochees ($- \cup$) and iambs ($\cup -$) in
the alexandrine or six-foot line, although other rhythmic feet
naturally come to be used in German poetry, especially the
dactyl ($- \cup \cup$). Line length in music cannot be regulated in
the same way as in a poem, but the use of the rhythmic foot
is considered in some detail, especially, as we might expect,
with regard to rhetorical impact and 'affective' expression.
Mattheson considers the topic in the *Capellmeister*, in a chapter called 'Von den Klang=Füssen' (164–70).[34] He gives the
spondee (— —; ♩ ♩) pride of place, not least for practical
reasons: 'hat billig unter allen rhythmis die Ober=Stelle, nicht
nur wegen seines ehrbaren und ernsthafften Ganges; sondern
auch weil er leicht zu begreifen ist', but also deals with the
pyrrhichius (♫ ♫) for 'schnelle oder feurige Bewegung', the
iamb (♩ ♩), characterized as 'mäßig lustig, nicht flüchtig',

---

[33] See also Wulf Arlt, 'Zur Handhabung der "inventio" in der deutschen
Musiklehre des frühen achtzehnten Jahrhunderts', in Buelow and Marx (eds.), *New
Mattheson Studies* (Cambridge 1983), 371–91.

[34] Walter Serauky indicates that an earlier consideration of metre in music was
made by Isaak Vossius (*De poematum cantu et viribus Rhythmi*, 1673); this may have been
a more immediate source for Mattheson than Opitz. See the article 'Affektenlehre'
in Friedrich Blume (ed.), *Die Musik in Geschichte und Gegenwart: allgemeine Enzyklopädie
der Musik*, 17 vols. (Kassel 1949–1986), vol. 1, cols. 113–21 (117).

the trochee (♩ ♩: 'zu Wiegen= oder Schlaf=Liedern'), the multi-purpose dactyl (♩ ♫) and the anapaest (♫♩), along with a number of other melodic feet. Again there is little mystery here. When Mattheson reveals that a molossus (♩ ♩ ♩) 'hat drey lange Sylben oder Klänge, und drücket eine Schwierigkeit, oder was mühseliges ziemlich wol aus', or that the tribrach (♫♩) occurs 'grössesten Theils in Giguen, und was mit denselben verwandt ist', even the musical lay person will guess that this does not so much constitute a doctrine of composition as an attempt at analysis of what most composers do intuitively. More important for this discussion is the strong sense of a theoretical relationship between music and language, which, as emerges in the treatment of pauses, is also a practical relationship.

The pause or 'rest' in the musical line is a device which Mattheson not only perceives as closely related to textual and rhetorical practice (a pause will occur to clarify meaning, or to heighten effect), but also as something which should come as naturally to the composer as the expression of the *Affekte*. In a section of his *Kern Melodischer Wißenschafft* entitled 'Von den Einschnitten der Klang=Rede', he is almost embarrassed by the need to elucidate:

Vor etlichen Jahren hat ein grosser Dichter, als etwas sonderbares, entdecken wollen, daß es mit der Music in diesem Stücke fast eben die Bewandniß habe, als mit der Rede=Kunst. . . . Die Ton=Künstler mögen sich wohl schämen, daß sie hierin so saumselig gewesen sind. (p. 71)

The same reproach is repeated almost word-for-word in the *Capellmeister* (p. 181).

The most extensively discussed feature of musical rhetoric, both in the early modern period and in modern criticism, is without question the use of figures. They are widely defined: Athanasius Kircher considers even the rest or pause a figure, in its standard musical usage for the expression of sighs, or grief.[35] The figure is a musical analogy which can add depth and meaning to a text. Two short examples from Reinhard

---

[35] See Albrecht D. Stoll, *Figur und Affekt: Zur höfischen Musik und zur bürgerlichen Musiktheorie der Epoche Richelieu*, 2nd edn. (Tutzing 1981), 38.

Ex. 1. Clelia (II. vi)

Ex. 2. Octavia (II. v)

Keiser's score for Feind's Hamburg libretto *Octavia* (1705)
illustrate this kind of word-painting (Exx. 1 and 2).[36]

The relation between text and music is clear, even though
these are not the kind of figures listed by the theorists of
*musica poetica*. Dietrich Bartel, author of a modern *Handbuch
der musikalischen Figurenlehre*, in which he lists over 150 musical rhetorical figures, maintains that there is no consistent
doctrine.[37] I find George Buelow's argument convincing:

> Many of the musical figures . . . originated in attempts to explain or justify
> irregular . . . contrapuntal writing. Although proceeding contrary to the rules
> of counterpoint, such passages were found to be suitable for dramatizing
> affective expression of the texts . . . What German theorists rationalized
> was a natural and common element in the craft of every composer.[38]

Even attitudes to the freer application of such sound-painting
are inconsistent. Mattheson pours scorn on the modish use of
musical figures to illustrate a text like 'zitterndes Gläntzen
der sprudlenden [*sic*] Wellen' because of technical problems

[36] Reinhard Keiser, *Octavia*, ed. Friedrich Chrysander, in *Händelgesellschaft:
Händels Werke, Supplemente* 6 (Leipzig 1902), 95, 99.

[37] Dietrich Bartel, *Handbuch der musikalischen Figurenlehre* (Hamburg 1985), 7.

[38] Article 'Rhetoric and Music', in *New Grove*, 15. 793–803 (800).

in the singing: 'wegen des hi, hi, hi, und hu, hu, hu, im Zittern und Sprudlen, sehr wiederlich [sic] klinget, und, mit einem Wort, recht gezwungen'; for this reason he recommends that figures should be used in the accompaniment rather than in the melody (Capellmeister, 201–2).

One of the most difficult issues in early modern music theory is that of the tonalities. It cannot be ignored in a consideration of the Hamburg opera, because it is Mattheson again who devotes a section of his Neu-eröffnetes Orchestre to a discussion of their affective 'meanings'. That Mattheson applied tonalities in a manner consistent with his own theories has been shown by Buelow with reference to the opera Cleopatra (1704).[39] How far they are received or applied by other composers can only be speculated on, possibly fruitlessly, although Hugo Leichtentritt has observed a keen concern with the choice of key in the operas and oratorios of Handel, who is known to have been influenced at least by Keiser during his time in Hamburg.[40] It is chiefly worth noting that much of what Mattheson writes about key 'affects' is roughly predictable: for example, his characterization of the minor keys as generally gentle and sad, of F major, the pastoral key, as suited to the expression of virtues such as love or constancy, and of D major (the trumpet and timpani key) as sharp and military.

Early musical rhetoric is, then, less arcane than it might initially appear. There is a great wave of music theory in Europe in the early modern period, but this is likely to have arisen at least in part from the excitement engendered by the observation of strong audience reactions to the new dramatic music of opera. Composers acquire an awareness of their own potential to affect fellow human beings, and are keen to enhance this ability by developing their understanding of how the power of music works, especially in conjunction with the language of the operatic text. The 'figures' they identify and discuss are not so much an early form of

[39] George G. Buelow, 'An Evaluation of Johann Mattheson's Opera, Cleopatra (Hamburg, 1704)', in H. C. Robbins Landon and Roger E. Chapman (eds.), Studies in Eighteenth-Century Music: A Tribute to Karl Geiringer on his Seventieth Birthday (London 1970), 92–107.

[40] See Hugo Leichtentritt, Music, History and Ideas (Cambridge, Mass. 1938), 143–4.

leitmotif as standard musical devices explained in terms of fashionable ideas about their acoustic effects. The musical rhetoric which will concern us in opera in fact functioned more simply than the systems of figures, affections, and tonalities might suggest, and is closely linked to the rhetoric of the text. Before we move on to musical examples, however, we need to take a brief look at the practical conditions of performance.

### Practice (i): The Elements of Opera

The component parts of opera that spring most readily to mind are recitative (madrigal-style through-composed verse) and aria, whose strophic verse is generally reflected in a structured musical form. These two elements did not, of course, suddenly spring into being in the first opera (generally assumed to have been *La Dafne,* by the Florentine *Camerata* members Ottavio Rinuccini [text] and Jacopo Peri [music], Florence 1598):[41] their origins were in madrigal drama, *intermedi* (musical intermissions in drama), and folk-song. The newness of opera did, however, lead to some discussion of the merits and possibilities of its most prominent components.

Early recitative has been seen as a response to Plato's advice to let the notes and the rhythm follow the speech. If the text is to dominate in this way, it must be perfectly comprehensible to a listener, something which can only be achieved if the musical accompaniment neither challenges the textual dominance in its complexity (an argument against counterpoint), nor prevents the words from being sung in their normal speech rhythm. Donington makes the point that this should not tempt us to class recitative as a 'natural' form: 'Recitative is not nature; it is a convention for suggesting nature by quite unnaturalistic contrivance. Above all, the primary consideration of recitative is dramatic expressiveness.' The primary consideration of aria, on the other hand, is

---

[41] Robert Donington points out that the usual date cited, 1597, is in fact Florentine old-style dating, and corresponds in the modern calendar to the year 1598. See Donington, *The Rise of Opera* (London 1981), 104.

musical expressiveness.[42] One early theorist, Scheibe, describes the musical antithesis between recitative and aria in terms of the textual opposition between verse and prose, with the recommendation, 'man soll . . . überhaupt das *Recitativ* nicht als verse [*sic*] *scandir*end, sondern als *Prosa* das ist redend *componir*en, denn so bekommen die . . . Wörter ihren gemäßen Ausdruck'.[43] In his reflections on recitative, Barthold Feind reminds us of the close links between music and language which are particularly evident in this form:

> Wenn etwas gefraget/ erzehlet/ anbefohlen oder abgelesen wird/ so hat ein jedes in der Music seine eigene Regel/ Thon und Harmonie. Ein Semicolon, Punctum, Signum interrogandi, Exclamationis, Colon und Comma hat seine Gesetze und Cadence . . . so wird man fast ein *certium quid* unter Singen und Sprechen bemercken/ welches man vom gantzen Recitativ sagen muß . . .[44]

Feind complains about too-complex or aria-style accompaniment to recitative, 'die nicht anders als verdrieslich seyn kan/ weil man kein Changement hat/ und fast durch das continuirliche durcheinander Schwermen der Instrumenten betäubet wird' (*Gedancken*, 78–9); *arioso* or *obbligato* recitative is, in his view, only allowable for the expression of especially strong emotion.

Typically, it is Mattheson who gives us the most detailed discussion of recitative. He notes that it has 'keine förmliche Melodie', but 'die Freyheit, daß [diese Art zu singen] sich nach der gemeinen Ausrede richtet, und mit allerhand Ton=Arten spielet' (*Kern*, 97). It is rhythmically flexible: 'Der Recitativ hat wol einen Tact; braucht ihn aber nicht: d.i. der Sänger bindet sich nicht daran' (ibid.). He stresses the need for the rhythm to follow that of speech, and for the text to be readily comprehensible, and concludes with the admonition that recitative is by no means secondary in importance or less demanding of a composer's skill: 'durch nichts verräth sich und seine Ungeschicklichkeit ein Componist mehr, als durch einen preshafften [= bresthaften] und hanenbüchenen Recitativ'.

---

[42] Donington, *The Rise of Opera* (London 1981), 89–90.
[43] In Benary, *Die deutsche Kompositionslehre*, 81.
[44] Barthold Feind, *Gedancken von der Opera*, in *Deutsche Gedichte*, 74–114 (78). Hereafter referred to in the text as *Gedancken*.

The extent to which recitative can heighten dramatic tension is demonstrated by Andrew McCredie with reference to Christoph Graupner's Hamburg operas, *Dido* and *Antiochus und Stratonica* (both 1707).[45] McCredie shows how the alternation of different kinds of recitative (the *secco, accompagnato*, and motivic orchestral varieties), the deliberate use of suggestive tonalities, and recurrent ornamentation not unlike leitmotif in recitative sections can create impressive dramatic effects. Here as much as in aria the rhetoric of the text can be effectively supported in the music.

The term 'aria' is first used in Domenico Mazzochi's score for *La catena d'Adone* (Rome 1626), although here it is applied not only to solo songs, but also to duets and larger ensembles.[46] For Feind, in his introduction to *Simson*, the aria is '[die] Seele musicalischer Schau=Spiele' (p. 270). This is an idea he had already expressed a year earlier, in *Gedancken von der Opera*, where he gives a more detailed explanation of the form:

Die Arien sind fast in der Opera die Erklährung des Recitatifs, das zierlichste und künstlichste der Poesie/ und der Geist und die Seele des Schauspiels. Ich habe schon gesagt . . . daß dieselbe nicht durch das blosse Metrum oder gröbern Druck vom Recitatif müssen unterschieden werden/ sondern/ daß dieselbe ein Morale, Allegorie, Proverbium und Gleichnis . . . haben müssen/ . . . entweder auf das/ was im Recitatif gesaget worden/oder üm eine neue Lehre/ Unterricht oder Raht zu geben. (p. 95)

Two interesting related aspects of the early German aria emerge. On a superficial level, the aria is visually (through the heavy print and spacing) as well as rhythmically (through the metre) distinct from recitative even in the libretto. It is also distinguished by its textual content, which is less literal and more abstract than the recitative, on which it reflects or comments. A link with the *Reyen* of Baroque drama is evident, which provide a similar allegorical, reflective, or didactic commentary on the action, and in which an authorial voice can break into the dramatic happenings to guide audience reactions. In opera this provides opportunities not only for

---

[45] Andrew D. McCredie, 'Christoph Graupner as opera composer', in *Miscellanea Musicologica* 1 (1966), 74–116 (93–4).

[46] See Grout, *Short History of Opera*, 62.

the librettist, but also for the composer, who can use the space offered by the aria for musical expression to sway audience sympathy, whether by delicate instrumentation and lilting melodies for an exemplary heroine, or by darker bass accompaniment, racing rhythms, and sliding chromatism for a more threatening character. We can give Mattheson the last word on this, who, from a musical point of view, expresses exactly the same opinions as Feind from his textual perspective:

denn eine Arie soll eigentlich nichts anders sein/ als ein wohlgefaßter/ mit einem gewissen Affect versehener/ nachdencklicher Haupt=Spruch/ und Axioma, das durchgehends auff diejenige Materie, davon es handelt/ seinen Nutzen oder seine application haben könnte. (*Critica Musica,* I. 104)

By the late seventeenth and early eighteenth centuries, a fairly extensive range of sounds was available in the orchestra, with which composers were keen to experiment. There is no doubt that the sound of an instrument, because it differs in its evocations from the sound of any other, is an essential factor in manipulating the reaction of a listener to music. The brief discussion of the opera orchestra which follows can only give an idea of the sound repertoire available; it will touch on the instruments in the context of their family groups, and attempt to indicate the kind of sound-painting they or their groups tend to support.

Reference to the musical Baroque as the *Generalbaßzeitalter* reflects a basic shift in compositional style that took place in the period, namely from traditional polyphony, or *musica antica*, to the accompanied monody of *musica moderna*. In early seventeenth-century Italy, the terms *prima pratica* and *seconda pratica* came to be used for the old and the new styles respectively. Because the accompanying thorough-bass or *basso continuo* provided an harmonic substructure, virtuoso melodic lines for one or more voices could be composed in a way that would not have been possible in the old polyphonic style; hence the development of opera and oratorio was inseparable from that of the *seconda pratica*.

The most common continuo instrument was the harpsichord. Other accompanying instruments included the lute (which in the Baroque was a larger instrument with more bass strings than the Renaissance lute), the viola da gamba

and the triple harp.[47] The continuo might be supported
by bass strings or bassoon. Small chamber groups including strings or woodwind could also form the accompaniment;
these were commonly used in the arias of the Hamburg
opera.

The basic bowed string in the orchestra was the viol (also
called viola da gamba or leg fiddle). There were various differently pitched versions of this instrument, which gradually
came to be replaced during the eighteenth century by the
violoncello. The viola da braccio or arm fiddle also existed
in different forms; the tenor viol corresponds to the modern
viola, and the descant viol or violetta picciola, mentioned by
Daniel Speer in the third 'leaf' of his *Vierfaches musikalisches
Kleeblatt* (1697), to our modern violin.[48] Speer also lists
among the strings the six-stringed 'Bass-Violon', pitched a
fifth lower than its cousin, the viola da gamba. Because these
strings were strung with natural gut, without metal wrapping,
and played with short light bows, they produced a more
transparent, less brilliant sound quality than the one we are
accustomed to today. The viola d'amore, on the other hand,
was characterized by its resonant sound quality, which was
created by a set of metal strings vibrating in sympathy with
the gut strings on which the instrument is played. In early
German opera the bowed strings characteristically accompany
entries of furies and other wild spirits, and express emotional
and physical excitement. Pizzicato strings form the standard
accompaniment for dream-states or secretive, tender scenes,
and mutes support a stage atmosphere of ghostliness or magic.
The dark sound of the double bass lends itself to underworld
scenes and the supernatural, sometimes in conjunction with
other bass instruments such as the bassoon.

Under the influence especially of Keiser in Hamburg the
woodwind section was used to imaginative effect. *Flöten* were

[47] For much of the information on early instruments given in this section
I am indebted both to Wilhelm Kleefeld's detailed account in 'Das Orchester der
Hamburger Oper 1678–1738', in *SIM* 1 (1899–1900), 219–89, and to the article
by Jeremy Montagu of the Bate Collection, Oxford, in Julie Anne Sadie (ed.),
*Companion to Baroque Music* (London 1990), 366–75.
[48] Daniel Speer, *Grundrichtiger Unterricht der musikalischen Kunst oder Vierfaches
musikalisches Kleeblatt* (Ulm 1697; repr. Leipzig 1974), 188–260.

in their basic form recorders, although the transverse flute, called *flûte d'Allemagne* or *flûte traversière*, was also in use. All were wooden, and had a soft sound quality that lent itself to the sound-painting of such things as light breezes and rustling leaves. Keiser uses the transverse flute to great effect when he sets it against a background of pizzicato strings for the slumber scene aria 'Kühle Winde, saust gelinde' in *Tomyris* (1717).[49] The Hamburg scores also contain occasional parts for *Zuffolo*, a small set of pan-pipes. Oboe and bassoon (*Fagott*) had developed by the third quarter of the seventeenth century from the Renaissance shawm (*Schäfer-Schalmei*) and dulcian. The origins of the former make it an obvious choice for pastoral scenes; Staden's score for the pastoral *Seelewig* requires as many oboes and flutes as violins. Bassoons, as was noted above, are favourite instruments for dark and dangerous effects: Kleefeld cites a five-bassoon aria in *Octavia* (the heroine of which is being betrayed by her husband, Nero) as an example of their use for the expression of guilt and, specifically, adulterous love.[50]

The most important member of the brass section was the trumpet, in North German opera most commonly the *Cammerthon* trumpet in D.[51] Trumpet playing is traditionally associated with royal entrances, and the instrument was officially one of state, which could only be played by members of the trumpeters' guild. Its sound is evocative of military scenes; we have observed that this led to the association of its key, D major, with warlike and strong *Affekte*.

If music and text in opera constitute a special kind of rhetoric, as the early modern theorists would have us believe, then the singer is the orator who must perform it effectively. The vocal effects which can be achieved by a skilled singer were clearly in the minds of librettists like Feind, who is emphatic in his opinion that singing is the ultimate form of rhetorical declamation:

---

[49] Nr. 27 in Keiser, *Die Großmüthige Tomyris* (Hamburg 1717), repr. ed. Klaus Zelm (Munich 1975).

[50] Kleefeld, 'Das Orchester', 266.

[51] See Andrew D. McCredie, 'Instrumentarium and Instrumentation in the North German Baroque Opera' (unpublished doctoral thesis, University of Hamburg 1964), 220.

Ich glaube auch nicht/ daß ein vernünfftiger Mensch leicht in Abrede seyn werde/ daß man nicht im Singen einer Rede zehnmal mehr Nachdruck geben könne/ als in der Declamation und simplen Sprache; Denn was ist wol das Singen anders/ als die Erhöhung der Rede und Stimme mit der höchsten Krafft und Nachdruck? (*Gedancken*, 79)

Christoph Bernhard puts his faith in the intellectual ability of singers to interpret a text in such a way as to excite the intended response in the listener; this he calls 'cantar alla Napolitana oder d'affetto', which 'bestehet . . . darinnen, daß der Sänger fleißig den *Text* beobachtet und nach Anleitung [desselbigen] die Stimme *moderirt*. . . . Solches geschieht auf zweyerley Weiße, einmahl in Beobachtung der blosen Worte, zum andren in Anmerckung ihres Verstandes.'[52] Bernhard is, however, adamant that affective expression on the part of the singer should restrict itself to voice control. He answers his own rhetorical question, 'ob ein Sänger auch die im *Texte* befindlichen *affecten* mit dem Gesichte und Geberden darstellen solle? So ist zu wissen, daß ein Sänger fein sittsam, und ohne alle *Minen* singen soll' (p. 37). In this he differs from the later theorist, Mattheson, who devotes an entire chapter of his *Vollkommener Capellmeister* to 'Geberden=Kunst'.

Ideas about the use of differently pitched voices reflect the general tendency, also observed in the use of the orchestra, to give music emblematic meaning. High notes suggest lofty character and the low registers, baseness. Soprano and tenor voices were therefore considered suitable for the expression of heroic virtue, while the bass parts were usually written for fools or villains. When Monteverdi wrote his *Incoronazione di Poppea* (first composed for Venice in 1642), it was natural that the parts of both lovers, Nero and Poppea, should be sung by castrati; in Hamburg operas the latter were replaced by women sopranos (the castrati were as expensive as they were popular), and tenors took the leading male roles.

Ideally, then, the singing voice should carry and fulfil the rhetorical potential offered by the combination of text and music. The calibre and training of individual singers, as well as the stresses placed on orchestral players by improvisation

---

[52] *Von der Singe-Kunst oder Manier* (1645[?]), in Müller-Blattau, *Die Kompositionslehre Heinrich Schützens*, 31–9 (36). Further references are given in the text.

and on their instruments by the unstable temperature (and smoky atmosphere) of a taper-lit opera house, are the variables which must temper any assumptions about the sounds produced and their effects on an audience.

## Practice (ii): The Interaction of Music and Text

While the emotional arousal of the listener is a frequently stated aim in early modern discussions of composition, orchestration, and singing, some passages suggest that this is the means to an end, rather than an end in itself.

The writers of opera are clearly interested in their public. Mattheson's recommendations to the up-and-coming *Capellmeister* betray his interest in the manipulation of people's physiological and psychological reactions to music: 'Die Lehre von den Temperamenten und Neigungen . . . leiste[t] hier sehr gute Dienste, indem man daraus lernet, die Gemüther der Zuhörer, und die klingenden Kräffte, wie sie an jenen wirken, wol zu unterscheiden' (*Capellmeister*, 15). Such an interest is more than an expression of the mercenary considerations forced on a commercial opera house like Hamburg. In 1650, Kircher is already observing audience responses to opera in Rome: 'was aber die Scenische Comödien-Music noch heutigs Tags zu Rom vor Wunder-Würckungen habe/ das ist nicht zu beschreiben: die Bewegung ist oftmal so groß und heftig/ das die autores [= auditores] überlaut anfangen zu schreien/ seufzen/ weinen/ sonderlich in casibus tragicis.'[53] The excesses of the human affections or passions may present a danger, but the emotions are also perceived as the path to virtue. Mattheson elucidates: 'Wo keine Leidenschaft, kein Affect zu finden, da ist auch keine Tugend', before going on to state the true purpose of musical manipulation of the affections as he sees it: 'das ist die rechte Eigenschaft der Music, daß sie eine Zucht=Lehre vor andern sey' (*Capellmeister*, 15).

One may choose to doubt Mattheson. His ideas may be pure theory and have no bearing on musical practice, or they

---

[53] Kircher, *Musurgia universalis*, 546; in Hirsch's translation, p. 134. Compare Damman, *Der Musikbegriff im deutschen Barock*, 228.

may form part of a rhetorical exercise designed to enhance music's theoretical status, or simply reflect the *Opernstreit* which sought to establish early opera's moral value. But the composers of the period were working within a tradition which finds clear expression in the music of Johann Sebastian Bach, to name a famous example, and persists in the work of later eighteenth-century composers such as Haydn: a tradition founded on the belief that music's primary function is to praise God. It is an interesting aspect of early opera, as it distinguishes itself from oratorio, that a break with this tradition begins. Opera is soon recognizably directed at its human audience, and not at the divinity. Yet its writers still feel an obligation to concern themselves with moral improvement. Some librettists were naturally less adept, or less concerned with moral issues than others; but it is important that those who saw themselves as tone-setters, like Mattheson, were genuinely persuaded of the influence their medium could have on other human beings. Observations like Kircher's of audience reactions to a performance suggest that they were not mistaken. This final section will investigate the rhetorical efficacy of a combination of music and text by looking more closely at the interaction of score and libretto specifically in portrayals of women and Turks in some of the Hamburg texts for which the music has survived.

*Turks and Christians: The Arias from* Cara Mustapha

Music theorists from the early modern period give us an indication of Western receptivity to sounds from other cultures. In his influential *Syntagma musicum* (1619), Michael Praetorius provides illustrations and descriptions of a variety of non-European musical instruments. Turkish music receives special attention, but there is nothing complimentary in this; Praetorius calls it 'Lumpen-Music', finds it barbaric and noisy, and finally decides that it is another indication of the general ill will of the Prophet of Islam: 'Denn es hat Mahomet alles was zur frölichkeit dienlich/ alß Wein und Saytenspiel in seinem ganzen Lande verbotten/ unnd an deren stadt eine Teuffels Glocke unnd Rumpelfaß mit einer schnarrenden und

kikakenden Schalmeyen verordnet/ . . .'[54] An anecdote from
Werckmeister's *Harmonologia Musica* (1702) illustrates the
general resistance to non-European sounds: 'Der vortreffliche
Kepler führe auch ein solch Exempel in seiner Harmonia
mundi an, von einem türkischen Priester, welcher all Morgen
auf die Erde gefallen und dergleichen verwirrte Melodien
zu Keplers Greuel gesungen habe.'[55] The enthusiasm for
'Turkish' opera and ballet seems to have sprung from a greed
for the visual spectacle of oriental opulence or decadence
rather than from aural curiosity, and there is a consensus
among modern critics that the oriental ambience is not
reflected in the score of early opera.[56] This view is based
on the fact that genuine imitations of foreign sounds are
not in evidence, yet this does not necessarily mean that composers had no interest at all in constructing the musical
oriental. Having established that eighteenth-century *alla turca*
style has little in common with real Turkish music, Roland
Würtz is nonetheless persuaded that an *idea* of 'Turkishness'
is musically present: 'Im Singspiel des 18. Jahrhundert finden
wir das Türkische in drei Komponenten: im dramatischen
Stoff, in der davon abhängigen Bühnenbild-Kostümkunst
und im Musikalischen.'[57] A distinction needs to be made
between genuine interest in understanding and imitating
another culture—which does not characterize seventeenth- or
eighteenth-century *Turquerie*—and the Western will to exoticize
a cultural Other. A distinctive 'oriental' style is evident in
early French opera; Lully's *Bourgeois Gentilhomme* (1670),

---

[54] Cited in Angelika Bierbaum, 'Exotische Klangwelten—Europäische Klangphantasien: Musikalische Exotismus', in Hermann Pollig *et al.* (eds.), *Exotische
Welten—Europäische Phantasien: Ausstellung des Instituts für Auslandsbeziehungen und
des Württembergischen Kunstvereins* (Stuttgart 1987), 270–7 (271).

[55] Hermann Kretzschmar, 'Allgemeines und Besonderes zur Affektenlehre', in
*JMP* 18 (1911), 63–78 (66). Kretzschmar approves of the early modern response he
cites, and illustrates that fear of the cultural Other is as alive in the early twentieth
as it was in the seventeenth century when he continues: 'Wir könnten uns diese
Praxis etwas ad notam nehmen und mit unserer Hingabe an allerhand Ausländer
etwas sparsamer sein. In der Befreundung mit rassenfremder Musik liegt die Gefahr,
daß der heute so wie so schon unempfindlicher gewordener Sinn für den Affekt
sich weiter abstumpft und ganz verloren geht.'

[56] See for example the article 'Exoticism', in Stanley Sadie (ed.), *The New Grove
Dictionary of Opera*, 4 vols. (London 1992), 2. 96.

[57] Roland Würtz, 'Das Türkische im Singspiel des 18. Jahrhunderts', in *Das deutsche
Singspiel im 18. Jahrhundert* (Heidelberg 1981), 125–38 (125).

for example, features a chorus in garbled 'Turkish' sung to pseudo-Turkish music, and anticipates the orientalizing style of Rameau's *Les Indes Galantes* (1735), with its exotic instruments and unusual chromatics and modulation.[58] Certain elements come to characterize 'Turkish' music (we find them later in Mozart's *Entführung*): military style, especially drums, repetitive rhythms, loudness, and minor keys, which are experienced as strange, or 'other' than the major.

Librettists are aware of the effects to be achieved with 'strange' music. In *Simson* (1709), Barthold Feind uses dance music to render the Philistines' worship of Dagon striking, but also primitive and animalistic; it is 'dem Gesange der Vögel ähnlich'.[59] Lucas von Bostel sets the scene for his libretto, *Cara Mustapha* (1686),[60] with a chorus of Janissaries who accompany the entrance of the Emperor Mahomet (Mehmed IV) at the beginning of Act 1. Bostel is not only looking to exoticize, however. As we saw in Chapter 1, he has political reasons for portraying the Turk in terms of strange and threatening alterity. Here I shall investigate the arias composed by Johann Wolfgang Franck for the opera (no recitative score survives), and consider their role in programming audience responses to the Turks and the Christians of the piece.

Mustapha himself (the historical Kara Mustafa Köprülü, who led the second unsuccessful siege of Vienna in 1683) is the most threatening character in Bostel's two-part libretto. The opera celebrates the final victory of the Austro-Hungarian army, and the audience can only savour this triumph to the full if the Turkish anti-hero who is defeated incorporates all they

---

[58] See Bierbaum, 'Exotische Welten', 272, and Miriam Karpilow Whaples, 'Exoticism in Dramatic Music, 1600–1800' (UMI microfilmed doctoral thesis, University of Indiana 1958), 121. This analysis of Rameau's opera is in direct contradiction to what is maintained in the 'Exoticism' article (n. 63).

[59] Barthold Feind (text), Christoph Graupner (music), *Der Fall Des grossen Richters in Israel/ SIMSON, Oder: Die abgekühlte Liebes=Rache der DEBORA* (Hamburg 1709). Libretto in Meyer, *Die Hamburger Oper*, 1. 255–333 (277).

[60] Lucas von Bostel (text), Johann Wolfgang Franck (music), *Der Glückliche Groß=Vezier CARA MUSTAPHA, Erster Theil/ Nebenst Der grausahmen Belagerung/ und Bestürmung der Käyserlichen Residentz=Stadt WIEN. Anderer Druck* (Hamburg 1686); repr. in Meyer, *Die Hamburger Oper*, 1. 173–248; *Der Unglückliche CARA MUSTAPHA Anderer Theil/ Nebenst Dem erfreulichen Entsatze der Käyserlichen Residentz=Stadt WIEN* (Hamburg 1686); repr. with arias from both operas in *Hamburger Opernarien im szenischen Kontext*, ed. Werner Braun (Saarbrücken 1988).

Ex. 3

rau-ben        bren-nen        schän-den

have ever feared about the Ottomans. As the most threatening of the characters, Mustapha is therefore also the most
'Turkish' from an audience perspective. These two aspects,
the Turk and the threat, are linked in Franck's music.

Mustapha is not only morally but vocally the lowest of the
characters: he is the only protagonist to sing bass. Franck uses
the low range for sound-painting at appropriate moments
in the text. The demonic associations of the deep voice are
brought out in Mustapha's aria, 'Will mich die Verfolgung
drükken' (1. I. ix; no. 10)[61] in which the lowest notes for the
voice fall emblematically on the word 'Höllen'. In his first solo
aria, 'Blut von Feinden oder Freunden ist mir alles gleiche viel'
(1. I. ii; no. 3), his voice sinks on the words 'morden' and
'rauben' from C below middle C to the G below that, and
the high point of Mustapha's treason is strikingly marked
by the lowest point of the aria, when the last two syllables of
'ja das Reich mag untergehn' fall from the low G to C two
octaves below middle C: the music underlines the sense of
the final word.

'Blut von Feinden' musically conveys the destructive energy
of the anti-hero. The words 'rauben, brennen, schänden'
follow the arpeggio up on the beat, separated by pauses which
contribute to a sense of 'hopping' passion (Ex. 3).

---

[61] I give first the part of the opera (1 and 2) with the act and scene, then the number of the aria in Braun's edition. For the sake of simplicity in this chapter I have
also followed Braun's orthography, which differs from that in the Hamburg libretto.

There is a similar sense of urgency in the rests which separate 'sterben, verderben, vergehen' in Mustapha's 'Kommet ihr Furien' (1. III. xi; no. 23). Mozart later uses the same technique in Osmin's 'Erst geköpft, dann gehangen' from *Die Entführung aus dem Serail* (1782); this suggests that the device comes to characterize a recklessly vengeful (Turkish) character.

Where the other players in the piece tend to sing solo arias in 3/1 or 3/2 tempo, in minims and breves which allow them space for didactic reflection, Mustapha's solos are in quicker 3/4 and 4/4 time.[62] Franck creates idiomatic parts for bowed strings in dense repeated rhythms which achieve a tremolo effect suggestive of high dramatic action or confrontation, as for example in aria no. 3 above. The beating semiquavers are reminiscent of those we shall find accompanying the heroine's part in Keiser's *Tomyris*. The associations are warlike, suited to the type of the aggressive Turk as well as to an Amazonian ruler.

The arias for *Cara Mustapha* are almost exclusively notated with violin accompaniment above the thorough-bass; the anti-hero is the only one of the characters to be accompanied by the clarin or clarino, in 'Eifer erwache' (2. I. xi; no. 32). Clarinos are high-register trumpets, and would have contributed to a militant characterization of this protagonist.[63] Mustapha is therefore musically distinct not only from the Christian characters, but also from the other Turks in the opera. The only character who is almost equally in the grip of destructive passion is the Sultan's mother, Zaime, who is unhappily in love with the anti-hero. Like his, her arias contain extravagant melismatic figures, but where his fall on 'danger' words such as 'Schlangen' (1. III. xi; no. 23) and 'Rache' (2. I. xi; no. 32), hers illustrate a lover's frustration on 'Streit' (1. I. viii; no. 9) and a desperation to quench passion's flames on 'vorleschen' [= löschen] (1. I. x; no. 11).

---

[62] Time signatures are not necessarily an indication of tempo. Kircher, however, suggests in 1650 that note length is an indication of speed; minims and crotchets therefore suggest a slower tempo than quavers or semiquavers. See Robert Donington, *Baroque Music: Style and Performance* (London 1982), 13.

[63] See Reine Dahlqvist and Edward H. Tarr, article 'Clarino' in *The New Grove Dictionary of Musical Instruments*, ed. Stanley Sadie, 3 vols. (London 1984), I. 405–6. Dahlqvist and Tarr suggest that the trumpet is a military type, and was used as the 'clairon' in the French army from 1822 (p. 405).

Ex. 4

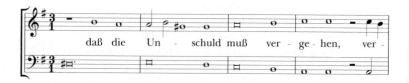

The musical portrayal of the two positively understood Turks in the piece, Baschlari and Ibrahim, is more likely to attract audience sympathy. The couple are finally separated when Mustapha's desire for Baschlari leads him to plot Ibrahim's death, and they sing some of the most affecting pieces in the opera. Ibrahim's last aria, sung just before he is strangled, 'Kanstu dieses Unrecht sehen' (7th *Vorstellung*; no. 42), has the air of a lament in slow 3/1 time. Minims, semibreves, and breves dominate; the only crotchets occur on the first syllable of 'vergehen' (Ex. 4).

The same crotchet pattern returns in an orchestral reminiscence after the singer has stopped, in a plaintive echo of the idea of Ibrahim's passing.

Baschlari's arias express harassment and persecution. Her first solo aria, 'Schikkung, warum läßtu mich nimmer ungeplaget' (II. i; no. 14), is in a major key (B flat), but modulates into the relative minor (g) on the word 'beklaget', which refers to the necessity of Ibrahim's departure to join Mustapha's forces. This is a premonition of the three minor arias she sings after the death of Ibrahim at Mustapha's hand: 'Ibrahim, geliebte Seele' (2. III. v; no. 44) in a, 'Scheiden, ach! betrübtes Scheiden' (2. III. v; no. 45) in e, and 'Lieb! ach Liebe' (2. III. vi) in c. Chromatism, identified by Mattheson as imitative of sadness, also characterizes Baschlari's arias, for example no. 44 (Ex. 5).

Ex. 5

in be-trüb-ter Ein-sam-keit,

Formal repetition links 'betrübt' and 'Einsamkeit' in an expression of the sorrow of Baschlari's widowed state, while a sliding undertone of sadness is provided by the slow climbing chromatism in the bass. The change back to the major key (B flat again) in aria no. 47 'Rache, zur Rache' (2. III. vi) is all the more striking, in 3/4 time and quick dotted rhythms, when Baschlari abandons her mourning for revenge on the demonic Mustapha.

The Christian pair, Manuela and Gasparo, are musically both linked with and distinguished from their Turkish counterparts Ibrahim and Baschlari. An interesting comparison can be drawn between the first solo arias sung by the two women. Both express a will to accept fate stoically, but where Baschlari's 'Schikkung warum läßtu mich nimmer ungeplaget' (1. II. i; no. 14) is in slow 3/1 time throughout, Manuela's overtly Christian 'Das Kreuz, so mir Gott aufgelegt' (1. I. viii; no. 8) begins in 3/1 and changes in a da capo section at the end into faster 4/4 tempo. The words of the aria in this section, 'Die Tugend soll indes allein mein Trost und stäte Freude sein', suggest that a move is occurring here from Christian resignation to Christian hope; this is reflected in the quicker rhythm and marks a difference between the hope that is offered to the Christian and the mere resignation available even to a positively portrayed Muslim.

Both couples sing duets in the tenor/soprano range, underlining their oneness in love. Gasparo and Manuela, however, have four duets to Baschlari's and Ibrahim's one, and audience attention is therefore directed more strongly at the Christian than at the Turkish pair. Love duets are a popular element in opera, and those of Gasparo and Manuela show simple melodies interwoven in phrase and counterphrase. When singing together they generally sing just a third apart, one voice shadowing the other. This not only illustrates their closeness, but the uncomplicated harmony makes the duet accessible to an audience, who might almost sing along and therefore feel drawn into the romantic situation.

The arias from *Cara Mustapha* show no deliberately exoticizing features in the music, unless one sees Mustapha's 'warlike' repeated rhythms as an echo of Janissary military music, the only form of Turkish music really received by Western composers in the seventeenth and eighteenth centuries. Bostel's libretto does reveal some 'Turkish' colour, especially in the choruses. We have observed that a chorus of Janissaries opens Act 1; this chorus reappears with the Sultan, Mahomet, in the course of the opera (1. I. vi; 2. III. xii; 8th *Vorstellung*). Dances also provide an oriental spectacle; the first act closes with a dance of Turkish pages ('Ein Itchoglan nebenst einer Itchoglane'), the second with 'ein Tantz von zweyen Tartarischen Mord=Brennern mit brennenden Fackeln', and in the third a kind of mini-tournament between two German and two Turkish combatants is danced on stage (1. III. vii). For these, however, Franck's music has not survived. Miriam Whaples concludes her discussion of exoticism in early dramatic music with the observation: 'we have found no instance of musical exoticism before 1800 which uses non-European devices not also found in the European vocabulary.'[64] It is important to note that 'real' Turkish elements are not *necessary* in the music to sway audience sympathies away from the figure of the Turkish tyrant, Mustapha, towards the more positively portrayed characters in the piece. It is sufficient that he is recognizably *other* than the positive, Christian-style protagonists; in music as in language, rhetorical categorization can be effectively achieved within the dominant idiom.

### Exemplary and Wicked Women

Beginning with the rise of opera in the seventeenth century, McClary has observed composers' efforts to develop 'a musical

---

[64] Whaples, 'Exoticism in Dramatic Music', 263.

semiotics of gender: a set of conventions for constructing "masculinity" or "femininity" in music'. She suggests that the images projected by this semiotic system are 'rhetorically generated', or produced with a particular effect more or less consciously in mind.[65] Music may thus complement the gendering rhetoric we have been identifying in early modern dramatic texts, including libretti.

Women in early opera more often appear as positive than as negative examples. The librettists facilitate recognition of the special virtues their heroines embody with such explanatory opera titles as *Zenobia Oder Das Muster rechtschaffener Ehelichen Liebe* (Händel/ Mattheson, Hamburg 1722), *Leonilde Oder Die siegende Beständigkeit* (Schürmann/ Fiedler, Brunswick *c.*1704), *Die Edelmühtige [sic] Octavia* (Keiser/Feind, Hamburg 1705), or *Die Großmüthige Tomyris* (Keiser/Hoë, Hamburg 1724; another version, Hasse/ Keiser/ Lalli, Wolfenbüttel 1749). Full versions of Reinhard Keiser's scores for the latter two operas are available.[66] The two libretti show two quite different approaches to the portrayal of an exemplary woman, and provide an opportunity to look more concretely at the rhetorical workings of text and music.[67]

Keiser's *Octavia* uses the popular Claudius Drusus Germanicus (Nero) material. Monteverdi's and Busenello's *Incoronazione di Poppea* (1642) portrayed the adulterous relationship between Nero and his lover, Poppea, without attempting to awaken audience sympathies for the abandoned Empress Octavia; but the title of Barthold Feind's libretto, *Die Edelmühtige Octavia*, immediately betrays a change in perspective. In this opera, Poppea does not appear at all, and Nero's infidelity is instead exemplified in his attempt to seduce Ormoena, Queen of Armenia, who is visiting the Roman court on a peace mission with her husband, Tiridates. Of central interest in Feind's opera is the wifely conduct of Octavia in the face of her husband's adultery: Octavia agrees to

[65] Susan McClary, *Feminine Endings: Music, Gender and Sexuality* (Minneapolin, Minn. 1991), 7, 9.
[66] See nn. 35 and 48.
[67] Barthold Feind, *Die Römische Unruhe. Oder: Die Edelmühtige Octavia.* Libretto in *Deutsche Gedichte*, 115–74; Johann Joachim Hoë, *Die Großmüthige Tomyris* (Hamburg 1717). Libretto SUB HH. Further references are given in the text.

commit suicide when Nero wants to be rid of her, and perceives herself as the one at fault on the grounds that she has
failed him. More trivial operatic love-confusion is provided
by an unhistorical passion for the empress on the part of
Piso (familiar from Lohenstein's *Epicharis* as the instigator
of a revolt against Nero), as well as by a small group of minor
characters: Clelia, Fabius, and Livia, who function solely as
frustrated lovers. The final reunion of Octavia and her repentant husband, Nero, as well as a pardon for the instigator of
the Pisonian rebellion (on the grounds that he prevented
the empress from committing suicide) suggest that historical
veracity is not Feind's first priority. Of greater importance is
the moral improvement to be culled from the material, and
in a prologue the librettist explains the potential of his text
and its message in the context of opera:

Beliebter Leser. Diejenige [*sic*]/ so keine Schaubühne der Eitelkeit
unbestiegen gelassen/ und das weiche Pflaster der sinnlichen Lüste an
alle Ecken betreten/ gehen offtmahls mit weit anderer Absicht an einen
Ort/ von welchem ihr verblendtes Gemüht manchmal unverhofft mit einer
Erleuchtung zurücke kehret/ ... Dies senkt sich am allerersten in verhärtete
Gemühter ein/ und läst einen kräfftigen Nachdruck nach sich/ zumahl
wenn die Music, die ohne dem eine schier übermenschliche Krafft/ das
Hertz zu bewegen/ an sich hat/ dazu kommt/ und die in der Poesie enthal-
tene Sitten-Lehren durch eine verborgene Wirckung lebhaffter und
annehmlicher macht. (p. 117)

The distribution of the voice parts in Keiser's score marks
the difference from Monteverdi's opera in which the lovers,
Nero and Poppea, celebrate their union in a musical unity of
(descant) pitch. Keiser makes Nero a bass, at the other end
of the scale from Octavia's symbolically soaring soprano. The
low voice is not inevitably a sign of villainy, since Seneca,
too, sings bass, but it does provide for striking juxtapositions
in the score.

Early in the first act our sympathy is engaged for the
betrayed empress by her plaintive D minor aria, 'Geliebte
Augen/ sagt/ wo zielt ihr hin' (I. iv). In this bipartite aria,
chromatism provides the cramped melodic movement recommended by the theorists for the expression of sadness,
while the 12/8 tempo and slurred dotted rhythms allow for

a graceful delivery by the soprano voice. This is followed by another aria, introduced by Nero's brief deep recitative 'Hör' auch ein Wort von mir', in which the emperor's bass provides a striking contrast. The form is again bipartite, but where the two sections of Octavia's aria were complementary, Nero's are antithetical and reflect his inconstancy. In the first half, the minor key from the previous aria modulates into its relative major, F. The associations of this key with the pastoral, and therefore with love and constancy, seem ironic in the light of Nero's infidelity, but in fact he is singing about an ideal here and not about reality, as we recognize from the subjunctive mood of the text:

> Wär' ein Mensch der Sinnen Meister/
> Wenn Vernunfft ihm wiederspricht/
> Ach so liebt' er manchmahl nicht.

In the second half, after an 'aber' has brought us back into the emperor's unfaithful reality, the minor key returns, and the bass voice sinks in an admission of subjugation to passion:

> Aber allzu starcke Krafft
> Unser Geister/
> Zwinget uns zur Leidenschaft!

We are only in the fourth scene of the opera here, and already the music is directing our reactions to the protagonists. The textual characterizations will take longer to develop; Nero has yet to reveal the depths of his iniquity by planning Octavia's death as a means of clearing a path to Ormoena, and the empress herself is only beginning to establish her ideal status.

Feind leaves us in no doubt about the latter. Towards the end of Act II, when Octavia is on the point of committing suicide, the librettist resorts to the use of one of the most persuasive ideas available to him, namely that of the *imitatio Christi*. This signals an ideal martyr; it is the same method used by Gryphius in his *Carolus Stuardus* and *Catharina von Georgien* to idealize the monarch, and by Postel for his good Turk, Ibrahim, in *Cara Mustapha*. Feind uses the language of martyrdom even though Octavia in fact survives; it is a form of metaphorical shorthand that sets the stoic ideal she represents against Nero's and Ormoena's passion-driven wickedness. In a *vanitas* aria, he puts words in the mouth of his heroine that align the Roman empress firmly with the Christian ideal, and hence establish her beyond doubt as an exemplary character:

> Hinweg/ hinweg/ du Dornen=schwangre Krone/
> Weg Scepter/ weg/ du Bild der Eitelkeit/
> Mich blendet nicht mehr euer Strahl                    (II. xv)

This recitative is accompanied by violins and viola as well as the standard thorough-bass, for heightened affective expression. It is preceded, in scene vi, by Octavia's last aria before she discovers Nero's plan to kill her, a piece which is clearly designed to awaken any still-slumbering audience sympathies: 'Wallet nicht zu laut/ Silber=helle Bach=Cristallen', which uses the poetic devices of repeated 'l' sounds to remind us of the soft natural motion of 'wallen', and later 's' sounds to anticipate the 'Gelispel' of the water mentioned at the end of the da capo section—the word reminds us of the child-like, innocent status of the apparently doomed empress. Keiser uses flute and violin accompaniment in triplets and 3/8 time to echo the water's movement, and to create an atmosphere of lightness and simplicity which reinforces the innocence of Octavia's words:

> Last die Wässerlein/
> Weil wir traurig seyn/
> Mit Gelispel niederfallen!   (II. vi)

The music is also working on audience responses to the other characters. I have suggested that Nero's aria is an early indication of his bondage in the dark depths of the passions, and Ormoena's first aria (I. v) points up the differences between her as the recipient of Nero's passion and Feind's ideal of woman in this opera, Octavia. It is interesting that Ormoena's text is Italian, not because this is an unusual occurrence in the Hamburg opera—Keiser was notorious for his use of borrowed Italian arias—but because it is given to her, as a foreigner in the opera, to sing the first aria in a foreign tongue. (Ormoena and Tiridates are from Armenia, and may have been made up as black characters on stage.)[68] It is guaranteed to bring her less audience sympathy than Octavia's German aria of the previous scene, not only because Italian was not readily comprehensible to most of the audience in Hamburg, but also because its fast virtuoso style contrasts strongly with the graceful simplicity of 'Geliebte Augen', and with the Empress's immediately subsequent recitative lament, 'verlassene, verlassene Octavia'. In rhetorical terms, Ormoena's music is seductive and sophisticated, Octavia's childlike and simple, and hence much closer to ideally innocent womanhood.[69] Octavia does follow in scene vi with her own Italian aria, 'Geloso sospetto'; but this is the only aria she sings in the foreign language, and represents her one lapse from the stoic ideal into a language of passion, emphasized by fast dotted rhythms.

The libretto develops Ormoena's portrayal only slowly. Her negative characterization by Feind culminates fairly late in Act II, when she makes what may be construed as homosexual overtures to Octavia. The empress's response demonizes her rival's sensual appeal: 'O weh! es rühren mich selbst ihre schwarze [*sic*] Flammen' (II. x). But the music has already shown that Ormoena, unlike Octavia, is sexually inconstant. Her first response to Nero's suggestion that he should murder Octavia to marry her is reluctance:

> Es streiten mit reitzender Blüthe
> In meinem Gemüthe/
> Liebe/ Treue/ Glück und Ehr.     (II. ii)

This is contradicted and her inconstancy emphasized by the unusual technique of juxtaposing this aria with another one for the same protagonist, this time in Italian, in which Ormoena confirms her surrender to Nero ('Caro amante') in a graceful, dance-like 6/4 time that is far from suggesting the internal conflict her previous aria purported to express.

---

[68] If this was the case, it would make Nero's passion appear all the more perverted and reprehensible. An Armenian giantess is used as a symbol of the sexual degeneracy of Lohenstein's Ibrahim Sultan.

[69] McClary discusses this phenomenon in operas by Monteverdi. See Susan McClary, 'Constructions of Gender in Monteverdi's Dramatic Music', in *COJ* 1/3 (1989), 203–23 (211–12).

As well as developing the character of Ormoena, the selfish seductress, Keiser's score supports Feind's textual portrayal of a figure they both perceive as an ideal: a married woman who subordinates her own ego utterly to that of her husband. Octavia's self-sacrifice is rewarded by her unhistorical reunification with Nero, and Feind has his heroine spell out the nature of the wifely 'Edelmut' she incorporates in a last recitative:

> Ein Weib/ das edelmühtig ist
> Hegt keine Rache im Gemühte/
> Es preist vielmehr der Götter Güte
> Die endlich nach so langer Trauer=Nacht/
> In Rom die Ruh/ bei uns die Gunst hat wiederbracht.    (III. xv)

There can be no question of a critical audience response to Octavia's subservience, because the musical framework in which it takes place is designed to provoke only positive sentiment towards this character. While Ormoena's virtuoso arias have a dynamism which is as threatening as the marriage-breaking potential of her sexuality, Octavia's tend to show a simplicity suited to a woman who responds to the authority of her husband like a child to its father. In this opera the rhetoric of Keiser's music, as Feind predicted in his prologue, entirely supports that of the text.

There is a different approach to the idealization of woman in another of Keiser's operas, *Die großmüthige Tomyris* (1717), written this time in conjunction with the librettist Johann Joachim Hoë,[70] who produced a translation of an Italian libretto, *L'Amore di figlio non conosciuto*. Hoë names Domenico Lalli as the original author, and is clearly less interested than Feind, in his *Octavia* libretto, in creating his own version of the main protagonist. The retitling of the piece by Keiser and Hoë suggests, nonetheless, that they are interested in portraying a heroic woman. This is borne out when the librettist dedicates the text to his famous contemporary, the Countess (and fellow librettist)[71] Maria Aurora von Königsmarck, whom

[70] A compact disc of a live performance of this opera in Ludwigshafen in 1988 (conductor: Hans-Martin Linde) is available on EMI CDS 7494662.
[71] Königsmarck was the author of the libretto *Die drey Töchter Cecrops* (music by J. W. Franck [?]), which was performed at Ansbach in 1679 and at the Hamburg opera in 1680.

he compares panegyrically with the heroine of the opera. Hoë appends a lengthy prologue, in which he discusses traditions of misogyny and the defence of women.[72]

The semantic differences between 'Edelmut' and 'Großmut' are not great, but Tomyris is nonetheless a very different kind of heroine from Octavia. She is a widow, and remains unmarried (unusually!) even at the close of the opera, since the man she loves is revealed to be her son. She is closer to the type of the virgin warrior queen epitomized in Spenser's Britomart, echoes of whom are to be found in another great dramatic widow, Gryphius's Catharina.

Keiser's musical portrayal of Tomyris underlines the difference in type. The opera is characterized by the recurring key of D major, the trumpet and timpani key (although these instruments are not written into the score) described by Mattheson as warlike and headstrong. Choruses in praise of the Messagete queen who defeated Cyrus the Great are sung at the beginning of the first two acts, and are in D, as are four of Tomyris's arias. Three of these may be seen as a group: 'Amor, fache nicht die Flammen' (II. iii) expresses attempted resistance to the *Affekt* of love, which is then anthropomorphized and reproached in 'Tu lusinghi, o crudo amore' (III. v), while the *aria furiosa*, 'Rase nur gegen dich selbsten, Barbar' (III. vii), with its frenetic demisemiquavers, eloquently betrays the grip passion has on the queen despite her will to resist. Melismatic passages—'rase' ascends in demisemiquavers over four bars (10–13), and 'lache' extends over eight bars (30–7)—purport textually to refer to Tigranes, Tomyris's incognito son, but musically they reflect the madness which has gripped the queen herself. But the discrepancy between music and text here is apparent, not real, since the clear intention in the libretto is to portray Tomyris in thrall to a passion she tries vainly to resist.

Tomyris's other aria in D is far gentler: 'kühle Winde, saust gelinde' (II. xi). An obbligato accompaniment for transverse flute paints the natural background for the slumber scene, and recalls the use of *flauto dolce* accompaniment in Octavia's aria,

---

[72] Hoë sets ideal women against the negative examples chosen by the misogynists. This method of defence is the familiar basis for the idea of the *femme forte*.

Ex. 6. (I. vi)

so er-tö - - - te mich ____ mein Schmertz

'wallet nicht zu laut/ ihr Silber=helle Bach=Cristallen'. The soft sound of the flute won sympathy for Nero's mistreated empress, and here it does something similar for Tomyris. During this scene the ghost of Cyrus, along with the allegorical figures of Revenge and Murderousness ('die Mordsucht'), appear to the sleeping queen, raising the question of her guilt and hence questioning her role as an ideal heroine. The problem is solved by the descent of a cloud bearing Seleucus, Tomyris's son who died at Cyrus's hand, and the figures of Fate and Justice, who rule in favour of the warrior queen. One might argue, however, that her innocence was already established in the preceding aria, 'kühle Winde', since audience sympathy is musically engaged for the heroine before the accusing apparitions can textually question her ideal status.

Another interesting character in the opera is Meroë, Cyrus's daughter and therefore the opponent of Tomyris. Meroë, too, displays aggressive strength and an active determination which would be alien to a character like Octavia. The associations of militancy and regency that attach to Tomyris do not consistently characterize Meroë: her first appearance is not as a princess, but as a wandering astrologer (in male garb). She sings only one aria in D: 'Liebe, Rache, Zorn und Wut' (I. vi), but this supports the hypothesis that the regal 'warlike' key of the trumpet is used in this opera to depict qualities that, unlike Octavia's, are traditionally masculine. Meroë's revenge aria culminates in a perilous chromatic figure on 'ertöte', which textually appears to refer to Meroë herself. In fact the alarming high chromatism redirects the meaning of the sung word away from the character it overtly refers to and towards the object of her revenge, Tomyris (Ex. 6).

This is not the only occasion on which the threatening edge to Meroë's character, which sets her apart from Tomyris (the

Ex. 7. (II. v)

Viel-leicht, daß du ihn liebst?

Ex. 8. (I. xiii)

Ich fol-ge dir in al-lem.

incorporation of 'Großmut'), emerges musically in chromatism. Her mysterious prophesies in the guise of Magus the astrologer achieve a ghostly tone from the chromatics of her recitative (II. v), even though the audience know that they are pure charlatanism. Unlike Tomyris, who fails to conceal her passion for Tigranes—she betrays herself in musical pauses or sighs and painful chromatic asides—Meroë is expert in the art of dissimulation. There is an ironic cajoling sweetness in her attempt to wring a confession of love from the queen she hates for a man whom the audience know to be Meroë's own lover (Ex. 7).

There is further irony in her final response to Tigranes after she has instructed him firmly of his part in her plan to assassinate the queen: Keiser uses chromatism and avoids the tonic, which may betray an element of dissimulation in her apparent submissiveness (Ex. 8).

In these two operas, two conceptions of ideal womanhood are musically developed: Octavia, submissive and moving in the beauty of her arias, ideally provoking emulation specifically from women in the audience; and Tomyris the ruler, whose qualities are epitomized by the heroic key of D and who provides a more masculine ideal. Meroë, who dissimulates in slippery chromatics and would dominate, is an admonitory reminder of what happens when women who are not rulers behave in a masculine way (she is finally saved from punishment by the generosity of her partner's love), while Octavia's counterpart, Ormoena, leans towards the rhetoric of seduction that is a clear danger signal in her showy arias. In each case, suggestions made in the text are animated by the score, and the impression on an audience is deepened through persuasive aural effects.

The types of the exemplary and the alarming woman are developed alongside each other to particularly impressive effect by Keiser with another librettist, Johann Ulrich König, in their reworking of a Venetian opera, *La Fredegonda*, for the Hamburg stage in 1715, as *Fredegunda*.[73] They use their historical material with some discretion to achieve this. König makes it quite clear in his introduction that the treatment of history will be in the didactic tradition established in school drama:

Die Geschicht an sich selbst ist gantz bekandt/ und nur hin und wieder von dem Poeten/ den theatralischen Regeln zu gefallen/ anderst fingirt worden/ um nicht von dem rechten Zweck eines Schau=Spiels abzukommen/ welcher allezeit dahin gehen soll/ daß das Laster bestrafft/ die Tugend aber belohnt werde.

The historical Frédegunde was born around 545 AD and belonged to the entourage of Queen Audovère, wife of Chilpéric I of Neustria. She is described as 'belle, intelligente, mais aussi intrigante et ambitieuse'[74]—at all events, she contrived to make the king divorce Audovère, but, contrary to his hopes, he was obliged to marry his brother Sigebert's sister-in-law Galswinthe. Frédegunde, undeterred, had Galswinthe strangled in her bed and married Chilpéric. A war between the kingdoms of Chilpéric and his brother ensued, and Frédegunde had Sigebert assassinated. Sigebert's widow Brunehaut then married Chilpéric's son by his first marriage,

---

[73] Reinhard Keiser (music), Johann Ulrich König (text), *Fredegunda* (Hamburg 1715). Libretto in Meyer, *Die Hamburger Oper*, 2. 519–74. All references, unless otherwise stated, are to this edition of the libretto. The Venetian opera, *La Fredegonda*, was composed by Carlo Francesco Gasparini with a libretto by Francesco Silvani, and was performed in the Teatro Tron in S. Casciano in 1705, and (with a German translation) in Braunschweig in 1712 or 1716. Both libretti HAB. I have unfortunately been unable to consult Eulan von Brooks's MA diss., 'R. Keiser and his Opera Fredegunda: A Study in the History of Early German Opera' (N. Texas State University 1966).

[74] *Dictionnaire d'histoire de France PERRIN*, ed. Alain Decaux and André Castelot (Paris 1981).

Ex. 9

again threatening the position of Frédegunde, who had the young man killed. After Chilpéric's violent death in 584, Frédegunde reigned as guardian to her infant son until she died peacefully(!) in 597.

König follows Silvani in dispensing with the figures of Brunehaut and Audovère; Galsuinde and Fredegunda are retained as the central female characters. In contradistinction to *Octavia*, the opera carries the name of the demon woman rather than of her exemplary counterpart: didacticism is balanced by the wish for popular appeal, and the wicked character is bound to appeal. The alteration of certain historical details is consistent with the intention König declares of demonstrating a moral in the tale. In Act I a love affair is contrived between Fredegunda and a courtier, Landerich, which functions not only as the mechanism of her downfall when they are discovered by Chilperich, but also as an indication that her motives for marrying the king are entirely political. Like Lohenstein's dangerous heroines, Fredegunda subordinates emotion to ambition; Keiser lets her betray this musically in a recitative where she considers her relationship both to Chilperich and to Landerich (II. iv). Her ambition ascends with her notes (Ex. 9).

The most striking change in the historical record, however, is made in the form of a reversal, by which Fredegunda perishes and Galsuinde survives. Both König and his predecessor

Silvani thus ensure that vice is seen to be punished, virtue rewarded, even though the portrayal of Fredegunda in both libretti as a sinister, pagan figure leaves us with the impression that her punishment by death is inconclusive. Far from experiencing Christian fear of damnation, Fredegunda anticipates feeling rather at home in the Underworld. She dies without insight or regret, cursing Galsuinde and King Chilperich:

> In dieser Hoffnungs=vollen Lust
> Fahr' ich erfreut zur Höllen hin.
>
> .    .    .    .    .    .    .    .    .
>
> Ich will mit hundert Furien zur Seiten
> Und was ich greßlichs nur im Abgrund finden kan/
> Stets deine Ruh/ verhaßtes Paar/ bestreiten.          (V. iv)

This final descent into hell is anticipated in earlier scenes, in which Fredegunda exercises the supernatural powers of the witch. It is a literary *topos* that men's sexual attraction to women is caused by a kind of magical emanation from the female, and this idea is realized in an allegorical stage set in scene iv of the second act. As Fredegunda transforms the stage through 'Zauberey' into 'den Ort der Vergessenheit . . . woselbst alle nur ersinnliche Lust und Ergötzung anzutreffen', in order to further entrap Chilperich, the audience is led to infer her supernatural sexual power. In this paradisal place, which recalls the Garden of Eden and the destructive consequences of female sensuality, it is not surprising that Fredegunda is able to lull him to sleep and persuade him to co-operate in her plans. A sense of infernal threat is thus developed, and reaches its climax in Act IV, scene vi. The scene opens on a ghoulish vision of the temple of Hecate, widely known in the early modern period as the goddess of witches:

Auf einen einzigen Tritt der Fredegunden vertheilet sich ein in der Nähe liegender Hügel/ und zeigt ihre Zauberhöhle mit allerhand magischen Zubereitungen/ samt einem der Hecate gewidmeten Tempel/ welcher mit vielen verfallenen Gräbern umgeben/ und durch greßlicher Ungeheuer bewacht wird.

Fredegunda sprinkles human blood upon the altar and calls on her familiar spirits for support. At this point events take an interesting turn. We have observed that Lohenstein consistently implies that ambitious women who use their sexuality—the rhetoric of seduction—as a means to power must and will be suppressed by a loosely defined 'fate', which is opposed to their success. This is of course a reassuring idea as regards the masculinist status quo, and it is conveyed with a clarity verging on crassness at this point in König's libretto:

(Unter Donner und Blitz und einem heftigen Erdbeben erscheinet am Himmel eine feurige Schrifft.)
FRED. liest: Die Schickung hat der Höllen Macht gebunden/
Und unterdrücket Fredegunden.                                    (IV. iv)

The *deus ex machina* that was a veiled subtext in Lohenstein's drama is here a stage reality, and openly disarms the anti-heroine.

We are only in the penultimate act, however, and Fredegunda is not yet entirely quelled. She recovers herself in an evocation of one of the best-known sorceresses in Western literature, Medea:

So ist dann alles nun dahin?
Bestürmt mich Himmel Höll und Erde?
Wohlan! so zeige doch mein Sinn
Daß ich von allen gleich verlassen werde.
Ich will bey aller Noth/ die mich bedrohet/ lachen/
Und mit verjüngter Wuht/ die Colchos und Micen
Und Argos eh an einer Frau geseh'n/
Altar/ Tisch/ Tempel/ Thron und Bett zu nichte machen.   (IV. iv)

The references are to Medea as she is portrayed in Euripides' version of the legend; references to Colchos, Micene, Argos and 'verjüngen' (an art attributed to the Euripidean figure) link Fredegunda with the fearful woman who murders her own children (the librettist may have been thinking of the death of Chilpéric's son, for which the historical Frédegunde was responsible).[75] By the end of the scene, Fredegunda has

---

[75] Euripides was the first, it seems, to make of Medea a child murderer. Older versions of the legend describe the deaths of her children at the hands of the Corinthians. See J. J. Donner's 'Nachwort' in his German translation of *Medea* (Stuttgart 1988).

emblematically *become* Medea: she departs in a chariot drawn through the air by snakes, a typical feature of contemporary portrayals of Euripides' (anti-)heroine.[76] By this point it is perfectly clear why her downfall must be divinely ordained. Fredegunda, like Medea, is a peril to social stability, especially in a male-dominated society. What makes Medea's crime so alarming is her conscious inversion of the female role: she not only subordinates the emotion associated with motherhood to a wish for revenge—the unfeminine connotations of this were paraded for us by Melanthia and Rosimunda in the previous chapter—but, by depriving Jason of his sons and heirs, Medea subverts patrilinearity, and thus upsets an entire social system.

Galsuinde, on the other hand, displays the same male-oriented humility we found in Feind's Octavia. She has all the qualities of the *femme forte*: dignity befitting her social station, chastity and constancy when she rejects the sexual advances of her illicit admirer, Sigibert, and stoic patience as she bears her humiliation at the hands of Chilperich and Fredegunda with 'äußerste Gelassenheit' (II. vi). She is the type of the virgin warrior, but in the Christian tradition of Joan of Arc rather than that of the Amazon; for Galsuinde enters the combat as a declaration of her fealty to men (and more specifically to her unfaithful fiancé, Chilperich), not in order to challenge them. König adapts her aria in Act II, scene ii to emphasize this quality. In the German version of Silvani's libretto for Braunschweig, the aria is rendered:

---

[76] Medea is a popular figure in early modern opera. *Medea in Atene* by Antonio Gianettini (music) and Aurelio Aureli (text) was performed in Venice in 1678, and with a German translation in Wolfenbüttel in 1688 and 1692. The same opera, which deals (unusually) with events *after* Medea's flight to Athens following the Jason episode, was adapted in German for the Hamburg stage by Christian Heinrich Postel in 1695; in his introduction, Postel notes the popularity of the material. Even though there is no reference to the child murders in this opera, Medea makes a traditional appearance, 'auf einen Wagen von zweyen Drachen gezogen in der Lufft' (II. xv). A more Classical portrayal can be found in *Medea Vendicativa*, performed to mark the birth of Maximilian Emanuel, firstborn heir to the Duke and Duchess of Bavaria, in Monaco in 1662. This opera probably provided the inspiration for Johann Siegmund Kusser's (?) / Georg Kaspar Schürmann's (music) and Friedrich Christian Bressand's (text: revised by Schürmann) *Die an des Jasons Untreu sich rächende Medea* (Braunschweig 1724). Here, too, Medea appears as in Euripides, 'auf einem mit Drachen bespannten Wagen sitzend' to inform Jason that she has murdered their sons (III. xxi).

> Still/ Himmel! meinen Schmertz/
> Erquick mein mattes Hertz
> Durch gnädge Strahlen.
> Solt ich verachtet seyn?
> Bleibt nur die Hoffnung mein/
> So fliehen die Quahlen.

König provides a noticeably more militant, yet distinctly (positively) feminine version, which matches the determination of Galsuinde's virtue to that of Fredegunda's wickedness:

> Ich rüste mich aus Liebe
> Mit Unschulds=vollem Triebe
> Zu einem harten Streit:
> Nur Thränen sind die Waffen/
> Die mir den Sieg verschaffen
> Trotz aller Grausamkeit!

Keiser's music complements the aria's tone, in an animated 12/8 tempo, with thorough-bass and *unisoni* orchestra providing a complex backdrop in quavers and semiquavers to the melody.[77] A certain amount of emphatic sound-painting takes place, for example on the third line (Ex. 10).

König is prevented from portraying Galsuinde as a real martyr—although the historical record might have allowed him to do so—by the pressure to provide a positive ending. Yet her rejection of her lover, Sigibert, in favour of her badly behaved fiancé, Chilperich, can still be understood as an expression of the same kind of inner necessity that prompted Gryphius's Catharina to reject her royal suitor, Chach Abas, for the sake of her duty to Christ. It also echoes the behaviour of other married paragons, such as Feind's Octavia, re-enacting St Paul's dictum that man shall stand to woman as Christ to man.

Keiser's music heightens the contrast between the two ideas of woman; the score shows that the music of the saintly and the demon woman differentiates the two types as clearly as their metaphorical and emblematic textual portrayal. Fredegunda is given the first aria, 'Du verspottest die Schmertzen,

---

[77] An autograph of Keiser's score, with the telling subtitle 'Triumph der Unschuld', is held by the Staatsbibiothek Berlin (Musikabteilung).

Ex. 10

du verlachest die Thränen' (I. i).[78] It is in the militant key
of D, and shows fast melismatic passages that are an early
indication of her energetic character (Ex. 11).

Galsuinde sings the second; already a balance between the
two characters is being established. 'Lasciame piangere e poi
morir' is as startling a contrast to Fredegunda's aria as one
could wish for, and underlines their antithesis as types. It is
in B flat and a regular dotted 6/4 tempo, marked *larghetto*.
There is a simple chordal orchestral accompaniment above
Galsuinde's unhurried melody, which provides space for the
pathos of the text (Ex. 12).

Galsuinde's second, more determined aria was discussed
in the context of its text above. Fredegunda matches it

<hr/>

[78] The first line appears the other way around in the libretto: 'Du verlachest die
Thränen, du verspottest die Schmertzen'.

Ex. 11

Du ver-la - - - - - - - - - - - - chest die Thränen

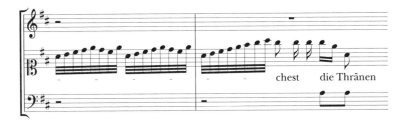

Ex. 12

La ____ scia - mi piangere e poi mo - rir

Ex. 13

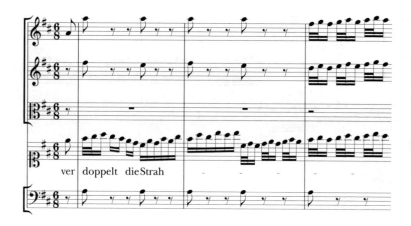

in Act II, scene iv with an aria in which she emphasizes her determination to gain power through her sexual appeal: 'Ihr reitzende Blicke verdoppelt die Strahlen'. The key is again D major, and the vitality of the anti-heroine is conveyed in her mobile 6/8 semiquavers and an energetic accompaniment (Ex. 13).

Ex. 14

Daß ich oft eu-res Al-tars Glut be-spritzt mit lau-em Men-schen-Blut

In the music as in the text, however, Fredegunda is at her most threatening in Act IV, scene vi. Jarring chromatics echo the description of her unnatural actions in the recitative (Ex. 14).

The aria in which she calls on the witch-goddess, Hecate, is the climax of Fredegunda's fearful potential, and Keiser does not let slip the opportunity to express it. A beating, repetitive orchestral accompaniment creates a strenuous and incantatory atmosphere that is maintained over 29 bars (Ex. 15).

After this it is unsurprising that nothing less than a fiery banner across the sky will put a stop to Fredegunda's machinations. The gravity of the divine pronouncement is felt chiefly in the bass (Ex. 16).

Keiser's and König's opera is one of the most dramatically effective portrayals of antithetical conceptions of woman on the early German stage. It was certainly one of the most frequently performed operas in Hamburg, forming part of the regular programme for twelve years after its first season in 1715. A large part of its effect is drawn from the dramatic opposition of the two extremes that constitute the idea of woman: the quietly subordinate and the seductively, rhetorically rebellious. The latter provides fascination for the duration of the performance; the former, reassurance and hence audience satisfaction at its close. The portrayal of both types of the feminine means that order is not only *implied* by its inversion (as it is, for example, in Lohenstein's ambitious heroines), but tangibly *demonstrated* in the ideal person of Galsuinde.

Ex. 15

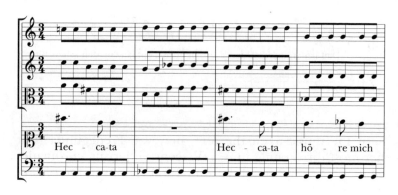

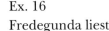

Ex. 16

## Conclusion

Music is felt to be a reflection of divine order, and to possess the power to influence those who are exposed to it. Both the early modern librettists and their composers display a determination to work together to realize the ordering, rhetorical potential of music and text, and while the newness of the operatic genre may provoke excitement, their persuasive intentions, like those of their dramatic forerunners, are socially conservative.

Catherine Clément has seen the spectator as a participant, particularly in opera, and links this with the music:

> he [*sic*] participates not only as a decorative extra but as an actor caught up in an identification for which he has paid. Risk-free identification: that is 'music'. . . . It drills deep; it grasps the story's deep structure for the spectator; it finds the phrase, the word, or the gesture that precipitates identification . . . The music makes one forget the plot, but the plot sets traps for the imaginary.[79]

Clément is writing about opera after Mozart, and presupposes that the text is hardly ever heard or understood. In early opera the case is different: music theory emphasizes the importance

---

[79] Catherine Clément, *Opera or the Undoing of Women*, trans. Betsy Wing, 2nd edn. (London 1989), 11–12.

of the text, and in practice libretti were read by the light of small tapers during performances, as wax droplets on surviving copies reveal. But Clément's reflections on music's power to effect identification—that is, to bring the audience in line with the intentions of the composer or librettist—constitute a modern recognition of its rhetorical power.

In conjunction with a text, the effects of music are in no way decreased. School dramatists of the seventeenth century employed the textual image as an aid to memory; more recently Anthony Storr has noted music's mnemonic effects: 'That music facilitates memory has been objectively confirmed by the study of mentally retarded children who can recall more material after it is given to them in a song than after it is read to them in a story.'[80] This speaks strongly for the rhetorical efficacy of music combined with text. Even if the librettists and composers of early opera had no access to such scientific confirmation, they are clearly aware of music's power not only to persuade but to imprint such persuasion on the memory, and they collaborate with the intention of realizing it.

Mustapha and Ibrahim, Tomyris and Meroë, Octavia and Ormoena, and Galsuinde and Fredegunda are all examples of the same kind of on-stage opposition we found in Gryphius's *Catharina von Georgien* (Catharina/Chach Abas) or *Cardenio und Celinde* (Celinde/Olympia). Such oppositions and antitheses seem to reach a high point on the opera stage, and become a necessary ingredient of almost every plot. This of course reflects the dramatic genre, which traditionally demands both conflict and resolution; but these operas are designed to demonstrate that resolution will always inevitably occur in a manner that stabilizes a pre-existing conception of order. Anxious, fascinating fantasies of chaos may (need to) be enacted in the world of the stage, but the reason they can be is that the puppets' strings are firmly in the hands of the dramatist, librettist, or composer.

[80] Anthony Storr, *Music and The Mind* (London 1992), 21.

# 5

# PERSUASIVE LAUGHTER:
# CARNIVAL, THEATRE, AND CONTROL

No study of outsiderdom and inversion in theatre could properly close without a consideration of comic drama and the role of that archetypal outsider, the fool. Comedy must also attract our attention because of its gendered position in the literary hierarchy: 'Comedy occupies a position in the structure of traditional literary discourses which is precisely parallel to that of 'female' in gender constructs: comedy is the "different", lesser, subordinate genre . . .'[1] It is in particular so-called 'low' comedy that occupies a subordinate position in literary theoretical thought. It has been widely assumed that farcical, carnivalesque comedy is inferior to what is sometimes called romantic comedy. The latter is 'high', the former is 'low', and, as in gender arrangements, the lower group is defined as inferior, or excess. Robert J. Alexander provides a perfect example of this in his description of the dramatic situation in Germany in the seventeenth century: 'Im 17. Jh. hat es an Lustspielen im herkömmlichen Sinne gemangelt. Abgesehen von vereinzelten Komödien von Gryphius, Weise, und vielleicht auch Reuter beherrschte das burleske Possenspiel die Bühne.'[2] Comedy in Germany was clearly rife; but at the same time it was, in Alexander's view, lacking.

Like femaleness, low comedy is held to pertain to the realm of earth and the body. This is evident in the Bakhtinian idea of carnivalesque mirth: 'Carnival laughter, Bakhtin implied, affirmed that the *human* comes from and will return to the *humus*, the soil, and that its earthy *humour* reminds man—who, in Western culture, stresses the gap between himself

---

[1] Susan Purdie, *Comedy: The Mastery of Discourse* (New York 1993), 120.
[2] Robert J. Alexander, *Das deutsche Barockdrama* (Stuttgart 1984), 35.

and Nature—of his more basic side.'[3] The generic 'man' here
does not mean woman. Carnival, fools, and the feminine are
all associated with what 'man' rejects: physicality, earthiness,
and chaos. Bakhtin found in carnival 'the peculiar logic of
the "inside out" (à l'envers) . . . a "world inside-out"'.[4] Yet
Bakhtin's 'grotesque body', the carnivalesque figure, symbolically displays an enlarged or extended phallus, and not
its inside-out opposite: the inverted phallus that is one early
modern conception of the vagina.[5] The carnival situation is
therefore, structurally speaking, the same situation as when
women wield power that is obviously phallic, or even when
women are positively characterized as *femmes fortes*, or Turks
as proto-Christians: ideas borrowed from one category are
superimposed, often in exaggerated form, over another.
In carnival the elements of the sensual, disorderly and corporeal that are usually attached to the Other—the opposing pole to masculine reason—are certainly allowed to
emerge. But the result is *not* an affirmation of inside-out,
vaginal, or feminine value, but a confirmation or (in the
exaggerated phallus) even a celebration of the power of the
norm.

There is a long-standing theory that difference and
superiority constitute our appreciation of the comic. Olson,
for example, has suggested that 'the persons whom we find
ridiculous are those whom we feel we can slight, and slight
deservedly and with impunity; to whom, therefore, we feel
superiority . . . and those who believe differently from us, e.g.
take seriously things which we do not. We therefore regard
them as unlike ourselves.'[6] This is not entirely satisfactory,
but Susan Purdie has recently augmented the idea with the
important basic element of *fear*. In order to gain comic
pleasure from superiority, the spectator must first have felt

[3] Richard Sheppard, 'Upstairs—Downstairs—Some Reflections on German
Literature in the Light of Bakhtin's Theory of Carnival', in Richard Sheppard (ed.),
*New Ways in Germanistik* (New York 1990), 278–315 (279–80).
[4] Mikhail Bakhtin, *Rabelais and His World*, trans. by Helene Iswolsky
(Bloomington, Ind. 1984), 11.
[5] See Jonathan P. Clark, 'Inside/out: Body Politics against Large Bodies', in *Daphnis*
20 (1991), 101–30.
[6] Elder Olson, *The Theory of Comedy* (Bloomington, Ind. 1968), 14–15.

insecurity about his/her superior position: she/he must in some way have perceived the comic object as a threat.[7]

This raises some questions about dramatic fools. If we laugh when the fool appears, does this mean that we perceive him or her as a (potential) threat? A carefully differentiated approach is necessary in order to establish what exactly we are laughing at; that is, who is in control of the comic discourse, and who is its butt? This chapter investigates the question of comedy and control, of how much of an Other the fool really is on the early German stage, and of a possible link between 'low' comedy—the carnivalesque—and the control of groups ideally classed as subordinate, such as the female and the oriental. Previous chapters have already demonstrated the extent to which the latter two groups are perceived as potentially threatening throughout the early modern period. Here I shall use the thread of order and inversion that has run through previous chapters to draw together ideas of woman and the non-Christian in the context of comedy, and to consider the relationship between *Trauerspiel*, *Lustspiel*, and *Singspiel*, and society's perception of itself on stage.

### 'Ein Thor muß Seines Gleichen sehn':[8] Comedy's Audience

There is a distinct relation between the gendered poles of value discussed in previous chapters and the conception of 'high' and 'low' theatre. In both cases one category is perceived as orderly or official, and one is unofficial, disorderly, or chaotic. Gottsched revealed his allegiance to such conceptions in drama when he described Martin Opitz's *Die Trojanerinnen* (1625), a translation of Seneca's *Trojan Women*, as 'den ersten Versuch einer *ordentlich* eingerichteten Tragödie' (my emphasis).[9] Opitz's Classical translations have been seen

---

[7] Purdie, *Comedy*, 59.

[8] This mocking remark is made to the audience by Negrodorus, the fool in Christoph Graupner's (music) and Barthold Feind's (text) *Amore Ammalato. Die krankende Liebe. Oder: Antiochus und Stratonica* (Hamburg 1707), I. ii.

[9] Johann Christoph Gottshed, *Nöthiger Vorrath*, 1. 184. Cited in Alexander, *Das deutsche Barockdrama*, 20.

as a first step in the development of a 'high' tradition of
German language theatre, and Gottsched automatically perceives the disappearance of folk or carnivalesque elements
as a move towards a more *orderly* drama.

   Gottsched, however, was deceived by the analogy between
'low' and 'high' theatre and an accepted binary system of
chaos and order. Just as dramatic order is founded on en-
coded (avoided) chaos, so the 'high' action of the play may
be affirmed and supported by the 'low', as Shakespearean
comedy demonstrates so clearly. Comic theorists before
Gottsched do not make his mistake: they involve 'low' methods
in the achievement of 'high' intentions, and express the closeness of the two in the metaphor of a healing pill, thinly cased
in sugar. Prefacing his play, *Eviana*, in 1696, M. Gottfried
Hoffmann applies the idea holistically to the dramatic genre:

Wer ... eine biblische oder sonst erbauliche Historie durch ein Drama
ausführet/ oder gewisse Glaubens=und Lebens=Lehren unter anmuthigen
Gedichten und Parabolischen Schau=Spielen vorstellet/ und solches zu
dem Ende thut/ daß er die Zuschauer in nützlichen und nöthigen
Dingen erbaue; der kömmt mir vor/ wie ein kluger Medicus, der herbe
Artzneyen durch ein süsses vehiculu dergestalt annehmlich machet/ daß
sie auch von den allereckelhaftesten Patienten können beliebet und nüt-
zlich eingenommen werden.[10]

The image is a common one, and is used at least as early
as 1597 by the French translator of Comes's *Mythologiae*.[11]
For Christian Weise, in an introduction to his historical
*Trauerspiel, Der Gestürtzte Marggraff von Ancre* (1681), it is an

---

[10] M. Gottfried Hoffmann, *Mit GOttes Hülffe! . . . Gefallene und wieder erhöhete
Eviana . . . Nebst einer Vorrede/ die von der Intention des Autoris ausführlich handelt* (Leipzig
1696). Grimmelshausen makes use of the same metaphor to excuse the antics of
his Simplicissimus: 'daß ich aber zuzeiten etwas possierlich aufziehe, geschiehet der
Zärtling halber, die keine heilsamen Pillulen können verschlucken, sie seien denn
zuvor überzuckert und vergüldt'. See Hans Jakob Christoffel von Grimmelshausen,
*Simplicius Simplicissimus: Der Abenteuerliche Simplicissimus Teutsch*, ed. Alfred Kellelat
(Munich 1985 [1975]), 485.
[11] '. . . que la Fable est tres-propre pour l'institution de la Ieunesse. Car tout ainsi
que l'estomach desgoust s'irrite & prouoque l'appetit par quelque viande commode
. . . aussi la Fable a ceste vertu & proprieté, de tellement chatouiller l'oreille des
enfans . . .' See *Mythologie c'est dire, Explication des Fables . . . Extraite du Latin de Noel
Le Comte, & augmentée de plusieurs choses qui facilitent l'intelligence du sujet* (Lyon: Paul
Frelon 1597[?]), A iij r. HAB. Compare Chapter 2 of this study.

apologetic commonplace: 'Und gleichwie nicht zu leugnen ist/ daß die gantze Begebenheit mit lustigen Erfindungen vermischet wird; Also wird ein jedweder recht urtheilen können/ man hätte dergleichen ernsthaffte Sachen/ nicht anders als harte Speisen/ mit einigen [sic] Zucker bestreuen müssen.'[12] The 'sugar' these writers see as a part of their work is clearly related to audience satisfaction. The presentation of orderly, 'high' values is made more attractive by adding carnivalesque elements of comic disorder. This does not as yet explain what exactly constitutes the satisfaction that is achieved, but modern theories of comedy help us to postulate an answer. It seems likely that comedy relies on the existence of a presupposed set of social codes or boundaries, which comic words or actions may break, or overstep. It is to this that Umberto Eco refers in an essay on the semiotics of the comic: 'In terms of a textual semiotics . . . one should say that tragic (and dramatic) texts are first of all supposed to establish both the common and the intertextual *frames* whose violation produced the so-called tragic situation. . . . in comedy . . . the broken frame must be *presupposed* but *never spelled out.*'[13] 'Frames' allow an audience to make sense of events, and are constituted by the expectations and taboos by which a society defines itself. Laughter confirms that the comic transgression is meaningful; that a proper rule is implicit and understood.[14] By overstepping the bounds of order, a fool or a comic action can remind us of the reassuring fact that they are there.

---

[12] In Christian Weise: *Sämtliche Werke*, ed. John D. Lindberg and Hans-Gert Roloff, vol. 1 (Berlin 1971), 10. This edition is henceforth referred to as *Werke*.

[13] Umberto Eco, 'The Frames of Comic "freedom"', in *Carnival!*, ed. Thomas A. Sebeok (Berlin 1984), 1–10 (4).

[14] Purdie, following Bakhtin, insists that comedy is in fact a dialogic or discursive exchange between the 'teller' and the audience; see Purdie, *Comedy*, 6, 14, *et passim.* One of Mikhail Bakhtin's best-known theories is of discourse as dialogic; he postulates, for example, that 'utterance . . . is constructed between two socially organized persons, and in the absence of a real addressee, an addressee is presupposed in the person, so to speak, of a normal representative of the social group to which the speaker belongs. . . . In the majority of cases, we presuppose a certain typical and stabilized social purview toward which the ideological creativity of our own social group and time is oriented'. From Volosinov and Bakhtin, *Marxism and the Philosophy of Language* (1929), in *The Bakhtin Reader*, ed. Pam Morris (London 1994), 58.

This is a long way from the joyful subversion in the Bakhtinian idea of carnival. Eagleton has criticized Bakhtin's conception because it is utopian, and fails to take into account the political control that licenses, for a limited period, the extraordinary carnival situation.[15] Whatever the case on the streets, the situation clearly changes when the carnivalesque is staged. When carnival moves into theatre, or, as Bakhtin would put it, acquires 'footlights',[16] the spectators are no longer licensed to participate, but only to observe. In early modern Germany, the players of the *Wanderbühne* might be separated from their audience only by a mutually agreed boundary or at most a raised platform; Shrovetide players tended to appear in an impromptu fashion in public houses, where arrangements for their performance might be made in an intimate, informal atmosphere.[17] But as theatre develops, the audience moves further and further away from the action, separated from it by the physical frame that demarcates the boundary between stage and auditorium. Only the direct address of the fool can still allow them, to a certain extent, to participate in the carnivalesque world. For this reason their comic satisfaction depends more and more on the reassurance that the comically disrupted world on stage is upside-down, that is, that their side of the frame is correct or the right way up. The carnivalesque, like the transgressive women we have considered, becomes a reminder rather than a rupture of the norm. This is emerging particularly from recent work on the German carnival play, or *Fastnachtspiel*. Shrovetide plays, which began to be written down in the fifteenth century, are the roots of early modern German dramatic comedy. We shall see their influence even in late seventeenth- and early eighteenth-century German language opera, and it is certainly worth considering some of the ways in which this popular, male-oriented genre functioned.

To describe the struggle between 'high' and 'low' culture, and their interpenetration in early modern Europe, Richard

---

[15] Terry Eagleton, *Walter Benjamin: Towards a Revolutionary Criticism* (London 1981), 148.

[16] Bakhtin, *Rabelais and his World*, 7.

[17] *Fastnachtspiele des 15. und 16. Jahrhunderts*, ed. Dieter Wuttke, 3rd edn. (Stuttgart 1989), 441–2.

Sheppard borrows Burke's terminology of the palimpsest.[18] He observes 'palimpsestic' traits in the work of two of the best-known writers of *Fastnachtspiel*, Hans Sachs and Jakob Ayrer, who alternate carnivalesque humour with expressions of anti-carnival sentiment.[19] The mix illustrates the futility of any theoretical attempt rigidly to separate the 'high' from the 'low'. Helen Watanabe-O'Kelly has demonstrated that the (usually) comic Shrovetide plays that coexisted with the (usually) serious biblical plays in the sixteenth century could convey entirely complementary messages: 'Auf alle Fälle muß man konstatieren, daß das ernste Bibeldrama und das derb-komische Fastnachtspiel die gleiche Absicht haben. Aus dem Bibeldrama lernen die Frauen, sittsam und still zu sein. Aus dem Fastnachtspiel lernen die Männer, sie durch Schläge so zu machen, wenn sie sich nicht fügen.'[20] The example of gender relations is not incidental. Comedy can reassure, and is therefore a good measure of subjects on which reassurance is required. The idea of the Turk in *Fastnachtspiel* relied on preconceptions of the Ottoman enemy; portrayals of women in 'low' comedy depend heavily on common anxieties about patriarchal power and its inversion, especially in marriage. Henpecked husbands frequently provide the butt, and comic satisfaction is achieved when such a man finally gains the upper hand that 'properly' behoves him.

A Shrovetide play like Jakob Ayrer's *Erziehung des bösen Weibes*[21] clearly perpetuates the medieval idea of woman observed in the work of Der Stricker in Chapter 2. The comic hero and fool who cannot control his wife here is Knörren Cüntzlein, a drunken farmer; his fool's status is signalled not only by the situation of non-authority in which we see him, but also by the diminutive form of his name and his social

---

[18] Sheppard, 'Upstairs-Downstairs', 283; compare P. Burke, *Popular Culture in Early Modern Europe* (New York 1978), 191.

[19] Sheppard, 'Upstairs-Downstairs', 293–4.

[20] Helen Watanabe-O'Kelly, 'Das Verborgene enthüllt: Das weibliche Publikum und die soziale Funktion des deutschen Dramas im 16. Jahrhundert', in Wolfram Malte Fues und Wolfram Mauser (eds.), *'Verbergendes Enthüllen': Zu Theorie und Kunst dichterischen Verkleidens: Festschrift für Martin Stern* (Würzburg 1995), 67–75 (75).

[21] Jakob Ayrer, *Die Erziehung des bösen Weibes*, 20 in *Fastnachtspiele des 15. und 16. Jahrhunderts*, ed. Dieter Wuttke, 2nd edn. (Stuttgart 1989).

standing and occupation.[22] The picture he paints of his wife
is a familiar evocation of feminine inversion:

> Dann mein Weib ist gar faul
> Und hatt ein böses Maul.
> Beym Tag thut sie umbleyern,
> Wil wol fressen und feyern
> Und biß an Mittag schlaffen,
> Lest sich nicht ziehen noch straffen.    (Stanza 2)

She demonstrates her inverted nature by beating both him
and his watching friend (stanza 64), but, as in Der Stricker's
tales, order is finally restored when Cüntzlein learns that the
proper solution is for *him* to beat *her* into obedience (stanza
72 ff.). Comic satisfaction is achieved not only because the
audience (which, as Watanabe-O'Kelly has inferred, would
have consisted almost exclusively of men)[23] can laugh at the
farmer as fool, but also because the 'happy' ending turns the
inverted world the right way up again, and the negation of
the potential threat of female dominance releases mirth.

Ayrer, who claims to have written the first German
*Singspiel* to be performed in Nuremberg,[24] is likely to have
been influenced by the presence of English players and
musicians in Nuremberg from 1596. *Die Erziehung des bösen
Weibes* is composed in six-line strophes, and performed to the
tune of a popular villanelle by Jacob Regnart, which I reproduce with its original text in Ex. 17.[25]

The choice of music corresponds to a method used in modern advertising, whereby the melody of a well-known song
reminds the listener of the words he/she is accustomed to
hear with it and hence of a certain textual idea or set of ideas.

---

[22] For a discussion of the prototypical function of the farmer/peasant as fool,
see Ninna Jörgensen, *Bauer, Narr und Pfaffe: prototypische Figuren und ihre Funktion
in der Reformationsliteratur*, trans. Monika Wesemann (Leiden 1988).

[23] Watanabe-O'Kelly, 'Das Verborgene enthüllt', 69.

[24] Ayrer's *Von dreyen bösen Weibern* (1598) closes with the words:

> Ihr Herrn, nembt also vor gut!
> Das ist das erste Spil,
> Daß man bey uns hie singen thut.

See Eckehard Catholy, *Das deutsche Lustspiel: Vom Mittelalter bis zum Ende der
Barockzeit* (Darmstadt 1968), 205 (n. 291).

[25] Reproduced in Wuttke, *Fastnachtspiele*, 288.

Ex. 17

Ve - nus, du und dein Kind, seid al - le bei - de blind,

und pflegt auch zu ver-blen - den, wer sich zu euch thut wen - den,

wie ich wol hab er - fah - ren in mei- nen jun-gen Jah - ren.

Here love is conceived of as feminine in the image of Venus (with Cupid), who is dangerous because she acquires power by causing blindness in men; the conceptual basis is familiar. In Ayrer's play, which is acted against the background of this textual meaning in the music, the consequences of male blindness are clear, but are resolved by the return of the man to *Vernunft* (in his recognition that he must beat his wife, not she him). The comic relief this induces is not dissimilar to the closure provided by the deaths of Lohenstein's great women.

The representation of female malice, especially within marriage, is a classic scheme both in Shrovetide plays and in the performances of the *Wanderbühne*;[26] it survives, then, in the presence of a mixed audience. The comic problem is that a woman makes a man the butt and thus assumes a form of mastery that offends against the gender hierarchy, and the situation is only resolved when the tables are turned, and the audience can laugh at her. Ayrer's Cüntzlein is a typical butt of *Fastnachtspiel* humour. He is derided as long as he allows his wife to dominate him, but derisive laughter becomes the

---

[26] Such a scheme is detailed by Monika Jonas, 'Idealisierung und Dämonisierung als Mittel der Repression: Eine Untersuchung zur Weiblichkeitsdarstellung im spätmittelalterlichen Schwank', in Sylvia Wallinger and Monika Jonas (eds.), *Der Widerspenstigen Zähmung: Studien zur bezwungenen Weiblichkeit in der Literatur vom Mittelalter bis zur Gegenwart* (Innsbruck 1986), 67–93 (70).

laughter of relief when the broken frame of male dominance
is finally mended, and the woman subdued. David Price
identifies this kind of conclusion as typical of sixteenth-
century German drama: 'German authors never present
gender inversion as an isolated form of transgression.
Instead, they reinforce inversion by explicitly reestablishing
male hierarchy in the aftermath of female disorder, even
though inversion by itself would affirm hierarchical order.'[27]
Carnivalesque reversal alone is an affirmation of the norm, or
frame. But just as König's Galsuinde will later stand opposite
Fredegunda on the opera stage to affirm the orderly standard
which the latter has perverted,[28] so here order is not only
implied but confirmed; a double dose of reassuring sugar is
strewn by the dramatic text.

The man who fails to restore order in this way, like
Thomas Mercator in Heinrich Julius von Braunschweig's
*Von einem Weibe*,[29] remains an object for derision. *Von einem
Weibe* (1593), features Meretrix (meaning harlot): a sly,
dishonest, cupidinous woman who is at pains to betray her
husband (whose name, Thomas Mercator, reminds us of
the foolish merchant of the *commedia dell'arte*, Pantalone). Her
lover is Thomas Amator, who as his name suggests is no
better than her husband, but simply another man. The only
other main character is a servant, Johan Bouset, who takes his
name from the English fool, John Posset. But it is not Johan
Bouset who is ultimately derided in the piece: on the contrary, the fool has the last laugh (with the audience) at the
expense of his master, who has failed to recognize his wife's
nature or assert a will to control her. The situation merits
analysis: the subordinate male, Thomas Mercator, occupies
the same structural position—that of the butt—as the woman
in Ayrer's play, and his status is therefore analogous to that
of the feminine. The comic servant, on the other hand, is

[27] David Price, 'When Women Would Rule: Reversal of Gender Hierarchy in
Sixteenth-Century German Drama', in *Daphnis* 20 (1991), 147–66 (166).
[28] See Chapter 4 of this study.
[29] Heinrich Julius von Braunschweig, *Von einem Weibe*, in *Von einem Weibe. Von
Vincentio Ladislao. Komödien*, ed. Manfred Brauneck (Stuttgart 1967). Following an
aristocratic vogue for keeping English players at court, Heinrich Julius von
Braunschweig (1564–1613) not only kept his own troupe, but was inspired to write
comic drama himself.

not the butt, but the master, controlling and directing audience mirth.

There is clearly a distinction to be made in early German drama between the controlling fool and the fool as butt. The butt is the non-conformer, male or female, but always on the side of social disorder. The controlling fool, on the other hand, understands and supports a normative frame, and his comic exchange with the audience depends on *shared* assumptions about the nature of the norm (order), if it is to lead to laughter. Dramatically the fool may be an outsider, because he takes no direct part in the action, which he may be licensed to turn on its head. Yet unlike the unruly women and effeminate men who invert without license, he is an ideological insider: the masterful or controlling fool is male and, in German language drama of the early modern period at least, a conservative social commentator.[30] He is thus implicated both in the evocation and in the normative negation of the *verkehrte Welt*: even as he participates in topsy-turvy comic events, he stands just far enough apart to sprinkle the sugar of reassurance that the inverted world of carnival is a controlled and therefore temporary one.

The same basic scheme is perpetuated in seventeenth-century comic drama and opera. The essential comic question remains: who is the master, and who is the fool?

*Comic (Dis)empowerment: The Fools of Christian Weise and Christian Reuter*

The comic plays of Christian Weise (1642–1708) demonstrate the power of the fool in a topsy-turvy world. The idea of the *mundus inversus*, or the reversal of accepted binary oppositions, has provoked literary anxiety since Antiquity.[31] Fear that

---

[30] Meyer comments: 'Dem Hofnarren wie dem Hanswurst ist eine konservative Gesinnung gemein . . . Dadurch wurde sie auch dem Bürgertum akzeptabel'. Reinhard Meyer, 'Hanswurst und Harlekin oder: Der Narr als Gattungsschöpfer: Versuch einer Analyse des komischen Spiels in den Staatsaktionen des Musik- und Sprechtheaters im 17. und 18. Jahrhundert', in Roland Krebs and Jean-Marie Valentin (eds.), *Théâtre, Nation & Société en Allemagne au XVIII<sup>e</sup> Siècle* (Nancy 1990), 18.

[31] See Michael Kuper, *Zur Semiotik der Inversion: Verkehrte Welt und Lachkultur im 16. Jahrhundert* (Berlin 1993), 10.

the ordered, hierarchical, God-given social scheme is prey
to disruption persists through the later Middle Ages and into
the early modern period, when the upside-down world is a
popular literary theme.[32] In a short prologue to his *Lust-Spiel/
Von der Verkehrten Welt* (1683), Weise draws on graphic representations of inversion from the mid-seventeenth century, and
explains his interest:

> Es ist etwas über dreissig Jahr/ als etliche artige Bilder zu Kauffe gien-
> gen/ darin die umgekehrte Welt durch artige und mehrentheils lächer-
> liche Erfindungen vorgestellet war. In dem nun viel artige MORALIA,
> und ich möchte fast sagen/ ein grosses Theil der Politischen Klugheit
> darunter verborgen liegt; Also daß der beste Staatsmann die umgekehrte
> Welt am geduldigsten vertragen muß/ wofern er in seiner Verrichtung
> etwas glückliches erhalten will: So ist diese INVENTION zu einem Lust-Spiele
> erwehlet . . .[33]

Weise's concerns are socio-political in a wide sense, and his
play inverts (and therefore defines) frames over a range of
social issues. By the end of Act I, four of the central hierarchical arrangements in capitalist patriarchal society have
been overturned: sellers are forced to pay buyers for goods
(I. iv); the master is made subservient to his servant (I. vii);
the power to choose a marital partner is allocated to women
rather than men (I. xii); and those empowered by education
are required to submit to the dictates of the untutored
(I. xiii–xiv). The key situation in the upside-down world, familiar from *Fastnachtspiel* as well as from more serious drama
(such as Lohenstein's *Cleopatra*), is depicted at the beginning
of Act II, when the stage reveals the Hercules-and-Omphale
scenario:[34] Simplicius the husband sits spinning, while his wife,
Duplicia (*nomen est omen*), deals with the family's financial

---

[32] See Heinrich Haxel, *Studien zu den Lustspielen Christian Weises (1642–1708): Ein
Beitrag zur Geschichte des deutschen Schuldramas* (Stettin 1932[?]), 50.
[33] Christian Weise, *Lust-Spiel/ Von der Verkehrten Welt/ Praesentiret in Zittau/ Den 4.
Mart. 1683*, in *Werke*, 12/1. 5. Further references are given in the text. The type
of illustration to which Weise refers is described by David Kunzle in his article 'World
Upside Down: The Iconography of a European Broadsheet Type', in Barbara A.
Babcock (ed.), *The Reversible World: Symbolic Inversion in Art and Society* (Ithaca, NY
1978), 39–94.
[34] Compare Daniel Casper von Lohenstein, *Cleopatra* (1680), II. 524. In *idem*,
*Afrikanische Trauerspiele*, ed. Klaus Günther Just (Stuttgart 1957), 73.

affairs. It is at this point that their maid, Scarabaea, turns to the audience and asks them to address the problem:

> Ihr Leute/ wie gefiel euch die umgekehrte Welt? Die Mutter drillt den Vater/ die Tochter herrscht über die Mutter/ ich bin Herr über die Tochter; Es fehlt noch ein Kinder-Mägdgen/ das mich in die CONTRIBU-TION nimt/ so hätten wir die Narren beysammen. (II. vi)

The oblique reference to the frame or proper rule is obvious; the *Narren* are those who fail to realize their social empowerment. Scarabaea's view is restated later by the philosopher, Democritus, who functions as a representative of order and *Vernunft* in this carnivalesque world and who in dialogue with the deposed king, Eleutherus, clarifies the didactic point that Weise's comedy is 'sugaring':

> DEMOCRITUS. Ich werde nochmals in meiner OPINION gestärket: Die Welt wäre nicht umgekehret/ wenn sie nicht von umgekehrten Leuten bewohnet würde.
>
> ELEUTHERUS. Knechtische Geister verdienen ein knechtisches Tractament.
>
> (II. xiv)

Those who surrender their mastery to become butts, then, deserve all they get. This interlude is literally reflective: a mirror is being held up, and comic 'failure' is reflected back into the society of the spectator as social comment.

That Weise intended his play to comment on the problems of contemporary society is suggested in the name of the character responsible for the inversions. Alamode, the fool, is in topsy-turvy fashion the judge and the master in the *verkehrte Welt*. His lieutenant, Spizwiz, swaggers through the piece in the manner of a *miles gloriosus*, or the *commedia dell'arte*'s Capitano (a character called Scaramuza also appears briefly in Act II, scenes vii–viii, but only recalls his predecessor from the *commedia* in name). Spizwiz and Alamode repeatedly perform an emblematic on-stage ritual, turning the other characters on their heads in order to reverse their perceptions of the world. By the penultimate act the two of them have even incited the women of Synesia to form an army, creating a situation fraught with inversions; not only do the women bear weapons while the men wear petticoats (IV. xix), but in traditional army style they have bonded, to form an

Amazonian 'Weiber-Gesellschaft' that stands in threatening
opposition to the unstated social norm: male-dominated
society (IV. xvii). This is the turning-point, at which the *verkehrte
Welt* is no longer tolerable for its male occupants, and a *deus
ex machina*—in the form of Apollo—intervenes to restore mastery to its conventional holders. Act V comprises Apollo's
judgements; this wise and just judge is the dramatic antithesis and correction of the Alamode figure. There is an
element of parable in the judgement passed; Alamode is
permitted to maintain a kingdom, but it is one in opposition
to the true kingdom of Eleutherus, into which Alamode's subjects will be free to move (V. xvii). An allegorical indicator
of the realms of Christ and Antichrist is almost certainly present in this, and adds considerable weight to Weise's comic
corrective. Apollo, god of poetry, is a suitable deity for the
fantasy land of Synesia; Weise brings on (or winches down)
a literary divinity to restore order in the dramatic world.

The dangers of inversion are equally central in the earlier
play, *Masaniello* (1682). Weise's portrayal of the Neapolitan
uprising led by a fisherman in 1647 is designated 'Trauer=
Spiel';[35] it nonetheless anticipates many of the concerns of
the *verkehrte Welt* comedy. Masaniello also features a fool,
Allegro: 'ein leibhafftiger Pickelhering', as a stage direction
describes him (III. viii).

As 'Pickelhering', Allegro is a more traditional and less
subversive fool than Alamode. 'Leibhafftig' suggests that he
is wearing some form of recognizable fool's costume, and he
frequently establishes contact with the audience in asides: both
of these things mark him as an outsider to the dramatic action.
Allegro is significantly the only offender to be pardoned
by the rebel leader, Masaniello, in a tyrannical judgement

[35] Christian Weise, *Trauer=Spiel Von dem Neapolitanischen Haupt=Rebellen Masaniello,
praesentiret in Zittau/ Den 11. Febr. M DC LXXXII*, in *Werke*, vol. 1. Further references
are given in the text. Weise's source is generally taken to be an Italian report of
the uprising that took place in Naples in 1647, Nescipio Liponari's *Relatione delle
Rivolutioni Popolari Successe nel Distretto, e Regno di Napoli Nel presente anno 1647 alli
7 Juglio* (Padua 1648), which was translated into German anonymously in the
same year. But Roger Thiel has pointed out that 'Nescipio Liponari' is in fact a
pseudonym for Alessandro Giraffi, and that this text is in fact the second edition
of Giraffi's *Le Rivolutioni di Napoli*. See Thiel, 'Constantia oder Klassenkampf? Christian
Weise's *Masaniello* (1682) und Barthold Feind's *Masagniello Furioso* (1706)', in *Daphnis*
17 (1988), 247–66 (251–2).

scene (II. xii); as a non-participant, the fool preserves his *carte blanche*. In the course of the play he attaches himself to both the revolutionary and the counter-revolutionary side. He has no ideological attachments: Allegro's concern is for his own physical well-being, and he has a typical clown's appetite for the material rather than the philosophical side of life, which enables him to provide an anti-tragic close to the piece, when Masaniello is dead and his revolutionary followers quashed: the play ends with an exchange between the fool and the victorious Captain, Prospero:

> PROSP. Die Nachwelt soll den Ruhm der Zeiten nicht vergessen.
> ALLEG. Der Koch hat angericht/ ihr Herren komt zum Essen.
>
> (V. xxv)

Allegro nonetheless displays a form of mastery. He has certain affinities with the Shakespearian wise fool, and in conversation with the nobles, who are frightened by the desperate, angry populace, he is able to assess their predicament and its causes: 'Ach wer das Werck mit den hohen Zöllen etwas niedriger gespannet hätte/ der dürffte sich nicht in das Castell/ als wie eine arme Bestie in ihr Fuchsloch verkriechen' (I. iv). When rebuked for his criticism, he reasons comically:

> Ich wil einmahl reden als ein PHILOSOPHUS. Die Tugend beschimpffet niemanden/ ATQUE ET SIC CONSEQUENTER: Die Warheit ist eine Tugend. ERGO ERGIUS ERGISSIME so beschimpffet meine Warheit niemanden. CONCEDO TOTUM ARGUMENTUM. (I. iv)

Allegro invites laughter here by apparently abandoning linguistic mastery in a foreign language, and exposing his inability to control forensic rhetoric. But the message is also earnest: in the topsy-turvy world of the play, in which the lower classes have assumed power, the fool paradoxically becomes the guardian of truth and wisdom. The inverted situation is spelt out when, in response to a commentary delivered by the child Arcos, Duke Torrecuso admits: 'Vor kurtzer Zeit haben wir die Warheit von einem Narren gehöret/ itzt muß ein kleines Kind den DISCURS CONTINUIren: Ach! unglückselige Zeit/ da solche Personen über uns urtheilen müssen' (I. vi). This topsy-turvy world is the product of the ascendancy of the lower classes. Roderigo, the Viceroy of Naples, is captured by rebels who wish to dictate terms regarding flour prices and taxes in the city, and laments: 'Unglückselige Herrschafft/ da ein Sclave über Standes Personen gebieten soll', to which Masaniello and his followers respond in the language of Alamode, the inverter: 'Das PRIVILEGIUM wollen wir haben/ oder die Stadt Neapolis soll sich umkehren' (I. xv).

Unlike Alamode, Allegro is not the perpetrator in the inverted world of Naples, but a satirical commentator. At the end of Act I, it is Allegro who shows to us the disruption of order that has occurred. Where the ultimate signal of the chaos that strikes Synesia under the influence of Alamode is the army of women, Naples under Masaniello is overrun with unsuitable armies, as Allegro explains: 'die Bürger machen ein Regiment zusammen/ die Weiber haben ihre COMPAGNIEN, die Bauren führen ihre SVADRONEN auff: ja die Kinder marchiren in ihrer Ordnung daher' (I. xxi). Two scenes later, his description becomes stage reality, in a truly carnivalesque procession; the fisherman-rebel with his followers and bandits precedes the citizens' army, the regiment of women led by Masaniello's wife, the children's battalion and the squadron of peasants. Bringing up the rear is the army Allegro has assembled to populate this *verkehrte Welt*, a host of infant fools or perverse cherubs who satirize military music, playing on their miniature pipes and drums (II. ii).

The carnival theme persists when we hear of Masaniello's meeting with the Viceroy. Instead of the fisherman's clothes that would behove his status in the ordered world, he is forced by court representatives to wear a silver jerkin; recalling the scene, the nobleman Ristaldi finds 'es war als ein umgekehrtes Fastnacht-Spiel' (IV. i). We are doubtless meant to see poetic justice in this; Masaniello has already turned Naples into something like a carnival city of costumes, demanding that women should wear short skirts or trousers —ironically to *prevent* disguise—and that priests should put off their long robes. It is therefore consistent that Masaniello himself, although ever more tyrannical in his behaviour, is gradually revealed as a carnival fool: like Alamode, or even

Nero in Lohenstein's *Epicharis*, he is the Lord of Misrule. Early in the play the Viceroy describes the rebel leader as 'ein närrischer Fischer-Bube' (I. iii), and the Cardinal echoes the judgement (IV. iii). Allegro makes the same point in typically sharp-witted fashion in an exchange with Masaniello's wife, Pasquella:

PASQU. Das soltu wissen/ wenn ich mit meinem Manne zu Bette gehe/ so schläfft ein Staats-Mann bey mir.
ALLEG. Und wenn ich mit eurem Manne zu Bette gehe/ so schläfft ein Narr bey dem andern.

(II. v)

The fisherman is finally literally driven mad when the Viceroy spikes his wine with poison; a crazed death is presented as just punishment for a destructive fool. Roderigo's wife, Leonisse, seems to express the view of the dramatist when she opines, 'So recht/ wer viel rothes Blut vergossen hat/ der muß in dem rothen Weine Blut und Gifft hinein sauffen' (V. iii).

The other, less serious, fools of the piece are the fisherwomen. Like the (comically or more seriously) demonized women of *Fastnachtspiel*, they display the vanity and dominance that are constructed as the opposite both of lower-class and of feminine virtue. It is Allegro again who sticks a pin into the balloon, reminding them and the audience of their real status. He mocks the will to command they have developed since their husbands gained power with clear reference to the gender problem: 'Ey/ kömt mirs heute so gut/ daß ich die liebe Obrigkeit in einem Weiber Kleide sehen kan?' (II. v), and undoubtedly gets a laugh of relieved satisfaction from his audience when he responds to Zeppa's socially unsuitable wish to be addressed as 'gnädige Frau' with comically veiled aggression:

ALLEG. Je du gnädige Mistfincke! wenn ich dir nun die Augen ausbrennte/ und klebte die Lücken mit Leime zu/ wem hätte ich doch unter den vornehmen Leuten was zu Leide gethan?

The women are finally more foolish even than the rebel, Masaniello. Having inverted the social order, Masaniello is prepared to put off his fine clothes and return to his fisherman's garb; but the women, as Villanella betrays, have become incurable fools in the matter of their finery: 'es gehet eine Sache vor/ darüber unsere Köpffe gar zu Narren werden' (IV. xv). The suggestion is that there is something more lastingly foolish in the female psyche, for where men will dress up only in carnival situations, women would do it all the time. Again Weise makes the idea visual: in the next scene, which opens the last act, Allegro appears disguised in women's clothes, and the effect is comical because even the clown is abased when he appears in the attire of the weaker, ridiculous sex (when women dress up as men, it is hardly ever funny). The male clown preserves his mastery by producing comedy at the expense of a female butt.

Masaniello's foolishness is of a more serious kind, however, and he is not exempted from the serious punishment of death. He has offended against the order of 'real' society rather than that of the fantasy realm of Synesia, where Alamode will effect his inverted judgements in the later drama (Masaniello anticipates these in the grotesque judgement scene of Act II, scene xii). As a man, even of the lower classes, his temporary empowerment is more credible, and therefore harder to ridicule, than that of the women. Allegro's function *vis-à-vis* Masaniello changes accordingly. When Pasquella preens herself on her husband's greatness, the clown turns to the audience to confirm the validity of the social frame Masaniello has violated: 'Ach wie wohl weiß der liebe GOtt sein Regiment zuführen! daß er in der Welt so viel arme Leute leben läst: denn er sieht wohl/ wie so gar wenig Leute sich in das Reichthum schicken können' (II. v). In Synesia, a mythological and poetic deity can restore order; in Naples the task must be undertaken by the Christian God and his representative in the world. The repentant rebels Arpaja and Formaggio return to their ruler like prodigal sons, reminding him: 'Ein Vater sorget auch vor das Auffnehmen seiner Kinder/ wenn sie den Untergang verdient haben' (V. xi).

In these dramas, Weise has provided us with two distinct types of the fool. One is the *Pickelhering*, like Allegro, who produces humour mainly by mocking others, and provides audience reassurance and thereby comic satisfaction by reiterating the existence of broken frames. The other is the fool who fails to correspond to social expectations, and is hence 'mad'—an undesirable outsider, in the Foucauldian sense[36]—and an object of (fearful) ridicule. Alamode falls more into this latter category, as the correspondences between him and the anti-hero of the earlier play, Masaniello, betray; it is only the change in the dramatic genre that allows his punishment to be comic where Masaniello's is serious. The women are not fools, but butts: Weise's treatment of the fisherwomen suggests that the will to disarm unruly women by making them into comic butts has not diminished since the *Fastnachtspiel*.

The butt, in Purdie's view, is deprived of linguistic or rhetorical agency: 'specifically, a Butt can be seen as denied discursive potency—the power to be an agent who has intentional effect in the world.'[37] Unlike the active clown, who can make spectators laugh at others as well as himself, the butt is—or is rendered—passive, and is delivered up to the mastery of the audience, expressed in derision. Purdie goes on to consider the audience psychology that makes the degradation or abjection of the butt amusing: 'to be psychically effective . . . this abjection must follow from the Butt's first being accorded power—Butts are precisely degraded from their power to construct and define us, within their language-making'.[38]

We know that the comedy *Die Ehrliche Frau zu Plißine* (1695) and the tragicomedy *Der ehrlichen Frau Schlampampe Krankheit und Tod* (1696)[39] were written as satires attacking Anna Rosine Müller, the landlady who had evicted their author, Christian Reuter (1665–?1712) and a fellow-student from her house in Leipzig.[40] Even without this knowledge it is not difficult to identify Reuter's butt. The frontispiece of *Die Ehrliche Frau* shows Schlampampe standing feet apart, supporting considerable girth, with her hands planted on her hips. This is not only (as Catholy has remarked) a

---

[36] Michel Foucault, *Madness and Civilization: A History of Insanity in the Age of Reason*, trans. Richard Howard (London 1995 [1967]).

[37] Purdie, *Comedy*, 59.     [38] Ibid.

[39] Both in Christian Reuter, *Schlampampe. Komödien*, ed. Rolf Tarot (Stuttgart 1977 [1966]).

[40] See Tarot's afterword in ibid. 177–95 (178).

parody of the seventeenth-century 'Repräsentationspose',[41] but also an aggressively unfeminine stance that underlines the picture of conventional comic unattractiveness—that is, non-conformity to the gender norm—that the artist is at pains to create.

Each of the plays has an independent comic figure who is male. In *Die Ehrliche Frau* it is Laux, a 'lustiger Bothe', in the later play, the servant Lorentz; each appears only briefly, and fulfils a dramatic convention rather than assuming any significant role. Comic foolishness (but no deliberate or active foolery) is provided by the women in the dramas, and the term 'Narr' is applied predominantly to them. Charlotte uses it of her mother, Schlampampe (*Die Ehrliche Frau*, I. ii) and of her sister (I. viii); the lawyer, Cleander, applies it to the whole family (III. ii). In the latter play, *Der Ehrlichen Frau Schlampampe Krankheit und Tod*, the landlady's two daughters are driven by foolish ambition to set out in quest of a noble title, and are comically punished for this breach of class convention when their carriage lands in a muddy rut. Clarille's hopes—'Wenns nur niemand erfähret/ daß es uns so närrisch gegangen ist' (II. iii)—are implicitly rendered futile by the laughter of an assembled theatre audience.

Schlampampe has been seen by critics as the real comic figure of the piece.[42] The definition needs to be tighter, however, for she is not a fool in the manner of Allegro or the operatic buffoons we shall come to, even though she does share some of the attributes of the type. Her name, like that of Weise's quick-witted clown, is 'speaking', and suggests the gluttony of the Hanswurst (*schlampampen*), but also the insulting, specifically female appellation *Schlampe*.[43] She has the fool's tendency to aspire beyond her proper social position: where Allegro babbled in Latin, Schlampampe chooses French-sounding names for her equally aspiring daughters, Charlotte and Clarille. She even fits a fool's role by establishing contact with the audience in asides, but generally in such a way as to encourage the spectators to laugh *at* her, rather than with her. Schlampampe's status is determined not by

---

[41] Catholy, *Das deutsche Lustspiel*, 173.
[42] See e.g. ibid. 170.      [43] Ibid. 171-2.

foolery, but by her foolishness or stupidity, as Reuter has one of the students observe: 'Die Frau Schlampampe scheinet wohl eine **Ehrliche**/ aber auch dabey eine sehr dumme **Frau** zu seyn' (*Die Ehrliche Frau*, II. xi).

In both plays the idea of the foolish or inverted world is replicated in the microcosm of Schlampampe's household, ruled as it is by women. Cleander comments to the audience: 'Ich glaube auch nicht daß es in der Welt thörichter und närrischer kan zugehen als in denselben [*sic*] Hause' (ibid., III. i). In this he briefly assumes the fool's privilege of direct contact *ad spectatores*; but the real control of foolery at others' expense is reserved for the clever students, Edward and Fidel, whose tricks make them the masters, and the three women their butt. Schlampampe herself is never the wit, despite the mirth she causes. Even at her funeral derisive farce prevails, for both Lorentz and Lysander fail to deliver the traditional mark of dignity, the *Leichenpredigt*, successfully. The death of the butt, it seems, cannot be tragic, because the butt is by definition the outsider (as Masaniello finally was), and identification leading to sympathy is therefore precluded.

The rhetorical power to direct comic effect and events, and to make us laugh at Schlampampe, is reserved by the author for the men in both plays. As the butt, the unfemininely dominant landlady is disarmed. Because she cannot make the audience laugh except in derision, she is also linguistically or rhetorically disempowered, and if we return to the frontispiece of Reuter's *Ehrliche Frau*, we find that not only is Schlampampe depicted there in an obviously masterful, masculine pose, but that within the picture is incorporated her favourite turn-of-phrase, 'So wahr ich eine ehrliche Frau bin'. The phrase is clearly intended to eliminate the possibility that any claim preceding it might be refuted, and as such is highly rhetorical. Schlampampe therefore has, or attempts to have, a stake in the masculine game of rhetoric, and it is no coincidence that even the title of Reuter's piece ridicules her favourite, manipulative turn-of-phrase. Schlampampe's unfeminine claims to mastery, linguistic and domestic, make her threatening, and it is from them that her comic degradation and her casting as the abject fool or butt must follow.

*Comic Reassurance in Opera*

By the end of the seventeenth century, the clown or more masterful type of the fool is well on the way to being the undisputed ruler of vernacular opera. Not all librettists willingly granted him a place in their texts. In Hamburg, Barthold Feind complained bitterly, expressing the view that love of the fool was the unfortunate expression of a lack of audience refinement: 'die grösseste bassesse eines mauvait gout [*sic*] und schlechten Esprit des Auditorii'.[44] This is not to say that Feind himself dispensed with the popular figure: so-called *Hanswürste* came to characterize the Hamburg texts in particular, and also feature in the German language libretti of other centres, notably Braunschweig-Wolfenbüttel. Their function is occasionally to be the butt, and often to construct it: to direct audience mirth at an object that might otherwise appear threatening.

One comic figure who obviously reassures on potentially alarming points is Desbo, the clownish servant in a version of Fiocci's and Aureli's *Helena Rapita da Paride* adapted for the Braunschweig stage around 1708.[45] This should arrest our attention in view of the extreme threat to male society associated with the legend of Helen, who was held culpable for the fall of Troy. In his fool's function as a source of conventional wisdom, Desbo first warns Paris's companion, Arminoe, who is in love with Helen, that beautiful women have vengeful natures. The idea is a now-familiar commonplace, but potentially disturbing, and within the space of an aria Desbo backtracks, playing down the threat with a reassuring reminder that, once roused, such women may easily be placated by a simple (male) embrace:

| | |
|---|---|
| Se sono offese | Wenn man sie einmahl beleidiget/ |
| E vilipese | Oder nicht genug ehret/ |
| Parlano subito | Reden sie alsbald |

[44] Barthold Feind, *Gedancken von der Opera*, in *idem*, *Deutsche Gedichte: Faksimiledruck der Ausgabe von 1708*, ed. W. Gordon Marigold (Berne 1989), 103.

[45] Pietro Antonio Fiocci (music), Aurelio Aureli (text: adapted by Valente), *Helena Rapita da PARIDE. . . . Oder Die vom Paris geraubte HELENA* (Braunschweig 1708[?]). Libretto: HAB.

| Di vendicarsi,    | Von lauter Rache.                     |
| Ma bene spesso    | Aber insgemein                        |
| Un solo amplesso  | Ist nur eine freundliche Umarmung     |
| Basta per trarle  | Schon vermögend genug/                |
| Fuori di duol.    | Sie wieder zu besänfftigen.    (II. xvi) |

The dangers of feminine allure are also the topic of a standard comic aria performed by Bressand's fool, Phorbas, in
the two-part Hamburg opera *Hercules Unter denen Amazonen*
(1694).[46] He and his master, Ismenus, have fallen into the
hands of the Amazons, and Phorbas compares the situation
ironically with social constructs familiar to the audience
before he launches into an aria:

> Bey uns gehts eben so/ das liebe Frauenzimmer,
> Trägt immer
> Gleichmässiges Verlangen/
> Jedoch auff andre weis/ das Männervolck zu fangen.
>
> **Aria.** 1.
> Ein angenehmes Weibgen
> Von jung und zartem Leibgen
> Ist eine Mause=Fall/
> Da mancher bleibt behangen/
> Und plötzlich wird gefangen
> Von der verführischen [*sic*] Sirenen schmeichel=Schall;
>
>   . . . . . . . . . .
>
> 2.
> Der Lockspeck seind die Blicke/
> Die Worte seind die Stricke/
> Die lauren überall/
> Und wer sich nicht läst warnen/
> Besitzt in ihren Garnen/
> Und findt/ daß ihm zuletzt sein naschen wird zu Gall (I. ix)

The tone is lighthearted, but the choice of theme is anything
but coincidental. In the introductory recitative I have cited,
Phorbas links his and Ismenus's physical capture by the
Amazons to the idea of men's sexual entrapment by women;
the comic link that is thus established makes women the butt,
because it reminds the audience that in real society men are
more economically powerful and therefore more desirable

---

[46] Johann Philipp Krieger (music), Friedrich Christian Bressand (text), *Hercules
Unter denen Amazonen* (Hamburg 1694). Libretto: SUB HH.

'captives' for marriage than women. This in turn distracts attention from the shameful situation on stage, where the two men have literally been taken captive by victorious women in combat. The potential threat or inversion inherent in the idea of successful warrior women is defused because Phorbas uses his fool's licence to be inappropriately flippant in a serious dramatic situation, and can remind the audience through his levity of the actual social *mores* that associate women with domesticity, and not with the battlefield.

Operatic buffoons do also sing comic arias in which men are the butt. In Graun's and Schürmann's *Iphigenia in Aulis* (1731) at Braunschweig, for example, a fool called Thersites performed an aria warning young women against men's dishonest intentions:[47]

> O ihr verliebten Venus-Sieger/
> Beym Glase Wein beherzte Krieger/
>   Ihr liegt [= lügt] wenn ihr das Maul aufthut.
> Ihr Mägdgens/ traut den Helden nicht
> Sie scheinen ehrlich von Gesicht/
>   Sind doch Betrieger/
>   Ja Ehren=Bieger/
>     Der Schalck steckt ihnen unterm Hut.     (I. ix)

Since the plot of the opera involves a young woman being lured to her death with a promise of marriage, the warning is perhaps under- rather than overstated. The aria echoes a similar piece in Postel's Hamburg libretto, *Die wunderbar= errettete Iphigenia* (1699),[48] on which Schürmann's version is based almost verbatim. In both operas, the fool sings about the phenomenon of love in fairly general terms, without making women specifically the butt; this is, after all, a story in which the central female figure is clearly of the virgin martyr rather than the witch type, and is therefore unthreatening. It is interesting that the only dangerous female character in the opera, Clytemnestra, is rendered incapable by madness when she hears of her daughter's fate, and thus joins the fool as an outsider who can no longer influence events.

---

[47] Karl Heinrich Graun (music), Georg Kaspar Schürmann (text), *Iphigenia in Aulis* (Wolfenbüttel 1731). Libretto: HAB.

[48] Reinhard Keiser (music), Christian Heinrich Postel (text), *Die wunderbar=errettete Iphigenia* (Hamburg 1699), libretto in *Die Oper*, ed. Willi Flemming (Leipzig 1933), 255–308 (263).

Fools in opera allay not only the anxieties that are felt about women in a Christian patriarchy, but also the threat posed by non-Christians. In Strungk's and Köhler's *Esther* the comic figure, Jethur, privileges women, at least white women, over blackness, even while he comically attacks them:[49]

> 1.
>
> Aus dem besten Helffenbein
> Ist gemacht das Frauenzimmer;
> Darümb wils vom Erdklos immer
> Frey und nie beherrschet seyn:
> Denn die harten Köpffchen kommen
> Und sind her von Bein genommen.
>
> 2.
> Wil man schon was Schwartzes bleichen/
> Dennoch bleibts bey schwartzer Art . . .    (II. i)

But the aspect of the oriental which usually concerns opera buffoons is not colour, but religion. If they are non-Christians, they will even make a butt of their own creed. Hadar, the fool in Graupner's and Feind's *Simson* (1709), 'mistakenly' announces that roast pork will be served at a Jewish feast,[50] and Barac in the first part of Franck's and Bostel's *Cara Mustapha* (1686) ridicules the Muslim veto on alcohol in a comic aria, while displaying his scorn for the Prophet by getting drunk:

> Hat uns nicht Mahomet schändlich betrogen/
>     Wann er den Wein in Verachtung gebracht/
> Hat der Verführer nicht heßlich gelogen/
>     Wann er Wein=Trincken zur Sünde gemacht?
> Wer so verachtet den edelen Wein/
> Muß wol ein Narre mit Mahomet seyn.[51]

[49] Nikolaus Adam Strungk (music) and Johann Martin Köhler (text), *Die Liebreiche/ Durch Tugend und Schönheit Erhöhete Esther* (Hamburg 1680). Libretto: HAB.

[50] Christoph Graupner (music) and Barthold Feind (text), *Der Fall des grossen Richters in Israel/ Simson, Oder: Die abgekühlte Liebes-Rache der Debora* (Hamburg 1709). Libretto in Reinhart Meyer (ed.), *Die Hamburger Oper: Eine Sammlung von Texten der Hamburger Oper aus der Zeit 1678–1730*, 4 vols. (Munich 1980–4), 2. 255–333 (281).

[51] Johann Wolfgang Franck (music) and Lucas von Bostel (text), *Der Glückliche Grosz-Vezier Cara Mustapha, Erster Theil* (Hamburg 1686). Libretto in Meyer, *Die Hamburger Oper*, 1. 171–248 (243). Mozart takes up the theme again in his *Entführung aus dem Serail*; in Act II the Turkish 'fool' Osmin performs a drunkenness aria with Pedrillo.

The comedy signals the arbitrariness of non-Christian religious customs. Barac's equation of his own status with that of the Prophet—'ein Narre mit Mahomet'—is also a claim to superiority. He, Barac, does not eschew wine; therefore Mahomet is the butt or the abject fool, and the suggestion is conveyed that all true Muslims are fools of this type (while the utter superiority of Christians is reassuringly confirmed). The tone of *Cara Mustapha* is celebratory, for the action revolves around the recent defeat of the Ottomans at Vienna in 1683, and the antics of the Turkish clown help the Hamburg audience to enjoy to the full the sense of relief that this major defeat of a centuries-old enemy must have engendered.

Contrary to what may have been our expectations, based on the 'superiority' theory of the comic, the German clown is clearly not a disempowered figure. His ability to make the audience laugh, and particularly to construct a butt for their laughter, confers on him a noteworthy level of mastery within the comedy. Both this and his unique position as an outsider to the dramatic action (even when he is embroiled in it in some way, he does not generally affect the course of events) reflect a special relationship between the clown and the dramatist or librettist; it is presumably no coincidence that clowns are almost invariably male, and almost invariably Christian. Jethur, Strungk's Jewish clown in *Esther*, is not a real exception, because in this Old Testament opera all the characters are Jewish; Barac the Turk is more unusual, because Bostel had a choice of Turks and Christians in *Cara Mustapha*. His decision may well have been determined by the dictum of comic 'lowness' that only allowed protagonists of inferior social status to be fools: in European Christendom, Turks are by definition of lower standing than Christians.

A similar hierarchical pattern is in evidence in the tendency to make women (and Turks and Jews, in *Cara Mustapha* and *Simson*) the butt. The comic punishment or abjection of the butt may be effected by the author or his clown, and produces satisfaction because it is reassuringly normative—the world is put the right way up at the expense of the unruly character. About a century later, Schiller describes this method euphemistically as 'eine sanfte Ermahnung'.[52] In fact Schiller's essay is a lucid account of the personal and social control that comedy, by identifying the abject fool, can exercise. He notes:

Wenn wir es unternehmen wollten, Lustspiel und Trauerspiel nach dem Maß der erreichten Wirkung zu schätzen, so würde vielleicht die Erfahrung dem ersten den Vorrang geben. Spott und Verachtung verwunden den Stolz des Menschen empfindlicher, als Verabscheuung sein Gewissen foltert.[53]

Schiller returns to the medical metaphor ('sugar on the pill') when he describes such methods as 'heilsam', but significantly makes no reference to comedy as a sweetener.

Is it really sugar, then, that the buffoon and the comic are adding to the texts considered? Feind, the self-confessed fool-hater, chooses what is perhaps a more accurate culinary metaphor to describe the function of his clown, Festus, in *Eugenia* (1695):[54]

Die Persohn des Festus is allhier gleichsahm als ein Gewürtz/ dessen Zusatz keine Speise verderbet/ sondern vielmehr derselben eine gewisse Schärffe giebet/ . . . so werden dadurch doch ein' oder andere Schwachheiten/ die im gemeinen Leben vorgehen/ gestraffet. (*Vorbericht an den Leser*)

A level of normative social control is certainly being exercised; but that in itself need not make an audience laugh. The key seems to be the element of relief or reassurance that the clown in the role of conservative social commentator and the butt as the punished inverter can provide. The last section of this chapter will investigate carnivalesque inversion, its implications, and the comic reachievement of order more closely.

---

[52] Friedrich Schiller, 'Die Schaubühne als eine moralische Anstalt betrachtet' (1784/1802), in *idem, Vom Pathetischen und Erhabenen: Schriften zur Dramentheorie*, ed. Klaus L. Berghahn (Stuttgart 1970), 3–13 (7).

[53] Ibid.

[54] Johann Philipp Förtsch (music) and Christian Heinrich Postel (text), *Die heilige Eugenia, Oder Die Bekehrung der Stadt Alexandria zum Christentum* (Hamburg 1695). Libretto: SUB HH. Compare also the discussion of this opera in Chapter 3.

*The Romantic and the Carnivalesque: From Gender-Bending to Married Order*

Performances by groups of Italian actors are recorded in German-speaking areas from 1568, by English players from 1585. The latter enjoyed such popularity that by the first half of the seventeenth century they were being emulated by German ensembles, who also called themselves *Englische Komödianten*. Musicians accompanied the first English strolling players on the Continent, and were in fact known and admired there even before the advent of the acting companies; there is evidence that a group of English fiddlers, trumpeters, and pipers were active at the Prussian court of Königsberg from 1556 to 1584.[55] Given the difficulties in comprehension experienced by German audiences, one of the main charms of the English performances was likely to have been the music that went with them. Trumpets and drums were played during fights or duels, horns for hunting scenes, and strings accompanied lovers' trysts, conventions which were therefore already familiar to the audience that later encountered them in opera.[56]

The plays of the Italian actors or *commedia* could easily be followed by a German-speaking audience because of their standard format. Although the pieces were often improvised, they were constructed from the 'building blocks' of programmatic situation comedy, and stock figures or 'masks'; these might include a pair of old men or *vecchi*, one usually a wealthy merchant (Pantalone), the other semi-intellectual (Dottore); two or more comic servants or *zanni*; a military figure who is both boastful and cowardly (Capitano); and two or more pairs of lovers or *inamorati*. One of the comic servants acquired the name Scaramuccio/a, or later, especially in Venice, Arlecchino.[57] The hilarity provoked by the *comici* does

---

[55] Jerzy Limon, *Gentleman of a Company: English Players in Central and Eastern Europe 1590–1660* (Cambridge 1985), 17.

[56] Hans-Albrecht Koch, *Das deutsche Singspiel* (Stuttgart 1974), 3.

[57] Compare Kenneth and Laura Richards, *The Commedia dell'Arte: A Documentary History* (Oxford 1990), 2. Scaramuccio or Scaramuzza was one especially successful example of the comic characters that were originally the property of a particular actor, their creator, but the name came to be used more generally to designate the comic figure. See Judith Popovitch Aikin, *Scaramutza in Germany: The Dramatic Works of Caspar Stieler* (University Park, Pa. 1989), 165.

not rely on innuendo or wordplay, but on the tangible, visual, and sensual situation; favourite confusions are mistaken identity (often as a result of disguise or cross-dressing) and love intrigue, whereby the lines of desire between characters are inevitably crossed. It is no coincidence that such confusions anticipate the plots of early opera; the *commedia dell'arte* feeds into Italian madrigal comedies, which are arguably the direct forerunners of Italian opera.[58] A striking example of the way the *commedia* traditions could find their way into German language opera is Telemann's *Pimpinone* (1725), composed for the Hamburg stage with a libretto by Johann Philipp Praetorius. Thematically the opera is a forerunner of Pergolesi's famous *La serva padrona* (1733), and caricatures the fortunes of a wealthy old man and a spirited female servant. The character types of the *commedia* are immediately perceptible here, and in fact the comic material can be traced back to Venice in 1708, where a three-part *intermezzo* called *Pimpinone*, by Tomaso Albinoni (music) and Pietro Pariati (text) was performed with an *opera seria*, *Astarto*. In 1717, a similar *intermezzo* called *Griletta e Pimpinone* was performed at Vienna, where Pariati had been employed since 1714, and five years later Albinoni's opera *I veri amici* appeared at Munich with *Vespetta e Pimpinone*, an *entr'acte* whose Italian libretto corresponds to the German of Praetorius's Hamburg text, which we must therefore regard as a translation.[59] It seems that Italian comedy informs the German tradition in a kind of pincer movement, coming up through the 'low' echelons of sixteenth- and early seventeenth-century folk performances, but also down through 'high' Italian opera (or, more specifically, the *intermezzi*) at the German courts into German language opera and *Singspiel*.

Both the *comici dell'arte* and the strolling players in Germany thrived on plot complications driven by disguise

[58] Orazio Vecchi's *L'Amfiparnaso*, for example, which may have been performed in Modena as early as 1594, is described by Hellmuth Christian Wolff as 'die erste größere komische Oper'. See Wolff, *Geschichte der komischen Oper: Von den Anfängen bis zur Gegenwart* (Wilhelmshaven 1981), 12. Among the cast of Vecchi's piece are Pantalone, Il Dottor Gratiano, Capitan Cardon, and a character called Zanni.

[59] This migration of comic material is traced by Liselotte de Ridder, 'Der Anteil der Commedia dell'Arte an der Entstehungs- und Entwicklungsgeschichte der komischen Oper: Studie zum Libretto der Oper im 17. Jahrhundert' (unpublished doctoral thesis: University of Cologne 1970), 187–91.

and mistaken identity. Weise and Reuter (the latter in particular under the influence of Molière)[60] make some use of the same devices. In particular, the carnivalesque device of assuming unsuitable clothes became a stock feature in the romantic plots of early opera in Germany.

Weise's Allegro achieved comic effect by dressing up as a woman. The assumption of an artificially high voice was part of his performance, a device which in opera can extend into comic falsetto singing. In most of the German language libretti, however, it is women who dress up as men, and the intention is not to parody the male, but usually to achieve an erotic goal. It is to this end that Lavinia becomes 'Cleantes' in the Hamburg adaptation of Steffani's and Mauro's *Il Trionfo del Fato* (1699),[61] Meroë is disguised as 'Magus' in Keiser's and Hoë's *Tomyris* (1717),[62] and Semiramis in Schürmann's *Ninus und Semiramis* (1730) serves her beloved Ninus in the guise of 'Orgontes' long before he discovers her true sex.[63]

This kind of costuming produces erotic tension, as the audience knows or guesses what the prospective partner does not, but it is also a comic device: the men are in fact being harmlessly gulled. But female cross-dressing in these operas has a further function. Women do not 'properly' pursue men; this is carnivalesque behaviour that turns the social order upside-down. Because these women take on external masculine characteristics, their active pursuit of a partner may appear more acceptable to an audience. The *verkehrte Welt*

[60] Reuter's source for *Die Ehrliche Frau*, whether direct or via the *Wanderbühne*, is Molière's *Précieuses Ridicules*. See Walter Hinck, *Das deutsche Lustspiel des 17. und 18. Jahrhunderts und die italienische Komödie* (Stuttgart 1965), 140.

[61] Agostino Steffani (music) and Ortensio Mauro (text: trans. by Gottlieb Fiedler), *Il Trionfo del Fato Oder Das Mächtige Geschick Bei Lavinia und Dido* (Hamburg 1699). Libretto: SUB HH.

[62] Reinhard Keiser (music) and Johann Joachim Hoë (text), *Die Großmüthige Tomyris* (Hamburg 1717). Libretto: SUB HH. The text is reprinted with the score in *Die Oper: Kritische Ausgabe von Hauptwerken der Operngeschichte*, vol. 1, ed. Klaus Zelm (Munich 1975). *Tomyris* was also performed at Braunschweig in 1724.

[63] Georg Kaspar Schürmann (music[?]), librettist unknown, *Ninus Und Semiramis* (Wolfenbüttel 1730). Libretto: HAB. The source for the text is *Nino overò La Monarchia Stabilitata* by Stefano Benedetto or Giorgio Maria Rapparini (?), performed with music by Johann Hugo Wilderer in Braunschweig in 1709. Libretto: HAB.

of costumed gender-bending thus confirms a frame in which the world is reassuringly the right way up.

There is an interesting instance of disguise in Bononcini's and Noris's version of the Semiramis material, *Semiramide Overò La Reina Creduta Re*, which was performed in Braunschweig with a German translation in 1708.[64] The action is drawn from a later period in Semiramis's life than in Schürmann's opera, and the heroine has become an anti-heroine by murdering Ninus, the husband she won in the earlier piece. In order to conceal her crime, she is posing as king, but is forced for practical reasons also to appear occasionally as herself, the queen. To add to the confusion she has fallen in love with one of her generals, Aribarzanes. It is therefore no surprise when Semiramis bewails the gender problems that assail her (the German parallel translation follows):

Son donna amante, e son Reina, e serva;
Anzi son Re trà questa
Clamide studiata: e quando d'essa
Comperto hò il sen; dove sue faci ardenti
Pose l'arcier bambino;
Seramide, sono e sembro Nino.

Ich bin ein verliebt Weibs=Bild/ eine Königin und eine Magd;
Auch bin ich der König in dieser
verstellten Tracht: und wann ich mit derselben
meine Brust bedecket habe/ worinn der Liebes=Schütze
seine brennende Fackeln aufgestecket hat[;]
Ich bin die Semiramis, und man hält mich vor den Ninus.     (I. iv)

The two guises of Semiramis signal the dichotomy of the masculine and the feminine in ambitious and powerful women. We have seen that women who aspire to rule are generally perceived both in opera and drama as threatening, and she is no exception: she has, after all, murdered her husband in order to accede to absolute power. But the threat Semiramis incorporates is defused in an unusual manner at the opera's conclusion, in that its existence is simply denied. To understand how this happens, we need to draw an analogy with the idea of the heroic woman, the paradoxical effect and

[64] Marc'Antonio Bononcini (music) and Matteo Noris (text), *Semiramide Overò La Reina Creduta Re . . . Semiramis Oder Die vor König gehaltene Königin* (Braunschweig 1708). Libretto: HAB. Further references are given in the text.

appeal of which depends on the presupposition that the generality of women are weak and unheroic. The threat of female fortitude is thus reduced in the same moment that it is evoked. Something similar happens in Aribarzanes' dénouement speech at the end of Noris's libretto, when the people are clamouring for the supposed king and the heir apparent to be executed on charges of tyranny; a bloody conclusion to the opera seems inevitable. Yet the moment Semiramis's womanhood is discovered, the weight of the crime that would require her death is suddenly reduced. Aribarzanes explains:

> Reina; ed'ora il veggo?
> Ingannasti regnando in varii modi
> Io scuso in petto feminil le frodi.

> Ist diß die Königin? nun sehe ichs/
> du hast auf mancherley Art diß Reich betrogen
> doch wird der Betrug weil es von einem Weibsbild geschehen
> desto eher zu vergeben seyn.

(III. xvii)

The threat of the powerful, masculine queen is retrospectively defused because it is simply denied. Women may be forgiven (Aribarzanes implies) because they are in fact without power, so we do not need to take their crimes seriously. This non-tragic conclusion is a form of comedy: disguise here turns the female tyrant into no more than a carnivalesque Lord of Misrule, who returns us to the security of reality as soon as the carnival is over and the clothes put off.

Lavinia's disguise in *Il Trionfo del Fato* is doubly carnivalesque, since she becomes not only a man, but black. As we have seen, black/white (like feminine/masculine) are opposing poles in the conceptual world of antitheses that characterizes early modern literature. Female cross-dressing can titillate especially *before* it is discovered onstage; colour swapping, by contrast, comes into its own particularly at the moment of dénouement. In Schürmann's and Fiedler's *Leonilde* (c.1704),[65] Sveno is in love with the heroine; but so

[65] Georg Kaspar Schürmann (music) and Gottlieb Fiedler (text), *Leonilde Oder Die siegende Beständigkeit* (Braunschweig c.1704). Libretto: HAB. Further references are given in the text.

is her adopted father, Gustavus, who as monarch chooses to banish his rival from the kingdom. Sveno returns to visit his beloved 'in Mohren=Gestalt' (II. x), and is of course eventually discovered by the king, who calls a guard to kill the black intruder. Leonilde grasps the moment to make her dramatic announcement.

> Hier ist/ mein König/ kein so schlecht Geblüthe/
> das von verachten Mohren=Pöbel stammt/
> der sich allhier lässt sehn/
> Ist der Sarmaten Printz. (III. iv)

Sveno's nobility and virtue shine all the more brightly because they are set off by the assumptions of evil and low character that go with blackness. The same point is spelt out in Bononcini's *Semiramide* libretto by Laodicea, Aribarzanes' secret wife who is also disguised as a moor. Her aria as black 'Nicea' links only whiteness with the virtue of constancy:

| | |
|---|---|
| Io bacio la catena | Ich küsse die Kette/ |
| Che schiava mi legò | die mich als eine Sclavin gefässelt. |
| Se qui servir a te | Weil ich bestimmt bin dir |
| Con bianca fe | mit weißer Treu zu dienen |
| Se ben nero hò il color, | ob ich gleich von Farbe |
| mi destinò. | schwartz bin. (I. xiii) |

When she is finally discovered by Nino, he is struck by the contrast between white Laodicea and her black counterpart:

> Ma: l'ancella d'Egitto
> Il color di la Notte
> Portava in faccia, e tu con bianco volto.
> Anche al'Alba fai scorno.
>
> Aber: das Weibs=Bild aus Egypten
> sahe so schwartz aus als die Nacht/
> und du beschämst mit deinem weissen Gesicht
> selbst die Morgenröthe. (III. vi)

The revelation of whiteness renders the beauty that is assumed to go with it all the more striking. Like gender-bending, colour-swapping is a carnivalesque device in opera that does not so much liberate the lower element (woman/ black) as confirm its place in a predefined, 'correctly' ordered hierarchical frame.

That frame, as we have seen in previous chapters, depends heavily on the social regulation of the sexes provided by marriage. Two distinct perceptions of marriage dominate in early modern comedy. One is that described by Gerhard Kaiser in his analysis of Gryphius's *Verliebtes Gespenst/ Die geliebte Dornrose* (1661), by which the characters' entry into the married state as the conclusion of comedy is equivalent to the martyr's entry into the blessed state of Heaven at the end of the martyr drama.[66] The 'high', norm-enforcing, non-carnivalesque prescription, particularly endorsed by Lutherans, is that the hierarchical order of marriage is a terrestrial mirror of the order of the divine. Characters who make the wrong choices at the worldly crossroads of gender relations enter, as Gryphius demonstrates in *Horribilicribrifax Teutsch* (1663; subtitled 'Wehlende Liebhaber'), a less blissful state, that may in an extreme form even be equated with Hell on earth.

This is closer to the 'low' perspective that emerges from popular writing, carnival, and *Fastnachtspiel*. Here a less exalted view of marriage emerges, which is in fact more bound up in the day-to-day problems of cohabitation and sexual relations. Watanabe-O'Kelly notes a change in the perspective on women as we move from 'high' to 'low': 'Die Ehe wird hier von einer ganz anderen Seite beleuchtet. Hier fehlen die beispielhaften Gattinnen, die sanften Märtyrerinnen. Sie werden durch keifende, geile, dumme, unflätige, fast monströse Frauen ersetzt . . .'[67] The question these pieces raise is which partner will dominate, but it is asked against a background of social expectations that dominance is a male prerogative, and that marriage is the approved institutionalization of this prerogative. Women who aspire to rule are, as we have seen, either demonized or ridiculed as butts. Carnival may license women to invert the gender hierarchy temporarily, but as soon as carnival becomes theatre, and the participants become spectators, comic satisfaction demands closure; the expectation of a return to normality or at least

[66] Gerhard Kaiser, *Die Dramen des Andreas Gryphius: Eine Sammlung von Einzelinterpretationen* (Stuttgart 1968), 279.
[67] Watanabe-O'Kelly, 'Das Verborgene enthüllt', 74.

an affirmation of normality (for example, the classification of the duped husband as *Narr*) is a condition of audience enjoyment. In this sense the comic has again become palimpsestic: both the Christian and the carnivalesque perspective are directed towards the reachievement of a comically disturbed, generally accepted (or rhetorically constructed) norm.

Christian Reuter's two *Singspiele, Des Harlequins Hochzeit-Schmauß* and *Des Harlequins Kindbetterin-Schmauß* (published with *Die Ehrliche Frau* in 1695),[68] are clear examples of the hybrid state of comedy by the end of the seventeenth century. They follow the form of the *intermezzi*, the popular comic playlets that punctuated the serious action of Italian opera. Although the style of Reuter's comedy is 'low', it depends heavily on the spectators' familiarity with 'high' conventions. Harlequin's wooing of Lisette, for example, is a parody of gallant metaphorical *acutezza*:[69]

> Mein süsser Bienen-Korb/ mein klares Urin-Glas/
> Verzeihe/ daß ich dich anrenn auf dieser Straß/
> Ich bin gantz verschammeriert/
> Weil niemand als mir gebührt
> zu üben
> das Lieben/
> mit dir du Raben-Aas.
>
> (*Hochzeit-Schmauß*, 60)

The comic effect springs from the audience's recognition that this language is unsuitable, and that terms like 'Raben-Aas' in fact belong to the 'low' vocabulary of the husband-within-marriage paradigm of *Fastnachtspiel*, rather than that of the hopeful lover of romantic comedy. Reuter's humour relies not only on the incongruity of language, but also of situation and genre. We expect pre-marital events to be the preserve of 'high' comedy, and to move romantically towards an idealized view of the married state that is significantly lacking in this carnivalesque piece; one of the first things we

---

[68] In *Schlampampe*, ed. Tarot, 57–110. Further references are given in the text.
[69] Of the kind recommended by Benjamin Neukirch in his *Anweisung zu Teutschen Briefen* of 1700; repr. in part in *Das Zeitalter des Barock*, ed. Albrecht Schöne (Munich: Beck 1988), 495–98.

discover in the companion play, *Harlequins Kindbetterin-Schmauß*, is that Lisette is to give birth just four months after the wedding.

The more conventional 'low' view of marriage finds its most frequent expression in the comic portrayal of the dominant wife, and the 'henpecked' husband (a reassuring choice of domesticated animal in the English metaphor!). In Christian Weise's version of the 'king for a day' theme, *Ein wunderliches Schau=Spiel vom Niederländischen Bauer* (1685),[70] the audience appetite for familiar domestic comedy is whetted by the comic servant, Lars: 'Botztausend die Weiber kommen/ und wollen ihre Männer heimholen/ das wird ein fein SPECTACUL werden' (I. iii). The direct address implicates the spectator in Lars's assumption that female dominance is a ridiculous sight, and thus defuses the threat of the women even before they are on stage. Farmer Krix's cry of alarm when he is apprehended by the vengeful women is, therefore, simply funny:

> KR. (*Schreyt.*) O Gevatter Mierten/ O Nachbar GOSCH, ô Schwager CLAS, ô steht mir nur dißmal bey/ ich will euch gerne nicht wieder verlassen.
>
> (I. iv)

A certain sympathy is apparent for the lot of the women, who are left to worry at home while their husbands squander their earnings getting drunk: Weise allows one of the farmers' wives to arouse audience concern for the wife and newborn child of the missing farmer, Mierten:

> BRÜTTE. Ich weiß was sie die Nacht vor ein Hertzeleid verführet hat/ ich halte immer die Mutter und das Kind wird davor bezahlen müssen.
>
> (II. xiii)

But the comedy of the piece relies on the unspoken premiss that, within a partnership, it is the role of the man to attempt to return to his 'carefree' pre-marital lifestyle, and the role of the woman—who is traditionally the predator, and has entrapped her husband—to put a spoke in his wheel. It is this view that excites the farmer of the title, Mierten, and it proves to be the catalyst for his adventure:

---

[70] Christian Weise, *Ein wunderliches Schau=Spiel vom Niederländischen Bauer*, in *Werke*, vol. 12/2. Further references are given in the text.

Hey sa! COURAGE! Da steht ein Mann/ der die Frau in Wochen liegen hat/ und der sich auff seine eigne Hand lustig machen darff. Hey sa! Da steht ein Mann/ der Geld hat/ und der sich um die gantze Welt nichts schieret/ wenn er nur vor der Frauen Friede hat! Ach schade/ daß die Weiber nicht zehnmahl nach einander in Wochen liegen sollen/ da solte erst ein köstlich Leben um uns Männer seyn. (I. v)

The tribulations that Mierten later undergoes at the hands of the duke and his court, who make of him their butt or abject fool when they make him a nobleman for a day, may be seen as a punishment for his irresponsible attitude towards his marriage. Nonetheless, it is this attitude and the spectators' comprehending response to it that allows the marital comedy in the piece to function.

The 'low' comedy of gender relations propagated by the fool on the opera stage follows a similar pattern. In Förtsch's and Postel's *Heilige Eugenia* (discussed in Chapter 3) the buffoon, Festus, initially decides to curry favour with women by performing an aria that attacks men:

> Ihr falschen Heuchler ins gemein/
>  Es sind nur süsse Lügen
> Ihr wollet mit geschmincktem Schein/
>  Die Mädgens nur betriegen
> Wenn sich ein gantzes Schock beklagt/
> Hat einer doch kaum wahr gesagt. (I. xv)

He is subsequently robbed by female gypsies, declares, 'ein Schelm mag mehr auff Weiber Seite treten', and by the second act he is comically caricaturing women as repressive wives:

> 1.
> Ja/ ja/ ja/
> Wer einmahl sich verbunden
>  Zu einer Frauen=Pflicht/
> Der muß zu allen Stunden
>  Auffpfeiffen/ wenn sie spricht.
> Ja/ ja/ ja/
>  Sonst sind die Ruhten da.
> 2.
>  Nein/ nein/ nein/
> Ich will es wohl verschweren/
>  Bin ich nur einmahl frey/
> Und nimmer wiederkehren

> Zu diesem sauren Brey.
> Nein/ nein/ nein/
> Ich müßt ein Narre seyn.    (II. vii)

This is the standard fool's approach to marriage, and is echoed by Barac, the Turkish clown in part two of *Cara Mustapha*, who engages with his audience by lapsing into a most un-Turkish *Plattdeutsch* to insult women and the marital state:

| | |
|---|---|
| Iß et nich genoeg bekant | [Ist es nicht genug bekannt, |
|    Watt öffters vor Verdreet | was oft für Verdruß |
| Mit sick bringt de Echte-Stand / | der Ehestand mit sich bringt, |
|    Wo mennig Mann drin schweet/ | in dem mancher Mann so schwitzt, |
| Dat he de kolde Pisse krigt | daß er die kalte Pisse kriegt, |
| Wenn ein Xantippe plaegt so dicht | wenn ein Xantippe ihn so plagt, |
|    Dat he sick mut beklagen | daß er sich beklagen muß: |
|    Och/ wo bin ick bedragen! | ach, wie bin ich betrogen worden!] |

(Part 2, III. ii)

A solution is found to the vexed question of women, men, and marriage in the comic interludes that punctuate Strungk's and Köhler's *Esther*. The librettist's treatment of the biblical material recalls a piece from the strolling players' repertoire, called *Comoedia von der Königin Esther und hoffertigen Haman* (published in 1620),[71] in which the action is repeatedly interrupted by the domestic battle between the fool, Hans Knapkäse, and his wife over who is 'Herr im Hause' (p. 41). His status as abject fool is confirmed when she finally emerges as the master. There are various 'low' influences at work here. The dominance of women is a familiar signal from the carnivalesque *verkehrte Welt* that also finds expression in *Fastnachtspiel* and popular drama. Koch, on the other hand, has asserted that when comic servants appear in pairs, like Hans Knapkäse and Fraw, we can be certain that the *commedia dell'arte* has exercised its influence.[72]

Strungk's libretto interweaves the 'high' with the 'low' in a manner typical of early opera, and has parts for three buffoons: a court jester called Tallas, the Jew, Mara, and her

---

[71] Reprinted in *Spieltexte der Wanderbühne*, ed. Manfred Brauneck, 4 vols. (Berlin 1970–5), 1. 3–77. Watanabe-O'Kelly also refers to serious 16th-cent. treatments of the Esther material by Naogeorg, Pfeilschmidt, and Murer; see Watanabe-O'Kelly, 'Das Verborgene enthüllt', 70.

[72] Hans-Albrecht Koch, *Das deutsche Singspiel* (Stuttgart 1974), 9.

husband, Jethur. Tallas's function is familiar: when, in the opening scenes, the court is alarmed by the unwifely disobedience of Queen Vasthi, the clown plays down the threat in a comic commentary:

> So gehts/ wenn man
> Nach schönen Frauen trachtet!
>
> .   .   .   .   .   .
>
> Es könt' ein' arge Dirn'
> Auch leicht mein klug Gehirn
> Als Zwirn
> Verwirrn                                   (I. iii)

'Low' marital comedy provides a pendant to the 'high' conjugal problems at court when Jethur and Mara join a fools' debate. Jethur, predictably, agrees with Tallas:

> Gewiß! der Narr hat wahr gesagt/
> Und gleichwohl ist er nie geplagt
> Mit einem bösem Weibe;
>
> .   .   .   .   .   .
>
> Ich aber hab' ein böses Ungeheuer;
> Ja ärger als das Fegefeur:
>
> .   .   .   .   .   .
>
> Deßwegen schweig' ich lieber still'/
> Und lasse sie nur schalten/ wie sie wil   (I. iv)

Mara, equally predictably, disagrees with Jethur:

> Wie mancher Nabal ist zu finden/
> Der meinet/ wenn er als ein Narr
> Auff seinem steiffen Kopff verharr'/
> Er könne tapffer überwinden!
> Und ob gleich sein' Abigail
> Mehr Klugheit hat im kleinen Finger;
> Doch hält er Sie/ als Sich/ geringer/
> Und ruffet nur: Ich wil! Ich wil!         (I. v)

The quarrel is resolved in a favourite dramatic *topos*, the judgement scene.[73] Social correctness is personified in the

---

[73] Weise's *Verkehrte Welt* concludes in this way (see above). Allegorical judgement scenes are also a feature of the *Reyen* in *Trauerspiel*; examples are the chorus that follows Act II of Lohenstein's *Cleopatra*, or that concluding the second act of Hallmann's *Urania*. In both cases the judgement made is highly relevant to our understanding of the action.

272 CARNIVAL, THEATRE, AND CONTROL

adjudicating figure of 'Höffligkeit', who pronounces authoritatively on the problem:

> Das Frauen=Volck ist/ wie ein Ey/
> Mit Schwachheit von Natur beleget;
> Wer Sie nicht auff Händen träget/
> Der stösset ihre Gunst entzwey:
> Drumb sollen feine Manns=Personen
> Mit Ungemach sie stets verschonen     (II. vi)

A social contract is confirmed, whereby women like Mara will
give up claims to a precedence based on 'mehr Klugheit
. . . im kleinen Finger' in return for the protection offered
by courtly gallantry or *Höflichkeit*. The solution ought to be
simply comical, since Jethur is no gallant and Mara clearly
a strong-minded woman; but, oddly, she appears to be satisfied with this judgement, even though it is based on a 'high'
conception of gender relations that sits uneasily with the 'low'
world of the clown.

   *Dei ex machina* more usually resolve the 'high', romantic
action in opera than quarrels in the comic interludes.
Schürmann's and Frauendorf's *Zerstörte Troia* (1724),[74]
for example, is concluded by Venus, Juno, and Pallas, who
descend on a cloud to unite the warring parties in a startling happy ending: Menelaus is reconciled with Helen, Ajax
is united with Cassandra, and Polyxena survives to marry
Pyrrhus. This is the kind of celebratory finale one might expect
in a piece designed for ducal wedding festivities, but in fact
Schürmann's *Troia* was composed for the Braunschweig fair.
One explanation for the proliferation of nuptials might be
that this opera has no clown, and the love interest created
by the build-up to these unlikely unions punctuates and
relieves the tragic potential of the mythological situation in
the same way as the interference of the buffoon does in other
libretti.

   When the move towards marriage and the activities of a
fool do combine on the opera stage, the level of comic reassurance becomes almost stifling. *Thalestris*, an opera written

[74] Georg Kaspar Schürmann (music) and Johann Christoph Frauendorf (text:
adapted by Schürmann), *Das Zerstörte Troia...* (Wolfenbüttel 1724). Libretto:
HAB.

for Hamburg by Förtsch and Postel in 1690,[75] draws on the ever-titillating legendary history of the Amazons, and tells the story of Queen Thalestris's oppression by the tyrant Neobarzanes and her eventual rescue by the young hero Orontes. It is also an opera about marriage. The Amazon legend is exciting precisely because of the anxiety aroused by the idea of a society that is not only matriarchal, but excludes men entirely, except in their reproductive function and, in some versions, as slaves. Significantly, Postel feels it necessary to preface his libretto with a fifteen-page discussion of misogyny, the *femme forte*, and the virtues of the female sex: if marriage within a patriarchy is considered an effective way of controlling the subversive, inverting potential of women, then the idea of a society which excludes both this institution and its institutors will shake the security of the status quo. It cannot surprise us that in *Thalestris* the fool Sbiocco provides a reminder of the conventional 'reality' of marriage early on, in a long comic aria from which I shall cite only three of seven stanzas:

1.
Wer den Ehstand wil erwehlen
　　Vor der Jugend Lieblichkeit/
Wird in allen Stücken fehlen
　　Darauff er sich hat gefreut
Weil von Jungfern/ Wittwen/ Frauen/
　　Keiner auff ein Haar zu trauen.

2.
Die ihr stets geputzet sehet/
　　Nimt das Hauß nur schlecht in acht/
Und die wie ein Färcken [= Ferkel] gehet/
　　Wird mit wenig Lust betracht.
Junge wollen immer schertzen/
　　Und die Alten bringen Schmertzen.
　　.　.　.　.　.　.　.

5.
Ist sie klug/ sie wil regiren/
　　Ist sie dum/ O welche Pein!
Reiche lassen Hoffarth spühren/

[75] Johann Philipp Förtsch (music) and Christian Heinrich Postel (text), *Die Groß=Müthige Thalestris, Oder Letzte Königin der Amazonen* (Hamburg 1690). Libretto: SUB HH.

Arme tragen wenig ein.
Adeliche laßen selten
    Uns mehr als die Diener gelten.        (I. x)

The tone of the aria is entirely lighthearted, and the ideas
it contains are not original: some of the same themes featured in Mara's and Jethur's marital quarrel in Esther, and
all occur in earlier popular plays. Yet it is precisely the hack-
neyed nature of these jokes that reminds spectators that
marriage, while absent at this point in the opera from the
Amazon community, is the long-standing and secure basis of
their own society. Sbiocco's aria also makes it clear that men
are in control of marriage: the 'wer' of the first stanza is indubitably masculine. Unlike the Amazons, real women do not
have the power to offer or withhold marriage; it is for men
to decide whether the married state is preferable to 'der
Jugend Lieblichkeit'.

Later in the opera, two young Amazons, Marthesia and
Evandra, are confronted with Sbiocco, and they sing him a
(shorter) answering aria that recalls Mara's complaints
about marriage in Esther:

1.
Die der Liebe sich ergeben/
    Und der Männer falschen Schein/
Werden gar gewiß erleben
    Daß sie recht betrogen sein/
Wenn die Eh verknüpfft die Hände/
Hat die Freude schon ein Ende.
2.
Ist er reich so muß sie hören/
    Daß sie ihm nichts zugebracht.
Ist er geitzig muß sie lehren/
    Wie er schindet Tag und Nacht/
Sie muß allen Närrschen Grillen
Untergeben ihren Willen.        (II. xiv)

Superficially, there is no loading of the dice in this opera
regarding men, women, and marriage: each sex comically
rejects the idea of being wedded to the other. The difference, however, is that Sbiocco's aria suggests that men have
the power to reject or accept marriage in a society where the

institution is a given; Marthesia and Evandra can only reject
it against the background of the Amazon community where
it does not exist, and the movement of the opera is towards
a correction, in a patriarchal sense, of this state of affairs.
Thalestris is the last queen of the Amazons, because she ends
the operatic action by disbanding the matriarchal state. She
appeals to her subjects to submit to the institution of marriage for the sake of order:

> Ihr aber/ ihr großmütgen Amazonen,
> Bedencket doch wie wir der gantzen Erden
> Ein Scheusal gleichsam sein/
> In dem wir so unordentlich beywohnen
> Den Männern/ unser Land zu mehren/
> Und diesen Schimpff nicht länger zu ernehren/
> Hab' ich an Printz Orontes mich ergeben          (III. xviii)

Her intention to marry Orontes is couched in terms that
suggest a conqueror/ conquered relationship. The metaphor
of the war of love, the *Venuskrieg*, is a popular one in German
gallant literature at the end of the seventeenth century, but
here it is used with particular effect. The battle skills of the
Amazons traditionally enabled them to retain their matriarchal independence, yet here the warlike Amazon surrenders
herself ('sich ergeben') to a male 'victor'; marriage in this
romantic comedy is a solution to the problem of the carnivalesque inversion of the Amazon community. Far from
licensing such inversion, even for the temporary duration of
the opera, the fool is there to remind us of the frame of order
that is masculine supremacy and marriage in the patriarchal
state.

The domestic anxieties caused by dominant wives pale
beside the sense of threat a politically active woman can
engender. Observing that the 'böse Frau' and the henpecked
husband are a favourite comic duo in the work of early
dramatists such as Hans Sachs, Barbara Becker-Cantarino
notes, 'das allerlächerlichste aber ist das Frauenregiment'.[76]
The relief of laughter is greatest where we have begun by

---

[76] Barbara Becker-Cantarino, 'Die Böse Frau und das Züchtigungsrecht des
Hausvaters in der frühen Neuzeit', in Wallinger and Jonas, *Der Widerspenstigen Zähmung*
(Innsbruch 1986), 117–32 (119).

feeling most anxiety, and in comedy may replace the destruction or damnation of the threatening character found in the
*Trauerspiel.*

Christian Weise deals with the problem of the politically
aspiring woman in a comedy with the tendentious title *Die
bosshafte und verstockte Prinzessin Ulvida aus Dennemarck* (1685).[77]
The genre allocation is mine; Weise does not call his play a
*Lust-Spiel,* possibly out of a sense that this dramatic form is
unsuited to a royal history. Opitz, after all, dictated that
comedy 'bestehet in schlechtem [= schlichtem] wesen unnd
personen'.[78] By the end of the seventeenth century, however,
things had changed, in theory as well as in the examples of
dramatic practice we have already considered. According to
Albrecht Christian Rotth in 1688, the new comedy 'nimt nicht
allein Possierliche und lächerliche Verrichtungen zu ihrer
Fabel/ sondern auch offtmal wichtige/ Gottesfürchtige/
lobenswürdige'.[79]

That the tone of *Ulvida* is not entirely serious is evident
as soon as the comic figure, Svinekof (a Danish fool), leaps
out during the *Vorspiel* to give an aggressive account of his
presence:

Ach ihr Fantasten, was woltet ihr doch machen wenn ich aus der
COMOEDIE bliebe. Ist die COMOEDIE ein Ring so bin ich ein Edelstein: Ist
sie eine Nuß, so bin ich der Kern: Ist sie ein Kalbs-Braten, so bin ich der
Nieren: Ist sie ein Schöpsenkopff so bin ich das Zünglichen, und ist sie
Sauerkraut so bin ich die Bratwurst. (p. 461)

The first act opens with a dialogue that demonstrates the carnivalesque nature of Ulvida's relationship with her husband,
Ubbo. She is keen to usurp power in the absence of her
brother, the king, and her conversation with the more cau-
tious Ubbo reads like a royal case of Shrovetide henpecking:

[77] Christian Weise, *Die bosshafte und verstockte Prinzessin Ulvida aus Dennemarck,* in
*Werke,* vol. 2. Further references are given in the text.
[78] Martin Opitz, *Buch von der Deutschen Poeterey* (1624), ed. Cornelius Sommer
(Stuttgart 1970), 27.
[79] Christian Albrecht Rotth, *Vollständige Deutsche Poesie in drey Theilen* (Leipzig 1688),
200–1. Cited in Judith P. Aikin, 'Happily Ever After: An Alternative Affective Theory
of Comedy and Some Plays by Birken, Gryphius, and Weise', in Hans Wagener
(ed.), *Absurda Comica: Studien zur deutschen Komödie des 16. und 17. Jahrhunderts,*
(Amsterdam 1988), 55–76 (64).

UBBO. Es ist gefährlich.

ULVIDA. Wir sind zu furchtsam.

UBBO. Die Furcht stehet uns an.

ULVIDA. Ein Mann soll sich schämen, daß er die Worte gegen einem Frauenzimmer führet.

(I. i)

Rhetorically, Ulvida is wearing the trousers, and she uses commonplace assumptions about masculinity and femininity to manipulate her husband. The tendency to parody various established 'high' ideas about women is the most interesting characteristic of Weise's Danish princess. Later in the play, when her sibling returns in the nick of time to catch her committing high treason, Ulvida unexpectedly casts herself in the role of the female martyr, posing as a heroic Catharina von Georgien faced with a ruthless tyrant:

ULVIDA. (*Ad spectatores.*) Und das ist ein tyrannischer Jäger der ein schwaches WeibsBild als eine wilde Pestie TRACTIRen will. . . . Und ist dieses nicht ein Königliches Gemüthe welches einen solchen Tyrannen so tapffer begegnen kan?

(II. i–ii)

It is significant that she moves into the mode of the fool, addressing the spectators directly, to take up this position, since the most likely intended audience response is derisive mirth. Just in case anyone has been taken in by Ulvida's affecting performance, Weise has her betray herself before the end of the act: 'Nun der Affen Tantz wäre vor diesesmahl gehalten' (II. x), and her maid confirms that her behaviour springs from sheer cockiness, and the belief that her brother will not have her executed: 'Gewiß die Leuthe müßen sich über ihre Großmüthigkeit verwundern, aber hätte es mit dem Tode sollen ein Ernst werden, so wäre das Leyd gewiß aus einen andern Thone gegangen' (II. xi).

But the show goes on. In debate with the king, Ulvida bewails her lack of linguistic mastery with considerable rhetorical deftness: 'Ein schwaches Weibesbild hat die Worte nicht allemahl in ihrer Gewalt' (III. xiv). When her mild-mannered suitor, Scotto, appears, the princess drastically thrusts upon him the role of oppressor of her martyred femininity:

O ist keine Steinklüffte in Dennemarck übrig welcher mich vor diesen grimmigen Tyger Thier verbergen kan? Ach da kommt das Reisende [= reissender] Thier, welchen ich meine Ehre, meine Redlichkeit, und mich selber aufopffern soll. (III. xiv)

From a modern point of view, one cannot help wondering how close Ulvida comes to the truth when she accuses her brother of tyranny; he is, after all, threatening her with rape in an enforced second marriage, as the priest darkly hints: 'Der Himmel helfe, daß es die PRINCESSIN so weit nicht kommen läßt, sie wird erfahren daß gewaltsame Hochzeiten auch möglich seyn' (III. xiv). In this sense she is potentially subject to oppression. She does not, however, display the passive stoicism in her suffering that is the essential qualification of the female martyr of early modern drama: a distinct and unfeminine willingness to help herself is evident when Ulvida persuades Scumbart to murder her new husband on their wedding night. The heinousness of her attempted crime, which attacks not only the man and his rights of possession but the romantic idyll associated with marriage, ensures that Ulvida forfeits audience sympathy to the end.

Weise makes it quite clear that his anti-heroine is a threatening character, above all in her incorrigible will to overturn male supremacy. One of the things that makes her dangerous is her ability to use her femaleness and assumptions about femininity to achieve political ends: like an early modern dramatist, she is using established signals or rhetorical categories—such as the martyr/ ideal wife—to manipulate the response of her on-stage audience. For Ulvida, rhetoric works seductively, when she barters with sexual favours for Ubbo's support—'Wer mir gefallen will der muß großmüthig seyn' (I. i)—and associatively, when she parodies the clichés of ideal womanhood. Ulvida is the type of dangerously articulate female character we have met in the plays of Lohenstein, even though Weise turns the drama into a fairly lightweight piece, and not into *Trauerspiel*. Where Lohenstein disarmed his heroines by showing them properly penitent in death, Weise defuses the threat of a 'bosshafte und verstockte Prinzessin' by making her the comic butt. We laugh at her bombastically unconvincing performances, and even at her final fate: imprisonment with her beloved Ubbo, who is by no means as sure as Ulvida that such enforced togetherness is really the fulfilment of his dreams.

## Conclusion

When Eckehard Catholy describes the *Fastnachtspiel* as the first instance of German secular drama, this does not mean that the genre treats only entirely secular themes, or only with an entirely secular message.[80] The point is that the Shrovetide plays, like other forms of 'low' comedy, are worldly or world-centred, and concentrate on issues which, although they often involve a Christian scheme of order, are located in this world rather than the next. 'Low' comedy on the German stage seems to reaffirm rather than to subvert the 'high' values of order. This is reflected in the palimpsestic integration of carnivalesque elements from the Shrovetide play and other forms of popular theatre into romantic comedy, with its powerfully normative underlying frame.

Even theatre, like opera, that has claims to 'high' or didactic status may be coloured and enlivened by elements of the carnivalesque such as disguise, the exchange of gender roles, and the marital squabbles the latter produces. The inversions or subversions of carnival, however (if we accept that there is any real subversion involved) are contained and controlled in the world of the stage, on which carnival acquires 'footlights' and becomes quite distinct from the auditorium. The subversive elements which were an overt part of carnival become mere suggestions of themselves: titillating ideas followed by the immediate reassurance which —in place of licence—now provides the comic relief or satisfaction of the event. The instigator of control is often the figure we might expect to be the most carnivalesque, the fool or clown, and the need for comic reassurance seems to develop as demands on theatre become 'higher'. Where, for example, Hans Knapkäse in the *Wanderbühne* version of

---

[80] See Eckehard Catholy, *Fastnachtspiel* (Stuttgart 1966), 80.

*Esther* is allowed to remain an abject male fool who cannot 'wear the trousers', his successor Jethur in Köhler's libretto is reinstated in his proper position through the imposed ruling of an allegorical representative of social *mores*.

Dramatic ideas of marriage in particular reveal the interworkings of the 'high' and the 'low'. The metaphysical dimension of marriage, as an allegory of the (feminine) human soul wooing Christ, has a long history in theological thought.[81] The marital union is analogous with divine union, and in 'high' comedy may even function as an alternative to death in the martyr drama. Comic punishment provides a similar reminder by analogy of its more earnest counterpart; women like Ulvida, who would remain in a carnivalesque position 'on top', are punished and disempowered when they are made the abject butt: a comic alternative to the damnation and destruction meted out to König's Fredegunda and her kind in more serious stage situations. In fact, the 'low' comic perspective on marriage complements the 'high' one, even though it does not achieve the same metaphysical dimensions. Its portrayal of chaos (the woman in charge) versus order (the man in charge) affirms the seventeenth-century Christian conception of a cosmic scheme based on antithesis, and there is—as the changing treatments of the *Esther* material illustrate—increasing pressure not to leave the mastered man as fool, but to show on stage the resolution of the conflict and the reachievement of a stable male hegemony.

The structural analogies between the comic and the serious plot show that serious and more lightweight German theatre in the seventeenth century can be treated not as separate, but as related entities. In both, the social threat that constitutes the action can be finally resolved by the defeat, comic or serious, of a person or persons perceived as wrongly empowered. These persons may be peasants (especially in early comedy), disruptive fools (such as Alamode or Masaniello), non-Christians, or women. What the four groups have in common is that they are resistant to *Vernunft*,

---

[81] For example in Origen's interpretation of the Song of Songs, promoted by Bernard of Clairvaux in the 12th cent., and in the poems of the 17th-cent. German Jesuit Friedrich Spee. See Aikin, 'Happily Ever After', 62–3.

and are therefore likely causes of chaos.[82] In fact, comic portrayals of women seem to be most common, and those of non-Christians almost incidental when they do occur. This may be because the latter group generates more unease than comedy can contain; for most people in European Christendom, non-Christians were, after all, an unknown quantity in their daily life, whereas women were obviously seen to be controlled by a hierarchical gender system.

What differentiates dramatic comedy from *Trauerspiel* is its ending, which does not generally involve death. For Susan Purdie, the comic conclusion is 'where the power of comedy inheres, for the status quo-affirming "happy endings" it shares with other genres [such as early opera, S.C.] are produced in conjunction with the discursive mastery of joking.'[83] The 'discursive mastery of joking', whether it is practised by the author or his clown, is what ensures that the 'right' characters or groups receive comic punishment, or become the butt. The audience enters into a dialogic agreement with the joker that its members are different from the butt they deride, and thereby assume the superiority that is comic satisfaction: an Other is isolated. As Schiller's musings on comedy suggested, however, the idea of the Other is not confined to the stage. Conceptions and infringements of 'rightness' or order are reflected back and forth within the terms of the dialogic agreement between stage and auditorium, whereby the discursive master—the author and/or his clown—has rhetorical control. The audience is rewarded for its concurrence in a normative, hierarchical value system with comic gratification, or what Purdie calls a 'doggy bag': if the happy ending is compatible with social agency in the world, then 'the effect is rather like being given a doggy bag so that you can take your empowerment home with you'[84]—a reward for those who share in the masculinist, Christian-centred worldview of these early modern authors.

Although the Silesian dramatists considered in earlier chapters appear to exclude the more obviously carnivalesque or farcical aspects of popular theatre from their work, they too

---

[82] See James A. Parente, Jr, 'Baroque Comedy and the Stability of the State', in *GQ* 56/3 (1983), 419–30 (426).
[83] Purdie, *Comedy*, 116.      [84] Ibid. 117.

provide the 'doggy bag' of audience gratification, when norms are enforced and order imposed. Even in *Trauerspiel,* the return to order follows its disruption by unauthorized agents: a typically carnivalesque situation. The distinction, as in the case of Weise's *Lustspiel von der verkehrten Welt* as opposed to his *Trauerspiel, Masaniello,* is in the degree of punishment or reward. Lohenstein's heroines die because their transgressions against the social ideal are such that audience satisfaction or reassurance could not otherwise be achieved, while a protagonist like Gryphius's Catharina is of such exemplary magnitude that the secular paradigm of happy marriage is transfigured to become a glorious metaphysical union.

Other playwrights such as Weise, Reuter, Hallmann, and the librettists with whose work theirs so clearly interacts, assimilate aspects of the carnivalesque more overtly. Fools, disguise, and other elements of traditional 'low' theatre intermingle with pastoral and romantic plots. The opera stage especially, with its sensual musical and visual appeal, seems to have offered an ideal platform for the perpetuation of carnival.

The interesting feature of carnival is that, despite the controlled release it may provide, it remains potentially disruptive. Stallybrass and White identify the festival as a 'specific calendrical ritual', but the concept also as 'a mobile set of symbolic practices, images and discourses which were employed throughout social revolts and conflicts'.[85] Exactly this emerges from Weise's treatment of the revolution in *Masaniello.* If theatre is to gratify its audience, rather than provoking anxiety, then its carnivalesque elements must be strictly controlled by the stage.

---

[85] Peter Stallybrass and Allon White (eds.), *The Politics and Poetics of Transgression* (London 1986), 15.

# CONCLUSION: THEATRE AND THE RHETORIC OF OTHERNESS

The early modern idea of the world as *theatrum mundi* makes the stage a peculiarly significant location. God may be the divine puppeteer, but in terrestrial theatres men [*sic*] pull the strings, and can impose order and certainty on a fictive world that mirrors an ideal image of their own. Order and chaos are polarized within a system that is comprehensible and therefore controllable: chaos is defined as *other* than the ideal norm. Within a masculinist Christian system, the feminine and the non-Christian are perceived as threatening; they are therefore classified on the side of chaos, whereby the orderly process of their categorization is one means of containing the potential threat. In both 'high' and 'low' theatrical forms—*Fastnachtspiel*, school drama, or the hybrid form of opera—it becomes the accepted function of the play to maintain or at least reiterate the subordinate position of these ideas in a way that appears both 'natural' and indubitable, and, in doing so, to control the definition of alterity. In this process the dramatist (or librettist or composer) becomes something akin to a rhetorically skilled and persuasive advocate for an idealized status quo. The drama or opera as a rhetorical exercise provides 'proof' to the audience-jury that certain values associated with their society are both *true* and *right*. What is more, the audience comes to demand this as a necessary prerequisite of dramatic resolution and satisfaction.

It has not been the intention of this study to overplay the separateness of opera and drama as theatrical forms in the early modern period; in fact, the overlaps in form and content should have become clear. But there clearly are some distinctions to be drawn. Opera is a high point in the development of secular theatre in the period. This is a natural result of its function at the courts, where it serves the *Repräsentation* of the ruler's worldly status (as well as often providing allegorical confirmation of the divine rights of princes). Opera amalgamates the sensual appeal developed in Jesuit and Protestant school theatre and in popular European traditions to a secular end: to titillate and gratify an audience to the greatest possible extent, using music, words, and the visual effects achieved by machinery, emblematic tableaux, and sumptuous stage décor. It also assimilates the carnivalesque devices of disguise, intrigue, and the licence of the clown that had long existed in popular theatre. While the pedagogical form and content of school drama is directed primarily towards the boys who act in it, opera depends on the approval of mixed audiences. It must therefore provide a paradigm for ideally feminine as well as ideally masculine behaviour: this is what differentiates the ideality of a character like Feind's Octavia from Gryphius's Catharina or Lohenstein's Epicharis. While the latter two are in fact pattern-cards for masculine behaviour, the former incorporates more specifically feminine qualities, above all the will to self-subordination that is portrayed as essential to marital, and hence social, stability.

The classification of certain groups as 'other'—a non-ideal reflection of an ideal Self—neither begins nor ends in the early modern period, nor of course is it an exclusively European phenomenon. There is a school of thought that would frown on the ahistorical application of such words as sexism and racism to periods prior to our century, even though twentieth-century sexism and racism clearly have their roots in a historical process of defining alterity. By the early nineteenth century, Hegel (in the *Phänomenologie des Geistes* of 1807) had produced a formal philosophical explanation of the ways in which human beings constitute personal identity by reference to that which they are *not*, and had thereby provided a theoretical stimulus for influential modern thinkers such as Freud and Lacan. This is not the place for a full discussion of the complications of the divided individual. But from a political perspective the process of defining self and world seems to become particularly problematic when it is not so much personal as group identity which is at stake, and when that identity is bound into social power structures.

What *is* historically specific about the material treated here is how drama becomes established in the early modern period as a powerful rhetorical genre: one that seeks to teach and hence to influence. Its rhetorical aspirations are carried over into and developed in opera: musical rhetoric is one of the burning themes of the early modern period in Europe, and discussion of it is closely bound up with the development of opera as the newest dramatic genre. There is a tangible sense of excitement when composers and librettists explore the possibilities of marrying words and music on the stage, and audience responses seem to have confirmed the emotive power of the combination.

The earlier chapters of this study set out to demonstrate that women, blacks, and Turks are rhetorically related groups for early modern writers: inconstancy, devilishness, and the triumph of passion over reason are ideas associated with all three. Oriental or non-Christian protagonists, such as Lohenstein's Sultan Ibrahim and Gryphius's Shah Abas, tend to move within their own spheres, which they control despotically. Tyrants override the power of language because they have the power to destroy. Because rhetoric is generally understood as the force of reason or *Vernunft*, however, they thereby position themselves on the side of chaos, which is also the side of the feminine. This is important in terms of dramatic semiotics: if the oriental (male) can be categorized with women, he becomes 'like' women in Christian society, that is, controlled by the Christian male. The threat he might constitute to that society is thus contained. In a similar way, women who attempt to participate in the masculine rhetorical competition are doomed to fail. Only figures like Gryphius's Catharina, who is licensed by a divine patriarchal authority to oppose a feminized oriental male, are exceptions to the rule—and even she must prove her utter subjugation to that authority in martyrdom. Within the drama, female pro- tagonists cannot usually be allowed to win the game of lan- guage because of the reversal of power relations this would imply. In this, the stage mirrors as well as reinforcing social reality: the 'weapons' of rhetoric, or gendered commonplaces which have been evolved as a means of controlling the idea of woman, are bound to serve women imperfectly as disputative tools. In other words, as long as 'weibisch' remains an insult, woman's rhetorical position cannot be a strong one.

Dramatic tension requires opposing forces. The polarity of characters and ideas on the stage is a means by which rhetorically trained playwrights can manipulate the expectations of their audience. After all, the play's the thing; and assumptions about gender, colour, and religion can all be used to heighten the dramatic impact. For a skilled playwright, prejudices and commonplaces are a gift horse: because certain ideas (for example about gender) are firmly fixed, the writer is in a position to play with the expectations of his audience, and thereby to achieve particular dramatic effects. Once the polar arrangement of categories such as male–female has been linguistically defined, ideas may be cross-assigned, or categories 'jumped'. The dramatic impact can be increased by the paradoxical device of attributing ideal masculinity to a woman, and chaotic femininity to a man. This is what is happening, structurally speaking, when we find a Turk or Muslim displaying the characteristics of an ideal Christian, or a woman who incorporates exemplary masculinity—like the *femme forte*. The rhetorical effect depends on the surprise element, and that works particularly well when the paradox is visible on stage—in the figure of an armoured woman, for example. In both drama and opera, idealized characters jostle with their demonized counterparts, and exemplary with admonitory fates; polarity is inverted, and order may be achieved through paradox. This is what makes it possible for the idea of witchcraft or the spectacle of carnival to refer back to and support an ideal of Christian order while overtly representing pagan or even antichristian chaos.

On the other hand, the very necessity of enacting and re-enacting the process of fixing order and chaos betrays the futility, in teleological terms, of the endeavour. Theatre audiences may take a 'doggy bag' of satisfaction,[1] in the form of constructed order and defeated chaos, home with them, and this might be an important result for the dramatist, the schoolboy, or the opera box-office. But it is in the nature of doggy bags that their contents will be diminished, and that they need repeated refilling. Historical work on the early

---

[1] Susan Purdie, *Comedy: The Mastery of Discourse* (New York 1993), 117. Compare the Conclusion to Chapter 5 of this Study.

modern period has recently tended to stress the precarious nature of European identities in a period of rapid and in some ways radical change: Tatlock, for example, describes the stabilizing endeavour in the popular prose works of Eberhard Werner Happel as 'the repeated negotiation of issues of authority, identity, and value . . . Happel's prose works on the Turks addressed the cultural anxieties of the burgeoning economy of late seventeenth-century Hamburg, and . . . offered a strategy by which at least momentarily to deny the existence of these anxieties.'[2] The strategy, it seems, is to provide a distraction rather than a solution: 'at the very moment when Happel's merchant readers might have perceived their own world as chaotic, as driven by something arbitrary that they did not understand, Happel tells them that the chaos is elsewhere—in the East'.[3] Newman has seen in the phenomenon of schoolboy actors perform-ing sexually and politically charged female roles a further sign of cultural anxiety regarding 'the instability and fluidity of male and female behaviour and identity in central Europe at the time'.[4] While ideal women are clearly as effective tools as their demon counterparts in the stabilizing of the male–female hierarchy on stage, the repetitive structures in the portrayal of both extremes betray that stability is never quite achieved. Writing of English Renaissance tragedy, Dympna Callaghan has suggested that the dramatists place 'gender issues in centre stage', and in doing so reveal 'the precarious status of phallic power, which encodes the disruptions its seeks to forestall . . .'.[5] In other words, wherever a hierarchy is constructed, the insecurity of the *Herr und Knecht* rela-tion will follow.[6] The difficulty with categories is maintaining their boundaries. Callaghan finds this problem reflected in the idea of woman as inconstant; the definition is bound

[2] Lynne Tatlock, 'Selling Turks: Eberhard Werner Happel's Turcica (1683–1690)', in *CG* 28 (1995), 307–35 (309, 319).

[3] Ibid. 328.

[4] Jane O. Newman, 'Disorientations: Same-Sex Seduction and Women's Power in Daniel Casper von Lohenstein's *Ibrahim Sultan*', in *CG* 28 (1995), 337–56 (353).

[5] Dympna Callaghan, *Woman and Gender in Renaissance Tragedy: A Study of King Lear, Othello, The Duchess of Malfi and The White Devil* (New York 1989), 1.

[6] See Georg Wilhelm Friedrich Hegel, *Phänomenologie des Geistes*, in *Gesammelte Werke*, ed. Wolfgang Bonsiepen and Reinhard Heede, vol. 9 (Hamburg 1980), 114.

in more closely with the difficulties of defining ('fickleness and instability')[7] than with the object it would contain.

Edward Said is presumably drawing on the juridical connotations of theatre when he takes it as a metaphor for orientalist discourse: this, he argues, represents an attempt 'at one and the same time to characterize the Orient as alien and to incorporate it schematically on a theatrical stage whose audience, manager and actors are *for* Europe, and only for Europe'.[8] It is noticeable that, just a few lines previously, Said described the 'figures' and 'tropes' of the orientalist vocabulary: both also standard features of forensic rhetoric. This connection between theatre and the juridical process— the 'uncovering' of 'facts'—puts the drama in a special position with regard to the persuasive communication of reassuring 'truths'.

Despite a generally negative attitude to the texts, some eighteenth-century criticism of the authors of school drama reflects interestingly on truth and proof in early modern rhetorical practice: Johann Jakob Breitinger, for example, despite his (wilful?) failure to comprehend Lohenstein's rhetorical and pedagogical motivation, shows perspicuity in his reading of that author. One of his complaints is that Lohenstein's characters speak in an overtly rhetorical style: 'gleichwie sie auch bey einem Sprach=Lehrer in die Schule gegangen waren [*sic*]';[9] Breitinger thus recognizes exemplary rhetoric without giving credit for didactic intent, but he is quick to identify the persuasive use of metaphor, and notes irritably: 'daß die Personen, welche Lohenstein ... auf den Schauplatz führet, durch lauter Gleichnisse dencken, durch Gleichnisse einander bestraffen, widerlegen, überführen. Die Gleichnisse sind ihre Gründe, und die Einbildungs=Kraft ist ihre Vernunft' (p. 470).[10] He later describes these metaphors or similes as 'Beweise' (p. 473), recognizing the same

[7] Callaghan, *Woman and Gender*, 109.

[8] Edward W. Said, *Orientalism: Western Conceptions of the Orient* (New York 1978), 71–2.

[9] Johann Jacob Breitinger, *Critische Abhandlung Von der Natur den Absichten und dem Gebrauche der Gleichnisse ... Durch Johann Jacob Bodmer besorget ...* (1740), repr. ed. Manfred Windfuhr (Stuttgart 1967), 227.

[10] Breitinger is here referring to Lohenstein's novel, *Arminius*.

metaphorical structures of proof and precedence identified by twentieth-century critics such as Schöne and Wichert.[11] Most interestingly, Breitinger's discussion of Lohenstein culminates in a critique of metaphorical practice which brings the Enlightenment scholar close to modern theorists: he attacks 'einen allgemeinen Irrthum in ansehung [*sic*] des Gebrauches und der Absichten der Gleichnisse . . . der seinen Ursprung eben von der Lohensteinischen Schreibart hat, und darinn bestehet, daß ein grosser Theil unserer Poeten die Gleichnisse mißbrauchet, die Wahrheit der Sätze dadurch, als ob es Gründe wären, zu befestigen' (p. 479). Breitinger is anticipating far more modern linguistic theorists when he problematizes metaphor's claim to truth. More than a century later, in a wider-reaching essay which deals with this difficulty in all human language, Nietzsche would take up the point more sharply: 'Was ist also Wahrheit? Ein bewegliches Heer von Metaphern, Metonymien, Anthropomorphismen, kurz eine Summe von menschlichen Relationen, die, poetisch und rhetorisch gesteigert, übertragen, geschmückt wurden, und die nach langem Gebrauche einem Volke fest, canonisch und verbindlich dünken . . .'[12] In our century, Barthes has called this aspect of human commication 'myth', and described the principal of myth as the transformation of the historical into the 'natural': 'pour le lecteur de mythe . . . tout se passe comme si l'image provoquait *naturellement* le concept, comme si le signifiant *fondait* le signifié: le mythe . . . est constitué par la déperdition de la qualité historique des choses: les choses perdent en lui le souvenir de leur fabrication.'[13] Both Nietzsche and Barthes are concerned with the *loci communes* of everyday language, which have become sufficiently familiar to pass as truth. Both theorists posit a process by which constructed ideas lose the memory of their constructedness— a process which is a deliberate technique in rhetoric. It seems

[11] Albrecht Schöne, *Emblematik und Drama im Zeitalter des Barock* (Munich 1964), 64 ff.; Adalbert Wichert, *Literatur, Rhetorik und Jurisprudenz im 17. Jahrhundert: Daniel Casper von Lohenstein und sein Werk* (Tübingen 1991), 267. Compare Chapter 2 of this study.
[12] Friedrich Nietzsche, 'Über Wahrheit und Lüge im aussermoralischen Sinne' (1873), in *Werke*, ed. Giorgio Colli and Mazzino Montinari (Berlin 1973), vol. 3/2. 369–84 (374).
[13] Roland Barthes, *Mythologies* (Paris 1957), 237, 251.

that we urgently need to look beyond the didactic authority of early modern tropes to their lasting implications in language as truth categories, or signifiers.

While women are frequently and fascinatingly *portrayed* in early theatre, they are seldom present as creators of the powerful genre; neither as dramatists/librettists nor as composers. Like the non-Christian characters and comic butts who play alongside them, women are defined rather than defining in the dramatic world. And the definitions that evolve during this time of political and social upheaval prove lasting in a way that is worthy of note. Haugwitz showed us Mary Stuart defined by the English court as a destructive reincarnation of Helen of Troy, but finally as an example of the *imitatio Christi* that must signal an ideal character. Just over one hundred years later, in 1800, Schiller's Maria Stuart is cursed by Paulet as 'diese Helena' (I. i), and her destructive sexual power is illustrated by Paulet's son Mortimer, in a speech which echoes the tyrannical passion, also aroused by a woman, of Bostel's Mustapha:[14]

> Mag der Welten Band
> Sich lösen, eine zweite Wasserflut
> Herwogend alles Atmende verschlingen!
> —Ich achte nichts mehr! Eh' ich dir entsage,
> Eh' nahe sich das Ende aller Tage.          (III. vi)

Like Gryphius's Catharina, Hallmann's Sophia, Haugwitz's Maria Stuarda, or even Lohenstein's Cleopatra, Schiller's Maria is transformed into an admirable character because she puts behind her the 'rhetoric of seduction' that constitutes feminine power, in preparation for death. While Schiller does not focus on the problem of language in the same way as Haugwitz did,[15] Elisabeth's persuasive advisers (arguing, in the later play, *for* rather than against Maria) nonetheless run into problems regarding the rhetorical categorization of women that recall the situation of Haugwitz's *Königlicher Rath*. Attempting to excuse Maria using the commonplace of feminine weakness, Talbot touches precisely the nerve in Elisabeth that was Beal's downfall in Haugwitz's play:[16]

---

[14] Compare *Cara Mustapha*, Part 1, II. vii.
[15] Compare Chapter 2 of this study.     [16] Compare *Maria Stuarda*, I. 168 ff.

TALBOT. . . . Denn ein gebrechlich Wesen ist das Weib.
ELISABETH. Das Weib ist nicht schwach. Es gibt starke Seelen
In dem Geschlecht—Ich will in meinem Beisein
Nichts von der Schwäche des Geschlechtes hören.

(*Maria Stuart*, II. iii)

One of the interesting things that emerges from the famous confrontation scene in Schiller's play is the inability of these two powerful, royal women to preserve or even fully to achieve rhetorical ethos. What begins as a dignified encounter, in which rhetoric will play a crucial part—Maria prays 'O Gott, gib meiner Rede Kraft' (III. iv)—degenerates into an exchange of personally motivated insults that finally destroys both women's claims to rhetorical credibility. More than one hundred years on from the plays of Haugwitz and Lohenstein, drama still shows women—necessarily?—unsuccessful in the rhetorical game of life.

Other familiar features of the early modern dramatic system also recur in the work of later generations. Schiller's Johanna in the *Jungfrau von Orleans* (1801) relies for much of her dramatic effect on the paradoxical impact associated with the *femme forte*. We observed with reference to vengeful women in plays of the early modern period that women who usurp masculine roles may be seen as admirable, but also run the risk of being perceived as witches;[17] this is what happens to Schiller's Johanna after her initial triumphs (V. i). By the end of the play she has been transfigured, however, and dies with martyr status; as does Hebbel's Mariamne in *Herodes und Mariamne* of 1849. The latter in particular fulfils precisely the function we have come to expect of heroic women: that of teaching men by example how *they* ought to behave. As Mariamne goes to her death, Titus observes:

Ich staune, daß ein Weib mich lehren soll,
Wie ich als Mann dereinst zu sterben habe! (V. vi)

The element of surprise associated with stoic constancy in woman is as clear as Mariamne's exemplary function here.

With reference to early modern drama and opera, we observed that classifying or rhetorically defining groups

[17] Compare Chapter 3 of this study.

perceived as potentially threatening can do much to contain the sense of threat. When Mozart (or his librettist, Gottlob Stephanie) has the Turkish gaoler in *Die Entführung aus dem Serail* (1782) sing an aria in praise of wine, he is continuing in the tradition established by early modern composers and librettists, whereby non-Christian religions may be drawn into the category of the comic or made the butt. With the settling of the 'Ottoman threat', portrayals of the Turk become rare in German literature after the early eighteenth century. But the *plus ça change* maxim comes to mind when one considers current discourse regarding Turkish residents in Germany. Anxiety about their presence and their 'otherness' is clearly rife; and terms such as the derogatory 'Kanake'— etymologically a South Sea islander, hence a typically generalizing collective category—are rhetorically only as pernicious as a verb like 'türken', meaning to cheat or fake.

From the early eighteenth century to the mid-twentieth, the idea of the Jew seems to have superseded that of the Turk in German literature;[18] but again, familiar patterns are in evidence. Jews are treated as both idealized examples for a Gentile audience (for example, in Lessing's *Nathan der Weise*) and as dangerous bringers of chaos and destruction. This is not the only way in which they become the new 'Turks' of the literary imagination. Ritchie Robertson has recently described the 'feminizing' of the Jew in turn-of-the-century Germany and Austria.[19] We have observed that the categorization as feminine of a group perceived as threatening is a rhetorical measure—one that suggests that the group in question *can* and *must* be socially controlled, as women are or ought to be— and it is certainly one feature of German characterizations of the Jew that continues into National Socialist rhetoric of the 1930s and 1940s. While literary Turks may have been going out of date by 1742, the use of the rhetorical feminine certainly was not.

---

[18] During the early modern period the Jew is not a trope in German literature in the same way as the Turk. However, the early modern image of the Jew is a topic that deserves fuller consideration in its own right.

[19] Ritchie Robertson, 'Historicizing Weininger: The Nineteenth-Century German Image of the Feminized Jew', in Bryan Chevette and Laura Marcus (eds.), *Modernity, Culture and 'the Jew'* (Cambridge 1998).

# BIBLIOGRAPHY

PRIMARY SOURCES

*Early Modern Drama and Prose*

ANDERSEN, JÜRGEN, *Orientalische Reise=Beschreibunge . . . Heraus gegeben durch Adam Olearium*, repr. ed. Dieter Lohmeyer (Tübingen: Niemeyer 1980 [1669]).

AYRER, JAKOB, *Schröckliche Tragedi. Vom Regiment und schändlichen Sterben des türckischen Keisers Machumets des Andern dis Namens, wie er Constantinopel eingenommen und gantz grausam tyrannisirt*, in *Ayrers Dramen*, ed. Adelbert von Keller, vol. 2 (Tübingen: Bibliothek des litterarischen Vereins 1865), 737–809.

—— *Die Erziehung des bösen Weibes: Ein schöns neus singets Spil . . .*, in *Fastnachtspiele des 15. und 16. Jahrhunderts*, ed. Dieter Wuttke, 3rd edn. (Stuttgart: Reclam 1989), 288–309.

BACON, FRANCIS, 'De dignitate et augmentis scientiarum', in *The Works of Francis Bacon*, ed. James Spedding *et al.*, vol. 1 (London: Longmans 1889).

BOCCACCIO, GIOVANNI, *De Claris Mulieribus*, trans. Heinrich Steinhöwel, ed. Karl Drescher (Tübingen: Bibliothek des Litterarischen Vereins 1895).

BRAUNECK, MANFRED, ed., *Spieltexte der Wanderbühne*, 4 vols. (Berlin: de Gruyter 1970–5).

BREITINGER, JOHANN JACOB, *Critische Abhandlung Von der Natur den Absichten und dem Gebrauche der Gleichnisse . . . Durch Johann Jacob Bodmer besorget . . .* (1740), ed. Manfred Windfuhr (Stuttgart: Metzler 1967).

BURMEISTER, JOACHIM, *Musica Poetica*, ed. Martin Ruhnke (Kassel: Bärenreiter 1955 [1606]).

COMES, NATALIS [= Natale Conti], *Natalis Comitis Mythologiae, sive explicationis fabularum, Libri decem . . .* (Frankfurt 1588).

—— *Mythologie, c'est dire, Explication des Fables . . . Extraite du Latin de Noel le Comte, & augmentée de plusieurs choses qui facilitent l'intelligence du sujet* (Lyons: Paul Frelon 1599 [1597?]).

DESCARTES, RENÉ, *The Passions of the Soul*, trans. Stephen H. Voss (Indianapolis: Hackett 1989).

FEIND, BARTHOLD, *Deutsche Gedichte*, ed. W. Gordon Marigold (Berne: Lang 1989 [1708]).

GRIMMELSHAUSEN, HANS JAKOB CHRISTOPH VON, *Satyrischer Pilgram*, ed. Wolfgang Bender (Tübingen: Niemeyer 1970).

GRIMMELSHAUSEN, HANS JAKOB CHRISTOFFEL [*sic*] VON, *Der abenteuerliche Simplicissimus Teutsch*, ed. Alfred Kelletat, 9th edn. (Munich: dtv 1985).

GRIMMELSHAUSEN, HANS JAKOB CHRISTOFFEL VON *Lebensbeschreibung der Erzbetrügerin und Landstörzerin Courasche*, ed. Klaus Haberkam and Günther Weydt (Stuttgart: Reclam 1986).

GRYPHIUS, ANDREAS, *Gesamtausgabe der deutschsprachigen Werke*, ed. Marian Szyrocki and Hugh Powell (Tübingen: Niemeyer 1963– ).

HALLMANN, JOHANN Christian, *Sämtliche Werke*, ed. Gerhard Spellerberg, 3 vols. (Berlin: de Gruyter 1975–87).

HAPPEL, EBERHARD WERNER, *Gröste Denckwürdigkeiten der Welt Oder so-genannte RELATIONES CURIOSAE . . . ,* 5 vols. (Hamburg 1683).

HARSDÖRFFER, GEORG PHILIPP, *Frauenzimmer Gesprächspiele*, ed. Irmgard Böttcher, 8 vols. (Tübingen: Niemeyer 1968–9 [1644]).

HAUGWITZ, AUGUST ADOLPH VON, *Prodromus Poeticus, Oder: Poetischer Vortrab*, ed. Pierre Béhar (Tübingen: Niemeyer 1984 [1684]).

HAUGWITZ, AUGUST ADOLF [*sic*] VON, *Schuldige Unschuld oder Maria Stuarda*, ed. Robert R. Heitner (Berne: Herbert Lang 1974).

HEINRICH JULIUS, Duke of Braunschweig, *Von Einem Weibe/ Wie dasselbige ihre Hurerey für ihrem Ehemann verborgen/ . . .* (1593), in *Von einem Weibe. Von Vincentio Ladislao. Komödien*, ed. Manfred Brauneck (Stuttgart: Reclam 1967).

HOFFMANN, M. GOTTFRIED, *Mit GOttes Hülffe! M. Gottfried Hoffmanns/ Lyc. Laub. Rectoris, Gefallene und wieder erhöhete Eviana . . . Nebst einer Vorrede/ die von der Intention des Autoris ausführlich handelt* (Leipzig: Friedrich Lanckischens Erben 1696).

KÖNIG, JOHANN ULRICH, *Theatralische geistliche/ vermischte und Galante Gedichte/ . . .* (Hamburg and Leipzig: Johann von Wiering 1713).

—— 'Untersuchung Von dem Guten Geschmack In der Dicht= und Rede=Kunst', in *Des Freyherrn von Canitz Gedichte . . . Nebst Dessen Leben, und einer Untersuchung . . . ausgefertiget von Johann Ulrich König . . . ,* 3rd edn. (Berlin and Leipzig: A. Haude and J. C. Spener 1750).

KORNMANN, HEINRICH, *Mons Veneris, Fraw Veneris Berg/ Das ist/ Wunderbare und eigentliche Beschreibung der alten haydnischen und Newen Scribenten Meynung/ von der Göttin Venere . . .* (Frankfurt a.M.: Jacob Fischer 1614).

LE MOYNE, PIERRE, *La Gallerie des Femmes Fortes* (Paris: Sommaville 1647).

LOCHNER, JAKOB HIERONYMUS, *Rosimunda oder Die gerochene Rächerin. Trauer=Spiel/ entworffen von dem Pegnitz=Schäfer Amyntas* (Frankfurt and Leipzig: Joachim Wilden sel. Erben 1676).

LOHENSTEIN, DANIEL CASPER VON, *Türkische Trauerspiele*, ed. Klaus Günther Just (Stuttgart: Hiersemann 1953).

—— *Römische Trauerspiele*, ed. Klaus Günther Just (Stuttgart: Hiersemann 1955).

—— *Afrikanische Trauerspiele*, ed. Klaus Günther Just (Stuttgart: Hiersemann 1957).

—— *Großmüthiger Feldherr Arminius*, 2 vols., ed. E. M. Szarota (Hildesheim: Olms 1973).

—— *Cleopatra. Trauerspiel* (1661), ed. Ilse-Marie Barth and Willi Flemming (Stuttgart: Reclam 1985 [1965]).

LUTHER, MARTIN, D. *Martin Luthers Werke: Kritische Gesamtausgabe* (Weimar: Hermann Böhlaus Nachfolger 1883– ).

—— 'Vorrede über den Propheten Daniel', in *D. Martin Luther, Die gantze Heilige Schrifft*, ed. Hans Volz (Munich: Rogner & Bernhard 1972).

MATTHESON, JOHANN, *Das Neu-Eröffnete Orchestre* . . . *Mit beygefügten Anmerckungen Herrn Capell=Meister Keisers* (Hamburg: Benjamin Schillers Witwe 1713; facs. Ann Arbor: UMI Books on Demand 1993).

—— *Das Beschützte Orchestre, oder desselben Zweyte Eröffnung/* . . . (Leipzig: Zentralantiquariat der DDR/ Kassel: Bärenreiter 1981 [1717]).

—— *Critica Musica* (Amsterdam: Frits Knuf 1964 [1722–5]).

—— *Kern Melodischer Wißenschafft* (Hildesheim: Olms 1976 [1737]).

—— *Der Vollkommene Capellmeister*, ed. Margarete Reimann (Kassel: Bärenreiter 1954 [1739]).

—— *Die neueste Untersuchung der Singspiele, nebst beygefügter musikalischen Geschmacksprobe, liefert hiermit Aristoxenus der jüngere* (Hamburg: Christian Herold 1744).

NEUKIRCH, BENJAMIN, *Benjamin Neukirchs Anthologie. Herrn von Hofmannswaldau und andrer Deutschen auserlesene und bißher ungedruckte Gedichte erster theil*, ed. Angelo George de Capua and Ernst Alfred Philippson (Tübingen: Niemeyer 1961 [1697]).

OPITZ, MARTIN, *Buch von der deutschen Poeterey*, ed. Cornelius Sommer (Stuttgart: Reclam 1970).

PRAETORIUS, JOHANNES [= Hans Schulze], *Catastrophe Muhammetica Oder das Endliche Valet, Und Schändliche Nativität Des gantzen und nunmehr vergänglichen Türckischen Reichs/* . . . (Leipzig: Johann Barthol Oelers 1664).

RENOUARD, NICOLAS, (trans. anon.) *Le Jugement de Paris Das Urtheil des Schäffers Paris* (Leipzig: Heinrich Nerlich 1638).

REUTER, CHRISTIAN, *Schelmuffskys Curiöse und sehr gefährliche Reisebeschreibung zu Wasser und Lande*, ed. Ilse-Marie Barth (Stuttgart: Reclam 1964).

—— *Schlampampe. Komödien*, ed. Rolf Tarot (Stuttgart: Reclam 1977).

RIEMER, JOHANNES, *Werke*, ed. Helmut Krause, 4 vols. (Berlin: de Gruyter 1979).

ROSENPLÜT, HANS, *Des Turken vasnachtspiel*, 39 in *Fastnachtspiele aus dem 15. Jahrhundert*, ed. Adelbert von Keller (Stuttgart: Bibliothek des litterarischen Vereins 1853; repr. Darmstadt 1965), 1. 288–304.

SACHS, HANS, *Hans Sachs Werke*, ed. A. von Keller and E. Goetze, 26 vols. (Tübingen: Bibliothek des litterarischen Vereins 1870–1908).

SHAKESPEARE, WILLIAM, *The Tragedy of Antony and Cleopatra*, ed. Barbara Everett (New York: New American Library 1964).

—— *The Tragedy of Othello The Moor of Venice*, ed. Alvin Kernan (New York: New American Library 1963).

—— *Titus Andronicus*, ed. J. C. Maxwell (London: Routledge 1993 [1953]).

SPEE, FRIEDRICH VON, *Cautio Criminalis oder Rechtliches Bedenken wegen der Hexenprozesse*, trans. Joachim-Friedrich Ritter (Munich: dtv 1982).

SPEER, DANIEL, *Grundrichtiger Unterricht der musikalischen Kunst oder Vierfaches musikalisches Kleeblatt* (Leipzig: Peters 1974 [1697]).

SPRENGER, JAKOB, and HEINRICH INSTITUTORIS, *Der Hexenhammer* (1487), trans. J. W. R. Schmidt (Munich: dtv 1993 [1982]).

STOSCH, BALTZER SIEGMUND VON, 'Danck= und Denck=Seule des ANDREAE GRYPHII' (1665), repr. in *Andreas Gryphius*, ed. Heinz Ludwig Arnold, 2nd edn. [= Text und Kritik 7/8, 1980].

SZAROTA, ELIDA MARIA, *Das Jesuitendrama im deutschen Sprachgebiet: Eine Periochen-Edition*, 4 vols. (Munich: Fink 1979–87).

TACITUS, *The Annals of Imperial Rome*, trans. Michael Grant, 2nd edn. (London: Penguin 1989 [1956]).

*Theatrum Malorum Mulierum, Oder Schau=Platz Der Bosheit aller bösen und Regier=süchtigen Weiber über ihre Männer . . .* (Hunßfeld: Carl Kalte=Schahl [?] *c.*1700).

THOMA, HIERONYMUS, *Titus und Tomyris oder Traur=Spiel Beygenahmt Die Rachbegierige Eyfersucht* (Steffen: Joseph Dieterich Hampel 1662).

WEISE, CHRISTIAN, *Politischer Redner/ Das ist: Kurtze und eigentliche Nachricht/ wie ein sorgfältiger Hofemeister seine Untergebene zuder Wohlredenheit anführen sol . . .* (Leipzig 1683; repr. Kronberg/Ts: Scriptor 1974).

—— *Christian Weisens Comödien Probe/ Von Wenig Personen/ In einer ernsthafften Action Vom Esau und Jacob/ Hernach in einem Lust=Spiele Vom Verfolgten Lateiner: Nebst einer Vorrede De Interpretatione Dramatica* (Leipzig: Jacob Gerdesius 1696).

—— *Komödie von der bösen Catharine*, in *Die Gegner der zweiten schlesischen Schule*, 2. Teil, ed. Ludwig Fulda (Berlin: Spemann 1873).

—— *Sämtliche Werke*, ed. John D. Lindberg and Hans-Gert Roloff (Berlin: de Gruyter 1971– ).

WERDER, PARIS VON DEM, *Viertzig Durchläuchtige Frauen Oder Deroselben Viertzig Heroische Reden/ Samt ihren eigentlichen Abbildungen/ . . . in Teutsch übergesetzet. Erster Theil* (Jena: Georg Sengenwalden 1654).

WUTTKE, DIETER (ed.), *Fastnachtspiele des 15. und 16. Jahr hurderts*, 3rd edn. (Stuttqovt: Reclam 1989).

*Libretti*

(The librettist's name is followed by that of the composer in square brackets).

ANTON ULRICH, Duke of Braunschweig and Lüneburg [Johann Jakob Loewe(?)], *Amelinde oder: Die triumphierende Seele . . .* (Wolfenbüttel 1657), in *idem, Werke*, ed. Rolf Tarot (Stuttgart: Hiersemann 1982), vol. 1/1.

—— *Andromeda, Ein Königliches Fräulein aus Æthiopien . . . in einem Singe=Spiel . . .* (Wolfenbüttel 1659), in *idem, Werke,* ed. Rolf Tarot (Stuttgart: Hiersemann 1982), vol. 1/1.

—— *Iphigenia, ein Königliches Fräulein . . . In einem Singe=Spiel . . .* (1661), in *idem, Werke,* ed. Rolf Tarot (Stuttgart: Hiersemann 1982), vol. 1/2.

—— *Des Trojanischen Paridis Urtheil/ Von dem Goldenen Apffel der Eridis* (1662), in *idem, Werke,* ed. Rolf Tarot (Stuttgart: Hiersemann 1982), vol. 2/2.

AURELI, AURELIO [Antonio Giannettini], *Medea in Atene. Drama per Musica . . .* (Wolfenbüttel 1688).

—— [Pietro Antonio Fiocco], *Helena Rapita da Paride Drama per Musica . . . Oder Die vom Paris geraubete Helena. In einem Singe=Spiel . . .* (Braunschweig 1708[?]).

BOSTEL, LUCAS VON [Johann Wolfgang Franck], *Der Glückliche Grosz-Vezier Cara Mustapha, Erster Theil* (1686), in Meyer, *Die Hamburger Oper,* vol. 1. 171–243.

—— [Johann Wolfgang Franck], *Der Unglückliche Cara Mustapha Anderer Theil/ Nebenst Dem erfreulichen Entsatze der Käyserlichen Residentz=Stadt Wien* (Hamburg 1686).

BOXBERG, CHRISTIAN LUDWIG [Nikolaus Adam Strungk], *Agrippina in einer Opera . . .* (Leipzig 1699).

BRESSAND, FRIEDRICH CHRISTIAN [Johann Siegmund Kusser], *Julia, In einem Schau=Spiel . . .* (Wolfenbüttel 1690).

—— [Johann Siegmund Kusser], *Cleopatra, Sing=Spiel . . .* (Wolfenbüttel 1691).

—— [Johann Philipp Krieger], *Hercules Unter denen Amazonen/ In einer Opera . . .* (Hamburg 1694).

—— and GEORG KASPAR SCHÜRMANN [Johann Siegmund Kusser and Georg Kaspar Schürmann], *Die an des Jasons Untreu sich rächende Medea, In einer Opera . . .* (Wolfenbüttel 1724).

ELMENHORST, HINRICH [Johann Wolfgang Franck], *Die Macchabaeische Mutter mit ihren Sieben Söhnen. In einem Singe=Spiel vorgestellet* (Hamburg 1679).

FEIND, BARTHOLD [Reinhard Keiser], *Die Römische Unruhe. Oder: Die Edelmühtige Octavia. Musicalisches Schau=Spiel* (Hamburg 1705), in *idem, Deutsche Gedichte,* ed. W. Gordon Marigold (Berne: Lang 1989), 121–74.

—— [Reinhard Keiser], *Die Kleinmühtige Selbst=Mörderin Lucretia. Oder: Die Staats=Thorheit des Brutus. Musicalisches Trauer=Spiel* (Hamburg 1705), in *idem, Deutsche Gedichte,* ed. W. Gordon Marigold (Berne: Lang 1989), 175–250.

—— [Reinhard Keiser], *Masagniello furioso. . . . Die Neapolitanische Fischer= Empörung. Musicalisches Schau=Spiel* (Hamburg 1707), in Meyer, *Die Hamburger Oper,* 2. 191–254.

FEIND, BARTHOLD [Christoph Graupner], *Amore Ammalato, Die krankende Liebe. Oder: Antiochus und Stratonica. Musikalisches Schauspiel*... (Hamburg 1707), in *idem, Deutsche Gedichte*, ed. W. Gordon Marigold (Berne: Lang 1989), 394–454.

—— [Christoph Graupner], *Der Fall des grossen Richters in Israel/ Simson, Oder: Die abgekühlte Liebes-Rache der Debora* (Hamburg 1709), in Meyer, *Die Hamburger Oper*, 2. 255–333.

FEUSTKING, FRIEDRICH CHRISTIAN [Reinhard Keiser and Ruggiero Fedeli], *Almira, Königin von Castilien*... (Weißenfels 1704).

—— [Johann Mattheson], *Die betrogene Staats=Liebe/ Oder: Die Unglückselige Cleopatra Königin von Egypten* (Hamburg 1704).

FIEDLER, GOTTLIEB [Georg Kaspar Schürmann], *Leonilde Oder Die siegende Beständigkeit In einem Singenden Schau=Spiel*... (Braunschweig *c.*1704).

FRAUENDORF, JOHANN CHRISTOPH [Georg Kaspar Schürmann], *Das verstöhrte Troja. In einem Singe=Spiel vorgestellet*... (Braunschweig 1706).

—— adapted by Schürmann [Georg Kaspar Schürmann], *Das Zerstörte Troia, In einer Opera*... (Wolfenbüttel 1724).

GRIMANI, VINCENZO [Georg Friedrich Händel], *Agrippina* (Hamburg 1718).

HINSCH, HINRICH [Reinhard Keiser], *Mahumeth II* (Hamburg 1696).

—— [Christoph Graupner], *Dido, Königin von Carthago* (Hamburg 1707).

HOË, JOHANN JOACHIM [Reinhard Keiser], *Das zerstörte Troja, Oder: Der durch den Tod Helenen versöhnte Achilles*... (Hamburg 1716).

—— [Reinhard Keiser], *Die Großmüthige Tomyris* (Hamburg 1717).

—— [Reinhard Keiser], *Die Großmüthige Tomyris, In einer Opera vorgestellet* (Wolfenbüttel 1724).

KÖHLER, JOHANN MARTIN [Nikolaus Adam Strungk], *Die Liebreiche/ Durch Tugend und Schönheit Erhöhete Esther, In einem Singe=Spiel*... (Hamburg 1680).

KÖNIG, JOHANN ULRICH [Reinhard Keiser], *Fredegunda* (Hamburg 1715), in Meyer, *Die Hamburger Oper*, 2. 519–74.

LALLI, DOMENICO, and GEORG KASPAR SCHÜRMANN (trans.[?]) [Reinhard Keiser and Georg Kaspar Schürmann(?)], *Die Großmühtige Tomyris in einer Opera vorgestellt*... (Wolfenbüttel 1749).

Librettist unknown [Johann Wolfgang Franck], *Semele, In einem Sing=Spiel*... (Hamburg 1681).

Librettist unknown [Johann Hugo Wilderer], *Nino Overò La Monarchia Stabilita. Drama per Musica*... *Ninus Oder Die befestigte Monarchie In einem Sing=Spiele*... (Braunschweig 1709).

Librettist unknown [Johann Philipp Käfer(?)], *Der Asiatischen Banise Andere Abtheilung/*... (Coburg 1714).

Librettist unknown [Georg Kaspar Schürmann(?)], *Ninus und Semiramis In einer Opera*... (Wolfenbüttel 1730).

MATTHESON, JOHANN [Georg Friedrich Händel], *Zenobia Oder Das Muster rechtschaffener Ehelichen Liebe/ . . .* (Hamburg 1722).

MAURO, ORTENSIO, trans. Gottlieb Fiedler [Agostino Steffani], *Il Trionfo del Fato Oder Das Mächtige Geschick Bei Lavinia und Dido . . . In einem Singe=Spiel* (Hamburg 1699).

MEYER, REINHART, ed., *Die Hamburger Oper: Eine Sammlung von Texten der Hamburger Oper aus der Zeit 1678–1730*, 4 vols. (Munich: Kraus 1980–4).

MOTTE, ANTOINE HOUDAR DE LA, trans. Georg Philipp Telemann [Andr Cardinal Destouches and Georg Philipp Telemann], *Omphale in einem Sing=Spiele aus dem Französischen des Herrn de la Motte übersetzt und auf dem Hamburgischen Schauplatz aufgeführt*, in *Hrn. Hof=Raht Weichmanns Poesie der Nieder=Sachsen, durch den Fünften Theil fortgesetzet . . .* (Hamburg: Christian Herold 1738), 366–412.

NORIS, MATTEO [Marc'Antonio Bononcini], *Semiramide Overò La Reina Creduta Re. Drama per Musica . . . Semiramis Oder Die vor König gehaltene Königin/ In einem Singe=Spiel . . .* (Braunschweig 1708).

OPITZ, MARTIN, *Daphne* (1627), in *Gesammelte Werke*, ed. George Schulz-Behrend, vol. 4/1 (Stuttgart: Hiersemann 1989), 61–84.

PARIATI, PIETRO, trans. Johann Philipp Praetorius [Georg Philipp Telemann] *Die ungleiche Heyrath; oder, Das Herrsch=süchtige Camer Mädgen* [= *Pimpinone*] (Hamburg 1725).

POSTEL, CHRISTIAN HEINRICH [Johann Philipp Förtsch], *Die Groß=Müthige Thalestris, Oder Letzte Königin der Amazonen* (Hamburg 1690).

—— [Johann Philipp Förtsch], *Bajazeth und Tamerlan* (Hamburg 1695).

—— [Johann Philipp Förtsch] *Die heilige Eugenia, Oder Die Bekehrung der Stadt Alexandria zum Christentum. In einem Sing=Spiel vorgestellet* (Hamburg 1695).

—— [Antonio Gianettini], *Medea. In Einem Singe=Spiel vorgestellet* (Hamburg 1695).

—— [Reinhard Keiser], *Die wunderbar-errettete Iphigenia/ In einem Singe= Spiel* (1699), in *Die Oper*, ed. Willi Flemming (Leipzig: Reclam 1933), 255–308.

RICHTER, CHRISTIAN [Johann Theile] *Adam und Eva. Der erschaffene/ gefallene und auffgerichtete Mensch. In einem Singe=Spiel* (Hamburg 1678), in Meyer, *Die Hamburger Oper*, 1. 1–58.

SCHÜRMANN, GEORG KASPAR [Karl Heinrich Graun], *Iphigenia in Aulis, In einer Opera . . .* (Wolfenbüttel 1731).

—— (trans.) [Giovanni Verocai and Georg Kaspar Schürmann(?)], *Zenobia und Radamistus. In einer Opera . . .* (Wolfenbüttel 1742).

—— (trans. of Pietro Metastasio, Andriano in Siria [?]) [Giovanni Verocai and Georg Kaspar Schürmann], *Die getreue Emirena Parthische Prinzeßin/ in einer Opera . . .* (Braunschweig 1745).

SILVANI, FRANCESCO [Carlo Francesco Gasparini], *La Fredegonda. Drama per Musica* . . . (Venice 1705).

—— [Francesco Gasparini(?)], *Fredegonda. Drama per Musica . . . Fredegunda. In einem Singe=Spiel vorgestellet* (Braunschweig 1712 or 1716).

—— [Guiseppe Maria Orlandini], *Ernelinda. Drama per Musica. . . . Ernelinda In einer Opera vorgestellet* . . . (Braunschweig 1730).

STÖLZEL, GOTTFRIED HEINRICH(?), *et al.* [Reinhard Keiser and Gottfried Heinrich Stölzel], *Artemisia* (Hamburg 1715).

TELEMANN, GEORG PHILIPP [Georg Philipp Telemann], *Omphale in einem Singe=Spiel* . . . (Hamburg 1724).

ZENO, APOSTOLO [Antonio Caldara], *Semiramis in Ascalon In einer Opera* . . . (Wolfenbüttel 1736).


*Music*

FRANCK, JOHANN WOLFGANG, *Hamburger Opernarien im szenischen Kontext*, ed. Werner Braun (Saarbrücken: SDV 1988).

HAUFE, EBERHARD, ed., *Was in Liebes-Früchten wehlet: komische Arien der Hamburger Barockoper* (Weimar 1974).

KEISER, REINHARD, *Fredegunda. Triumph der Unschuld* (Hamburg 1715).

—— *Octavia*, ed. Friedrich Chrysander, in Händelgesellschaft: *Händels Werke, Supplemente* 6 (Leipzig: Stich und Druck der Gesellschaft 1902).

—— *Die großmütige Tomyris*, ed. Klaus Zelm (Munich: Henle 1975) [*Die Oper: Kritische Ausgabe von Hauptwerken der Operngeschichte*, vol. 1].

MATTHESON, JOHANN, *Cleopatra*, ed. George G. Buelow (Mainz: Schott 1975) [= *Das Erbe deutscher Musik*, vol. 69].


REFERENCE LITERATURE

BARON, JOHN H., *Baroque Music: A Research and Information Guide* (New York: Garland 1993).

BARTEL, DIETRICH, *Handbuch der musikalischen Figurenlehre* (Hamburg: Laaber 1985).

BLUME, FRIEDRICH, *Die Musik in Geschichte und Gegenwart: allgemeine Enzyklopädie der Musik*, 17 vols. (Kassel: Bärenreiter 1949–86).

BROCKPÄHLER, RENATE, *Handbuch zur Geschichte der Barockoper in Deutschland* (Emsdetten: Lechte 1964).

DÜNNHAUPT, GERHART, *Personalbibliographien zu den Drucken des Barock*, 2nd edn. (Stuttgart: Hiersemann 1990– ).

HENKEL, ARTHUR, and ALBRECHT SCHÖNE, eds., *Emblemata: Handbuch zur Sinnbildkunst des XVI. und XVII. Jahrhunderts* (Stuttgart: Metzler 1967; new edn. 1976).

MARCO, GUY A., *Opera: A Research and Information Guide* (New York: Garland 1984).

Répertoire Internationale des Sources Musicales (RISM) Arbeitsgruppe Deutschland e.V., ed., *Libretti in deutschen Bibliotheken: Katalog der gedruckten Texte zu Opern, Oratorien, Kantaten, Schuldramen, Balletten und Gelegenheitskompositionen von den Anfängen bis zur Mitte des 19. Jahrhunderts* (Munich: Saur 1992).

SADIE, STANLEY, ed., *The New Grove Dictionary of Music and Musicians*, 20 vols. (London: Macmillan 1980).

—— ed., *The New Grove Dictionary of Musical Instruments*, 3 vols. (London: Macmillan 1984).

—— ed., *The New Grove Dictionary of Opera*, 4 vols. (London: Macmillan 1992).

SONNECK, OSCAR GEORGE THEODORE, *Library of Congress Catalogue of Opera Librettos Printed before 1800*, 3 vols. (New York: Franklin 1914; repr. 1967).

THIEL, EBERHARD, and GISELA ROHR, Libretti: *Verzeichnis der bis 1800 erschienenen Textbücher* (Frankfurt a.M.: Klostermann 1970) [= *Kataloge der Herzog August Bibliothek, Wolfenbüttel*, vol. 14].

WISSOWA, GEORG, and KONRAT ZIEGLER, eds., *Paulys Real-Encyclopädie der Classischen Altertumswissenschaft, Neue Bearbeitung* (Stuttgart: Metzler 1894– ).


SECONDARY LITERATURE

ABERT, ANNA AMALIE, 'Die Barockoper: Ein Bericht über die Forschung seit 1945', in *Acta Musicologica* 41 (1969), 121–64.

—— 'Die Oper zwischen Barock und Romantik: ein Bericht über die Forschung seit dem Zweiten Weltkrieg', in *Acta Musicologica* 49/2 (1977), 137–93.

—— 'Libretto', in Blume, *Die Musik in Geschichte und Gegenwart*, vol. 4, cols. 708–27.

AIKIN, JUDITH POPOVITCH, ' "And they changed their lives from that very hour": Catharsis and Exemplum in the Baroque Trauerspiel', in *Daphnis* 10 (1981), 241–55.

—— *German Baroque Drama* (Boston: Twayne 1982).

—— 'Happily Ever After: An Alternative Affective Theory of Comedy and Some Plays by Birken, Gryphius, and Weise', in Wagener, *Absurda Comica*, 55–76.

—— 'The Comedies of Andreas Gryphius and the Two Traditions of German Comedy', in *GR* 63/3 (1988), 114–20.

—— 'Creating a Language for German Opera: The Struggle to Adapt Madrigal Versification in Seventeenth-Century Germany', in *DVjs* 62 (1988), 266–89.

AIKIN, JUDITH POPOVITCH, *Scaramutza in Germany: The Dramatic Works of Caspar Stieler* (University Park, Pa.: Pennsylvania State University Press 1989).

—— 'Libretti without Scores: Problems in the Study of Early German Opera', in McGlathery, *Music and German Literature*, 51–64.

ALEXANDER, ROBERT J., *Das deutsche Barockdrama* (Stuttgart: Metzler 1984).

ALT, PETER-ANDRÉ, 'Traditionswandel des Allegoriebegriffs zwischen Christian Gryphius und Gottsched', in *Europäische Barock-Rezeption*, ed. Klaus Garber (Wiesbaden: Harrassowitz 1991), 1. 249–79.

ANDERSEN, WARREN, 'Aristotle', in Sadie, *The New Grove Dictionary of Music and Musicians*, 1. 587–91.

—— 'Plato', in Sadie, *New Grove*, 14. 853–7.

ANKARLOO, BENGT, and GUSTAV HENNINGSEN, *Early Modern European Witchcraft: Centres and Peripheries* (Oxford: Clarendon 1993 [1990]).

ARLT, WULF, 'Zur Handhabung der "inventio" in der deutschen Musiklehre des frühen achtzehnten Jahrhunderts', in Buelow and Marx, *New Mattheson Studies*, 371–91.

ASMUTH, BERNHARD, *Daniel Casper von Lohenstein* (Stuttgart: Metzler 1971).

—— *Lohenstein und Tacitus* (Stuttgart: Metzler 1971).

—— 'Lohensteins Quelle und Vorlagen für die Epicharis', in Kleinschmidt, *Die Welt des Daniel Casper von Lohenstein*, 92–103.

ASTON, ELAINE, and GEORGE SAVONE, *Theatre as Sign-System: A Semiotics of Text and Performance* (London: Routledge 1991).

BABCOCK, BARBARA A., ed., *The Reversible World: Symbolic Inversion in Art and Society* (Ithaca, NY: Cornell University Press 1978).

BAKHTIN, MIKHAIL, *Rabelais and his World*, trans. Helene Iswolsky (Bloomington: Indiana University Press 1984).

—— *The Bakhtin Reader*, ed. Pam Morris (London: Arnold 1994).

BARNER, WILFRIED, 'Gryphius und die Macht der Rede: Zum ersten Reyen des Trauerspiels "Leo Armenius"', in *DVjs* 42 (1968), 325–58.

BARNER, WILFRIED, *Barock-Rhetorik: Untersuchungen zu ihren geschichtlichen Grundlagen* (Tübingen: Niemeyer 1970).

—— 'Rhetorik in Literatur, Unterricht und Politik des 17. Jahrhunderts', in Kleinschmidt, *Die Welt des Daniel Casper von Lohenstein*, 40–9.

BAROJA, JULIO CARLO, 'Witchcraft and Catholic Theology', in Ankarloo/Henningsen, *Early Modern European Witchcraft*, 19–43.

BARTHES, ROLAND, *Mythologies* (Paris: Éditions du Seuil 1957).

BARTMUß, ARWED WOLDEMAR, 'Die Hamburger Barockoper und ihre Bedeutung für die Entwicklung der deutschen Dichtung und der deutschen Bühne' (unpublished doctoral thesis, University of Jena 1924).

BECKER, GABRIELE, et al., *Aus der Zeit der Verzweiflung: Zur Genese und Aktualität des Hexenbildes* (Frankfurt a.M.: Suhrkamp 1977).

BECKER-CANTARINO, BARBARA, ' "Frau Welt" und "Femme Fatale": Die Geburt eines Frauenbildes aus dem Geiste des Mittelalters', in J. F. Poag and G. Scholz-Williams, *Das Weiterleben des Mittelalters in der deutschen Literatur* (Königstein/Ts. 1983), 61–73.

—— *Der lange Weg zur Mündigkeit: Frauen und Literatur in Deutschland von 1500 bis 1800* (Stuttgart: Metzler 1987).

—— 'Die Böse Frau und das Züchtigungsrecht des Hausvaters in der frühen Neuzeit', in Wallinger and Jonas, *Der Widerspenstigen Zähmung*, 117–32.

—— 'Dr. Faustus and Runagate Courage: Theorizing Gender in Early Modern German Literature', in Tatlock, *The Graph of Sex*, 27–44.

—— and JÖRG-ULRICH FECHNER, eds., *Opitz und seine Welt: Festschrift für George Schulz-Behrends* (Amsterdam: Rodopi 1990) [= *Chloe: Beihefte zum Daphnis*, vol. 10].

BÉHAR, PIERRE, 'Anton Ulrichs Ballette und Singspiele', in *Daphnis* 10/4 (1981), 775–92.

—— 'Dramaturgie et histoire chez Lohenstein: Les Deux Versions de Cleopatra', in Brinkmann, *Theatrum Europaeum*, 325–42.

—— *Silesia Tragica: Épanouissement et fin de l'école dramatique silésienne dans l'œuvre tragique de Daniel Casper von Lohenstein (1635–1683)*, 2 vols. (Wiesbaden: Harrassowitz 1988).

—— 'Vt Pictura Poesis: Lohenstein ou la dramaturgie picturale', in *Pictura et Poesis, TRAMES, collection allemand*, 3 (Limoges 1989), 27–63.

—— 'La Représentation du Turc dans l'Europe des XVIᵉ et XVIIᵉ siècles et l'œuvre de Callot', in *Jacques Callot (1592–1635): Actes du colloque de musée du Louvre et de la ville de Nancy des 25, 26 et 27 Juin 1992*, ed. D. Ternois (Paris 1993), 305–30.

—— ed., *Image et spectacle* (Amsterdam: Rodopi 1993) [= *Chloe: Beiheifte zum Daphnis*, vol. 15].

BENARY, PETER, *Die deutsche Kompositionslehre des 18. Jahrhunderts* (with: Johann Adolph Scheibe, *Compendium Musices*) (Leipzig: VEB Breitkopf & Härtel Musikverlag 1961).

BENJAMIN, WALTER, *Ursprung des deutschen Trauerspiels*, ed. Rolf Tiedemann, 5th edn. (Frankfurt a.M.: Suhrkamp 1990).

BENSON, PAMELA JOSEPH, *The Invention of the Renaissance Woman: The Challenge of Female Independence in the Literature and Thought of Italy and England* (University Park, Pa.: The Pennsylvania State University Press 1992).

BEST, THOMAS W., 'Gryphius's Cardenio und Celinde in its European Context: A New Perspective', in *Literary Culture in the Holy Roman Empire, 1555–1720*, ed. James A. Parente et al. (Chapel Hill and London: University of North Carolina Press 1991), 60–77.

BIANCONI, LORENZO, and THOMAS WALKER, 'Production, Consumption and Political Function of Seventeenth-Century Opera', in *Early Music History* 4 (1984), 209–96.

BIERBAUM, ANGELIKA, 'Exotische Klangwelten—Europäische Klangphantasien', in Pollig *et al.*, *Exotische Welten*, 270–7.

BILLMANN, ELSIE G., *Johann Christian Hallmanns Dramen* (Würzburg: Konrad Triltsch 1942).

BLACKWELL, JEANNINE, ' "Die Zunge, der Geistliche und das Weib': Überlegungen zur strukturellen Bedeutung der Hexenbekenntnisse von 1500–1700', in Wallinger and Jonas, *Der Widerspenstigen Zähmung*, 95–115.

BONIFATTI, EMILIO, 'Mond und Sonne in Andreas Gryphius' Catharina von Georgien', in Becker-Cantarino and Fechner, *Opitz und seine Welt*, 93–124.

BORGSTEDT, THOMAS, *Reichsidee und Liebesethik: Eine Rekonstruktion des Lohensteinischen Arminiusromans* (Tübingen: Niemeyer 1992).

BOVENSCHEN, SILVIA, *Die imaginierte Weiblichkeit: Exemplarische Untersuchungen zu kulturgeschichtlichen und literarischen Präsentationsformen des Weiblichen* (Frankfurt a.M.: Suhrkamp 1979).

BRANCAFORTE, CHARLOTTE, *Lohensteins Preisgedicht 'Venus': Kritischer Text und Untersuchung* (Munich: Fink 1974).

BRANDT, GEORGE W., ed., *German and Dutch Theatre, 1600–1848* (Cambridge: Cambridge University Press 1993).

BRAUN, WERNER, *Vom Remter zum Gänsemarkt: Aus der Frühgeschichte der alten Hamburger Oper (1677–1697)* (Saarbrücken: SDV 1987).

—— *Deutsche Musiktheorie des 15. bis 17. Jahrhunderts, II. Teil: Von Calvisius bis Mattheson* (Darmstadt: Wissenschaftliche Buchgesellschaft 1994).

BRAUNECK, MANFRED, *et al.*, eds., *Theaterstadt Hamburg* (Reinbek bei Hamburg: Rowohlt 1989).

BRAUNER, SIGRID, 'The Demonization of the Shrew: Witchcraft and Gender Relations in Shrovetide Plays by Hans Sachs', in *Daphnis* 20 (1991), 131–45.

BRAUNER, SIGRID, 'Gender and its Subversion: Reflections on Literary Ideals of Marriage', in Tatlock, *The Graph of Sex*, 179–98.

BRAUNGART, GEORG, 'Rhetorik, Poetik, Emblematik', in Glaser, *Deutsche Literatur*, 219–36.

BRENNER, INES, and GISELA MORGENTHAL, 'Der Sabbat als Ort der Verschwörung der Frauen gegen Ordnung und Vernunft', in Becker *et al.*, *Aus der Zeit der Verzweiflung*, 212–17.

BRENNER, ROSAMOND DROOKER, 'Emotional Expression in Keiser's Operas', in *MR* 33 (1972), 222–32.

BRIETZMANN, FRANZ, *Die böse Frau in der deutschen Litteratur des Mittelalters* (Berlin: Mayer & Müller 1912) [= *Palaestra* 42].

BRINKMANN, RICHARD, *et al.*, eds., *Theatrum Europaeum: Festschrift für Elida Maria Szarota* (Munich: Fink 1982).

BRÜCKNER, WOLFGANG, *et al.*, *Literatur und Volk im 17. Jahrhundert: Probleme populärer Kultur in Deutschland*, 2 vols. (Wiesbaden: Harrassowitz 1985).

BUELOW, GEORGE J., 'The Loci Topici and Affect in Late Baroque Music: Heinichens Practical Demonstration', in *MR* 27 (1966), 161–76.

—— 'An Evaluation of Johann Mattheson's Opera, *Cleopatra* (Hamburg, 1704)', in *Studies in Eighteenth-Century Music: A Tribute to Karl Geiringer on his Seventieth Birthday*, ed. H. C. Robbins Landon and Roger E. Chapman (London: Allen & Unwin 1970), 92–107.

—— 'Music, Rhetoric and the Concept of the Affections: A Selective Bibliography', in *Notes* 30 (1973–4), 250–9.

—— 'Rhetoric and Music', in Sadie, *The New Grove Dictionary of Music and Musicians*, 15. 793–803.

—— 'Johann Mattheson and the Invention of the Affektenlehre', in Buelow and Marx, *New Mattheson Studies*, 393–408.

—— 'Hamburg Opera during Buxtehude's Lifetime: The Works of Johann Wolfgang Franck', in *Church, Stage and Studio: Music and its Contexts in 17th-Century Germany* (Ann Arbor: UMI Research Press 1990).

—— and H. J. MARX, eds., *New Mattheson Studies* (Cambridge: Cambridge University Press 1983).

BUKOFZER, MANFRED F., *Music in the Baroque Era: From Monteverdi to Bach* (London: Dent & Sons 1947).

BURGER, HEINZ OTTO, 'Dasein heißt eine Rolle spielen: Das Barock im Spiegel von Jacob Bidermanns "Philemon Martyr" und Christian Weises "Masaniello"', in *idem, 'Dasein heißt eine Rolle spielen': Studien zur deutschen Literaturgeschichte* (Munich: Hanser 1963), 75–93.

BUTLER, JUDITH, *Gender Trouble: Feminism and the Subversion of Identity* (New York: Routledge 1990).

CALLAGHAN, DYMPNA, *Woman and Gender in Renaissance Tragedy: A Study of King Lear, Othello, The Duchess of Malfi and The White Devil* (New York: Harvester Wheatsheaf 1989).

CATHOLY, ECKEHARD, *Fastnachtspiel* (Stuttgart: Metzler 1966).

—— *Das deutsche Lustspiel: Vom Mittelalter bis zum Ende der Barockzeit* (Darmstadt: Wissenschaftliche Buchgesellschaft 1968).

—— 'Die deutsche Komödie vor Lessing', in *Die deutsche Komödie: Vom Mittelalter bis zur Gegenwart*, ed. Walter Hinck (Düsseldorf: Bagel 1977).

CHEESMAN, TOM, 'Performing Omnivores in Germany circa 1700', in David J. George and Christopher J. Gossip, eds., *Studies in the Commedie dell'Arte* (Cardiff: University of Wales Press 1993), 49–68.

CHRYSANDER, FRIEDRICH, 'Mattheson's Verzeichniss Hamburgischer Opern von 1678 bis 1728, gedruckt im "Musikalischen Patrioten", mit seinen handschriftlichen Fortsetzungen bis 1751, nebst Zusätzen und Berichtigungen', in *AMZ* 12 (1877; repr. Amsterdam: Frits Knuf 1969), cols. 198–200; 215–20; 234–6; 245–51; 280–2.

CHRYSANDER, FRIEDRICH, 'Die erste Periode der Hamburger Oper von 1678 bis 1681', in *AMZ* 12 (1877; repr. Amsterdam: Frits Knuf 1969), cols. 369–75; 385–91; 401–7; 417–24; 433–7; 449–53; 465–70; 481–6.

—— 'Die zweite Periode der Hamburger Oper von 1682 bis 1694, oder vom Theaterstreit bis zur Direction Kusser's', in *AMZ* 13 (1878), cols. 289–95; 304–12; 324–9; 340–6; 355–61; 371–6; 388–92; 405–10; 420–4; 439–42.

—— 'Die Hamburger Oper unter der Direction von Johann Sigismund Kusser 1693–1696', in *AMZ* 14 (1879), cols. 385–98; 401–8.

—— 'Geschichte der Hamburger Oper vom Abgange Kusser's bis zum Tode Schott's (1695–1702)', in *AMZ* 14, cols. 433–41; 447–59; 465–74; 481–3; 496–504; 513–21; 529–33.

—— 'Geschichte der Hamburger Oper unter der Direction von Reinhard Keiser (1703–1706)', in *AMZ* 15 (1880), cols. 17–25; 33–41; 49–55; 65–72; 81–8.

CLARK, JONATHAN P., 'Inside/out: Body Politics against Large Bodies', in *Daphnis* 20 (1991), 101–30.

CLARK, STUART, 'Inversion, Misrule and the Meaning of Witchcraft', in *Past and Present* 87 (1980), 98–127.

—— 'Protestant Demonology: Sin, Superstition and Society (*c*.1520–1630)', in Ankarloo and Henningsen, *Early Modern European Witchcraft*, 45–81.

CLÉMENT, CATHERINE, *Opera, or the Undoing of Women*, trans. Betsy Wing, 2nd edn. (London: Virago 1989).

COLVIN, SARAH, 'The Classical Witch and the Christian Martyr: Two Ideas of Woman in Hamburg Opera Libretti', in *GLL* 46/3 (1993), 193–202.

COWHIG, RUTH, 'Blacks in English Renaissance Drama and the Role of Shakespeare's Othello', in *The Black Presence in English Literature*, ed. David Dabydeen (Manchester: Manchester University Press 1985).

CULLEY, THOMAS D., *Jesuits and Music I: A Study of the Musicians Connected with the German College in Rome during the 17th Century and of their Activities in Northern Europe* (Rome: Jesuit Historical Institute 1970).

DAHLHAUS, CARL, 'Musica poetica und musikalische Poesie', in *Archiv für Musikwissenschaft* 23 (1966), 110–24.

—— 'Zum Affektbegriff der frühdeutschen Oper', in *Hamburger Jahrbuch für Musikwissenschaft* 5: *Die frühdeutsche Oper und ihre Beziehungen zu Italien, England und Frankreich* (Hamburg: Laaber 1981), 107–11.

DAMMANN, ROLF, *Der Musikbegriff im deutschen Barock* (Cologne: Arno Volk 1967).

DANIEL, NORMAN, *Heroes and Saracens: An Interpretation of the Chansons de Geste* (Edinburgh: Edinburgh University Press 1984).

—— *Islam and the West: The Making of an Image* (Oxford: Oneworld 1993 [1960]).

DARMON, PIERRE, *Mythologie de la Femme dans L'Ancienne France* (Paris: Editions du Seuil 1983).

DAVIES, STEVIE, *The Idea of Woman in Renaissance Literature: The Feminine Reclaimed* (Sussex: Harvester 1986).

DAVIS, NATALIE ZEMON, 'Women on Top: Symbolic Sexual Inversion and Political Disorder in Early Modern Europe', in Babcock, *The Reversible World*, 147–92.

DESCARTES, RENÉ, *The Passions of the Soul* (1649), trans. Stephen H. Voss (Indianapolis: Hackett 1989).

DIAKUN, GERTRUD, 'Märtyrertum und Selbstmord: Frauengestalten in Lohensteins Trauerspielen' (UMI microfilmed doctoral thesis, State University of New York at Buffalo 1983).

DOMMER, ARREY VON, 'Die deutsche Oper in Hamburg zu Ende des 17. und Anfang des 18. Jahrhunderts', in *AMZ* 2 (1864; repr. Amsterdam: Frits Knuf 1969), cols. 217–23; 233–7; 249–54; 273–7.

DONINGTON, ROBERT, *The Rise of Opera* (London: Faber 1981).

—— *Baroque Music: Style and Performance* (London: Faber 1982).

—— *Opera and its Symbols: The Unity of Words, Music, and Staging* (New Haven: Yale University Press 1990).

DRAEGER, HANS-HEINZ, 'The Relation of Music to Words during the German Baroque Era', in Schulz-Behrend, *The German Baroque*, 123–44.

DYCK, JOACHIM, *Ticht-Kunst: Deutsche Barockpoetik und rhetorische Tradition*, 3rd edn. (Tübingen: Niemeyer 1991).

EAGLETON, TERRY, *Walter Benjamin: Towards a Revolutionary Criticism* (London: Verso 1981).

ECO, UMBERTO, 'The Frames of Comic "Freedom"', in *Carnival!*, ed. Thomas A. Sebeok (Berlin: Mouton 1984), 1–10.

EGGERS, DIETRICH, 'Die Bewertung deutscher Sprache und Literatur in den Schulactus von Christian Gryphius' (unpublished doctoral thesis, University of Mainz 1967).

EGGERS, WERNER, *Wirklichkeit und Wahrheit im Trauerspiel des Andreas Gryphius* (Heidelberg: Winter 1967).

EMRICH, WILHELM, *Deutsche Literatur der Barockzeit* (Königstein/Ts.: Athenäum 1981).

FERRARIS, FRANCESCA, 'Exotismus und Intertextualität: Die literarische Kuriositätensammlung', in Wilhelm Kühlmann and Wolfgang Neuber, eds., *Intertextualität in der frühen Neuzeit: Studien zu ihren theoretischen und praktischen Perspektiven* (Frankfurt a.M.: Lang 1994), 465–84.

—— and SABINE WAGNER, 'Stellung und Funktion des Exotismus in der deutschen Literatur der frühen Neuzeit', in *Frühneuzeit-Info* 3/2 (1992), 113–14.

FERRIS, LESLEY, *Acting Women: Images of Women in Theatre* (Basingstoke: Macmillan 1990).

FLAHERTY, GLORIA, *Opera in the Development of German Critical Thought* (Princeton: Princeton University Press 1978).

—— 'Mattheson and the Aesthetics of Theatre', in Buelow and Marx, *New Mattheson Studies*, 75–99.

FLEMMING, WILLI, ed., *Das Schlesische Kunstdrama* (Leipzig: Reclam 1930) [= *Deutsche Literatur in Entwicklungsreihen, Barockdrama* 1].

—— ed., *Die deutsche Barockkomödie* (Leipzig: Reclam 1931) [= *Deutsche Literatur in Entwicklungsreihen, Barockdrama* 4].

—— ed., *Die Oper* (Leipzig: Reclam 1933) [= *Deutsche Literatur in Entwicklungsreihen, Barockdrama* 5].

—— 'Der deutsche Barockmensch und sein Theater', in *Maske und Kothurn* 7 (1961), 197–208.

FLÖGEL, CARL FRIEDRICH, *Geschichte der komischen Litteratur*, 4 vols. (Leignitz and Leipzig: David Siegert 1784).

FORSTER, LEONARD, *The Temper of Seventeenth-Century German Literature: An Inaugural Lecture delivered at University College London* (London: Lewis 1952).

FRICKE, GERHARD, *Die Bildlichkeit in der Dichtung des Andreas Gryphius* (Berlin: Junker und Dünnhaupt 1933).

FROTSCHER, GOTTHOLD, 'Die Affektenlehre als geistige Grundlage der Themenbildung J. S. Bachs', in *Bach-Jahrbuch* (1926), 90–104.

FUBINI, ENRICO, *The History of Music Aesthetics*, trans. M. Hatwell (Basingstoke: Macmillan 1991).

FUCHS-SUMIYOSHI, ANDREA, *Orientalismus in der deutschen Literatur: Untersuchungen zu Werken des 19. und 20. Jahrhunderts, von Goethes West-Östlichem Divan bis Thomas Manns Joseph-Tetralogie* (Hildesheim: Olms 1984).

GABEL, GERNOT UWE, 'Johann Christian Hallman: Die Wandlung des schlesischen Kunstdramas im Ausgang des 17. Jahrhunderts' (UMI microfilmed doctoral thesis, Rice University, Houston, Texas 1971).

GAJEK, KONRAD (ed.), *Das Breslauer Schultheater in 17. und 18. Jahrhundert* (Tübingen: Niemeger 1994).

GERSTENBERG, W., *Zur Geschichte des deutschen Türkenschauspiels I: Die Anfänge des Türkenschauspiels im 15. und 16. Jahrhundert* (Wissenschaftliche Beilage zum Programm des königlichen Gymnasiums zu Meppen 1902).

GHISI, FEDERICO, 'Carnival Songs and the Origins of the Intermezzo Giocoso', in *MQ* 25 (1939), 325–33.

GIBSON, WENDY, *Women in 17th Century France* (Basingstoke: Macmillan 1989).

GILLESPIE, G. E. P., *Daniel Casper von Lohenstein's Historical Tragedies* (Columbus: Ohio State University Press 1965).

GILLESPIE, GERALD, *Garden and Labyrinth of Time: Studies in Renaissance and Baroque Literature* (New York: Lang 1988).

—— 'Lohenstein's Epicharis: The Play of the Beautiful Loser', in *idem*, *Garden and Labyrinth of Time*, 193–224.

—— 'Humanist Aspects of the Early Baroque Opera Libretto after the Italian Fashion (Opitz, Harsdörffer, Anton Ulrich)', in A. Martino, ed., *Beiträge zur Aufnahme der italienischen und spanischen Literatur in Deutschland im 16. und 17. Jahrhundert* (Amsterdam: Rodopi 1990) [= *Chloe: Beihefte zum Daphnis*, vol. 9], 151–70.

—— 'Passion, Piety and Politics: Lohenstein's Ibrahim Sultan and Tristan L'Hermite's Osman', in Parente *et al.*, *Literary Culture in the Holy Roman Empire*, 78–88.

—— and GERHARD SPELLERBERG, eds., *Studien zum Werk Daniel Caspers von Lohenstein* (Amsterdam: Rodopi 1983) [= *Daphnis* 12/2–3].

GLASER, HORST ALBERT, *Deutsche Literatur: Eine Sozialgeschichte*, vol. 3: *Zwischen Gegenreformation und Frühaufklärung: Späthumanismus, Barock 1542–1740* (Reinbek bei Hamburg: Rowohlt 1985).

GOLDSCHMIDT, HUGO, *Studien zur Geschichte der italienischen Oper im 17. Jahrhundert* (Hildesheim: Olms 1967).

GRIMM, REINHOLD, and WALTER HINCK, *Zwischen Satire und Utopie: Zur Komiktheorie und zur Geschichte der europäischen Komödie* (Frankfurt a.M.: Suhrkamp 1982).

GROUT, DONALD J., 'German Baroque Opera', in *MQ* 32 (1946), 547–87.

—— *A Short History of Opera*, 2nd edn. (New York: Columbia University Press 1965).

GUGREL-STEINDL, SUSANNE, and MARGARETE BICAN-ZEHETBAUER, 'Figurenkonstellation im Drama des 17. Jahrhunderts im deutschsprachigen Raum Oder: Von Tugend und Untugend, (Frauen)Schönheit und (Ohn)Macht' (unpublished doctoral diss., University of Vienna 1991).

GUIRGUIS, FAWZY D., 'Bild und Funktion des Orients in Werken der deutschen Literatur des 17. und 18. Jahrhunderts' (unpublished doctoral thesis, University of Berlin 1972).

HAAS, ROBERT, *Die Musik des Barocks* (Wildpark-Potsdam: Athenaion 1928).

HABERKAMM, KLAUS, 'Scherz-Spiel als Sprech-Spiel: Andreas Gryphius' Liebes-Spiel "Horribilicribrifax"', in Helmut Arntzen, ed., *Komödien-Sprache: Beiträge zum deutschen Lustspiel zwischen dem 17. und dem 20. Jahrhundert* (Münster: Aschendorff 1988), 1–22.

HALL, EDITH, *Inventing the Barbarian: Greek Self-Definition through Tragedy* (Oxford: Clarendon 1989).

HALSTED, DAVID, 'From School Theater to Trauerspiel: Lohenstein's *Agrippina* as Systematic Analysis', in *Daphnis* 22 (1993), 621–39.

—— *Poetry and Politics in the Silesian Baroque: Neo-Stoicism in the Work of Christophorus Colerus and his Circle* (Wiesbaden: Harrassowitz 1996).

HAMBURGISCHE STAATSOPER *et al.*, eds., *300 Jahre Oper in Hamburg* (Hamburg: Hans Christians 1977).

HANNING, BARBARA RUSSANO, *Of Poetry and Music's Power: Humanism and the Creation of Opera* (Ann Arbor: UMI Research Press 1980 [1969]).

HARMS, WOLFGANG, *et al.*, eds., *Illustrierte Flugblätter des Barock: Eine Auswahl* (Tübingen: Niemeyer 1983).

HARRIS, ELLEN T., *Handel and the Pastoral Tradition* (London: Oxford University Press 1980).

HARRIS-SCHENZ, Beverley, *Black Images in Eighteenth-Century German Literature* (Stuttgart: Heinz 1981).

HASTY, WILL, 'The Order of Chaos: On Vanitas in the Work of Andreas Gryphius', in *Daphnis* 18/1 (1989), 145–57.

HAUFE, EBERHARD, *Die Behandlung der antiken Mythologie in den Textbüchern der Hamburger Oper 1678–1738* (Frankfurt a.M.: Lang 1994; repr. of doctoral diss., University of Jena 1964).

HAUG, WALTER, ed., *Formen und Funktionen der Allegorie: Symposion Wolfenbüttel 1978* (Stuttgart: Metzler 1979).

HAXEL, HEINRICH, *Studien zu den Lustspielen Christian Weises (1642–1708): Ein Beitrag zur Geschichte des deutschen Schuldramas* (Stettin: Ostsee-Verlag 1932[?]).

HAY, DENYS, *Europe: The Emergence of an Idea*, 2nd edn. (Edinburgh: Edinburgh University Press 1968).

HAYS, HOFFMANN R., *The Dangerous Sex: The Myth of Feminine Evil* (London: Methuen 1966 [1964]).

HEGEL, GEORG WILHELM FRIEDRICH, *Phänomenologie des Geistes*, in *Gesammelte Werke* ed. Wolfgang Bonsiepen and Reinhard Heede, vol. 9 (Hamburg: Felix Meiner 1980).

HENDRICKS, MARGO, and PATRICIA PARKER, eds., *Women, 'Race', and Writing in the Early Modern Period* (London: Routledge 1994).

HICKMANN, ELLEN, 'Michael Praetorius über heimische und fremdländische Volksinstrumente', in Brücker, *Literatur und Volk*, 319–40.

HILLEN, GERD, *Andreas Gryphius' 'Cardenio und Celinde': Zur Erscheinungsform und Funktion der Allegorie in den Gryphischen Trauerspielen* (The Hague: Mouton 1971).

—— 'Allegorie im Kontext: Zur Bestimmung von Form und Funktion der Allegorie in literarischen Texten des 17. Jahrhunderts', in Haug, *Formen und Funktionen der Allegorie*, 592–604.

HINCK, WALTER, *Das deutsche Lustspiel des 17. und 18. Jahrhunderts und die italienische Komödie* (Stuttgart: Metzler 1965).

HOFFMANN, KONRAD, 'Alciati und die geschichtliche Stellung der Emblematik', in Haug, *Formen und Funktionen der Allegorie*, 515–34.

HOFFMEISTER, GERHART, ed., *German Baroque Literature: The European Perspective* (New York: Ungar 1983).

HONEGGER, CLAUDIA, ed., *Die Hexen der Neuzeit: Studien zur Sozialgeschichte eines kulturellen Deutungsmusters* (Frankfurt a.M.: Suhrkamp 1978).

HUBER, WOLFGANG, 'Das Textbuch der frühdeutschen Oper: Untersuchungen über literarische Voraussetzungen, stoffliche Grundlagen und Quellen' (unpublished doctoral thesis, University of Munich 1957).

HUFF, STEVEN R., 'The Early German Libretto: Some Reconsiderations based on Harsdörffer's "Seelewig"', in *ML* 69 (1988), 345–55.

HUGHES-HALLETT, LUCY, *Cleopatra: Histories, Dreams and Distortions* (London: Vintage 1991).

HULTSCH, PAUL, 'Der Orient in der deutschen Barockliteratur' (unpublished doctoral thesis, University of Breslau 1936).

INGEN, FERDINAND VAN, 'Wahn und Vernunft, Verwirrung und Gottesordnung in Cardenio und Celinde des Andreas Gryphius', in Brinkmann, *Theatrum Europaeum*, 253–90.

IWASAKI, EIJIRO, ed. *Begegnung mit dem 'Fremden': Grenzen—Traditionen—Vergleiche: Akten des VIII. Internationalen Germanisten-Kongresses, Tokyo 1990*, 11 vols. (Munich: iudicium 1991).

JAACKS, G., 'Hamburg als Zentrum geistige und musikalische Kultur im Barock', in Hamburgische Staatsoper *et al.*, *300 Jahre Oper in Hamburg*, 36–49.

JAHN, BERNHARD, 'Ist die musikalische Figurenlehre eine Hermeneutik? Probleme und Perspektiven beim Umgang mit einem analytischen Verfahren aus der Barockzeit', in *Germanica Wratislaviensia* 93 (Wroclaw 1992), 172–90.

—— '*L'Adelaide* und *L'Heraclio* in Venedig, Breslau und Hamburg: Transformationen zweier Bühnenwerke im Spannungsverhältnis zwischen Musik- und Sprechtheater', in *DVjs* 68 (1994), 651–94.

—— 'Das Libretto als literarische Leitgattung am Ende des 17. Jahrhunderts? Zu Zi(e)glers Roman *Die Asiatische Banise* und seinen Opernfassungen', in Sent, *Die Oper*, 143–70.

JANOTA, JOHANNES, 'Zur Rezeption mittelalterlicher Literatur zwischen dem 16. und 18. Jahrhundert', in Poag and Scholz-Williams, *Das Weiterleben des Mittelalters in der deutschen Literatur*, 37–46.

JARRAT, SUSAN C., and NEDRA REYNOLDS, 'The Splitting Image: Contemporary Feminisms and the Ethics of *êthos*', in James S. Baumlin and Tita French Baumlin (eds.), *Ethos: New Essays in Rhetorical and Critical Theory* (Dallas: Southern Methodist University Press 1994), 37–64.

JOHANNSMEIER, ROLF, *Spielmann, Schalk und Scharlatan: Die Welt als Karneval: Volkskultur im späten Mittelalter* (Reinbek bei Hamburg: Rowohlt 1984).

JONAS, MONIKA, 'Idealisierung und Dämonisierung als Mittel der Repression: Eine Untersuchung zur Weiblichkeitsdarstellung im spätmittelalterlichen Schwank', in Wallinger and Jonas, *Der Widerspenstigen Zähmung*, 67–93.

JONES, ELDRED D., *Othello's Countrymen: The African in English Renaissance Drama* (London: Oxford University Press 1965).

312     BIBLIOGRAPHY

Jones, Eldred D., The Elizabethan Image of Africa (Charlottesville, Va.: University Press of Virginia 1971).

Jörgensen, Ninna, Bauer, Narr und Pfaffe: prototypische Figuren und ihre Funktion in der Reformationsliteratur, trans. Monika Wesemann (Leiden: Brill 1988).

Juretzka, Jörg C., Zur Dramatik Daniel Caspers von Lohenstein 'Cleopatra' 1661 und 1680 (Meisenheim am Glam: Hain 1976).

Just, K. G., Die Trauerspiele Lohensteins: Versuch einer Interpretation (Berlin: Schmidt 1961).

—— 'Das deutsche Opernlibretto', in Scher, Literatur und Musik, 100–6.

Kabbani, Rana, Europe's Myths of Orient (Bloomington: Indiana University Press 1986).

Kaiser, Gerhard, Die Dramen des Andreas Gryphius: Eine Sammlung von Einzelinterpretationen (Stuttgart: Metzler 1968).

Kâmil, Burhaneddin [Burhan Al-Din], 'Die Türken in der deutschen Literatur bis zum Barock und die Sultansgestalten in den Türkendramen Lohensteins' (unpublished doctoral thesis, University of Kiel 1935).

Kaminski, Nicola, Der Liebe Eisen=harte Noth: 'Cardenio und Celinde' im Kontext von Gryphius' Märtyrerdramen (Tübingen: Niemeyer 1992).

Katz, Ruth, Divining the Powers of Music: Aesthetic Theory and the Origins of Opera (New York: Pendragon 1986).

Keimer, Jürgen, 'Nicht Mensch—Nicht Gott—Nicht Teufel', in Poley, Unter der Maske des Narren, 202–7.

Keller, Elisabeth, Die Darstellung der Frau in Fastnachtspiel und Spruchdichtung von Hans Rosenplüt und Hans Volz (Frankfurt a.M.: Lang 1992).

Keller, Peter, Die Oper Seelewig von Sigmund Theophil Staden und Georg Philipp Harsdörffer (Berne: Paul Haupt 1977).

Kennedy, William J., 'Audiences and Rhetorical Strategies in Jodelle, Shakespeare, and Lohenstein', in Assays: Critical Approaches to Medieval and Renaissance Texts 1 (1981), 99–116.

Kirchner, Gottfried, Fortuna in Dichtung und Emblematik des Barock: Tradition und Bedeutungswandel eines Motivs (Stuttgart: Metzler 1970).

Kittler, Friedrich A., 'Rhetorik der Macht und Macht der Rhetorik: Lohensteins Agrippina', in Johann Christian Günther, ed. Hans-Georg Pott (Paderborn: Schöningh 1988), 39–52.

Kleefeld, Wilhelm, 'Das Orchester der Hamburger Oper 1678–1738', in SIM 1 (1899–1900), 219–89.

Kleinschmidt, Peter, et al., Die Welt des Daniel Casper von Lohenstein: Epicharis: Ein römisches Trauerspiel (Cologne: Wienand 1978).

Koch, Hans-Albrecht, Das deutsche Singspiel (Stuttgart: Metzler 1974).

Koebner, Thomas, 'Der Narr auf der Bühne', in Poley, Unter der Maske des Narren, 191–4.

—— and Gerhart Pickerodt, eds., *Die andere Welt: Studien zum Exotismus* (Frankfurt a.M.: Athenäum 1987).

KOHL, KARL-HEINZ, 'Cherchez la Femme D'Orient', in Sievernich/ Budde, *Europa und der Orient*, 356–67.

KÖNNEKER, BARBARA, *Wesen und Wandlung der Narrenidee im Zeitalter des Humanismus: Brant—Murner—Erasmus* (Wiesbaden: Steiner 1966).

KOPPLIN, MONIKA, 'Turcica und Turquerien: Zur Entwicklung des Türkenbildes und Rezeption osmanischer Motive vom 16. bis 18. Jahrhundert', in Pollig *et al.*, *Exotische Welten*, 150–63.

KRAFT, HELGA, 'Töchter, die keine Mütter werden: Nonnen, Amazonen, Mätressen', in *Mütter—Töchter—Frauen: Weiblichkeitsbilder in der Literatur*, ed. Helga Kraft and Elke Liebs (Stuttgart: Metzler 1993), 35–52.

KRÄMER, KRISTINE, 'Johann Christian Hallmanns Trauer-, Freuden- und Schäferspiele: Die Bedeutung des Fortuna-Konzeptes für die Vermischung der Dramenformen des Barock' (unpublished doctoral thesis, University of Berlin 1978).

KRAMER, MARTIN, 'Rhetorikunterricht und dramatische Struktur: Am Beispiel der consultationes', in Schöne, *Stadt—Schule—Universität—Buchwesen*, 261–75.

KRAUSE, HEINZ, 'Johann Beer 1655–1700: Zur Musikauffassung im 17. Jahrhundert' (unpublished doctoral thesis, University of Leipzig 1935).

KREIDT, DIETRICH, ' "Kann uns zum Vaterland die Fremde werden?": Exotismus und Schauspieltheater', in Pollig *et al.*, *Exotische Welten*, 248–55.

KREMER, MANFRED, 'Bauern-, Bürger- und Frauensatire in den Zittauer Komödien Christian Weises', in Wagener, *Absurda Comica*, 99–118.

KRETZSCHMAR, HERMANN, 'Allgemeines und Besonderes zur Affektenlehre', in *JMP* 18 (1911), 63–78, and 19 (1912), 65–78.

KUNZLE, DAVID, 'World Upside Down: The Iconography of a European Broadsheet Type', in Babcock, *The Reversible World*, 39–94.

KUPER, MICHAEL, *Zur Semiotik der Inversion: Verkehrte Welt und Lachkultur im 16. Jahrhundert* (Berlin: VWB 1993).

LAKOFF, GEORGE, *Women, Fire, and Dangerous Things: What Categories Reveal about the Mind* (Chicago: University of Chicago Press 1987).

—— and Mark Johnson, *Metaphors We Live By* (Chicago: University of Chicago Press 1980).

LARSEN, LAWRENCE S., 'Una Poenitentium: Levels of Sin and Sanctity in Albertinian Women', in James Hardin and Jörg Jungmayr, eds., *'Der Buchstab tödt—der Geist macht lebendig': Festschrift zum 60. Geburtstag von Hans-Gert Roloff*, 2 vols. (Berlin: Lang 1992), 2. 697–708.

LEICHTENTRITT, HUGO, 'Reinhard Keiser in seinen Opern: Ein Beitrag zur Geschichte der frühen deutschen Oper' (unpublished doctoral thesis, Friedrich-Wilhelms-Universität Berlin 1901).

LEICHTENTRITT, HUGO, *Music, History and Ideas* (Cambridge, Mass.: Harvard University Press 1938).

LEVINE, LAURA, *Men in Women's Clothing: Anti-Theatricality and Effeminization, 1597–1642* (Cambridge: Cambridge University Press 1994).

LEWIS, ANTONY, and NIGEL FORTUNE, eds., *Opera and Church Music 1630–1750* (London: Oxford University Press 1975) [= *New Oxford History of Music*, vol. 5].

LIMON, JERZY, *Gentleman of a Company: English Players in Central and Eastern Europe 1590–1660* (Cambridge: Cambridge University Press 1985).

LINDBERG, DIAN IGOR, 'Literary Aspects of German Baroque Opera: History, Theory and Practice (Christian H. Postel and Barthold Feind)' (UMI microfilmed doctoral thesis, University of California 1964).

LINDBERG, JOHN D., 'The German Baroque Opera Libretto: A Forgotten Genre', in Schulz-Behrend, *The German Baroque*, 87–122.

LOOMBA, ANIA, *Gender, Race, Renaissance Drama* (Delhi: Oxford University Press 1992).

—— 'The Color of Patriarchy: Critical Difference, Cultural Difference, and Renaissance Drama', in Hendricks and Parker, *Women, 'Race', and Writing*, 17–34.

LOOSE, H.-D., 'Hamburg vor 300 Jahren: Wirtschaft—Gesellschaft—Politik', in Hamburgische Staatsoper *et al.*, *300 Jahre Oper in Hamburg*, 28–35.

LÜHNING, HELGA, 'Metastasios "Semiramide riconosciuta": Die verkleidete Opera seria oder: Die Entdeckung einer Gattung', in Klaus Hortschansky, ed., *Opernheld und Opernheldin im 18. Jahrhundert: Aspekte der Librettoforschung: Ein Tagungsbericht* (Hamburg: Wagner 1991), 131–8.

LUNDING, ERIK, 'Das Schlesische Kunstdrama: Eine Darstellung und Deutung' (unpublished doctoral thesis, University of Copenhagen 1939).

LUPTON, PHILIP WADSLEY, 'Die Frauengestalten in den Trauerspielen Daniel Casper von Lohensteins [*sic*]' (unpublished doctoral thesis, University of Vienna 1954).

LYNCH, ROBERT DONALD, *Opera in Hamburg 1718–1738: A Study of the Libretto and Musical Style*, 2 vols. (Michigan: Ann Arbor 1980).

McCLARY, SUSAN, 'Constructions of Gender in Monteverdi's Dramatic Music', in *COJ* 1/3 (1989), 203–23.

—— *Feminine Endings: Music, Gender, and Sexuality* (Minneapolis, Minn.: University of Minnesota Press 1991).

MACLEAN, IAN, *Woman Triumphant: Feminism in French Literature 1610–1652* (Oxford: Oxford University Press 1977).

McCREDIE, ANDREW D., 'Instrumentarium and Instrumentation in the North German Baroque Opera' (unpublished doctoral thesis, University of Hamburg 1964).

—— 'Christoph Graupner as opera composer', in *Miscellanea Musicologica* 1 (1966), 74–116.

McGLATHERY, JAMES M., ed., *Music and German Literature: Their Relationship since the Middle Ages* (Columbia, Oh.: Camden House 1992).

McGOWAN, MARGARET M., 'The Origins of French Opera', in Lewis and Fortune, *Opera and Church Music*, 169–205.

McLEOD, GLENDA, *Virtue and Venom: Catalogs of Women from Antiquity to the Renaissance* (Ann Arbor: University of Michigan Press 1991).

MAJER, HANS GEORG, 'Die Türken—Gegner des Westens am Ende des 17. Jahrhunderts', in Hubert Glaser, ed., *Kurfürst Max Emanuel: Bayern und Europa um 1700* (Munich: Hirmer 1976), 1. 362–72.

MANNACK, EBERHARD, 'Lustspiele', in Glaser, *Deutsche Literatur*, 295–309.

MARIGOLD, W. GORDON, 'Aspekte der Komödie und des Komischen in Hamburg 1600–1708', in Wagener, *Absurda Comica*, 15–35.

—— 'Politics, Religion and Opera: Problems of the Hamburg Opera, 1678–1720', in *Mosaic* 18/4 (1985), 49–60.

MARQUART, ALFRED, 'Der Mond an Nil und Euphrat', in Pollig *et al.*, *Exotische Welten*, 256–61.

MARTINI, FRITZ, 'Masaniello, Lehrstück und Trauerspiel der Geschichte', in *Orbis Litterarum* 25 (1970), 171–96; repr. in *Masaniello. Trauerspiel*, ed. Martini (Stuttgart: Reclam 1978 [1972]).

MARTINO, ALBERTO, *Daniel Casper von Lohenstein: Geschichte seiner Rezeption*, trans. Heribert Streicher (Tübingen: Niemeyer 1978).

MARX, HANS JOACHIM, 'Geschichte der Hamburger Barockoper: Ein Forschungsbericht', in *Hamburger Jahrbuch für Musikwissenschaft 3: Studien zur Barockoper* (Hamburg: Wagner 1978), 7–34.

MASSON, PAUL-MARIE, 'French Opera from Lully to Rameau' in Lewis and Fortune, *Opera and Church Music*, 206–66.

MENHENNET, ALAN, 'The Death of Lohenstein's Agrippina', in *Quinquereme: New Studies in modern languages* 6/1 (1983), 28–38.

—— 'Virtue and Vanity: Thoughts on the Beginning and End of Lohenstein's Epicharis', in *OGS* 16 (1985), 1–12.

MERCHANT, W. MOELWYN, *Comedy* (London: Methuen 1972).

METZGER, ERIKA A., and MICHAEL M. METZGER, *Reading Andreas Gryphius: Critical Trends 1664–1993* (Columbia, Oh.: Camden House 1994).

MEYER, REINHART, 'Hanswurst und Harlekin oder: Der Narr als Gattungsschöpfer: Versuch einer Analyse des komischen Spiels in den Staatsaktionen des Musik- und Sprechtheaters im 17. und 18. Jahrhundert', in Roland Krebs and Jean-Marie Valentin, eds., *Théâtre, Nation & Société en Allemagne au XVIIIᵉ Siècle* (Nancy 1990).

MEYER-KALKUS, REINHART, *Wollust und Grausamkeit: Affektenlehre und Affektdarstellung in Lohensteins Dramatik am Beispiel von 'Agrippina'* (Göttingen: Vandenhoeck & Ruprecht 1986).

MÖSER, JUSTUS, *Harlekin oder Vertheidigung des Groteske-Komischen (1777)*, in *Harlekin: Texte und Materialien*, ed. Henning Boetius (Bad Homburg v.d.H.: Gehlen 1968), 9–37.

MÜLLER, OTHMAR, *Drama und Bühne in den Trauerspielen von Andreas Gryphius und Daniel Casper von Lohenstein* (St Gallen: Gegenbauer 1967).

MÜLLER-BLATTAU, Joseph, *Die Kompositionslehre Heinrich Schützens in der Fassung seines Schülers Christoph Bernhard* (Kassel: Bärenreiter 1963 [1926]).

MÜSCH, BETTINA, *Der politische Mensch im Welttheater des Daniel Casper von Lohenstein: Eine Deutung seines Dramenwerks* (Frankfurt a.M.: Lang 1992).

NELSON, T. G. A., *Comedy: An Introduction to Comedy in Literature, Drama, and Cinema* (Oxford: Oxford University Press 1990).

NEUMANN, OTTO, 'Studien zum Leben und Werk des Lausitzer Poeten August Adolph von Haugwitz (1647–1706)' (unpublished doctoral thesis, University of Greifswald 1937).

NEUMEISTER, SEBASTIAN, 'Cenobia und Cleopatra: Das Liebeskalkül bei Calderón und bei Lohenstein', in *Beiträge zur Aufnahmne der italienischen und spanischen Literatur in Deutschland im 16. und 17. Jahrhundert*, ed. A. Martino (Amsterdam: Rodopi 1990), 385–97.

NEWMAN, JANE O., 'Mierten's Wife, or: (Dis)locating the Site/Sight of Meaning in Christian Weise's Ein wunderliches Schau-Spiel vom Niederländischen Bauer (1685)', in *MLN* 105/1 (1990), 512–35.

—— 'Innovation and the Text Which is not One: Representing History in Lohenstein's >Sophonisbe< (1669), in *Innovation und Originalität* (*Fortuna Vitrea* vol. 9), ed. Walter Haug und Burghart Wachinger (Tübingen: Niemeyer 1993), 206–38.

—— 'Sex "in Strange Places": The Split Text of Gender in Lohenstein's *Epicharis*' (1665), in Tatlock, *The Graph of Sex*, 349–82.

—— 'Disorientations: Same-Sex Seduction and Women's Power in Daniel Casper von Lohenstein's *Ibrahim Sultan*', in *CG* 28 (1995), 337–56.

NIESCHMIDT, H. W., 'Emblematische Szenengestaltung in den Märtyrerdramen des Andreas Gryphius', in *MLN* 86 (1971), 321–44.

NIETZSCHE, FRIEDRICH, 'Über Wahrheit und Lüge im aussermoralischen Sinne' (1873), in *Nietzsche Werke: Kritische Gesamtausgabe*, ed. Georgi Colli and Mazzino Montinari (Berlin: de Gruyter 1973), vol. 3/2. 369–84.

NOLLE, ROLF WERNER, *Das Motiv der Verführung: Verführer und 'Verführte' als dramatische Entwürfe moralischer Weltordnung in Trauerspielen von Gryphius, Lohenstein und Lessing* (Stuttgart: Heinz 1976).

OLSEN, SOLVEIG, *Christian Heinrich Postels Beitrag zur deutschen Literatur: Versuch einer Darstellung* (Amsterdam: Rodopi 1973).

—— *Christian Heinrich Postel (1658–1705): Bibliographie* (Amsterdam: Rodopi 1974).

OLSON, ELDER, *The Theory of Comedy* (Bloomington: Indiana University Press 1968).

OPITZ, CLAUDIA, 'Der aufgeklärte Harem: Kulturvergleich und Geschlechterbeziehungen in Montesquieus "Perserbriefen"', in *Feministische Studien* 2 (1991), 22–56.

ÖZYURT, SENOL, *Die Türkenlieder und das Türkenbild in der deutschen Volksüberlieferung vom 16. bis zum 20. Jahrhundert* (Munich: Fink 1972).

PALISCA, CLAUDE VON, 'Prima Prattica', in Sadie, *The New Grove Dictionary of Music and Musicians*, 15. 228–9.

PALMER, D. J., *Comedy: Developments in Criticism: A Casebook* (London: Macmillan 1984).

PAPE, WALTER, 'Der fremde Blick der Komik: Das Vertraute und das Fremde in Komik und Komödie', in Iwasaki, *Begegnung mit dem 'Fremden'*, 6. 106–16.

PARENTE, JAMES A., Jr., 'Baroque Comedy and the Stability of the State', in *GQ* 56/3 (1983), 419–30.

—— et al., eds. *Literary Culture in the Holy Roman Empire, 1555–1720* (Chapel Hill: University of North Carolina Press 1991).

PARKER, PATRICIA, 'Fantasies of "Race" and "Gender": Africa, Othello, and Bringing to Light', in Hendricks and Parker, *Women, 'Race', and Writing*, 84–100.

PAUSCH, HOLGER A., ed., *Kommunikative Metaphorik: Die Funktion des literarischen Bildes in der deutschen Literatur von ihren Anfängen bis zur Gegenwart* (Bonn: Bouvier 1976).

PERRIG, ALEXANDER, 'Erdrandsiedler oder die schrecklichen Nachkommen Chams: Aspekte der mittelalterlichen Völkerkunde', in Koebner, *Die andere Welt*, 31–87.

PIRROTTA, NINO, 'Commedia dell'Arte and Opera', in *MQ* 41 (1955), 305–24.

PLUME, CORNELIA, *Heroinen in der Geschlechterordnung: Wirklichkeitsprojektionen bei Daniel Casper von Lohenstein und die 'Querelle des Femmes'* (Stuttgart: Metzler 1996).

POLEY, STEFANIE, ed., *Unter der Maske des Narren* (Stuttgart: Hatje 1981).

POLLIG, HERMANN, et al., eds., *Exotische Welten—Europäische Phantasien: Ausstellung des Instituts für Auslandsbeziehungen und des Württembergischen Kunstvereins* (Stuttgart: Institut für Auslandsbeziehungen 1987).

—— 'Exotische Welten, Europäische Phantasien', in *idem, Exotische Welten*, 16–25.

POWELL, HUGH, *Trammels of Tradition: Aspects of German Life and Culture in the Seventeenth Century and their Impact on Contemporary Literature* (Tübingen: Niemeyer 1988).

PRAZ, MARIO, *Studies in Seventeenth-Century Imagery*, 2 vols. (London: Warburg Institute 1939).

# 318

BIBLIOGRAPHY

PRICE, DAVID, 'When Women Would Rule: Reversal of Gender Hierarchy in Sixteenth-Century Drama', in *Daphnis* 20 (1991), 147–66.

PURDIE, SUSAN, *Comedy: The Mastery of Discourse* (New York: Harvester Wheatsheaf 1993).

QUANT, REINHOLD, and HEINZ BECKER, eds., *Quellentexte zur Konzeption der europäischen Oper im 17. Jahrhundert* (Kassel: Bärenreiter 1981).

REICHARDT, JOHANN FRIEDRICH, *Über die Deutsche comische Oper nebst einem Anhange eines freundschaftlichen Briefes über die musikalische Poesie* (Hamburg 1774), repr. ed. Walter Kolneder (Munich: Katzbichler 1975).

REULING, CHARLOTTE, *Die komische Figur in den wichtigsten deutschen Dramen bis zum Ende des XVII. Jahrhunderts* (Stuttgart: Göschen 1890).

REYNIER, GUSTAVE, *La Femme au XVIIᵉ siècle: ses ennemis et ses défenseurs* (Paris: Tallandier 1933 [1929]).

RICHARDS, KENNETH, and LAURA RICHARDS, *The Commedia dell'Arte: A Documentary History* (Oxford: Blackwell for the Shakespeare Head Press 1990).

RICHTER, KARL, 'Die Verwandlung des Harlekin', in Poley, *Unter der Maske des Narren*, 195–201.

RIDDER, LISELOTTE DE, 'Der Anteil der Commedia dell'Arte an der Entstehungs- und Entwicklungsgeschichte der komischen Oper: Studie zum Libretto der Oper im 17. Jahrhundert' (unpublished doctoral thesis: University of Cologne 1970).

ROBERTSON, RITCHIE, 'Historicizing Weininger: The Nineteenth-Century German Image of the Feminized Jew', in Bryan Chevette and Laura Marcus, eds., *Modernity, Culture and 'the Jew'* (Cambridge: Polity 1998).

ROBINSON, MICHAEL F., *Opera before Mozart* (London: Hutchinson University Library 1966).

ROLOFF, HANS-GERT, 'Die Funktion der szenischen Bildlichkeit im deutschen Drama des 16. Jahrhunderts', in Béhar, *Image et spectacle*, 285–312.

ROOS, KEITH L., *The Devil in 16th-Century German Literature* (Berne: Lang 1972).

ROPER, LYNDAL, *Oedipus and the Devil: Witchcraft, Sexuality and Religion in Early Modern Europe* (London: Routledge 1994).

ROSAND, ELLEN, *Opera in Seventeenth-Century Venice: The Creation of a Genre* (Berkeley: University of California Press 1991).

RUDWIN, MAXIMILIAN JOSEF, *Der Teufel in den deutschen geistlichen Spielen des Mittelalters und der Reformationszeit* (Göttingen: Vandenhoeck & Ruprecht and Baltimore: The Johns Hopkins Press 1915).

SADIE, JULIE ANNE, ed., *Companion to Baroque Music* (London: Dent 1990).

SADIE, STANLEY, *History of Opera* (Basingstoke: Macmillan 1989).

SAID, EDWARD W., *Orientalism: Western Conceptions of the Orient* (New York: Pantheon 1978).

SCHADE, RICHARD ERICH, 'Thesen zur literarischen Darstellung der Frau am Beispiel der Courasche', in Brückner *et al.*, *Literatur und Volk*, 227–44.

—— *Studies in Early German Comedy 1500–1650* (Columbia, Oh.: Camden House 1988).

SCHARLAU, ULF, *Athanasius Kircher (1601–1680) als Musikschriftsteller: Ein Beitrag zur Musikanschauung des Barock* (Marburg: Görick & Weiershäuser/ Kassel: Bärenreiter-Antiquariat 1969).

SCHER, STEVEN PAUL, ed., *Literatur und Musik: ein Handbuch zur Theorie und Praxis eines komparatistischen Grenzgebietes* (Berlin: Erich Schmidt 1984).

—— ed., *Music and Text: Critical Enquiries* (Cambridge: Cambridge University Press 1992).

SCHILLER, FRIEDRICH, 'Die Schaubühne als eine moralische Anstalt betrachtet', in *idem, Vom Pathetischen und Erhabenen: Schriften zur Dramentheorie*, ed. Klaus L. Berghahn (Stuttgart: Reclam 1970).

SCHILLING, MICHAEL, 'Allegorie und Satire auf illustrierten Flugblättern des Barock', in Haug, *Formen und Funktionen der Allegorie*, 405–18.

—— *Imagines Mundi: Metaphorische Darstellungen der Welt in der Emblematik* (Frankfurt a.M.: Lang 1979).

SCHINGS, HANS-JÜRGEN, *Die Dramen des Andreas Gryphius: Eine Sammlung von Einzelinterpretationen* (Stuttgart: Metzler 1968).

—— 'Consolatio Tragoediae: Zur Theorie des barocken Trauerspiels', in *Deutsche Drametheorien: Beiträge zu einer historischen Poetik des Dramas in Deutschland*, ed. Reinhold Grimm (Frankfurt a.M.: Athenäum 1971), 1–44.

SCHLUMBOHM, CHRISTA, 'Die Glorifizierung der Barockfürstin als "Femme forte"', in August Buck *et al.*, eds., *Europäische Hofkultur im 16. und 17. Jahrhundert*, 3 vols., (Hamburg: Hauswedell 1981), 1. 112–22.

SCHOLZ WILLIAMS, GERHILD, 'On Finding Words: Witchcraft and the Discourses of Dissidence and Discovery', in Tatlock, *The Graph of Sex*, 45–66.

SCHÖNE, ALBRECHT, *Emblematik und Drama im Zeitalter des Barock* (Munich: Beck 1964).

—— *Säkularisation als sprachbildende Kraft: Studien zur Dichtung deutscher Pfarrersöhne* (Göttingen: Vandenhoeck und Ruprecht 1968).

—— ed., *Stadt—Schule—Universität—Buchwesen und die deutsche Literatur im 17. Jahrhundert* (Munich: Beck 1976).

SCHREIBER, [Caroline Christiane Helene] IRMTRAUD, *Dichtung und Musik der deutschen Opernarien 1680–1700* (Wolfenbüttel: Hallmeyer 1935).

SCHULDES, LUIS, *Die Teufelsszenen im deutschen geistlichen Drama des Mittelalters* (Göppingen: Kümmerle 1974).

SCHULZ-BEHREND, GEORGE, ed., *The German Baroque: Music, Literature, Art* (Austin: University of Texas Press 1972).

SCHWAB, RAYMOND, *The Oriental Renaissance: Europe's Rediscovery of India and the East, 1680–1880*, trans. G. Patterson-Black and V. Reinking (New York: Columbia University Press 1984).

SCHWARZ, HANS-GÜNTHER, 'Die Metapher im Drama', in Pausch, *Kommunikative Metaphorik*, 129–40.

SCHWEIGER-LERCHENFELD, AMAND FREIHERR VON, *Die Frauen des Orients in der Geschichte, in der Dichtung und im Leben* (Vienna: Hartleben 1904).

SENT, ELEONORE (ed.), *Die Oper am Weißenfelser Hof* (Rudolstadt: Hain 1996).

SERAUKY, WALTER, 'Affektenlehre', in Blume, *Die Musik in Geschichte und Gegenwart*, 1 (1949–51), cols. 113–21.

SHEPHERD, SIMON, *Amazons and Warrior Women: Varieties of Feminism in Seventeenth-Century Drama* (Brighton: Harvester 1981).

SHEPPARD, RICHARD, 'Upstairs—Downstairs—Some Reflections on German Literature in the Light of Bakhtin's Theory of Carnival', in Sheppard, ed., *New Ways in Germanistik* (New York: Berg 1990), 278–315.

SIEVERNICH, GEREON, and HENDRIK BUDDE, *Europa und der Orient 800–1900* (Gütersloh: Bertelsmann Lexikon Verlag 1989).

SIMON, ECKEHARD, 'Der Türke in Nürnberg: Zur Türkenpolemik nach 1453 und "Des Türcken vasnachtspil"', in Iwasaki, *Begegnung mit dem 'Fremden'*, 7. 322–8.

SKRINE, PETER, 'A Flemish Model for the Tragedies of Lohenstein', in *MLR* 61 (1966), 64–70.

—— *The Baroque: Literature and Culture in Seventeenth-Century Europe* (London: Methuen 1978).

—— 'An Exploration of Hallmann's Dramas', in *GLL* 36/3 (1983), 232–40.

—— 'German Baroque Drama and Seventeenth-Century European Theatre', in Parente, *Literary Culture in the Holy Roman Empire*, 49–59.

SMITH, PATRICK J., *The Tenth Muse: A Historical Study of the Opera Libretto* (London: Gollancz 1971).

SÖRENSEN, BENGT ALGOT, ed., *Allegorie und Symbol: Texte zur Theorie des dichterischen Bildes im 18. und frühen 19. Jahrhundert* (Frankfurt a.M.: Athenäum 1972).

SPAHR, Blake LEE, *Andreas Gryphius: A Modern Perspective* (Columbia, Oh.: Camden House 1993).

SPELLERBERG, GERHARD, 'Eine unbekannte Quelle zur Epicharis Daniel Caspers von Lohenstein', in *Euphorion* 61 (1967), 143–54.

—— *Verhängnis und Geschichte: Untersuchungen zu den Trauerspielen und dem 'Arminius'-Roman Daniel Caspers von Lohenstein* (Bad Homburg v.d.H.: Gehlen 1970).

—— 'Nachwort', in Hallmann, *Mariamne* (Stuttgart: Reclam 1973), 189–211.

—— 'Das schlesische Barockdrama und das Breslauer Schultheater', in Kleinschmidt, *Die Welt des Daniel Casper von Lohenstein*, 58–69.

—— 'Ratio Status und Tragoedia. Bemerkungen zur Wandlung des barocken Trauerspiels bei Hallmann', in *Virtus et Fortuna: Zur deutschen Literatur zwischen 1400 und 1720: Festschrift für Hans-Gert Roloff*, ed. Joseph P. Strelka and Jörg Jungmayr (Berne: Lang 1983), 496–517.

SPERBERG-McQUEEN, M. R., 'Deceitful Symmetry in Gryphius's *Cardenio und Celinde*: Or What Rosina Learned at the Theater and Why She Went', in Tatlock, *The Graph of Sex*, 269–94.

SPIES, OTTO, *Der Orient in der deutschen Literatur I: Die unmittelbaren Einflüsse während des Mittelalters* (Kevelaer: Butzon & Berker 1950).

STACKHOUSE, JANIFER GARL, *The Constructive Art of Gryphius' Historical Tragedies* (Berne: Lang 1986).

STALLYBRASS, PETER, and ALLON WHITE, eds., *The Politics and Poetics of Transgression* (London: Methuen 1986).

STEFAN, INGE, and SIGRID WEIGEL, *Die verborgene Frau: Sechs Beiträge zu einer feministischen Literaturwissenschaft* (Berlin: Argument 1988).

STEINHAGEN, HARALD, and BENNO VON WIESE, eds., *Deutsche Dichter des 17. Jahrhunderts* (Berlin: Schmidt 1984).

STERNFELD, F. W., 'The First Printed Opera Libretto', in *ML* 59 (1978), 121–38.

—— *The Birth of Opera* (Oxford: Clarendon 1993).

STILES, ANDRINA, *The Ottoman Empire 1450–1700* (London: Hodder & Stoughton 1989).

STOLL, ALBRECHT D., *Figur und Affekt: Zur höfischen Musik und zur bürgerlichen Musiktheorie der Epoche Richelieu*, 2nd edn. (Tutzing: Hans Schneider 1981).

STOLL, BRIGITTE, 'Frauenspezifische Verwendung von mystischem Traditionsgut im *Geistlichen Frauenzimmer-Spiegel* des Hieronymus Oertl', in Dieter Breuer, ed., *Religion und Religiosität im Zeitalter des Barock* (Wiesbaden: Harrossowitz 1995), 477–85.

STORR, ANTONY, *Music and the Mind* (London: Harper Collins 1992).

SUSINI, EUGÈNE, 'Claude Malingre, Sieur de Saint-Lazare, et son histoire de Catherine de Géorgie', in *Études Germaniques* 23 (1968), 37–53.

SYNDRAM, KARL ULRICH, 'Der erfundene Orient in der europäischen Literatur von 18. bis zum Beginn des 20. Jahrhunderts', in Sievernich and Budde, *Europa und der Orient*, 324–41.

SZAROTA, ELIDA MARIA, *Künstler, Grübler und Rebellen: Studien zum europäischen Märtyrerdrama des 17. Jahrhunderts* (Berne: Francke 1967).

—— *Geschichte, Politik und Gesellschaft im Drama des 17. Jahrhunderts* (Berne: Francke 1976).

—— 'Lohensteins Epicharis', in Kleinschmidt, *Die Welt des Daniel Casper von Lohenstein*, 104–11.

SZAROTA, ELIDA MARIA, *Stärke, dein Name sei Weib!: Bühnenfiguren des 17. Jahrhunderts* (Berlin: de Gruyter 1987).

TATLOCK, LYNNE, ed., *The Graph of Sex and the German Text: Gendered Culture in Early Modern Germany 1500–1700* (Amsterdam: Rodopi 1994) [= Chloe: Beihefte zum Daphnis, vol. 19].

—— 'Selling Turks: Eberhard Werner Happel's Turcica (1683–1690)', in *CG* 28 (1993), 307–35.

TAUBALD, RICHARD, 'Die Oper als Schule der Tugend und des Lebens im Zeitalter des Barock: Die enkulturierende Wirkung einer Kunstpflege' (unpublished doctoral thesis, University of Erlangen-Nuremberg 1972).

TEKINAY, Alev, *Materialien zum vergleichenden Studium von Erzählmotiven in der deutschen Dichtung des Mittelalters und den Literaturen des Orients* (Frankfurt a.M.: Lang 1980).

THIEL, ROGER, 'Constantia oder Klassenkampf? Christian Weises *Masaniello* (1682) und Barthold Feind's *Masagniello Furioso* (1706)', in *Daphnis* 17 (1988), 247–66.

THOMAS, GARY C., 'Musical Rhetoric and Politics in the Early German Lied', in McGlathery, *Music and German Literature*, 65–78.

THORNTON, LYNNE, 'Frauenbilder. Zur Malerei der "Orientalisten"', in Sievernich/ Budde, *Europa und der Orient*, 342–67.

TREDER, UTA, *Von der Hexe zur Hysterikerin: Zur Verfestigungsgeschichte des 'Ewig Weiblichen'* (Bonn: Bouvier 1984).

TURBAYNE, Colin Murray, *The Myth of Metaphor* (New Haven: Yale University Press 1962).

UEDING, GERT, *Klassische Rhetorik* (Munich: Beck 1995).

—— and BERND STEINBRINK, *Grundriß der Rhetorik: Geschichte-Technik-Methode* (Stuttgart: Metzler 1986).

UNGER, HANS-HEINRICH, *Die Beziehung zwischen Musik und Rhetorik im 16.–18. Jahrhundert* (Würzburg 1941; repr. Hildesheim: Olms 1985).

VALENTIN, JEAN-MARIE, 'Une représentation inconnue de l'Epicharis de Lohenstein (Sion, 1710)', in *Études Germaniques* 24 (1969), 242–8.

VICKERS, BRIAN, *In Defence of Rhetoric* (Oxford: Clarendon 1997 [1988]).

VOßKAMP, WILHELM, 'Daniel Casper von Lohensteins Cleopatra: Historisches Verhängnis und politisches Spiel', in Walter Hinck, ed., *Geschichte als Schauspiel: Deutsche Geschichtsdrama: Interpretationen* (Frankfurt a.M.: Suhrkamp 1981), 67–81.

WADE, MARA R., *The German Baroque Pastoral 'Singspiel'* (Berne: Lang 1990).

—— 'Geist- und weltliche Dramata: Hecuba, Dafne, Judith, Antigone: The Dramatic Works and Heroines of Martin Opitz', in Becker-Cantarino and Fechner, *Opitz und seine Welt*, 541–59.

WAGENER, HANS, ed., *Absurda Comica: Studien zur deutschen Komödie des 16. und 17. Jahrhunderts* (Amsterdam: Rodopi 1988) [= Daphnis 17/1 (1988)].

WALDECK, PETER B., *Weighing Delight and Dole: A Study of Comedy, Tragedy and Anxiety* (New York: Lang 1989).

WALLINGER, SYLVIA, and MONIKA JONAS, *Der Widerspenstigen Zähmung: Studien zur bezwungenen Weiblichkeit in der Literatur vom Mittelalter bis zur Gegenwart* (Innsbruck: Institut für Germanistik an der Universität Innsbruck 1986).

WALSÖE-ENGEL, INGRID, *Fathers and Daughters: Patterns of Seduction in Tragedies by Gryphius, Lessing, Hebbel and Kroetz* (Columbia, Oh.: Camden House 1993).

WATANABE-O'KELLY, HELEN, 'Barthold Feind, Gottsched, and Cato—or Opera Reviled', in *Publications of the English Goethe Society* 55 (1984/5), 107–23.

—— 'Barthold Feind's Libretto Octavia (1705) and the "Schuldrama" Tradition', in *GLL* 35/3 (1982), 208–20.

—— 'Lohenstein, Haugwitz, und das Türkenmotiv in deutschen Turnieren des Barock', in Iwasaki, *Begegnung mit dem 'Fremden'*, 7. 348–55.

—— 'Das Verborgene enthüllt: Das weibliche Publikum und die soziale Funktion des deutschen Dramas im 16. Jahrhundert', in Wolfram Malte Fues and Wolfram Mauser, eds., *'Verbergendes Enthüllen': Zu Theorie und Kunst dichterichen Verkleidens: Festschrift für Martin Stern* (Würzburg: Königshausen & Neumann 1995), 67–75.

—— 'Sei mir dreimal mehr mit Licht bekleidet: German Poems by Women to their Mentors in the Seventeenth Century', in *CG* 28 (1995), 255–64.

WEIGEL, SIGRID, 'Das Weibliche als Metapher des Metonymischen', in Albrecht Schöne, ed., *Kontroversen, alte und neue: Akten des VII. internationalen Germanisten-Kongresses* (Tübingen: Niemeyer 1986), 6. 108–18.

—— 'Die nahe Fremde—das Territorium des 'Weiblichen': Zum Verhältnis von 'Wilden' und 'Frauen' im Diskurs der Aufklärung', in Koebner, *Die andere Welt*, 171–99.

—— 'Die geopferte Heldin und das Opfer als Heldin: Zum Entwurf weiblicher Helden in der Literatur von Männern und Frauen', in Stefan and Weigel, *Die verborgene Frau*, 138–52.

WHAPLES, MIRIAM KARPILOW, 'Exoticism in Dramatic Music, 1600–1800' (UMI microfilmed doctoral thesis, University of Indiana 1958).

WHITE, HAYDEN, 'Form, Reference and Ideology in Musical Discourse', in Scher, *Music and Text*, 288–319.

WICHERT, ADALBERT, *Literatur, Rhetorik und Jurisprudenz im 17. Jahrhundert: Daniel Casper von Lohenstein und sein Werk* (Tübingen: Niemeyer 1991).

WIEDEMANN, CONRAD, 'Bestrittene Individualität: Beobachtungen zur Funktion der Barockallegorie', in Haug, *Formen und Funktionen der Allegorie*, 574–91.

WIESNER, MERRY E., *Women and Gender in Early Modern Europe* (Cambridge: Cambridge University Press 1993).

WILSON, W. DANIEL, *Humanität und Kreuzzugsideologie um 1780: Die 'Türkenoper' im 18. Jahrhundert und das Rettungsmotiv in Wielands 'Oberon', Lessings 'Nathan' und Goethes 'Iphigenie'* (New York: Lang 1984).

WINDFUHR, MANFRED, *Die barocke Bildlichkeit und ihre Kritiker: Stilhaltungen in der deutschen Literatur des 17. und 18. Jahrhunderts* (Stuttgart: Metzler 1966).

WINNINGTON-INGRAM, R. P., 'Pythagoras', in Sadie, *The New Grove Dictionary of Music and Musicians,* 15. 485.

WOLFF, HELLMUTH CHRISTIAN, *Die Venezianische Oper in der zweiten Hälfte des 17. Jahrhunderts* (Bologna: Forni 1975 [1937]).

—— *Die Barockoper in Hamburg* (1678–1738), 2 vols. (Wolfenbüttel: Möseler 1957).

—— *Oper: Szene und Darstellung von 1600 bis 1900* (Leipzig: VEB 1968).

—— 'Italian Opera from the Later Monteverdi to Scarlatti', in Lewis and Fortune, *Opera and Church Music,* 1–72.

—— 'Italian Opera 1700–1750', in Lewis and for tune, *Opera and Church Music,* 73–163.

—— 'Die Hamburger Oper 1678–1738', in Hamburgische Staatsoper et al., *300 Jahre Oper in Hamburg,* 72–91.

—— *Geschichte der komischen Oper: Von den Anfängen bis zur Gegenwart* (Wilhelmshaven: Heinrichshofen 1981).

WUNDER, HEIDE, *'Er ist die Sonn', sie ist der Mond': Frauen in der frühen Neuzeit* (Munich: Beck 1992).

WÜRTZ, ROLAND, 'Das Türkische im Singspiel des 18. Jahrhunderts', in *Das deutsche Singspiel im 18. Jahrhundert* (Heidelberg: Winter 1981), 125–38.

ZELLER, KONRADIN, *Pädagogik und Drama: Untersuchungen zur Schulkomödie Christian Weises* (Tübingen: Niemeyer 1980).

ZELM, KLAUS, *Die Opern Reinhard Keisers: Studien zur Chronologie, Überlieferung und Stilentwicklung* (Munich: Musikverlag Emil Katzbichler 1975).

—— 'Zur Verarbeitung italienischer Stoffe auf der Hamburger Gänsemarkt-Oper', in *Hamburger Jahrbuch für Musikwissenschaft 5: Die frühdeutscher Oper und ihre Bezeihungen zu Italien, England und Frankreich* (Hamburg: Laaber 1981), 89–106.

ZIMMERMANN, MARGARETE, 'Literarische Variationen über das Thema der Geschlechter im XVII. Jahrhundert', in *Germanisch-Romanische Monatsschrift* 42 (1992), 257–74.

# INDEX